PROFILES OF
CANADA

PROFILES OF
CANADA

Edited by
Kenneth G. Pryke
Walter C. Soderlund
University of Windsor

Copp Clark Pitman Ltd.
A Longman Company
Toronto

ISBN: 0-7730-5188-0

Editor: Claudia Kutchukian, Jane Lind
Design: Kyle Gell
Cover: Tom Thomson 1877–1917, *Tamaracks*, 1915. Oil on panel. 21.4 x 26.8 cm. McMichael Canadian Art Collection. Gift of Mr. R.A. Laidlaw. 1968.12
Typesetting: Carol Magee, Marnie Morrissey
Printing and binding: D.W. Friesen

Canadian Cataloguing in Publication Data

Main entry under title:

Profiles of Canada

Includes bibliographical references and index.

ISBN 0-7730-5188-0

1. Canada.   I. Pryke, Kenneth G., 1932–   II. Soderlund, Walter C.

FC51.P76 1992   971   C91-095079-2
F1008.P76 1992

Copp Clark Pitman Ltd.
2775 Matheson Blvd. East
Mississauga, Ontario
L4W 4P7

Associated companies:
Longman Group Ltd., London
Longman Inc., New York
Longman Cheshire Pty., Melbourne
Longman Paul Pty., Auckland

Printed and bound in Canada

  2 3 4 5   5188-0   96 95 94 93

Table of Contents

Acknowledgements

First of all, we would like to recognize the large degree of support given over a number of years to the Canadian Studies Program at the University of Windsor. Especially deserving of mention is the late Professor Paul Vandall, who for years pressed for the creation of the program, and to Professor Jerome Brown, who as Dean of Arts managed the program through the Senate. A high level of institutional support for Canadian Studies has continued under Professor Kathleen McCrone, Dean of the Faculty of Social Science.

During the actual planning stages of the book, the contributions of Adele Wiseman, writer in residence in the Department of English, were particularly helpful to us. As well, Adrien van den Hoven of the Department of French was extremely helpful to us at a number of stages. Indeed, the support we received for the project from all sides, especially from our contributors, was outstanding. Brian Henderson and Barbara Tessman of Copp Clark Pitman were always supportive of the project. David Taras of the University of Calgary read the manuscript and made a number of extremely helpful suggestions.

The work of preparing the manuscript was considerably eased by the efforts of Mrs. Lee Wilkinson and Mrs. Barbara Faria of the Department of Political Science and Mrs. Diane Lane and Mrs. Carmela Papp of the Department of History. Mrs. Lucia Brown, Mrs. Diane Dupuis, and Mrs. Pat Jolie of the Word Processing Centre worked countless hours on draft after draft of the manuscript, always without a complaint. Appreciation is also given to Mr. Ronald Welch who prepared some of the maps in the introduction and in chapter 1.

To commemorate his contribution to Canadian Studies at the University of Windsor, the royalties from the sale of this book will go to the Paul Vandall Memorial Fund. This fund will be used to support various programs to enrich Canadian Studies at the University of Windsor.

The Contributors

BARRY D. ADAM (Ph.D., Toronto) is professor of sociology at the University of Windsor and author of *The Survival of Domination* (1978) and *The Rise of the Gay and Lesbian Movement* (1987). He has published extensively on Canadian television news coverage of Nicaragua, the politics of AIDS, and mobility in the Ontario legal profession in such journals as the *Canadian Journal of Communication, Critical Sociology, Canadian Review of Sociology and Anthropology*, and the *Canadian Bar Review*.

IAIN BAXTER (M.F.A., Washington State) is associate professor in the school of visual arts at the University of Windsor. His unique blend of artistic techniques has earned him an international reputation.

RÉJEAN BEAUDOIN (Ph.D., McGill) teaches Québécois literature in the department of French at the University of British Columbia. His fields of research are nineteenth-century French-Canadian literature and the contemporary Québécois novel. In addition to several articles, he is the author of *Naissance d'une littérature: Essai sur le messianisme et le debuts de la littérature canadienne-française (1850–1890)* (1989). He has also contributed to radio programs at Radio-Canada (CBC) and is book editor of Québécois literature for the magazine *Liberté*.

STEPHEN BROOKS (Ph.D., Carleton) teaches political science at the University of Windsor. He is the author of *Who's in Charge? The Mixed Ownership Corporation in Canada* (1987), *Social Scientists and Politics in Canada: Between Clerisy and Vanguard* (with Alain Gagnon, 1988), *Public Policy in Canada* (1989), and *Business and Government in Canada* (with Andrew Stritch, 1991), and is the editor of *Political Thought in Canada: Contemporary Perspectives* (1984) and *Social Scientists, Policy and the State* (with Alain Gagnon, 1990).

ROBERT G. CHANDLER (M.S.W, Toronto) is associate professor of social work at the University of Windsor. His academic interests are in the areas of social welfare, social work with groups and families, social work and the workplace, and practice research methodology. He has contributed chapters to *Canadian Social Welfare* (1986) and *Evaluation of Employee Assistance Programs* (1988), as well as articles to *Juvenile and Family Court Journal* and *Employee Assistance Quarterly*.

LYNDA A. DAVEY (Ph.D., Université de Montréal), is assistant professor of French at Nipissing College. Having resided in Québec for a number of years, she is well-acquainted with the Québécois literary tradition.

IAN M. DRUMMOND (Ph.D., Yale) has been vice-dean and chair of the department of political economy at the University of Toronto. In 1975–1976, he was the first professor of Canadian studies at the University of Edinburgh. His research interests are in twentieth-century economic development, especially British, imperial, Canadian, and Russian/Soviet. Among his publications are *British Economic Policy and the Empire* (1972), *The Floating Pound and the Sterling Area* (1981), *Economics: Principles and Policies in an Open Economy* (1976), and (with R.S. Bothwell and J. English) *Canada 1900–1945* (1988) and *Canada since 1945* (1989).

JOAN HACKETT (Ph.D., Wayne State) retired from the school of dramatic art at the University of Windsor, 1989. During her teaching career she taught acting, directing, theatre history, as well as directing plays for the University Players. Her research interest focuses on modern and contemporary production of period plays. She has published articles on this subject in *Cue* and *Horizon*.

MAX J. HEDLEY (Ph.D., Alberta) is associate professor and head of the department of sociology and anthropology at the University of Windsor. He has conducted research into the way macro-social and economic processes contribute to the difficulties faced by family farms, and the transformation of rural communities and culture in the Canadian Prairies and northern New Zealand, and of Canadian fishermen and trappers. Since 1982 he has been involved in a co-operative University of Windsor–community research program at the Walpole Island First Nation.

J. RICHARD HERON (Ph.D., McMaster) is with the department of geography at the University of Windsor. His main research interests are the hydrology and climatology of arctic and subarctic Canada. He has conducted studies on permafrost hydrology, snowmelt, lake and river ice growth and break-up, and wetland hydrology. His work has appeared in the *Canadian Journal of Earth Sciences, Cold Regions Science and Technology, Arctic and Alpine Research,* and *Atmosphere-Ocean.*

FRANK C. INNES (Ph.D., McGill) taught at McGill before becoming the chair of the geography department at the University of Windsor. Historical and medical geographic studies of Canada have resulted from his recent research efforts, including a contribution to volume 2 of *The Historical Atlas of Canada.*

WILLIAM S. JACKSON (M.L.S., Wayne State) is a reference librarian at the Leddy Library at the University of Windsor.

TERENCE A. KEENLEYSIDE (Ph.D., London), formerly a foreign service officer with External Affairs, is now with the department of political science at the University of Windsor. His principal research interest has been Canadian foreign policy, with a particular interest in issues of human rights and Third World development. He is author of *The Common Touch* (1977), a novel about Canadian diplomacy in developing countries. In addition to several chapters in books, he has published articles on Canadian foreign policy in *International*

Journal, Journal of Canadian Studies, Canadian Public Administration, Canadian Journal of African Studies, and *Pacific Affairs.*

EDWARD KOVARIK (Ph.D., Harvard) teaches music history at the University of Windsor and is active in the Windsor area as a writer and lecturer. His area of specialization is music of the fifteenth and sixteenth centuries, and he has contributed articles and reviews on this subject to the *Journal of the American Musicological Society/Studies in Music* and *Notes of the Music Library Association.*

ROBERT M. KRAUSE is associate professor and head of the department of political science at the University of Windsor. His research interests are in the fields of Canadian federal and provincial politics and elite behaviour. He has published articles in journals such as the *Canadian Journal of Political Science, American Journal of Political Science,* and *Legislative Studies Quarterly.* As well, he has contributed chapters to numerous texts and most recently has co-edited *Introductory Readings in Canadian Government and Politics* (1991).

ANDRÉ LAMONTAGNE (Ph.D., Laval) teaches in the department of French at the University of British Columbia. His research focuses on the contemporary Québécois novel and narrative discourse theory. In addition to writing several items for the *Dictionnaire des oeuvres littéraires du Québec, Canadian Literature,* and *Nuit Blanche,* he has published research in journals such as *Protée.* His major work is *Les mots des autres: La poétique intertextuelle des oeuvres de fiction de Hubert Aquin* (1991).

LOUIS K. MacKENDRICK (Ph.D., Toronto) is professor of English at the University of Windsor. He is editor of *Probable Fictions: Alice Munro's Narative Acts* (1983) and author of *Robert Harlow and His Works* (1989), and *Al Purdy and His Works* (1990). He has published articles and chapters on Canadian comic fiction and on such writers as Elliot, Steinbeck, Pratt, Kroetsch, Lampman, and Leacock. His principal teaching and research interest is the modern and contemporary Canadian short story.

PAUL McINTYRE (D. Mus., Toronto), is a composer, pianist, and conductor and is a faculty member at the University of Windsor. Among his numerous compositions are several that were written especially for performance in Windsor, the most recent being "Matins for the Vigil of Assumption" (1989), a personal commentary on a widely reported local tragedy. He has orchestrated a number of early Canadian pieces, including the entire score of "The Widow" by Calixa Lavallée.

KENNETH McNAUGHT (Ph.D., Toronto) is professor emeritus in the department of history at the University of Toronto. He has enjoyed a distinguished career, having taught at universitities in Canada, Britain, the United States, and Germany. He is author of *A Prophet in Politics* (a biography of J.S. Woodsworth, 1959), *The Penguin History of Canada* (1988), and, with J.L. Granatstein, editor of *"English Canada" Speaks Out* (1991).

SANDRA PAIKOWSKY (M.A., Toronto) is associate professor at Concordia University, specializing in Canadian art history. She is also the curator of the Concordia Art Gallery. As well, she is the publisher and a co-editor of the *Journal of Canadian Art History/Annales d'histoire de l'art canadien*. In addition to presenting lectures to both the general public and specialists, she has written many exhibition catalogues and has contributed articles to various Canadian periodicals and publications.

KENNETH G. PRYKE (Ph.D., Duke) joined the department of history at the University of Windsor in 1963 and currently directs the interdisciplinary program in Canadian studies. His primary field of research involves nineteenth-century Canada, especially the Maritimes. His work, *Nova Scotia and Confederation, 1864–1865*, was published in 1979. In addition to writing several items for the *Canadian Dictionary of Biography*, he has published research in journals such as *Dalhousie Review*, *Histoire sociale/Social History*, and *Acadiensis*.

WALTER I. ROMANOW (Ph.D., Wayne State) professor emeritus at the University of Windsor where he founded the department of communication studies and served as chair of the department for two terms. As well, he has served as dean of student affairs and as dean of the faculty of social science. His research and publications focus on media–society relationships, media and political processes, and on policy considerations for Canadian mass media–telecommunications systems.

RALPH SARKONAK (Ph.D., Toronto) has taught at the University of British Columbia since 1983. He edited *The Language of Difference: Writing in QUEBEC(ois)* (1983) and co-edited with Richard Hodgson *Le Roman québécois comtemporain (1960–1986) devant le critique* (1989).

WALTER C. SODERLUND (Ph.D., Michigan) is professor of political science at the University of Windsor. His research interests focus on processes of political integration and the role of mass media in Canadian politics. He is co-author of *Canadian Confederation: A Decision-Making Analysis* (1979) and *Media and Elections in Canada* (1984). His research on Canada has appeared in journals such as *Canadian Journal of Political Science, Comparative Politics, Journalism Quarterly, Gazette*, and *Journal of Broadcasting & Electronic Media*.

RONALD H. WAGENBERG (Ph.D., London) teaches political science at the University of Windsor. He is co-author of *An Introduction to Canadian Government and Politics*, now in its fifth edition (1990), as well as *Canadian Confederation: A Decision-Making Analysis* (1979) and *Media and Elections in Canada* (1984).

❑ ❑ ❑ ❑ ❑ ❑ ❑

Introduction

Kenneth G. Pryke
Walter C. Soderlund

The Canadian experience, not an especially easy one to understand at the best of times, seems even more problematic now, with the future of the country itself in doubt. The past is frequently interpreted in the light of current concerns, and this book is no exception. It was written at a time in Canadian history when factors that had come more or less to be taken for granted (federalism, bilingualism, multiculturalism, and an economic system distinct from that of the neighbouring United States) were being called into question by significant numbers of Canadians. There is no question that some of the uncertainty, and indeed disappointment, brought about by current trends is reflected in the chapters that follow. For this we do not apologize, but rather point out to students that the mind set of a country has an impact on the way in which scholars interpret national experiences, whether these interpretations are of the recent or distant past. Had this book been written in 1982, or even five years ago, a number of treatments and interpretations would have been considerably different.

Indeed, we began thinking about this book approximately five years ago in the context of a multi-disciplinary introductory course on Canada that had been fashioned for the newly created honours program in Canadian studies at the University of Windsor. We had a definite idea regarding what we wanted included in the course, and, by and large, we had the faculty to provide lectures on these subjects. What we could not find was a text that provided an introductory overview of the various subjects for our students. From this need this book was born. Since then, a number of people (most of whom have been mentioned in the acknowledgements) have kindly offered suggestions concerning the range and organization of the material to be included in the text. Despite alterations in response to these comments, the basic conception of the book—an introductory text on Canada—has remained unchanged.

The material assembled in the following pages reveals five recurrent themes that are crucial to an understanding of the origins of Canada, the patterns it has followed in its development, its present status, and its future evolution.[1] As a diverse country, Canada promotes many differing views as to its character, strengths, and weaknesses. Thus, while the authors whose works are represented in this volume discuss many common themes, they do not, nor were they encouraged to, share the same perceptions and draw the same conclusions.

PHYSICAL SETTING

The first of these common interpretive themes deals with the physical setting of Canada—vast, harsh, northern, and regionally diverse. Modern technology can only modify, not eliminate, the impact of this reality. In addition to the chapter on geography by Innes and Heron, this theme is most evident in the chapters dealing with Canada's culture, especially its literature and art, and in those treating its history, society, politics, and the economy.[2]

Particularly relevant at the present time is the notion that Canada is a nation made up of different geographic regions. The contemporary preoccupation, not to say obsession, with regionalism has led to this term being used in a variety of ways. While many English Canadians take it as a point beyond dispute that Québec is a region, Québécois scholars insist that Québec consists of several regions. Others, particularly western scholars, occasionally contend that Ontario and Québec form a single region. Such different uses of the term make it necessary to approach the subject with care.

Regionalism usually refers to a section of the country that may embrace more than one province. Thus, Newfoundland, Nova Scotia, New Brunswick, and Prince Edward Island are collectively referred to as Atlantic Canada. Ontario and Québec stand alone, as does British Columbia. Manitoba, Saskatchewan, and Alberta comprise the Prairies.

Discussions of regionalism in Canada will, sooner or later, introduce the notion that Canada consists of five geographic regions that run north to south rather than east to west. Among the many questions raised about regionalism is how the popular east-to-west view of regions is related to regions as defined by geographers. If geographic factors can be seen to separate various sectors of the country, are there other geographic factors that have tended to direct relationships on an east–west basis? It is also pertinent to ask to what extent economic and social developments are determined, or controlled, by geographic factors. Can the development of mining in northern Ontario, or cereal production in the Prairies, be seen solely in terms of physical geography, or are such developments really the products of a variety of political and social decisions that turn potential into reality? The work of both physical and social geographers is important in understanding the nature of growth in Canada. It might also be asked whether geographic determinism is accepted more readily today by novelists and artists than by geographers and other social scientists.

Commentators often resort to the existence of regionalism as a justification for increasing the powers of the provincial governments and decreasing the role and function of the federal government. On the face of it, it is not at all clear why the existence of a region should properly lead to the enhancement of the powers of a provincial government. Historically, the enhancement of provincial powers has benefited the stronger provinces at the expense of the weaker ones. A case can, and should, be made that the existence of regions is a basic reason for the federal government to have a major role in policy making in Canada. Nonetheless, at the present time there is a major thrust towards what is termed the devolution of federal powers. This process, sometimes derisively referred to as turning Canada into a loose confederation of shopping malls, would have a major impact on every aspect of Canadian social policy. It is evident in a number of chapters that the federal government has had a major impact in a wide range of areas and that the types of changes now being suggested would bring drastic alterations to the country. Before approval is given to such a revolutionary change, it is essential that all reasons and justifications for the proposed changes be subject to detailed examination.

POPULATION

The second theme involves Canada's peoples and focuses on the fact that there are relatively few Canadians in relation to the physical space available. Further, this small population tends to be clustered in cities, which in turn are widely dispersed across the country. Canadians are thus faced with an anomaly: although they occupy a huge land mass, some of their most pressing problems arise from population density.

The population, in addition to being small in number, is also quite heterogeneous, with native peoples having completed the process of immigration long before the modern wave of immigration from Europe began in the 1600s. In more recent decades, immigration has expanded to include significant numbers of non-European peoples. The cultural and political interactions between key population groups within the country (native peoples, the French, the English, and the more recent immigrants), must be understood in order to arrive at any reasonably accurate assessment regarding where the country has come from and where it is going. In addition to the question of ethnicity, contemporary studies of society are deeply involved with questions concerning inequalities based on class and gender. These questions form the organizing theme for Barry Adam's chapter on Canadian society, while Robert Chandler's chapter on social policy focuses on the wide array of programs available to Canadians, many of which apply universally to the population and work as a whole to diminish inequalities based on wealth and social position.

IMPERIALISM AND COLONIALISM

A third theme, which is closely related to the previous one, is that French and British immigration to Canada occurred in the context of the policies of imperialism and colonialism undertaken by the two mother countries. In general, imperialism and colonialism have had disastrous effects on large areas of the globe. On any world-scale comparison, Canada has escaped with seemingly light damage, although when we begin to examine Canada's current problems more closely, the bitter legacies of the mother countries loom large. Chief among these are attitudes of superiority on the part of European peoples and the set of dominance relationships that flow from them.

This is seen most clearly in the way in which the culture and way of life of the native peoples were deemed to be inferior to those of "civilized" Europeans. This theme is dealt with extensively in Max Hedley's chapter on native peoples and in Kenneth Pryke's chapter on history. As we enter the 1990s, it is apparent that the policies of the past and the stereotypes on which they were built are no longer regarded as adequate by Canadian society at large, not to mention by native peoples themselves.

The second area in which the consequences of imperialism and colonialism continue to have a profound effect on Canada is in English–French relations. History, not to mention the contemporary political agenda, is seen quite differently by Francophones in Canada. Events associated with the English military victories in Acadia and Québec in the eighteenth century had a dramatic impact on the French-speaking people living there—deportation in the case of the former and attempted forced assimilation associated with the Durham Report in the latter. The chapter by Beaudoin and LaMontagne on French-Canadian literature gives a profound insight into the defensiveness and inward-looking character of French society in Canada. The political chapters by Wagenberg and by Krause and Soderlund explore the continuing relations between the two groups, in the context of federal–provincial relations and in the paradox of the Quiet Revolution, where growing political power on the part of French speakers within the province of Québec is associated with demands for even greater political autonomy. What is evident in relations between French and English Canadians from the time of the Conquest in 1759 to the Quiet Revolution in 1960 is that two cultures were not seen as equal partners in the Canadian experience. Unstated assumptions regarding French-Canadian inferiority on the part of English-speaking Canadians are difficult to fully comprehend, particularly on the part of those not on the receiving end of such an unequal relationship. But to appreciate the depth of Québécois alienation, one must understand the psychological consequences of colonialism. Unfortunately, the world is virtually a living laboratory for such study.

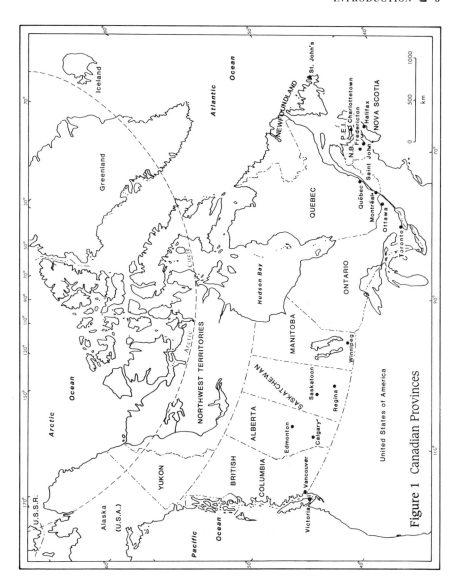

Figure 1 Canadian Provinces

CORE–PERIPHERY RELATIONS

A fourth theme again focuses on an unequal relationship, this time the relationship between the wealthy industrial provinces of Central Canada and the poorer peripheral provinces to the east and to the west.

Since the end of World War II, governments in Canada, both federal and provincial, have become responsible for maintaining employment and providing a level of social services that are roughly comparable across the country. This commitment has created major problems in public policy, since geography, population density, and past economic development policies have resulted in an unequal distribution of wealth across the country.

As one means of dealing with regional disparities, the federal government, particularly after 1957, adopted programs to promote economic development in the less developed areas of the country. While such programs have been introduced to help promote economic and social equality, they are criticized by political economists such as Stephen Brooks and mainstream economists such as Ian Drummond. Given the record of failure of these programs, what, if anything, is the alternative? Certainly the suggestion of an earlier royal commission that everyone in the Maritimes be given a one-way bus ticket to Toronto seems quite unacceptable to anyone who considers the staggering problems faced by Metropolitan Toronto.

Another important way of providing more or less uniform social policies across the country has been to develop an ingenious and innovative social welfare system. This system not only combines the private and public sectors, but frequently manages to involve the federal, provincial, and municipal governments in the administration of particular programs. As Robert Chandler indicates, social welfare programs have been a major achievement of postwar Canada, although welfare remains a highly contentious issue that all too often is seen in too narrow a context. While often seen as dealing primarily with the poor, it actually refers to programs, such as those covering health care, that are designed to provide services to the entire community.

To a significant extent, welfare programs have been funded by transfer payments from the federal government to provincial governments, structured in such a way as to benefit the economically deprived regions of the country at the expense of such prosperous provinces as Ontario and Alberta. The entire system is dependent on a highly complex system of funding, and any radical alteration in that system is likely to lead to the collapse of the welfare system that has developed over the past forty years. This is undoubtedly why some critics of the welfare system advocate the devolution of federal powers.

IMPACT OF THE UNITED STATES

The final theme that we will consider is the impact of Canada's geographic proximity to the United States. Clearly, this impact has been profound, and most would consider it at best a mixed blessing. Virtually every facet of Canadian life has been affected by developments in the United States starting as far back as the revolutionary war. Canada's political and economic systems, either overtly or subconsciously, were crafted with American models and experience in mind, although often the US experience was seen as something to be avoided. The American Revolution provided the impetus for large-scale Loyalist immigration to British North America. The American Civil War provided one of the direct causes of Confederation, as British–Union animosity seemed to set up the scenario whereby the victorious Union army would attack the British colonies.

As is the case with many areas of academic inquiry, scholars are not of one mind when it comes to assessing the importance of the American reality on Canadian historical development. In his thought-provoking epilogue, Kenneth McNaught sides with scholars such as Seymour Martin Lipset, who stress differences between Canada and the United States.[3]

The notion that Canada and the United States travel in parallel tracks may well have validity, especially for the period prior to World War II. But the chapter by Kovarik and McIntyre on music and the Hackett chapter on theatre point out that there has been extensive interaction between creative artists working in the two countries. As well, Terrence Keenleyside emphasizes the centrality of the United States in Canadian foreign policy, and both the Drummond and Brooks chapters demonstrate the historic interconnectedness of the two nations' economies.

Since the end of World War II, however, we would argue that the forces leading to a convergence between the two societies have increased dramatically. This is especially apparent in Walter Romanow's treatment of television, a medium that has been recognized as a cultural threat by a succession of Canadian governments and has led to the wholesale transmission of American popular culture and the values that underlie that culture into Canada. The chapter on politics by Krause and Soderlund likewise points to the Americanization of Canadian political processes, seen most vividly in techniques of electoral campaigning and, more recently, in the incorporation of the Charter of Rights and Freedoms into the Constitution, thereby creating an enhanced role for the judiciary in interpreting what Parliament can and cannot do with respect to legislation. As both Brooks and Drummond point out, the recently signed Free Trade Agreement with the United States signals the creation of a North American economic unit, in name as well as in fact. That there will be fall-out from this economic integration into other areas, especially into Canada's unique network of social programs, is a concern voiced in the Chandler chapter on social policy. In summary, Canada and the United States are indeed growing closer together on a number of dimensions and, in the vast majority of areas of convergence, it is Canadian society that is undergoing the greatest degree of change.

As American influence in Canada increases, the range of action open to the Canadian governments (both federal and provincial) inexorably decreases. Mainstream neo-classical economists recognize a very limited role for the state in economic development, and they would likely applaud as the range of state activity is restricted. However, reliance on the state is embedded in the political culture of this country, as much as this may be regretted by economists. Increased American influence in Canada will thus inevitably create controversy because it is a challenge to deeply held societal values.

THE ARTS AND CANADIAN IDENTITY

Asked to name ten people who have had the most influence on the country, most students would produce a list of politicians. Yet as the chapters on the arts emphasize, artists, musicians, and writers have had an important role in defining and shaping the country. This is easily recognized, but it is much more difficult to define the exact boundaries between culture and the political and economic spheres. The high priority and difficulty of defining Canadian culture in relation to the United States, Great Britain, and France, as well as between English and French Canadians, is made abundantly clear in Walter Romanow's chapter on telecommunications.

The cultural and intellectual traditions of the country are rooted in the culture of western Europe. This is certainly true with respect to our political traditions, but it is often seen as being a more critical issue in cultural areas. Is it consistent, however, to emphasize how our political institutions embody British ideals and simultaneously reject British and other European models in the field of the arts? Is Canada part of Western culture or should Shakespeare and Shaw be treated in Canada as "foreign" authors? In examining the chapters on the arts in Canada the reader should focus on the question, what is art? Canadian museums, for example, long followed the practice of assigning art historians to explain Roman statues but left wooden carvings created by native peoples to the attention of anthropologists. It is only in the past decade that this practice has been seriously questioned.

Recently the discussion concerning the role of art, and of culture in general, has moved forward with the contention that, if European culture is to be regarded as part of Canadian life, then a similar recognition should be given to the culture of non-European peoples who have a steadily increasing presence in Canada. Some commentators have begun to suggest that a formal acknowledgement of multiculturalism, as well as of native peoples and women, should replace the intellectual and cultural models drawn from Europe.

The sometimes heavy hand of our colonial past is explored in Kim MacKendrick's chapter on English-Canadian literature. As the author emphasizes, it is only in the recent past that English conventions have been replaced by a language that more adequately represents our experience and a perception that more truly expresses contemporary life.

English-Canadian literature provides an interesting parallel and contrast with French-Canadian literature. In Québec, there is even greater emphasis on the duty of the arts to define and protect the society than there is in English Canada. In spite of, or perhaps because of, the severe cultural restrictions, Québécois writers began to innovate sooner and in more ways than did their English counterparts.

All too often the arts were regarded with the suspicion that they were somehow subversive and that, unchecked, they would undermine decent, respectable society. As Joan Hackett's chapter on English-Canadian theatre points out, it was well into the twentieth century before Canadian theatre was able to overcome the taint of scandal and immorality that had so long surrounded it.

It is often stated that Canadians know little of their artistic past. The question might be asked whether this is because Canadians have achieved little or whether, for some other reason, Canadians prefer to downgrade or ignore achievements in the artistic field. This is particularly true of the field of painting, which is only now receiving serious scholarly attention. Artists in Canada were particularly attracted to landscapes, as Sandra Paikowsky points out, rather than to portrait painting, so it is understandable that her chapter on Canadian painting should concentrate on that area. Indeed, Canada's most well-known school of painters, the Group of Seven, was developing a sense of Canada in terms of landscape at the very time when Canadians were becoming more and more an urban people. The aggressive manner in which this art was promoted by both public and private bodies, as well as the marked popularity of this school of painters, bears witness to its strong appeal. It would be of value to investigate how such attitudes influenced the public's perception of its urban experience.

In the Kovarik and McIntyre chapter, one can see the depth and variety of music that developed from the period of early settlement. Significant as well is the tremendous expansion that took place in all of the arts following the establishment of the Canada Council. While the development of the arts in Canada prior to the 1950s should not be discounted, the role of government in fostering culture remains a significant feature in the development of the country.

CONCLUSION

It is evident from the various chapters in this book that, in most respects, Canada has been a very fortunate country whose record of national development has significant meaning for Canadians and for others. It is a wealthy country, both in terms of resources and people, and has evolved a distinctive national style. The various accounts make it abundantly clear that some of these accomplishments have involved serious injustices for large segments of the population. Evident too, is the fact that many of the long-held assumptions about the nature of the country and the policies it should adopt are currently under serious review. It is only through an examination of all aspects of Canadian life that the true nature of the country can be grasped.

Notes

[1] D.V. Smiley, *Canada in Question: Federalism in the Seventies*, 2nd ed. (Toronto: McGraw-Hill Ryerson, 1976), 184–99. W.L. Morton, "The Relevance of Canadian History," Canadian Historical Association *Annual Report* (1960): 1–21.

[2] The very act of naming an event or a place may in itself be significant. This important point is certainly evident in the chapter on literature in French where the authors trace the transition from French-Canadian literature to Québec literature to Québécois literature. The name or title may serve to indicate certain features or to suggest various inferences as to the nature of the identified object. The use of a name can be very simple, and designate a very basic, political act. This issue becomes relevant when considering how to deal with French place names. There is no ready formula, however, since established practices, which are by no means clear-cut, are currently undergoing change. Where appropriate the editors have used, following the model of the *Dictionary of Canadian Biography*, the 1987 issue of *Repertoire toponymique du Québec*.

[3] S.M. Lipset, *Continental Divide: The Values and Institutions of the United States and Canada* (New York: Routledge, Chapman and Hall, 1990).

Basic
Components

1

❏   ❏   ❏   ❏   ❏   ❏   ❏

Physical and
Social Geography

Frank C. Innes
J. Richard Heron

INTRODUCTION

Canada was invented as a political entity in 1867 following settlement by people of European origin with an agricultural heritage—hence their awareness of environmental restrictions for rural settlement. Much that has been written on the geography of this country has reflected the perceptions of these newcomers, the pioneers of a particular technology associated with a specific time and activity. For them, the soils formed over time by the interaction of geology and climate and the subsequent vegetation were critical elements, which together represented the raw materials of their resource base. The selection of farmland dictated the settlement patterns, the populated and the unpopulated areas of the country, and the traditional regions of Canada. The internal political framework, substantially completed by 1912, is inherited from the period when people were scattered over the vast lands and transportation by train was paramount. Now, although the physical geographic underpinnings are still apparent, they have acquired an altogether reduced significance in the light of a postindustrial economy based on urban places and their spheres of influence.

In Canada today, the 10 million square kilometres of territory stretch over six time zones for 5346 kilometres from Cape Spear, Newfoundland (53.9° west longitude) to the Yukon–Alaska border (141° west longitude). Next to Russia, Canada is the second largest country in the world. Like that other northern country, it displays a wide diversity of landscapes.

PHYSIOGRAPHY

For a country the size of Canada, it is not surprising that there is a wide diversity of landscapes. Within this diversity, however, it is possible to distinguish a number of physiographic regions (figure 1) that have been subjected to common geological events and that display similar landscapes.

❑ CANADIAN SHIELD

The Canadian (or Laurentian) Shield is the core of the North American continent and covers about 40 percent of Canada in a broad swath surrounding Hudson Bay. Although the shield is so large and often identified with Canada, it contains less than 10 percent of the population and has continually repelled permanent occupation since it has little agriculturally useful land.

Some of the oldest rocks in the world, almost 4 billion years old, are found in the Canadian Shield, which was formed between 1.7 and 2 billion years ago when continental drift brought at least seven micro-continents together and welded them into a single, geologically complex unit.[1] The mountains produced by the collisions were eroded away over the ages leaving a relatively low, undulating terrain, which may be quite rough in places. The local relief is generally less than 100 metres while the greatest elevations are found in the Torngat Mountains of Labrador and along the eastern coast of Baffin Island. The primary resource is the rich deposits of minerals found throughout the region. These range from precious metals (gold, silver, platinum), to speciality metals (cobalt, titanium, uranium), and the utilitarian metals (iron, nickel, copper, lead, and zinc). The result has been the development of this area in the form of mining towns that remain viable until the ore deposit is exhausted.

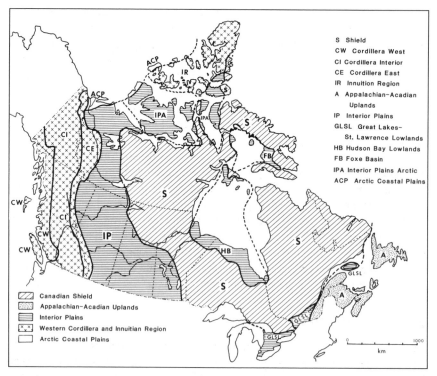

Figure 1A Physiographic Regions

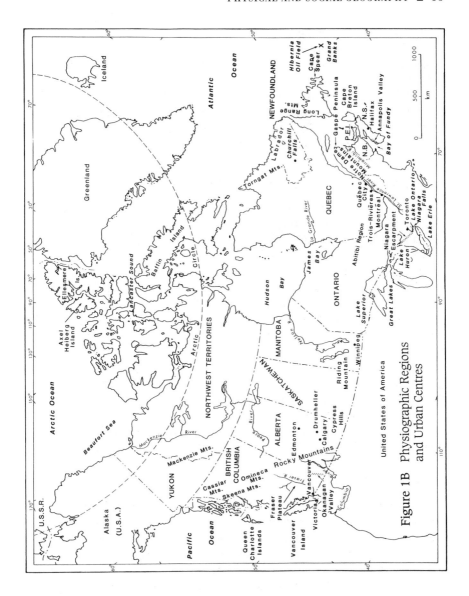

Figure 1B Physiographic Regions and Urban Centres

The impact of continental glaciation, which ended only about 10 000 years ago, is very evident. Ice scoured the surface of the land, removing the soil and creating innumerable small depressions in the rock. Thus, most of the Canadian Shield is bare rock or has extremely thin soil, while the depressions form lakes, ponds, or wetlands. Where glacial deposits are substantial, such as the Abitibi clay plain in northern Ontario and Québec, some farming is possible, but widespread, commercial agriculture is generally not feasible on the Canadian Shield. However, the soils are sufficient to sustain slow-growing, primarily coniferous forests that provide raw materials for the lumber and pulp-and-paper industries located in the southern part of the shield. Linked to the energy-intensive mining and pulp-and-paper industries was the harnessing of the hydro-electric power potential of the large northern rivers. Hydro development is continuing today, especially in northern Québec where the energy is being transferred to southern Canada and the United States.

❑ GREAT LAKES–ST. LAWRENCE LOWLAND

Surrounding the Canadian Shield is a group of plains, remnants of the sedimentary rock that once covered this area. Rocks geologically similar to the Canadian Shield provide the base material upon which the limestones, dolomites, sandstones, and shales that compose these lowlands and plains rest.

The most southerly of these plains is the Great Lakes–St. Lawrence Lowland. It is divided into separate areas where erosion exposed the Canadian Shield, and stretches from southwestern Ontario down the St. Lawrence Valley and incorporates Anticosti Island and small parts of Newfoundland. The rocks are generally horizontal, so the only major relief is provided by the Niagara Escarpment, which is up to 100 metres high, and by the Monteregion Hills, a series of granitic intrusions east of Montréal. The rest of the terrain is covered by glacial deposits and is gently rolling except for a large area consisting of eastern Ontario and western Québec, where deposition of sediments left by the former Champlain Sea produced an almost flat landscape. An excellent soil has developed, and this, in addition to its relatively southern position, has produced a prime agricultural area that has been maintained largely because of its proximity to the main population centres.

❑ INTERIOR PLAINS

The Interior Plains extend northward from the Canada–U.S. border into the Arctic. The region is gently rolling and the elevation increases in steps toward the West. The most prominent topographic features are the northwest-southeast-trending escarpments and the associated large hills or plateaus, which define three levels. The Manitoba Lowland (the lowest) is separated from the Saskatchewan Plains (middle level) by the Manitoba Escarpment, which is composed of large hills such as Riding Mountain. The highest level, the Alberta Plain, is delineated by the Missouri Coteau. Within the Alberta Plain there are a number of large, isolated hills. One such area, the Cypress Hills, was high enough to remain unglaciated. However, the glaciers left thick deposits of debris elsewhere, which developed into excellent soils that attracted nineteenth-century settlers. Meltwater discharge during deglaciation cut large, deep valleys, called coulees, into the plain. Where the glacier impounded this meltwater, glacial lakes in central Saskatchewan and southern Manitoba left relatively flat terrain when they drained. Where pronounced erosion continues, such as in the Drumheller area of Alberta, badland topography has developed. The Arctic Interior Plains have the same rolling topography except that the elevation increases eastward.

Since the rocks that compose the Interior Plains were laid down in a warm, shallow sea, the area is rich in coal and, especially, oil and gas. While Saskatchewan, Manitoba, and British Columbia have some oil, an area from Alberta northward to the Beaufort Sea contains most of it, either as conventional deposits or oil sands. The other primary mineral of this region is potash, mined in eastern Saskatchewan. These resources have provided alternatives to agriculture in recent years and adjustments to population distribution have reflected this development.

❏ HUDSON BAY LOWLAND AND FOXE BASIN

The Hudson Bay Lowland and the Foxe Basin are also composed of the remnants of the sedimentary rocks that once extended over the Canadian Shield. The Hudson Bay Lowland is extremely flat and is almost completely covered with muskeg: wetlands with thick deposits of peat; the Foxe Basin has substantial wetlands but also has drier upland areas. Both have oil potential, but no oil has yet been found.

❏ INNUITION REGION AND ARCTIC COASTAL PLAIN

Around the continental margins are zones where continental drift and the collision of continents have deformed the land, producing mountains. The Innuition Region is one of these. In the western Arctic, erosion has reduced the topography to upland and plateau surfaces, but on Axel Heiberg and Ellesmere Islands spectacular mountains topped with icecaps reach elevations of 2600 metres. The Arctic Coastal Plain is a narrow lowland strip running from the Mackenzie Delta along the edge of the Arctic Islands. Since the bedrock geology is similar to that of Alberta, substantial deposits of oil and gas have been found throughout the Innuition Region and the Coastal Plain, as well as offshore in the Beaufort Sea. However, the current costs of recovery are too high for commercial development.

❏ APPALACHIAN REGION

The Appalachian Region was formed during the collision of North America with Europe. The Notre Dame Mountains, from the Eastern Townships of Québec to the Gaspé Peninsula, are the highest remnants of the large mountains that have now been rounded by erosion. Eastern New Brunswick, Prince Edward Island, and parts of western Nova Scotia consist of a gently rolling terrain. Along New

Brunswick's Bay of Fundy coast, a series of hills about 450 metres high stretches toward western Cape Breton Island. Between these and the upland along Nova Scotia's east coast is the lowland area of the Annapolis Valley, which extends to the plateau interior of Cape Breton Island. In Newfoundland, the Long Range Mountains (800 metres) form the western side of the island while the remainder is an irregular plateau.

The area presented scattered lowlands suitable for agriculture, while mineral resources reflect the complex geology. Coal fields on Cape Breton Island support a steel industry and deposits of gypsum, potash, and lead/zinc are exploited. However, the potential wealth of the Maritime region lies offshore in the oil fields of Hibernia and Terra Nova on the Grand Banks and in the natural gas deposits of the Scotian Shelf, the traditional fishing areas. Only for Hibernia has the first stage of the new development started.

❑ WESTERN CORDILLERA

The Cordilleras of western North America were formed during the collision of the North American and Pacific plates, which still continues—as those who live along the San Andreas fault will readily recognize. Despite the complex topography and geology, the region can be subdivided into three parallel systems. The Cordillera East section is composed of sedimentary rocks that have folded and faulted to produce a spectacular mountain chain known as the Rockies in the south and the Mackenzie Mountains in the north. Coal deposits located here have been exploited since the late 1800s.

The Cordillera West region includes the mountains of Vancouver and the Queen Charlotte Islands, the Coast Mountains on the mainland, and a trough between them. The mountains are generally composed of igneous intrusions and reach altitudes of 4000 metres. Between these two mountain belts lies the Cordillera Interior, a mixture of mountains and high plateaus composed of igneous, metamorphic, and sedimentary rock. The Fraser Plateau in central British Columbia separates the Columbia Mountains in the southwest and the Skeena-Cassair-Omineca Mountains in northern British Columbia and the Yukon. Both the western and interior parts of the cordilleras are rich in the same types of minerals as are found on the Canadian Shield. These include gold, silver, lead, zinc, and specialty metals such as tungsten and molybdenum.

❑ CLIMATE

Due to its large size, Canada experiences a wide variety of climatic conditions that have been described by Hare and Morley.[2] These range from the temperate marine climate along the West Coast to polar conditions in the extreme north.

With a few exceptions, the Canadian climate can be characterized as harsh, with marked seasonality of the climatic components. The seasons are most pronounced north of the Arctic Circle (66.5° N), where extremes of light and darkness occur. In the summer, when the northern hemisphere is tilted toward the sun, this area receives twenty-four hours of sunlight each day, and in the winter, polar night brings continuous darkness. This seasonal variation in day length becomes less severe as one moves south, but still greatly influences the climate.

This is seen most clearly in the annual variation of air temperatures as shown in figures 2a and 2b. During the winter, all of Canada experiences subfreezing temperatures, with the exception of coastal British Columbia, where mean January temperatures remain just above freezing due to the moderating influence of the Pacific Ocean. The Atlantic Ocean is colder, so temperatures in Nova Scotia and Newfoundland fall below freezing. Even in southwestern Ontario, the most southerly point in Canada, winter temperatures are less than zero degrees Celsius. While the coldest areas are the mainland and islands of the Northwest Territories, minimum temperatures of minus thirty degrees Celsius or lower can occur everywhere but in the warm coastal areas.

In the summer, when the days are longer and the sun is higher in the sky, the average monthly temperatures increase to a more comfortable fifteen degrees Celsius or higher in the populated regions. The maximum daily temperatures frequently exceed thirty degrees Celsius in the southern portion of the country during the summer.

For many locations in the interior of the continent, the range of mean monthly air temperatures is about forty degrees Celsius and is even greater if the daily maximums and minimums are considered. On an annual basis, the Vancouver-Victoria region of British Columbia is the warmest, with mean temperatures of greater than ten degrees Celsius, while most of the Canadian population lives in areas where the mean annual is greater than zero degrees Celsius.

The harsh thermal regime has a number of important effects. Permafrost (ground with a temperature that does not rise above freezing, as seen in figure 2c), occurs in most of the Arctic and sporadic patches can be found in the northern parts of all but the Maritime provinces. This, along with the harsh winter climate, determines the northern limit of forest growth, the so-called tree line. A zone of low-growing tundra vegetation is found immediately to the north of the tree line, and in the Arctic Islands north of Lancaster Sound vegetation is sparse, growing only in favourable areas.

The temperature regime also limits crops to areas that have at least 1000 growing degree-days. As shown in figure 2d, this excludes the northern parts of Québec, Ontario, and Manitoba but reaches down the Mackenzie Valley. Commercial agriculture generally ends several hundred kilometres south to this line due to the uncertainty of the length of the growing season.

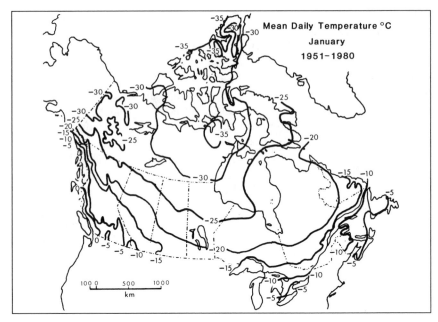

Figure 2A

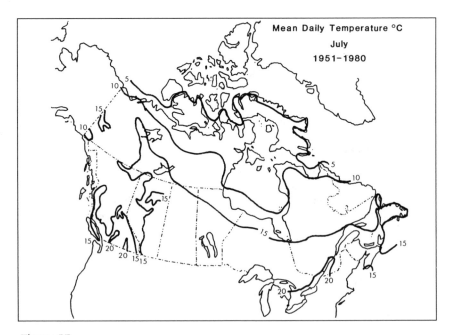

Figure 2B

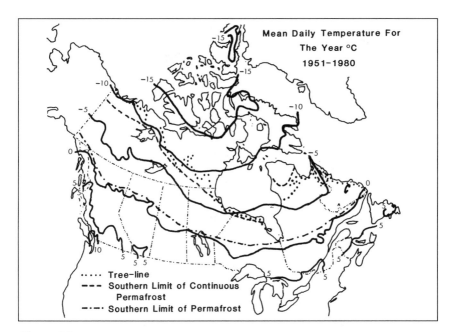

Figure 2C

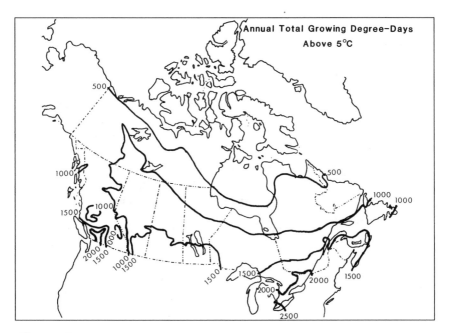

Figure 2D

The subfreezing winter temperatures cause ice to form on all the coastal and inland water bodies, except for parts of the Atlantic coast and the coast of British Columbia. This greatly impedes shipping in the Gulf of St. Lawrence and the Great Lakes, and eliminates navigation on the St. Lawrence Seaway and most other bodies of water. Hudson and James bays are arctic seas and the presence of melting sea ice for much of the summer causes the climate of the surrounding land to be much cooler. Thus, as is indicated in figure 2c, all the climatic zones, the permafrost boundaries, and the tree line are farther south relative to western Canada.

Most of Canada receives sufficient precipitation to support vegetation. Although there is no pronounced dry season, precipitation tends to increase in the summer. All parts of the country receive snow, but it may remain on the ground only a short time in the lower mainland of British Columbia and in southwestern Ontario. In the coastal mountains of British Columbia, temperate rain forests receive more than 2000 millimetres of precipitation annually. With the exception of mountainous or upland areas and coastal environments, the rest of the country gets less than 1000 millimetres of precipitation.

The area east of the Rocky Mountain foothills and south of a line from Edmonton to Winnipeg lies in the lee of the Western Cordillera, where most of the rain associated with the Pacific Ocean has been dropped. As a result, this region receives about 400 millimetres of precipitation or less. Evaporation is almost as great, so the region is semi-arid. Initially grassland, the prairies have rich soil and now produce a range of agricultural products, especially grain. However, drought is a problem and irrigation is employed in the driest areas in southeastern Alberta and southwestern Saskatchewan. A similar situation exists in the dry interior valleys and southern plateau of British Columbia. These warm valleys, such as the Okanagan Valley, are prime agricultural areas that require irrigation.

The other semi-arid region is the Arctic Islands, which receive less than 200 millimetres of precipitation annually. This area is referred to as a polar desert, and the lack of moisture after snowmelt limits vegetational growth in the most northern islands.

Canada is richly endowed with fresh water, much of which is stored in lakes and wetlands. There are more than 565 lakes larger than 100 square kilometres in area, and wetlands cover most of the Hudson Bay Lowland and up to 75 percent of some regions in the Canadian Shield.[3]

Water that is not consumed or evaporated will produce run-off into lakes and rivers. Except for a few catchments in southern Saskatchewan and Alberta that drain internally, as indicated in figure 3b, all areas produce some run-off. Approximately 50 percent of Canada, primarily the Prairie provinces and the Northwest Territories, produces between 100 and 200 millimetres of run-off. Greater run-off is generated east of the Great Lakes, and the mountains of British Columbia yield more than 2000 millimetres.

The two largest drainage basins are the Arctic and Hudson Bay catchments, which account for 33 and 37 percent of the area of Canada, respectively. The

Atlantic and Pacific catchments are much smaller, with areas of 19 and 10 percent, respectively, while internal drainage and rivers contributing to the Gulf of Mexico are less than 1 percent. The largest rivers, both with discharges of about 10 000 cubic metres per second, are the Mackenzie and the St. Lawrence. The total discharge of all Canadian rivers is about 105 000 cubic metres per second, one-twelfth of the total discharge for the world, but only half as large as that of the Amazon River.[4]

Abundant surface water has had a pronounced effect on the development of Canada. The large rivers, especially the St. Lawrence and those draining into Hudson Bay, served as gateways to the continental interior and the Western Cordillera for Europeans entering from the Atlantic, while innumerable lakes and smaller rivers composed the transportation routes on the Canadian Shield. Thus, many of Canada's major settlements came to be located along these waterways. Currently, only the St. Lawrence Seaway–Great Lakes system and the Mackenzie River are still used for commercial shipping, while the others are used for recreational purposes.

Rivers are also used to generate hydro-electricity in all provinces except Prince Edward Island. The largest of these installations are in Labrador (Churchill Falls), northern Québec (La Grande River), on the St. Lawrence and large tributaries, and in northern Ontario, northern Manitoba (Nelson River), and British Columbia (Peace and Columbia Rivers). Much of the output from these sites is sold to utilities in the United States.

❑ CLIMATE AND ENVIRONMENTAL CHANGE

As a result of the emission of carbon dioxide and other air pollution, or greenhouse gases, into the atmosphere, it is predicted that the air temperature may increase from two to five degrees Celsius in the southern part of the country and between two degrees Celsius (summer) and ten to fifteen degrees Celsius (winter) in the Arctic.[5] Scientists have only begun to consider the implications of this temperature rise and associated changes in precipitation, but it is clear that they will be far-reaching. Winter heating costs would drop and ice cover would decrease in the Arctic, on the Great Lakes, and in the Gulf of St. Lawrence, permitting year-round navigation at lower cost. However, recent studies have indicated that the effects of global warming are not all positive. While the growing season would increase, allowing agricultural areas to expand northward and productivity to increase, it would be necessary to alter the crops grown. Also, if precipitation decreases, drought could become more severe and the productivity of the Prairie grain fields may then drop as much as 75 percent. The forest ecozones would also shift northward between 100 and 900 kilometres and the productivity of the forest industry could rise. However, forest fires, insects, and diseases would also be expected to escalate. In the Arctic, melting permafrost would make construction more difficult and, along the coasts, rising sea level (half a metre or more) would inundate low-lying areas.

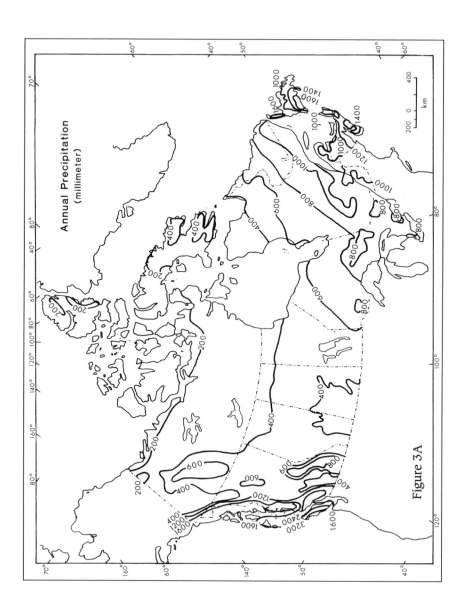

Annual Precipitation
(millimeter)

Figure 3A

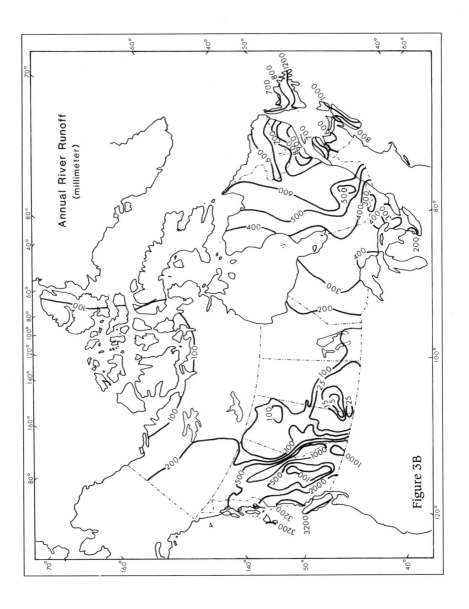

Annual River Runoff
(millimeter)

Figure 3B

SOCIAL GEOGRAPHY

"The geography of any country is what people see in it, want from it, and do with it."[6] Within this vast and varied land, unified by its northern setting, people have imprinted character and distinctiveness. They have done so to differing degrees over a span of some 15 000 years, but always as transients. Technology has dictated how much of an imprint they have made, as has the length of their stay, for Canadian peoples of all sorts have always been migrants, and still are. It is the exception for three generations to call the same locale, home.

❑ FOUNDING PEOPLES

The earliest arrivals, the native peoples, entered the continent from the Eurasian land mass skirting the polar icecap.[7] Almost certainly they came in waves; parties of hunters and gatherers of not more than a hundred or so at a time, moving ever onward seeking fresh game and driven by curiosity. Their environmental impact was modest, and their remains today are few, but their most recent arrivals have been labelled Indians and Inuit.

Today these peoples represent only 2 percent of the population of Canada. This means that in 1988 there were in Canada some 444 000 Indians and

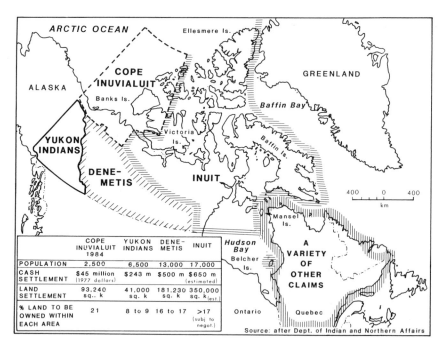

	COPE INUVIALUIT 1984	YUKON INDIANS	DENE-METIS	INUIT
POPULATION	2,500	6,500	13,000	17,000
CASH SETTLEMENT	$45 million (1977 dollars)	$243 m	$500 m	$650 m (estimated)
LAND SETTLEMENT	93,240 sq.. k	41,000 sq. k	181,230 sq. k	350,000 sq. k (est.)
% LAND TO BE OWNED WITHIN EACH AREA	21	8 to 9	16 to 17	>17 (subj to negot.)

Source: after Dept. of Indian and Northern Affairs

Figure 4   Native Land Claims in the North

slightly fewer than 33 000 Inuit, and in addition, about 98 000 Metis of mixed heritage.[8] The Inuit are the dwellers of the Far North beyond the tree line, the majority living on the coastal fringes of the Arctic Ocean, while others live in northern Québec and along the Labrador coast. They are recognized for their skilled use of the resources of land and sea, exploiting seal, fish, and caribou.[9] Theirs was a lifestyle that entailed much seasonal migration and, due partly to the numbers supported and the technology used, not infrequently involved feast and famine. When fishing or hunting were crowned with success, this was shared with all, but there were times of want, which effectively prevented the human population from overstepping the carrying capacity of the resource base.

This handful of people suffered invasion by Europeans over the last 200 years and especially since the 1920s. Missionaries and traders penetrated the Inuit homelands with crosses, rifles, and microbes. The Inuit lifestyle was changed, leading some to engage in exploitation of whales and Arctic fox for their foreign overlords in exchange for metal knives and pots. Airplanes appeared in their skies, and intrusive mines, trading posts, and later radar stations were scattered across their lands along with discarded oil drums and blowing plastic. In an accelerating process, their children were placed in white schools and educated in alien ways. They were encouraged to settle in government-subsidized housing, eat imported foods, dress in unaccustomed ways, and lose touch with their land and its resources. Some were supposedly fortunate and found limited opportunities for employment in this new world; others lapsed into dependence on handouts and alcohol.[10] The stress associated with these social changes has led to high rates of suicide, disease, and infant mortality. While there has been some improvement in these latter problems, the European lifestyle has brought with it increases in obesity, diabetes, and cardiovascular disease.[11]

More than 50 percent of the Inuit are under twenty-five years of age, and while their future is still in doubt, opportunities have been increasing in both the introduced economic sector and through a resurgence of more traditional activities. Thus, some have employment with oil companies and social and administrative agencies, some work as outfitters and guides within a growing tourist industry, and others work with soapstone and walrus ivory or have reverted to subsistence hunting and gathering and a rediscovery of traditional skills.

The Indian communities are similarly torn between traditional lifestyles and introduced ways, though they lived farther inland and farther south and were therefore subjected to European ways earlier and more completely. Their settlements are also small, usually fewer than 1000 inhabitants,[12] and a number are strung along the rivers such as the Mackenzie, where they call themselves Dene—"the people." In the Northwest Territories and Yukon there are no reserves in the sense that they are within the provinces of Canada, but recent government negotiations have offered them specific rights to large areas totalling 3.4 million square kilometres, or roughly 34 percent of Canada.[13] Fifty-eight percent of the inhabitants of these northern territories are native peoples, most of the south-erners being concentrated in the largest two or three of the sixty-four communities in the whole region. Here, again, abandoned wilderness is dominant, with population concentrated in settlements separated by great distances within a vast emptiness.

By far the majority of Indians and Metis live farther south within Canada's ten provinces. Here they represent a tiny minority, with some two-thirds still liv-ing on one of the 2242 Indian reserves, which total 25 954 square kilometres, an area roughly the size of Nova Scotia. Thus segregated, often on poor land and as designated wards of the federal government, which has recently been joined by provincial governments to provide health and community services, they have suffered from exclusion from Canadian society as a whole. This exclusion, how-ever, has allowed for their preservation as a distinct people. Although non-tradi-tional religion, medicine, and education have been thrust upon them, and some have opted out of reserve life and have been assimilated into Canadian society as a whole, there is today a resurgence of pride in a number of these communi-ties, and renegotiation of treaties and new arrangements with government are moving native groups toward self-government.

❑ EUROPEAN PEOPLES

Migrants from Europe reached Canada in the ninth or tenth centuries, but these Norsemen were brief visitors. Thus, even today there is some dispute over the significance of the L'Anse-aux-Meadows site in peninsula Newfoundland, as the place of their temporary sojourn.[14] There is no disputing, however, the arrival of fishermen off the eastern shores in the late 1400s, or of the subsequent settle-ment of Basques, French, and English: refugees from war-torn Europe and the limited economic opportunities of a class-ridden society.[15] True, their leaders had other motives—political, economic, and even evangelical—but the masses sim-ply sought a new start with the hope of a better life. Initially this was promised along the Atlantic seaboard through seasonal employment in the fishery and a return home with money to spend. The promise meant a temporary visit to an isolated frontier in company employ to make a "quick buck"—something still experienced by a small segment of Canadian society, be it on a hydro project in northern Québec or a drilling rig in the Beaufort Sea or the Hibernia oil field.

Canada, however, became a colony of settlement.[16] Men, then women and children, abandoned Europe, cleared the wilderness, and settled widely across the vast land wherever they perceived an opportunity for farming.[17] This pattern was to continue from 1611 to the 1930s. During the Great Depression farmers started to move on; large numbers sought urban employment instead, leaving behind the land. The frontier experience pitting humans against the harsh reali-ties of Canadian nature, be it in the forests of the Miramichi or the hayfields of the Peace River, is the stuff of Canada's past. True, pioneers tamed the wilder-ness, turning forests to fields, trees to grasses, and simplifying the ecology with imported species. The white pine, spruce, moose, and beaver gave way to oats, wheat, cows, and rabbits, but over large areas this was not to last. Since 1930 nature has been reclaiming rural Canada, especially in the East, as farmlands have been abandoned and people have retreated from the immediacy of wrestling with an unforgiving climate and deteriorating soils. Today only 4 percent of Canada's area is cultivated.[18]

❑ PATTERNS OF SETTLEMENT

The European economy was as much one of commerce as of agriculture, and for this, strategic locations for collecting, processing, and shipping were needed. Towns and cities were founded as the frontier became a producer of staple raw materials.[19] Thus, this marginal area saw a movement of people in, and fish, furs, lumber, wheat, and more recently minerals, out. Entrepreneurs combed the land for marketable resources to be shipped out by water, rail, and truck via corridors of exploitation snaking expensively across the vastness.[20] Where these routes met, or goods had to be trans-shipped from one mode of transportation to another, a town grew and provided a marketplace for local subsistence farmers, enabling them to move towards commercial production, capitalization, and mechanization.

❑ FRENCH CANADA

In New France, the precursor of modern Québec, this linear pattern was set by the St. Lawrence and the nodes of Québec City, Trois Rivières, and Montréal. Furs were the staple, and habitant farmers reluctantly grew oats and barley and raised a few animals when they could not engage in the fur trade. Later, as a seasonally-migrating, unskilled labour force, they were to provide the manpower needed to cut the eastern forests. Squared lumber floated down the rivers in rafts, and with technological change the smaller trees were cut for pulp and paper at the behest of British and American entrepreneurs. Not surprisingly, a number chose to leave, seeking their fortunes in the factories of New England. Others chose to stay, suffering poverty on the meagre lands while awaiting a better day. Thus French Canada was an overwhelmingly rural society until after World War II and the launching of the Quiet Revolution, having survived in the meantime the flow of masses of new immigrants heading up the river for points farther west. Then the French Canadians grasped control of their vast hydro resources by establishing Hydro-Québec, overhauled their educational system, and opened the province for business. Today, French Canada is confident in its new-found economic strength and is conscious of the immense water-power resources that provide it with sustainable energy, albeit at the expense of native people and the environment. What remains of the traditional rural population is aging and declining, while a new dynamism is expressed in numerous commercial enterprises and urban centres. These are dominated by Montréal, the main destination of out-of-province migrants and therefore much more cosmopolitan than Québec City, the old fortress and capital of the province.

Figure 5 shows the extent of French-speaking Canada,[21] but it should be noted that it has two very significant attributes. First, it is a larger area than the province of Québec, and second, it does not represent a culturally unified region. Thus, just as so-called English Canada is cosmopolitan and multiracial (including many whose mother tongue is not English), so there is a distinct difference between a Québécois Francophone, an Acadian Francophone, and a Montréal Haitian Francophone. Any notion that simplifies Canada into two monolinguistic "two nations" is downright wrong, and in any case ignores the founding native peoples, or first nations.

❏ URBANIZATION

Presently Canada is one of the most urbanized societies in the world, with well over 80 percent of its people living in towns and cities. These, in turn, are dominated by the three metropolitan nodes of Montréal, Toronto, and Vancouver, where one in three Canadians lives.

Toronto is the largest Canadian city and has the most diverse character, both in the variety of people who call it home and the kinds of employment they find there. Upwards of 70 000 people migrate to Toronto each year, many of whom come from overseas. Thus, especially in the core of the city, the population is extremely

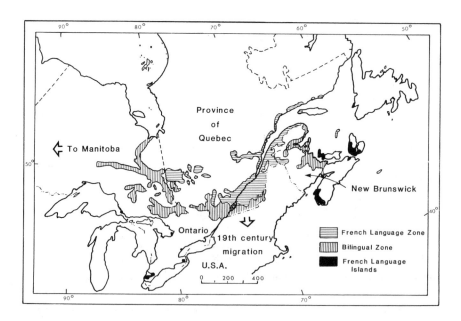

Figure 5 French Canada as of 1976

Source: After Cartwright (1980).

diverse. This has given rise to substantial growth during the 1980s as the city has sprawled along Lake Ontario onto some very productive agricultural land. This, in turn, has resulted in conflicts regarding land-use policy centred on this urbanization, which now takes in the neighbouring city of Hamilton and even the tender-fruit lands below the Niagara Escarpment.[22] Within the metropolitan region conflicts have also arisen between local governments, and of late this has been exacerbated by demands to enlarge the freeway system to relieve traffic congestion.

The geographical dominance of Toronto has developed from the strategic position it holds. Water frontage was initially important, as were nineteenth-century colonization roads to the north and west. Subsequently, rail links were built to the east, west, and north, tapping the rich farmland of southwest Ontario and the mineral and forest wealth of the Canadian Shield.[23] Additionally, the region benefited from the ease with which American coal could be brought across the lake to fuel early industrialization. Early in this century this was supplemented by cheap hydro power from Niagara Falls. Today, however, some 60 percent of Ontario power is generated by expensive nuclear plants along Lake Ontario and on Lake Huron. Historically, these advantages led to a concentration not only of manufacturing but of financial services and head offices of both provincial and national companies offering a wide range of employment opportunities, which in recent years have become increasingly service oriented.

Vancouver, the third of Canada's metropolitan core regional nodes is isolated from the Montréal-Ottawa-Toronto triangle, being some 2000 kilometres to the west. Facing the Pacific Ocean, backed by the Rocky Mountain cordillera, and overlooking the very restricted deltaic lowlands of the lower Fraser River, the city has always functioned as a significant port. At first Vancouver became a collecting point for the shipment of local timber and fishing products to west-coast American markets and those farther afield. Later, with the development of rail transportation across the mountains, it became a centre for the export of prairie grain, and more recently has handled large cargoes of minerals and coal for Asian markets. Meanwhile, numbers of prairie farmers attracted by the mild climate of the coast retired there and were joined in the 1960s by disaffected young people who saw the region as Canada's California. In the process, Vancouver developed as the dominant centre of the West and has accommodated an increasing number of peoples from homelands around the Pacific, adding an Asiatic component to the Canadian mosaic that contrasts with the largely European heritage of eastern Canada. Today, however, philosophies and heritages clash as exploitative natural-resource industries have depleted the forests and fisheries and will be forced to close down and move on if newer "green" thinking does not prevail to restore the economic base. Here, as elsewhere in Canada, little thought seems to have been given to planning for continued human resource-based activity, as the notion of moving on to new opportunities elsewhere has until now prevailed.

Second-rank urban centres give regional character to the other sections of Canada. Thus Halifax, the old military and naval garrison of the Maritimes, is the centre of this, the earliest area to be exploited by the rapacious Europeans. The region has seen better days: fishing and forestry are in decline, and in the nineteenth century much larger areas were farmed and the limited coal fields sustained the heavy manufacturing core of the nascent country. Now, as in other declining regions, subsidies and tourism, together with megaprojects such as the Hibernia development, hold the hopes and aspirations of those who have not relocated.

Likewise, Winnipeg, former gateway city to the Prairie West, is in relative decline along with its hinterland, and only the Albertan cities of Edmonton and Calgary hold prospects of continuing to flourish as long as oil and coal remain significant sources of energy. They have, however, failed to see a development of a full industrial base, perhaps reflecting the inertia of capital investment and the rise of postindustrial society. These communities maintain strong links north and south. As well, many people are derived from American settlers who have always been as conscious of the artificiality of the international border as of the tenuous nature of the ties eastward.[24] These folk inherited a land taken from the native buffalo hunters by a heterogeneous mixture of colonists dominated by Slavs recruited by Clifford Sifton, the Minister of the Interior in the 1890s, who had created the breadbasket of Canada. Railways, now frequently abandoned, along with the elevators that gave a distinctive vertical component to an otherwise horizontal landscape, are the relics of this region's past.

Not all the sheltering clumps of poplar remaining today mark the location of a homestead farm replete with a dugout to provide water in the hot summer months, for in the Prairies, too, many of the earlier settlers have left. Changing technology and alternative opportunities, together with grasshoppers, hail, and drought have resulted not only in abandoned farms, but also in strings of former service centres with decaying clapboard stores long since boarded up. The remaining agrobusinesses, heavily capitalized and indebted, are hardly a replacement for the former family-run farms. Once again, former occupancy patterns have become untenable and unsustainable without subsidy.

CONCLUSION

Canada was formerly interpreted through European eyes, which saw the vastness of the physical features in all their diversity and responded to the challenge of the conquest of this space and its northern climate. In this saga, these interpreters reflected their inherited background as the children of the initiators of worldwide colonialism. Now, their neat regional systems based on the appraisal and use of physical resources rather than human cultures and economies have been superseded by city-centred zones of dominance, for Canada today is a system of cities, not a scattering of farms. As such, it is inextricably linked to the American urban system and that of the world at large, and not to its particular set of physical geographic features. This means that people rather than minerals and crops are the resources of tomorrow, and Canada is starting to realize this fact.

Notes

[1] P.F. Hoffman, "United Plates of America: the Birth of a Craton," *Annual Review of Earth and Planetary Sciences* 16 (1988): 534–603.

[2] F.K. Hare and T.K. Morley, *Climate Canada* (Toronto: John Wiley and Sons, 1979), 230.

[3] Fisheries and Environment Canada, *Hydrological Atlas of Canada* (Ottawa: Supply and Services Canada, 1978), map 18.

[4] Ibid., map 22.

[5] D. Phillips, *The Climates of Canada* (Ottawa: Supply and Services Canada, 1990), 152.

[6] W. Watson, *Social Geography of the United States* (New York: Longman, 1979), 1.

[7] S. Yi and G. Clark, "The 'Dyuktai Culture' and New World Origins," *Current Anthropology* 26, 1 (1985): 1–13.

[8] Department of Indian and Northern Affairs, 1988, quoted in the *Globe and Mail* (14 June 1990).

[9] M. Sahlins, "The Original Affluent Society," in *Stone Age Economics* (Chicago: Aldine, 1972).

[10] U.F. Valentine and I.P. Taylor, "Native Peoples and Canadian Society: A Profile of Issues and Trends," in R. Breton, J.G. Reitz, and V. Valentine, eds., *Cultural Boundaries and Cohesion of Canada* (Montreal: Institute for Research on Public Policy, 1980), 45–135; and H. Kleivan, *The Eskimo of Northeast Labrador: A History of Eskimo-White Relations, 1771–1955* (Oslo: Norsk Polarinstitutt, 1966).

[11] J.P. Thouez et al., "Hypertension et 'modernité', chez les cris et les inuit du Nord du Québec," *The Canadian Geographer* 33, 1 (1989): 19–31.

[12] P.J. Usher, "The North: One Land, Two Ways of Life," in L.D. McCann, ed., *Heartland and Hinterland*, 2nd ed. (Scarborough: Prentice-Hall, 1987), 483–529.

[13] R. Platiel, "Hurdles Remain in Settling Native Land Claims," *Globe and Mail* (Toronto) 9 April 1990.

[14] R. McGhee, "Contact between Native North Americans and Medieval Norse: A Review of the Evidence," *American Antiquity* 49, 1 (1984): 4–26.

[15] R.C. Harris and G.J. Matthews, *Historical Atlas of Canada*, vol. 1, *From the Beginning to 1800* (Toronto: University of Toronto Press, 1987).

[16] A.G. Keller, *Colonization: A Study of the Founding of New Societies* (Boston: Ginn, 1908).

[17] J.L. Robinson, *Concepts and Themes in the Regional Geography of Canada*, rev. ed. (Vancouver: Talon Books, 1989).

[18] W. Simpson-Lewis et al., *Canada's Special Resource Lands: A National Perspective of Selected Land Uses* (Ottawa: Environment Canada, Land Directorate, 1979).

[19] G. Paquet, "Some Views on the Pattern of Canadian Economic Development," in T. Brewis, ed., *Growth and the Canadian Economy* (Ottawa: Carleton Library, 1968), 33–64.

[20] J. Vance, "The Corridor of Exploitation in the Shaping of Canadian Geography" (paper presented to American Association of Geographers Annual Meeting, Toronto, 1990).

[21] D.G. Cartwright, "Official-language Populations in Canada: Patterns and Contacts," Occasional paper 16 (Montreal: Institute for Research on Public Policy, 1980).

[22] R. Kreuger, "Urbanization of the Niagara Fruit Belt," *Canadian Geographer* 22, 3 (1978). This phenomenon is seen as well as in the lower Fraser Valley hinterland of Vancouver.

[23] J. Simmons and R. Simmons, *Urban Canada* (Toronto: Copp Clark Pitman, 1969).

[24] B.M. Barr and J.C. Lehr, "The Western Interior: The Transformation of a Hinterland Region," in L.D. McCann, ed., *Heartland and Hinterland*, 2nd ed. (Scarborough: Prentice-Hall, 1982).

Bibliography

Atmospheric Environment Service. *Climatic Atlas Climatique—Canada*. Map Series 1-5. Ottawa: Supply and Services Canada, 1978.

Bird, J.B. *The Natural Landscapes of Canada*. 2nd ed. Toronto: John Wiley and Sons, 1979.

Bostock, H.S. "Physiographic Subdivisions of Canada." In R.J.W. Douglas, ed. *Geology and Economic Minerals of Canada*. Ottawa: Department of Energy, Mines and Resources, 1969, 9–30.

Breton, R., J.G. Reitz, and V. Valentine. *Cultural Boundaries and the Cohesion of Canada*. Montreal: Institute for Research on Public Policy, 1980.

Cartwright, D.G. "Official-language Populations in Canada: Patterns and Contacts." Occasional Paper 16. Montreal: Institute for Research on Public Policy, 1980.

Fisheries and Environment Canada. *Hydrological Atlas of Canada*. Ottawa: Supply and Services Canada, 1978.

Graf, W.L., ed. *Geomorphic Systems of North America*. Centennial Special vol. 2. Boulder: Geological Society of America, 1987.

Hare, F.K., and M.K. Thomas. *Climate Canada*. 2nd ed. Toronto: John Wiley and Sons, 1979.

Harris, R.C., and G.J. Matthews. *Historical Atlas of Canada*, vol. 1, *From the Beginning to 1800*. Toronto: University of Toronto Press, 1987.

Head, C.G. *Eighteenth Century Newfoundland: A Geographer's Perspective*. Carleton Library 99. Toronto: McClelland & Stewart, 1976.

Hoffman, P.F. "United Plates of America: the Birth of a Craton." *Annual Review of Earth and Planetary Sciences* 16 (1988): 534–603.

Kerr, D., and D. Holdsworth. *Historical Atlas of Canada* vol. 3, *Addressing the Twentieth Century*. Toronto: University of Toronto Press, 1990.

McCann, L.D. *Heartland and Hinterland: A Geography of Canada*. 2nd ed. Scarborough: Prentice-Hall, 1987.

Phillips, D. *The Climates of Canada*. Ottawa: Supply and Services Canada, 1990.

Robinson, J.L. *Concept and Themes in the Regional Geography of Canada*. Vancouver: Talon Books, 1989.

Robinson, S.M. *A Social Geography of Canada, Essays in Honour of J. Wreford Watson*. Edinburgh: North British Publishing, 1988.

Trenhaile, A.S. *The Geomorphology of Canada*. Toronto: Oxford University Press, 1991.

Warkentin, J. *Canada a Geographical Interpretation*. Toronto: Methuen, 1968.

Wood, J.D. *Perspectives on Landscape and Settlement in Nineteenth Century Ontario*. Carleton Library 91. Toronto: McClelland & Stewart, 1975.

A Profile of Canadian History

Kenneth G. Pryke

INTRODUCTION

Until the 1970s, English-Canadian history was interpreted as a straightforward story that dealt with a limited number of themes.[1] This basic structure originated in the works of historians who were writing in the 1920s and 1930s and it survived relatively intact for almost forty years. This approach continues to have a strong popular appeal with respect to the idea of the state, and continues to influence discussions of national identity, especially vis-à-vis the United States. Its popularity cannot mask the fact that the underlying premises that gave it credibility have been systematically attacked by a new generation of scholars. No new syntheses have appeared, however, to replace the older views. Thus, the newer approaches exist in an uneasy and precarious partnership with long-established conclusions.

THE SEARCH FOR NATIONAL UNITY

A major goal of the English-Canadian historians during much of the twentieth century was to provide a sense of identity for the inhabitants of the gigantic land mass known as British North America.[2] This search for an identity was not restricted to historians, of course; it was undertaken by scholars from many disciplines. In the field of literature, for example, commentators with similar ideas reached conclusions that sometimes conflicted with and sometimes overlapped those reached in the field of history. Compare, for example, the views of a historian such as W.L. Morton concerning the role of Great Britain in the development of Canadian identity with the comments of Northrop Frye about Canada's "garrison mentality," or those of Margaret Atwood on the theme of "survival" in Canadian literature.[3] The overriding objective was to find some significance in the Canadian experience. This significance would at once provide a coherent rational bond between Canadians and a basis for separation from Great Britain and the United States.

The development of Canadian historiography was very much influenced by the prevailing tendency in the 1920s to view social and political influences as controlling political events. This view led people to see governments as agents of other interests and to view politics as less significant than the interests that they represented. Thus, rather than concentrating on constitutional and ideological issues, scholars sought to explain this country in terms of its geography and its economy. This was part of a movement that fostered the growth of the social sciences.

The new focus in Canadian history incorporated many, although certainly not all, of the intellectual trends that were being explored in the United States. One major influence on the importance of the frontier and regionalism in American history was the work of Frederick Jackson Turner. The strong emphasis he placed on the physical environment, or geography, had a definite appeal for those who were no longer satisfied with exploring the intricacies of constitutional lore. Another major American influence was provided by the earlier works of Charles Beard, who, in a famous book on the American constitution, purported to show how political decisions were determined by economic interests.[4]

THE STAPLE THEORY

Discussions of Canadian history frequently begin with a study of Harold Innis. During his long academic career at the University of Toronto, he published a number of works that provided some of the basic premises for the writing of Canadian history. The best known of these works, *The Fur Trade in Canada*,[5] concludes with the challenging statement that Canada was developed because of, rather than in spite of, its geography. This assertion that Canada has an essential physical unity might seem strange to those who fervently believe, whatever the geographers may say to the contrary, that Canada consists of five physical regions and that the development of each region has been shaped by its particular physical environment—it was no less startling when it was made in the 1930s. This statement was significant because it indicated, first, that Canada had an essential unity despite any North–South ties. Second, it suggested that Canada was not created by some historical accident or political absent-mindedness. Third, it showed that the role of the state was to adopt policies that would recognize the underlying geographic and economic reality of the country.

To propose that Canada had a natural unity that ran east and west indicated that the ties with Europe were stronger than those with the United States. Thus, claimed Innis, Canada formed part of the North Atlantic community. In terms of political ideology this position certainly differed from the American tradition, which from the time of the American Revolution frequently tried to minimize, if not totally disregard, the European influence on American society. Frederick Jackson

Turner was thus part of a very respectable and well-established tradition when he claimed that American liberty and freedom were derived from the frontier.

While other scholars developed the political and ideological aspects of Canada's North Atlantic links, Innis explored the issue of trade between British North America and Europe. In his work on the fur trade, and in his companion piece on the Atlantic fisheries, Innis developed the theory that the key to the economic development of Canada lay in the export of basic commodities, or staples. Certainly, for a long time the notion that European, and particularly British, markets were essential for a prosperous Canadian economy was as strongly held as is the contemporary view that Canada must at any and all cost retain access to American markets. This conviction reflected political factors, and the belief in the importance of British trade links remained long after their economic significance had faded. Thus, in the early 1930s Prime Minister Bennett fruitlessly sought preferential trade ties with Great Britain in an attempt to deal with problems caused by the Depression.[6]

At first glance the notion that Canada exported staples such as fur, fish, lumber, and wheat seems to be a self-evident explanation of the Canadian economy. What gave the staple theory its attraction was that it provided an explanation for the economic development of the country. The export of basic products stimulated the economy because of the need to provide certain services and materials. In the case of lumbering, camps had to be built for the workers, and ships had to be constructed for the conveyance of lumber to Great Britain. These developments, called forward and backward linkages, were seen as eventually leading to a mature economy; and they were viewed as politically important because they provided a means whereby Canada could establish a separate identity within the North Atlantic community.

Academics quickly recognized the potential of the staple theory for explaining Canadian development, yet it is curious that further studies of the Hudson's Bay Company and of the fur trade in the Canadian West did not build on the framework erected by Innis.[7] Indeed, in recent years his work has been the object of vigorous attacks. Part of the reason for this is that implicit in his approach was a strong presumption that the outcome of events was determined by technology. He assumed that the Iron Age technology of the Europeans was superior to the Stone Age technology of the native peoples, and therefore saw European domination of the native peoples and the complete disruption of native societies as inevitable. This theory was compatible with a general sense of superiority summed up in the belief that the Europeans discovered America. Further, there was the supposition that true settlements began only after the arrival of the Europeans, who believed in private property and exploited the natural resources. The European way of life contrasted with that of the native peoples who shared communal resources and who harvested, but did not develop, natural resources. Thus, the assumption of technological determinism drew on long established beliefs in material progress, and it was seen as entirely inevitable that the impersonal forces of history would sweep aside the native peoples.

What started out as a straightforward piece of economic history contained a number of ideological assumptions. This was apparent in the belief that the native peoples were manipulated by forces beyond their control. Similar assumptions were used to rationalize the defeat of New France by the British empire. In both cases there was a resort to technological determinism to explain these developments. Innis's position was that British technology was more advanced than that of the French, and hence that British goods were of better quality than those of the French. Furthermore, he saw the communication route used by the Hudson's Bay Company through Hudson Bay as superior to that through the Great Lakes used by the French. Added to this factor was the assumption that British social and political beliefs were more progressive than those of the French. Innis's analysis suggested that the French in North America were satisfied with a modified form of medieval land holding and that they revelled in chasing the chimera of the fur trade across half a continent. He contrasted them unfavourably with the settlers in the neighbouring New England colonies who promoted individual enterprise and developed self-reliant communities. Just as the Europeans brushed aside the native peoples, so the British overtook the French. The contention that the native peoples and the French both went down to defeat because they stood on the wrong side of history was akin to a modern morality play.[8]

The emphasis on the fur trade rather than on agriculture as the key element of the economy of New France was quite consistent with the thrust of the staple theory, which was to concentrate on exports. Economic activity that did not result in exports was regarded as a failed opportunity to achieve economic development. This same approach was applied to the development of British North America in the nineteenth century and it led to considerable focus on the export of such commodities as wheat and lumber. Essential for exports, and therefore seen as important for the growth of the country, was the construction of a transportation system that first took the form of canals, and by the 1850s, railways. The development of financial services such as banks was also necessary, not only to deal with exports, but to finance the many construction projects that were seen as essential. Issues concerning economic development had a very strong political component, especially for allocation of resources by the state; and they provoked some of the major disputes of the nineteenth century. Since such projects were regarded as essential for national development, it was all too easy to present any opposition, whether it be from farmers, Québec nationalists, the Maritimes, or any other source, as an indication of chronic discontent.

Issues concerning economic growth were thus central to the political agenda. Yet, at the same time, there was a curious distortion in the way in which the issue of development was treated. For example, burning thousands of acres of trees to produce potash for export was treated as an aspect of growth, rather than as an act of environmental destruction. This type of wholesale destruction was repeated with other resources, but this aspect of the economic growth of Canada has never been addressed in a coherent or consistent fashion.

Many of the ingredients in the saga of the development of Canada were given shape by Donald Creighton in a work originally published in 1937 under the title *The Commercial Empire of the St. Lawrence*. When the book was republished in 1956, the term "commercial" was deleted because it was as much a political history as a commercial one.[9] In this account, the St. Lawrence was presented as an essential link in both a transatlantic and a continental economic and political system. Unlike earlier authors who focussed on constitutions, political institutions, and politicians, Creighton's book stressed the role of merchants as the heroes responsible for creating the new country. This basic premise, enhanced by an imaginative writing style, had a tremendous and immediate impact on the perception of Canadian history.

POLITICAL ASPECTS OF NATIONAL UNITY

Some twenty years after first publishing his work on the St. Lawrence, Creighton developed his approach to Canadian unity in a two-volume biography of John A. Macdonald. As in his earlier work, there was a strong emphasis on the east-west linkage, which he perceived as being critical for the existence of the country. As befitted his subject, however, Creighton stressed the creation of political institutions, their nature, and the formation of policies essential for the development of Canada within the British orbit. The use of the biographical form as a device to present a political analysis was a significant break from the alliance of history with the social sciences that had existed since the 1920s. It also represented a markedly different approach from that used by Québécois historians, who were skeptical of the value of both political studies and of biographies.[10]

The Dominion of Canada presented by Creighton was emphatically British, and in his Canada the French Canadians continued to play a very negative role. This was particularly true with respect to the break-up of the Province of Canada. This body, which consisted of Canada West and Canada East, originally Upper and Lower Canada, had been created in 1840, in part to enable the British Canadians to control the French Canadians. According to this view, however, these expectations were not fulfilled because the latter had exploited their political position to obstruct economic growth and to continue their program of cultural survival.

In Creighton's account, Macdonald worked assiduously to keep the union functioning.[11] Ultimately, when even his tremendous talents were unable to deal with a conflict provoked by irresponsible politicians in both Canada East and Canada West, Macdonald undertook a vast reorganization of British North America. The basic justification for this movement, which resulted in Confederation in 1867, was thus seen essentially in terms of the priorities and objectives of the Province of Canada. The fundamental vision of the nation-building theme that emerged from this account was that the interests of the centre took priority over those of the periphery. After addressing pressing financial problems and pacifying British concerns provoked by the American Civil War, the country would find its proper destiny by claiming the Prairies as its own empire. While the benefits to Central Canada were stressed, it was much more difficult to determine how other areas were expected to benefit—other than by a voyeur's delight in the exploits of a neighbour. This cavalier disregard of the Maritimes actually reflected an all-too-common negativism towards that region in the writing of Canadian history.[12]

While the interests of the centre would control the country's agenda, according to Creighton the full potential of the country would remain threatened by the French Canadians' continued attempts to establish their own priorities. Creighton's view of Confederation obviously took very little account of the French Canadians, other than as disturbers of the country's harmony. He made his views explicit by contending that Canada was intended to be an English-speaking country with a French minority. He thus viewed with a suspicion amounting to hostility the creation of Manitoba as a bilingual province within Confederation in 1870. He also viewed with alarm the idea that took firm hold in the 1880s that the government of Québec, and not the central government in Ottawa, was the real protector of French rights in Canada.[13]

It is significant that the debate over the meaning and importance of Confederation to Canadian national development was carried on largely by English-Canadian historians. Thus, while there is a very impressive list of books and articles on Confederation in English, until very recently there were virtually none in French.[14] For French-Canadian historians Confederation marked not a commencement, but a continuation, of a long-established pattern.

While a number of historians challenged different aspects of Creighton's interpretation, the assertion that English–French relations formed the essential elements of Canadian history continued to be an integral factor in the centralist-oriented, nation-building approach. It was perhaps not surprising that such a perspective was not always shared by those on the periphery. There was no doubt that the four provinces of Nova Scotia, New Brunswick, Québec, and Ontario, which were united in 1867, as well as Manitoba, British Columbia, and Prince Edward Island, which were added in the following six years, were not strongly bound together. This situation, combined with the very reasons cited as justifying union, might have led to the conclusion that some form of decentralization would have been essential. On the contrary, however, the Macdonald form of governance, as defined by Creighton, involved the complete centralization of powers and the provinces were to be subordinated to the policies devised in Ottawa. Even those powers originally allocated to the provinces to solve the political impasse of 1864, which had been cited as a major justification for union, were to be exercised only in conformity with the wishes of Ottawa.[15]

The question soon arose as to how a country as diverse economically, politically, and socially as Canada could be administered. Policies adopted in Ottawa frequently benefited one area more than another. Sometimes these discrepancies were intentional, such as in the matter of freight rates. In other cases, the lack of financial resources meant that the adoption of one set of policies, which had a differential impact on different parts of the country, meant that others could not be undertaken. This was particularly true with respect to the opening of the Prairies and the building of the Canadian Pacific Railway in the 1880s.[16] During the Macdonald period the federal government was often able to have its own way. This was especially true with respect to the Maritimes, because the provincial governments were so short of revenue that they were virtually clients of the federal treasury.[17]

As controversy arose over public policies, it was inevitable, given the existence of provincial governments, that disputes would develop between the federal and various provincial governments. From one perspective, these disputes indicated a selfish, irrational opposition to reasonable policies that were essential for the development of the country. Furthermore, the attacks from the provincial governments were seen as attempts by those ministries to develop a Canadian version of the American "states rights" argument. Thus, the provinces and not the federal government would be the dominant political forces in the country. From this perspective, the growing number of complaints from the provinces merely reaffirmed the correctness of Macdonald's policies.

As long as the issue of the creation of a nation state remained a central concern of historians of Canada, the question of relations between the federal and the provincial governments would receive considerable attention. For Creighton, the growing attention to provincial powers and the recognition that provinces were supreme in those subjects assigned to them in the British North America Act formed the basis of a fundamental error.

In the opinion of another noted historian, William L. Morton, Creighton's conclusion was an elemental denial of the Canadian reality. Morton began his career by working in the history of his native province of Manitoba and he quickly realized that the Prairies had their own separate history. Later, Morton adopted the nation-state approach of Creighton, but he continued to be sensitive to provincial realities. Thus, he contended that the recognition of an active role for the provinces within Confederation, begun by Sir Wilfrid Laurier after he became prime minister in 1896, was essential for the survival of the country.[18]

The difference in approach of these scholars illustrates a basic disagreement as to the nature of the country. At the present time, practice (and to a large extent, belief) supports the view that the federal government is just one of the governments of Canada, and is in no way superior to the provincial governments. Yet, despite this dramatic shift in attitude, the standard historical accounts frequently continue to present Macdonald's attitudes towards the role of the federal government in Confederation in a highly favourable light.

Macdonald's approach was closely identified with his attitude to the development of the country. His policies were grouped by Creighton under the general term of the "National Policy." Included in this group of policies was the adoption of a protective tariff designed to promote Canadian manufactures, the building of the Canadian Pacific Railway, and the promotion of settlement in the West.

Presented in such a fashion, these policies appeared to present a coherent, well-integrated blueprint for the economic and political integration of Canada.

The construction of an east-west transportation and communication network would provide an obvious means of linking together the products manufactured in the newly-built factories in the East (a result of the tariff wall), with the newly-created markets in the West. At the same time, the growth of farming in the West would produce such foodstuffs as grain and cattle, which would utilize the railways to take advantage of markets in Great Britain. Although ostensibly concerned with economic issues, the very term "National Policy" indicated its political objective. The goal was to create a country with its primary linkage on an east-west axis, linked to Great Britain but achieving its own identity as a North American nation.

There was no doubting the appeal of the National Policy to Canadian historians, especially because of its apparent success during the Laurier period, which ran from his election in 1896 to the time of his defeat by Sir Robert Borden in 1911. Never before in history had an area been opened to settlement as quickly as were the Canadian Prairies. The sudden rush of grain onto world markets from the Prairies upset prices and caused serious repercussions in traditional grain-growing areas in the world. For years the United States had been the preferred destination for immigrants leaving Europe. Suddenly, Canada became attractive and for a decade more people came to Canada than to the United States. Canadians who for many years had sought opportunities in the United States now returned. They were joined by Americans who were much sought after by land companies because of their capital and their experience in dry-land farming. Immigrants came in such large numbers that the part of the total population that was neither British nor French in origin took on considerable proportions.[19]

It was easy to cite many examples of growth as proof that the National Policy was really effective. Some critics did suggest, however, that the National Policy existed only in hindsight and that the development of the country during the Laurier period was not the result of government policies. It was also quite possible that the extremely rapid expansion placed far too great a strain on the available resources and institutions. The growth in population of cities such as Winnipeg and Montreal created a demand for housing and social services that ould not be met. The opening up of new land was seen as a mark of progress, but vast areas were opened that required agricultural techniques that exceeded existing practices. Moreover, social bonds were strained by the perceived challenge created by the large influx of immigrants. Indeed, many of the social, political, and economic problems of the decades of the 1920s and the 1930s had their origins in the period of rapid growth under Laurier.

A significant feature of the debate that ensued was that it frequently revolved around the notion of the National Policy. Protest movements took the form of regionalism in both the Maritimes and the Prairies. The contention that the prosperity of Ontario was based on its manufacturing was quickly reversed to show that its position depended on the creation and maintenance of regional disparities.

But those who argued that the federal government merely represented the interests of large corporations in the East eventually tended to subordinate the antagonism to capitalism to a focus on regionalism.[20]

It was evident that the arguments of the political-nationhood historians did not go unchallenged. Indeed, their position on a number of questions led to a criticism that deepened over time. At the same time, it was equally significant that while their answers were often disputed, the debate turned on the issues they selected.

RELATIONS WITH THE UNITED STATES

Just as the debate over French–English relations and the nature of federal-provincial relations was an integral element of the nation-building approach, so too was the preoccupation with relations with the United States. The contention that Canada politically, socially, and economically formed part of the North Atlantic community merely established the nature of the argument. That Canada was a North American country was obvious and it had to be incorporated into the nation-building theme. The implications of this situation created a question of some controversy. At the first level, Canada shares a continent with the United States, although William L. Morton's contention that Canada is an arctic country served to emphasize the physical variety of the continent. While the impact of sharing a physical environment might be discounted, the overwhelming presence of the United States could not be ignored. As Morton noted, the need to continuously evaluate the relationship with the United States in light of changing circumstances is one of the permanent features of Canada's nationhood.[21]

While the all-pervasive influence of the United States is evident, so, too, is the fact that it is frequently selective. Thus, in 1935 William Lyon Mackenzie King fought, and won, an election campaign based, in part, on increasing economic ties with the United States as a means of delaying social reform in Canada. More recently, some endorsed the Free Trade Agreement as a means of curtailing social-welfare programs. Any assessment of the impact of the United States on Canada, of course, would depend on prior views concerning the real nature of Canada. In this regard it was notable that the nation-building theme should present the relationship as a conflict between differing political ideologies. William L. Morton, for example, saw the Canadian identity as inextricably intertwined with the British monarchy, a point that he underscored when he entitled his textbook on Canadian history, *The Kingdom of Canada*. This was a direct and effective way of separating the Canadian political ideology from the emphasis on individual rights and the stress on the revolutionary tradition that ostensibly marked the American political ideology. While contemporary social scientists often try to reduce politics to a conflict of interests, Morton contended that political ideologies do matter and that there was more than one legitimate nation in the New World. By emphasizing the monarchy, Morton obviously stressed the conservative nature of the Canadian political tradition. While there are many variants on this theme, much of the analysis of politics in nineteenth-century Canada did emphasize conservatism and loyalty to Great Britain as central to the Canadian tradition.[22]

The stereotypical view that Great Britain was an essential element in Canadian development and that the United States was a negative, disruptive force provided a coherent theme in Canadian history. Yet, as the twentieth century developed, Great Britain was less and less able, or willing, to play its assigned role. Moreover, concepts such as the monarchy gradually lost much of their credibility. In this respect it is noticeable that scholars such as Creighton and Morton did much of their work on the nineteenth century. Toward the end of his career, when Creighton applied his approach to the twentieth century, particularly the post-World War II period, it was quickly apparent that his approach was dependent on a set of historical circumstances that no longer existed. Rather than recognizing that Great Britain was no longer able to play its assigned role, Creighton blamed William Lyon Mackenzie King and the Liberal government for moving into the American orbit at the expense of the link with Great Britain.[23]

THE RISE OF REGIONALISM

During Creighton's final years as a scholar, the focus of Canadian history had already begun to develop a major shift in orientation. A thrust for "limited identities" began to break down the old insistence on one form of identity. Rather than regarding regional identities as disruptive and somewhat inferior, scholars began to concern themselves with a sense of identity rooted in a particular environment. This was the path originally explored by Morton, who had pointed out that the history of the Prairies was more than a thread in a national theme. With a sudden rush, the argument that the Prairies had economic, social, and political patterns of their own became a dominant theme among Western writers.[24] The explanation for this separation of the Prairies from the rest of Canadian society was found in its emphasis on agriculture and, especially, the production of cereal grains. No further analysis seemed necessary since a simple reference to the physical terrain seemed to provide a sufficient explanation. The history of the Prairies thus seemed to be simply geography in action. Prairie society was an outgrowth of physical features that were distinctive to that region. Yet, it was curious that this regionalism did not develop environmental or geographic concerns. Instead, it became a vehicle for expressing political grievances against the East. This was a type of regionalism that could declare that Ontario and Québec formed a single region because they held a balance of power in the country. Thus, the National Policy, which only a few years before had been presented as a means of creating a new nation, was now seen as a means of regional oppression and the device by which the glorious promise of the Prairies had been snatched away for the benefit of Ontario and Québec.[25]

There is no doubt that the cry of regionalism has been used by the provincial governments over the past number of decades as a tool against the federal government. The provincial governments have greatly increased their powers in the name of regionalism. While a maxim such as "Canada is a collection of regions" has gained widespread respectability, there is nonetheless a question as to the extent to which regionalism is really identifiable with provincial rights. Even the term "regionalism," which seems at first to be very straight-forward, is really very ambiguous. One should ask the question as to the precise source of this regionalism and what form it takes. Also, if that regionalism is rooted in a distinctive society, what happens to that regionalism as the society undergoes change? Obviously, although regionalism is a theme that animates much of the recent writing on Canadian history, it is not without some ambiguity as an interpretive device for the understanding of the subject.

There is no doubt that the wealth of recent studies on the various sections of Canada has considerably improved our understanding of the country. The benefits can be seen particularly in recent work on Atlantic Canada. For some time, studies on Canada ignored themes of particular importance to the Atlantic region. Subjects such as shipping were of less interest than the expansion of settlement onto the Prairies. Studies that dealt with subjects that were actually relevant to Atlantic Canada often ignored or discounted developments in that area. Implicitly—and sometimes explicitly—eastern Canada was presented as politically conservative and socially reactionary. Western Canada, on the other hand, was presented as politically progressive and socially innovative. It was noticeable that the concept of regionalism was particularly well developed with respect to the Prairies, and the notion that the West was the birthplace of popular democratic movements in Canada became widely accepted. Thus, emphasis was placed on the western origin of such worker movements as the One Big Union and on such political developments as the Progressive movement of the 1920s and the Co-operative Commonwealth Federation of the 1930s. The claims of the West did not go unchallenged by those who preferred to find the driving force for change in Ontario. This was true, for example, in the analysis of the struggle for women's suffrage and what was termed "maternal feminism."[26]

The notion that the settlements of the West, because of their very newness, were more open to innovation than the more settled communities of the East represented a Canadian version of the frontier thesis so long popular in the United States. The spate of historical studies in the past two decades, however, has produced a tremendous amount of new knowledge and a reexamination of long-accepted maxims. In the case of the Atlantic area, it has become apparent that many events, comparable to those elsewhere in the country, were either discounted or simply ignored altogether. In cases where the western approach was held up as the model by which others were to be judged, little allowance was made for different situations. The development of serious studies throughout the country has thus challenged some of the simple, although often unstated, premises underlying previous interpretations of Canadian history. The new work has provided us with a richer, more diverse, picture of Canadian development than we had before.

THE FRENCH-CANADIAN EXPERIENCE

If the issue of regionalism is a constant thread in the fabric of English-Canadian history, the nature of French–English relations forms its central design. Time and again, for example, this issue dominates the interpretation of the political development of the country. Thus, the policy of the English towards the French Canadians is usually central to an analysis of the extension of the British form of cabinet government to British North America in the 1840s.[27] Also, accounts of the union of the four colonies that formed the Dominion of Canada in 1867 focus on the attempts to reconcile the differing interests of the French and the English. The careers of political leaders, such as Sir John A. Macdonald, Sir Wilfrid Laurier, and William Lyon Mackenzie King, are minutely examined to determine their policies towards Québec and the French Canadians.

Issues involving French–English relations have undoubtedly been emphasized to the point of distortion. Thus, in dealing with domestic politics in Canada during World War I, most commentators have concentrated on showing how the introduction of conscription created a crisis and how isolated acts of violence had the potential to erupt into civil war.[28] Many English Canadians, however, were less concerned with conscription than they were with a war that threatened to destroy the very principles for which they ostensibly were fighting.[29] Furthermore, in examining developments in Québec, English-Canadian historians have often emphasized those aspects that dealt with the French-Canadian identity to the exclusion of all other issues. In stressing that issues involving French–English relations are the most significant for the development of Canada, historians have distorted the nature of the historical process and have thereby helped bring about the very situation that they have so often deplored.[30]

In dealing with the nature of society in Québec, English-Canadian historians have long preferred to present cultural factors as being decisive. Thus, the failure of Québec agriculture to keep pace with technical developments at the end of the nineteenth century is seen to be the result of a conservative, hidebound tradition that repudiated innovation and change. By resorting to cultural factors, these commentators have ignored such technical explanations as the composition of the soil or issues involving economic development, such as whether the Québec farmers had the capital necessary for the transition to new farming methods.[31]

The reliance on cultural factors as an all-embracing interpretation of Québec meant that the disproportionate control of the Québec economy by English-Canadian, British, and American interests was in reality a self-inflicted wound. The claim was lent a virtually impregnable credibility by the contention of Québécois intellectuals that their society was a rural society attached to the Roman Catholic Church, the French language, and the land. When Québec historians did begin to consider economic factors in the 1950s, they did so by examining the nature of the colony of New France and the impact of the British Conquest.[32] More recent scholarship, however, has emphasized how deeply Québec was affected by advances in such fields as physics, chemistry, and metallurgy at the end of the nineteenth century. Industrialization took place only in isolated pockets in the province and was not sufficiently strong to force a perception of Québec more in keeping with the new social and economic realities. The way in which old attitudes masked new realities can be seen in the famous paean to rural Québec, *Maria Chapdelaine*, which was set in the Lac St Jean region.[33] Missing from this work is any indication that this region was adjacent to a major hydro-electric plant and aluminum smelter. In this way public perceptions, and also many public policies, became increasingly separated from the economic and social realities of the province.

The economic developments that occurred in Québec during World War II destroyed any remaining credibility in the old belief that Québec had a rural economy. The new economic reality was not, however, transmitted into a new political orientation. The Union Nationale, under Maurice Duplessis, maintained a strong political control, largely by continuing to cater to a traditional demand for local control and by an extensive use of patronage. However, with the death of Duplessis in 1959 and the election of a Liberal administration under Jean Lesage in 1960, new political policies began to emerge. These explicitly recognized that Québec was an urban society. This recognition had been a development long hoped for by the English-speaking community, and especially the business community, which had expected to provide leadership for the Francophones. The result, however, was not what they had been expecting. The Québec state replaced the church as the principal guide of the people, and the long-established fragmentation of Québec was replaced by a demand that the provincial government take action on behalf of the people of Québec. The result was that Duplessis's defensive, and very negative, policy towards the federal government was quickly replaced in the 1960s. The new aggressive strategy succeeded in limiting the power of Ottawa to intervene in the economic and social life of Québec. At the same time, measures were undertaken to replace the English-speaking business elite with Francophones. What proved baffling for many Anglophones was the recognition that Québec, in becoming a modern, consumer-oriented society, had failed to identify with English Canada but instead had developed a sharply heightened sense of its own separate identity.

The dramatic shift in the perception of the nature of Québec society has resulted in an intense, ongoing reexamination of its past. Where once the outlines of Québec history were crystal clear, there is now uncertainty and serious questioning. This is particularly true of the role played by the Roman Catholic Church. The church that was once praised for being the guardian of Québec society now often stands condemned for having crippled the development of Québec to enhance its own position.[34]

Québec's focus on the value of modernity created a preoccupation with analysing the nature of a modern society, as well as on those conditions necessary to bring it about. While some were concerned with theories of economic development, others attempted to explain why the benefits of monopoly capitalism were not distributed equally across all regions. In looking at external factors, some commentators pointed out that Québec's economy had traditionally been oriented to the export trade with Great Britain, and the decline of that trade in the twentieth century affected Québec much more than it did Ontario, which had always been more oriented towards the United States. Others sought an explanation in terms of relations between regions. Québec was not alone in attempting to discover why economic development was concentrated in some areas and not others. Scholars in Atlantic Canada and the West have also resorted to dependency theories to explain their economic disadvantage. From the periphery of the country, Ontario and Québec constitute but a single region.[35] The attempt to explain Québec's economic position in terms of regionalism is popular, easy, and, in the long run, ambiguous and unsatisfactory.

Analyses of Québec's economy are one thing, but an explanation of the marked economic inequality of Francophones within that economy is quite another matter. While some commentators focused on theories of cultural division of labour, others tried to modify this approach by introducing theories of class.

The several theories developed to explain the general position of the Québec economy, and the position of Francophones within that economy, when considered separately, often had a degree of plausibility. However, none provided a complete explanation by itself and collectively the theories were often contradictory or incomplete. Theories of a cultural division of labour, for example, did not explain the relations between classes within the Francophone community. While particular explanations are still in dispute, the extensive work being done has explored critical issues for Québec and for Canada as a whole.[36]

CONCLUSION

The Québec history that has emerged in the last three decades has not only challenged traditional explanations but has explored new subjects and utilized sophisticated techniques that often were inspired by European scholarship. Although lacking the fervour of their Québécois colleagues, by the early 1970s English-Canadian historians were increasingly ignoring long-established approaches to Canadian history. The abandonment of the nation-building theme was due, in part, to a recognition of the viability and legitimacy of the long-discounted regions. Perhaps even more important was the growing skepticism of the significance of political issues. The extensive studies of Confederation, so popular in the 1960s, gave way in the 1970s to studies of social history.

The investigation of new subjects has produced a fresh perspective on many standard topics. This was certainly needed since many of the older approaches were extremely narrow and restrictive. Recent studies on the lumbering and steel industries, for example, have illustrated how the structure of these activities was altered by demographic changes in the work force.[37] Sensitivity to environmental concerns has also forced a reexamination of how natural resources were used.[38] Another fortunate outcome of the work has been to break down regional stereotypes in which reform movements were associated with the Prairies and conservatism with Atlantic Canada, while Ontario was accepted as providing the model for the country as a whole. This is certainly true with respect to recent work in both labour history and the history of women.[39]

The recent challenging and invigorating studies in Canadian history have pushed aside many of the older explanations. What they have yet to do, however, is to replace the nation-building theme with a more coherent framework. All too often a discussion of working conditions will be grafted onto a structure built around such political events as Confederation or the granting of cabinet government. What remains unclear is the extent of the connection between development in the political sphere and those in the economic and social spheres. The continued reliance on a political framework occurs more by default, however, than by design, because there is no unifying perspective binding together the various aspects of social history. While the field of social history is at present the most energetic and promising area in Canadian history, it is also fragmented and becoming increasingly specialized. Thus, while the overall image of Canada remains blurred, new perspectives on different aspects of Canadian society continue to emerge.

Notes

[1] For a comprehensive survey of Canadian history, see J.L. Finlay and D.N. Sprague, *The Structure of Canadian History*, 2nd ed. (Scarborough: Prentice-Hall, 1984). A useful bibliography is D.A. Muise, ed., *A Reader's Guide to Canadian History: Beginnings to Confederation* (Toronto: University of Toronto Press, 1982) and J.L. Granatstein and P. Stevens, *A Reader's Guide to Canadian History: Confederation to the Present* (Toronto: University of Toronto Press, 1982).

[2] For a detailed examination of English-Canadian history, see C. Berger, *The Writing of Canadian History*, 2nd ed.(Toronto: University of Toronto Press, 1986); for Francophone Canada, see S. Gagnon, *Québec and Its Historians: 1840 to 1920*, trans. Y. Brunelle (Montreal: Harvest House, 1982), and *Québec and Its Historians: The Twentieth Century*, trans. J. Brierley (Montreal: Harvest House, 1985).

[3] See the discussion of these issues by Professor MacKendrick in this volume.

[4] F.J. Turner, *The Frontier in American History* (New York: Holt, 1958); C.A. Beard, *An Economic Interpretation of the Constitution* (New York: Macmillan, 1956); a pertinent analysis can be found in D.W. Noble, *The End of American History: Democracy, Capitalism, and the Metaphor of Two Worlds in Anglo-American Historical Writing* (Minnesota: University of Minnesota Press, 1985).

[5] H. Innis, *The Fur Trade in Canada* (Toronto: University of Toronto Press, 1962). For a recent critique of this work, see W.J. Eccles, "A Belated Review of Harold Adams Innis' *The Fur Trade in Canada*," *Canadian Historical Review* 60 (Dec. 1979): 419–41.

[6] H.B. Neatby, *The Politics of Chaos: Canada in the 1930s* (Toronto: Macmillan, 1972).

[7] F. Pannekoek, *The Fur Trade and Western Canadian Society*, Canadian Historical Association, Historical Booklet no. 43 (Ottawa, 1987).

[8] W.J. Eccles, *France in America* (Vancouver: Fitzhenry & Whiteside, 1972); see also his monograph, *Canada Under Louis XIV, 1663–1701* (Toronto: McClelland & Stewart, 1964).

[9] D. Creighton, *The Empire of the St. Lawrence* (Toronto: Macmillan, 1956).

[10] Gagnon, *Québec and Its Historians: The Twentieth Century*.

[11] D.G. Creighton, *The Road to Confederation* (Toronto: Macmillan, 1964). The most reliable account of the Confederation period is P.B. Waite, *The Life and Times of Confederation, 1964–1967: Politics, Newspapers, and the Union of British North America* (Toronto: University of Toronto Press, 1962).

[12] E. Forbes, "In Search of a Post-Conferation Historiography," *Acadiensis* 8 (Autumn 1978): 3–21. See also his work *Maritime Rights: The Maritime Rights Movement, 1919–1927: A Study in Canadian Regionalism* (Montreal: McGill-Queen's University Press, 1979).

[13] For a contemporary analysis of French-Canadian attitudes in the post-confederation period, see A.I. Silver, *The French-Canadian Idea of Confederation, 1864–1900*

(Toronto: University of Toronto Press, 1982); J.-C. Bonenfant, *French Canadians and the Birth of Confederation*, Canadian Historical Association, Historical Booklet no. 21 (Ottawa, 1966). For a recent study of the post-confederation period, see P.-A. Linteau, R. Durocher, and J.-C. Robert, *Québec: A History, 1867–1929*, trans. R. Chados (Toronto: Lorimer, 1983).

[14] Bonenfant, *French Canadians and the Birth of Confederation*.

[15] For an examination of the post-confederation period see P. Waite, *Canada, 1874–1896: Arduous Destiny* (Toronto: McClelland & Stewart, 1971).

[16] For the most thorough and stimulating examination of the history of the Prairies, see G. Friessen, *The Canadian Prairies* (Toronto: University of Toronto Press, 1984).

[17] A number of useful studies on this period are to be found in D.J. Bercuson, ed., *Canada and the Burden of Unity* (Toronto: Macmillan, 1977).

[18] W.L. Morton, "The Relevance of Canadian History," Canadian Historical Association *Papers* (1960): 1–21. See also B.W. Hodgins and R.C. Edwards, "Federalism and the Politics of Ontario," in B.W. Hodgins et al., eds., *Federalism in Canada and Australia: The Early Years* (Waterloo: Wilfrid Laurier University Press, 1978), 43–60.

[19] H. Troper, *Only Farmers Need Apply: Official Canadian Encouragement of Immigration from the United States, 1896–1911* (Toronto: Griffin House, 1972); J. Burnet with H. Palmer, *"Coming Canadians": An Introduction to the Coming of Canada's Peoples* (Toronto: McClelland & Stewart, 1988); D. Avery, *"Dangerous Foreigners": European Immigrant Workers and Labour Radicalism in Canada, 1896–1932* (Toronto: McClelland & Stewart, 1979).

[20] D. Bercuson and P. Buckner, eds., *Eastern and Western Perspectives* (Toronto: University of Toronto Press, 1981).

[21] W.L. Morton, "The Relevance of Canadian History," 1–21. See also *The Kingdom of Canada: A General History from the Earliest Times*, 2nd ed. (Toronto: McClelland & Stewart, 1969).

[22] A key article in the discussion of the conservative tradition is S.F. Wise, "Upper Canada and the Conservative Tradition," *Profiles of a Province: Studies in the History of Ontario*, E.G. Firth, ed. (Toronto: Ontario Historical Society, 1967). A recent study of loyalty is D. Mills, *The Idea of Loyalty in Upper Canada, 1784–1850* (Montréal: McGill-Queen's University Press, 1988). A work that challenges aspects of this approach is J. Errington, *The Lion, the Eagle, and Upper Canada: A Developing Colonial Ideology* (Montréal: McGill-Queen's University Press, 1987).

[23] D. Creighton, *Canada's First Century, 1867–1967* (Toronto: Macmillan, 1970). This originally bore the working title of "Canada's Last Century." See also his *The Forked Road: Canada, 1939–1957* (Toronto: McClelland & Stewart, 1976).

[24] In addition to Friessen, see J.H. Thompson, *The Harvests of War: The Prairie West, 1914–1918* (Toronto: McClelland & Stewart, 1978); D. Owram, *Promise of Eden: The Canadian Expansionist Movement and the Idea of the West, 1856–1900* (Toronto: University of Toronto Press, 1980).

[25] For one example, see Bercuson, ed., *Canada and the Burden of Unity*.

[26] The conclusions in C.L. Bacchi, *Liberation Deferred? The Ideas of the English-Canadian Suffragists, 1877–1918* (Toronto: University of Toronto Press, 1983) are vigorously disputed by Maritime historians. See M. Conrad, "The Rebirth of Canada's Past: A

Decade of Women's History," *Acadiensis* 12 (Spring 1983): 140–61. See also E. Forbes, "The Ideas of Carol Bacchi and the Suffragists of Halifax," *Atlantis* 10 (Spring 1985): 119–26.

[27] W. Ormsby, *The Emergence of the Federal Concept in Canada, 1839–1845* (Toronto: University of Toronto Press, 1969). A recent and stimulating analysis of the subject is P. Buckner, *The Transition to Responsible Government: British Policy in British North America, 1815–1850* (Westport, CT: Greenwood Press, 1985).

[28] See especially A.M. Willms, "Conscription 1917: A Case for the Defence," *Canadian Historical Review* 37 (Dec. 1956): 338–51. This, and three other articles on conscription can be found in *Conscription 1917*, essays by A.M. Willms et al. Intro. by C. Berger (Toronto: University of Toronto Press, 1967).

[29] M. Shore, *The Science of Social Redemption: McGill, The Chicago School, and the Origins of Social Research in Canada* (Toronto: University of Toronto Press, 1987); D. Owram, *The Government Generation: Canadian Generation: Canadian Intellectuals and the State, 1900–1945* (Toronto: University of Toronto Press, 1986).

[30] R. Cook, *Canada and the French-Canadian Question* (Toronto: Macmillan, 1966); See also *Canada, Québec, and the Uses of Nationalism* (Toronto: McClelland & Stewart, 1986).

[31] For a comparison of agricultural development in Québec and Ontario, see J. McCallum, *Unequal Beginnings: Agriculture and Economic Development in Québec and Ontario until 1870* (Toronto: University of Toronto Press, 1980).

[32] G. Fregault, *Canadian Society in the French Regime*, Canadian Historical Association, Historical Booklet no. 3 (Ottawa, 1963) [first published in French, 1954]; see also his *The War of the Conquest* (Toronto: Oxford University Press, 1969) [first published in French, 1955]; M. Brunet, *French Canada and the Early Decades of British Rule, 1760–1791*, Canadian Historical Association, Historical Booklet no. 13 (Ottawa, 1963) [first published in French, 1962].

[33] L. Hemon, *Maria Chapdelaine, A Tale of the Lake St. John Country*, trans. with an introduction by W.H. Blake (Toronto: Macmillan, 1947).

[34] An illustration of a critical assessment of the church may be seen in the works of M. Brunet. Another illustration may be found in M. Rioux, "The Development of Ideologies in Québec," trans. G.L. Gold, in *Communities and Cultures in French Canada*, comp. G.L. Gold and M.-A. Tremblay (Toronto: Holt Rinehart & Winston, 1973), 260–79.

[35] E. Sager, "Dependency, Underdevelopment, and the Economic History of the Atlantic Provinces," *Acadiensis* 17 (Autumn 1987): 117–36. See also J.P. Bickerton, *Nova Scotia, Ottawa, and the Politics of Regional Development* (Toronto: University of Toronto Press, 1990).

[36] B. Young and J.A. Dickinson, *A Short History of Québec: A Socio-Economic Perspective* (Toronto: Copp Clark Pitman, 1988); K. McRoberts, *Québec: Social Change and Political Crisis*, 3rd ed. (Toronto: McClelland & Stewart, 1988); M.D. Behiels, *Prelude to the Quiet Revolution: Liberalism Versus Neo-nationalism, 1945–1960* (Montréal: McGill-Queen's University Press, 1985).

[37] C. Heron, *Working in Steel: The Early Years in Canada, 1883–1935* (Toronto: McClelland & Stewart, 1988); I. Radforth, *Bush Workers and Bosses: Logging in Northern Ontario, 1900–1980* (Toronto: University of Toronto Press, 1987).

[38] For a recent study that reflects environmental concerns, see B. Hodgins and J. Benedickson, *The Temagami Experience: Recreation, Resources, and Aboriginal Rights in the Northern Ontario Wilderness* (Toronto: University of Toronto Press, 1989).

[39] For an overview of women's history, see A. Prentice, P. Bourne, G. Cuthbert Brandt, B. Light, W. Mitchinson, and N. Black, *Canadian Women: A History* (Toronto: Harcourt Brace Jovanovich, 1988); Clio Collective, *Québec Women: A History*, trans. R. Gannon and R. Gill (Toronto: Women's Press, 1987).

Bibliography

Avery, D. *"Dangerous Foreigners": European Immigrant Workers and Labour Radicalism in Canada, 1896–1932*. Toronto: McClelland & Stewart, 1979.

Bacchi, C.L.. *Liberation Deferred? The Ideas of the English-Canadian Suffragists, 1877–1918*. Toronto: University of Toronto Press, 1983.

Beard, C.A. *An Economic Interpretation of the Constitution*. New York: Macmillan, 1956.

Behiels, M.D. *Prelude to the Quiet Revolution: Liberalism Versus Neo-nationalism, 1945–1960*. Montréal: McGill-Queen's University Press, 1985.

Bercuson, D., and P. Buckner, eds. *Eastern and Western Perspectives*. Toronto: University of Toronto Press, 1981.

Berger, C. *The Writing of Canadian History*. 2nd ed. Toronto: University of Toronto Press, 1986.

Bonenfant, J.-C. *The French-Canadian and the Birth of Confederation*. Canadian Historical Association. Historical Booklet no. 21. Ottawa, 1966.

Brunet, M. *French Canada and the Early Decades of British Rule, 1760–1791*. Canadian Historical Association. Historical Booklet no. 13. Ottawa, 1963 [first published in French, 1962].

Buckner, P. *The Transition to Responsible Government: British Policy in British North America, 1815–1850*. Westport, CT: Greenwood Press, 1985.

Burnet, J., with H. Palmer. *"Coming Canadians": An Introduction to the Coming of Canada's Peoples*. Toronto: McClelland & Stewart, 1988.

Clio Collective. *Québec Women: A History*. Trans. R. Gannon and R. Gill. Toronto: Women's Press, 1987.

Conrad, M. "The Rebirth of Canada's Past: A Decade of Women's History," *Acadiensis 12*, 2 (Spring 1983): 140–61.

Cook, R. *Canada and the French-Canadian Question*. Toronto: Macmillan, 1966.

Cook, R. *Canada, Québec, and the Uses of Nationalism*. Toronto: McClelland & Stewart, 1986.

Creighton, D.G. *Canada's First Century, 1867–1967*. Toronto: Macmillan, 1970.

Creighton, D.G. *The Empire of the St. Lawrence*. Toronto: Macmillan, 1956.

Creighton, D.G. *The Forked Road: Canada, 1939–1957*. Toronto: McClelland & Stewart, 1976.

Creighton, D.G. *The Road to Confederation*. Toronto: Macmillan, 1964.

Eccles, W.J. "A Belated Review of Harold Adams Innis, *The Fur Trade in Canada*," *Canadian Historical Review* 60 (Dec. 1979): 419–41.

Eccles, W.J. *Canada Under Louis XIV, 1663–1701*. Toronto: McClelland & Stewart, 1964.

Eccles, W.J. *France in America*. Vancouver: Fitzhenry & Whiteside, 1972.

Errington, J. *The Lion, the Eagle, and Upper Canada: A Developing Colonial Ideology*. Montréal: McGill-Queen's University Press, 1987.

Finlay, J.L., and D.N. Sprague. *The Structure of Canadian History*. 2nd ed. Scarborough: Prentice-Hall, 1984.

Firth, E.G., ed. *Profiles of a Province: Studies in the History of Ontario*. Toronto: Ontario Historical Society, 1967.

Forbes, E. "In Search of a Post-Confederation Historiography," *Acadiensis* 8 (Autumn 1978): 3–21.

Forbes, E. *Maritime Rights: The Maritime Rights Movement, 1919–1927: A Study in Canadian Regionalism*. Montréal: McGill-Queen's University Press, 1979.

Fregault, G. *Canadian Society in the French Regime*. Canadian Historical Association. Historical Booklet no. 3. Ottawa, 1963 [first published in French, 1954].

Fregault, G. *The War of the Conquest*. Toronto: Oxford University Press, 1969 [first published in French, 1955].

Friessen, G. *The Canadian Prairies*. Toronto: University of Toronto Press, 1984.

Gagnon, S. *Québec and Its Historians: 1840 to 1920*. Trans. Y. Brunelle. Montréal: Harvest House, 1982.

Gagnon, S. *Québec and Its Historians: The Twentieth Century*. Trans. J. Brierley. Montréal: Harvest House, 1985.

Gold, G.L., and M.-A. Tremblay, comps. *Communities and Cultures in French Canada*. Toronto: Holt, Rinehart & Winston, 1973.

Hemon, L. *Maria Chapdelaine: A Tale of the Lake St. John Country*. Trans. with an introduction by W.H. Blake. Toronto: Macmillan, 1947.

Heron, C. *Working in Steel: The Early Years in Canada, 1883–1935*. Toronto: McClelland & Stewart, 1988.

Hodgins, B.W., et al., eds. *Federalism in Canada and Australia: The Early Years*. Waterloo: Wilfrid Laurier University Press, 1978.

Hodgins, B.W. , and Jamie Benedickson. *The Temagami Experience: Recreation, Resources, and Aboriginal Rights in the Northern Ontario Wilderness*. Toronto: University of Toronto Press, 1989.

Innis, H.A. *The Fur Trade in Canada*. Toronto: University of Toronto Press, 1962 [First published, 1930].

Linteau, P.-A., R. Durocher, and J.-C. Robert. *Québec: A History, 1867–1929*. Trans. R. Chados. Toronto: Lorimer, 1983.

McCallum, J. *Unequal Beginnings: Agriculture and Economic Development in Québec and Ontario until 1870*. Toronto: University of Toronto Press, 1980.

McRoberts, K. *Québec: Social Change and Political Crisis*. 3rd ed. Toronto: McClelland & Stewart, 1988.

Mills, D. *The Idea of Loyalty in Upper Canada, 1784–1850*. Montréal: McGill-Queen's University Press, 1988.

Morton, W.L. *The Kingdom of Canada: A General History from the Earliest Times*. 2nd ed. Toronto: McClelland & Stewart, 1969.

Morton, W.L. "The Relevance of Canadian History," Canadian Historical Association *Historical Papers* (1960): 1–21.

Neatby, H.B. *The Politics of Chaos: Canada in the 1930s*. Toronto: Macmillan, 1972.

Noble, D.W. *The End of American History: Democracy, Capitalism, and the Metaphor of Two Worlds in Anglo-American Historical Writing*. Minnesota: University of Minnesota Press, 1985.

Ormsby, W. *The Emergence of the Federal Concept in Canada, 1839–1845*. Toronto: University of Toronto Press, 1969.

Owram, D. *The Government Generation: Canadian Generation: Canadian Intellectuals and the State, 1900–1945*. Toronto: University of Toronto Press, 1986.

Owram, D. *Promise of Eden: The Canadian Expansionist Movement and the Idea of the West, 1856–1900*. Toronto: University of Toronto Press, 1980.

Pannekoek, F. *The Fur Trade and Western Canadian Society*. Canadian Historical Association Historical Booklet no. 43. Ottawa, 1987.

Radforth, I. *Bush Workers and Bosses: Logging in Northern Ontario, 1900–1980*. Toronto: University of Toronto Press, 1987.

Sager, E. "Dependency, Underdevelopment, and the Economic History of the Atlantic Provinces," *Acadiensis* 17 (Autumn 1987): 117–36.

Shore, M. *The Science of Social Redemption: McGill, the Chicago School, and the Origins of Social Research in Canada*. Toronto: University of Toronto Press, 1987.

Silver, A.I. *The French-Canadian Idea of Confederation, 1864–1900*. Toronto: University of Toronto Press, 1982.

Thompson, J.H. *The Harvests of War: The Prairie West, 1914–1918*. Toronto: McClelland & Stewart, 1978.

Troper, H. *Only Farmers Need Apply: Official Canadian Encouragement of Immigration from the United States, 1896–1911*. Toronto: Griffin House, 1972.

Turner, F.J. *The Frontier in American History*. New York: H. Holt & Co., 1958.

Waite, P.B. *Canada, 1874–1896: Arduous Destiny*. Toronto: McClelland & Stewart, 1971.

Waite, P.B. *The Life and Times of Confederation, 1964–1967: Politics, Newspapers, and the Union of British North America*. Toronto: University of Toronto Press, 1962.

Willms, A.M. "Conscription 1917: A Case for the Defence," *Canadian Historical Review* 37 (Dec. 1956): 338–51.

Young, B., and J.A. Dickinson. *A Short History of Québec: A Socio-Economic Perspective*. Toronto: Copp Clark Pitman, 1988.

Social Inequality in Canada

Barry D. Adam

INTRODUCTION

Among the most fundamental questions that can be asked of any society is: Who holds wealth and power and why? It is a question for which almost everyone has some kind of personal theory, and it has inspired a rich research tradition in Canadian social science. The intent of this chapter is to sketch out some of the major findings that have emerged from scholarly investigation of this question, and that have begun to shape our understanding of social inequality in Canada.

On the face of it, Canada is a democratic nation in which citizens enjoy equality before the law, the right to elect their governments, and equal opportunity for economic advancement. But behind this image of formal equality, "everybody knows" there is a practical reality governed by distinctions stemming from wealth, status, and power. Some people have more of these things than others. The issues that arise are: How are these social goods distributed? Who is "successful" in our society and why? What are the implications of these distinctions for people in their everyday lives? This social reality is the preoccupation of this chapter.

WEALTH AND POWER

The obvious place to begin looking for answers to these questions is in the centres of money and power. Considerable attention has been devoted to the make-up of government and corporate institutions, especially to their top ranks. These include government cabinet ministers at both the federal and provincial levels,

Supreme Court judges, and the boards of directors of the largest corporations. Hardly anyone in Canada escapes the impact of decisions made by these office-holders.

As Michael Parenti points out in his review of corporate power, investment decisions made by business executives have a wide-ranging influence.[1] The decision to build or to close factories can guarantee the prosperity or decline of whole cities or regions. Mining towns from Schefferville, Québec[2] to Sudbury, Ontario[3] and Kimberley, British Columbia have been particularly hard hit by "boom-and-bust" cycles, as have manufacturing cities dependent on steel (such as Sydney, Nova Scotia or Hamilton, Ontario), car assembly (Windsor, Ontario), or pulp and paper (Ocean Falls, British Columbia). Corporate decision making, then, has considerable impact upon economic growth or decline within Canada. In addition, in an era of multinational corporate economies, capital can be moved almost instantaneously across national boundaries, giving major corporations the power to play one political jurisdiction off against another in securing the most favourable conditions for production, be they tax concessions, capital grants, special hydro rates, labour legislation, minimum wage rates, and so on. The result can be the export of jobs towards more modern or less expensive plants in the country of the corporate head office or a transfer of industries to Third World nations offering lower labour costs. These kinds of capital move-ments affect the wealth of Canada as a whole and have repercussions on a wide range of institutions dependent on government revenues, such as schools and universities, hospitals, pensions, social welfare, and municipal works.

The creation (or cutback) of employment, in turn, greatly affects both migra-tion patterns and immigration policies, including number and employment quali-fications necessary for immigrants. These movements of people shape the compositions of the national population, the growth of cities, and the natural environment. A "side effect" of industrial expansion, better understood today than ever before, is ecological change, which includes the release of toxic sub-stances into the air, water, and food supply, destruction of forests through log-ging and acid rain, and problems of global warming and deterioration of the ozone layer. These changes can have far-reaching effects upon the health and livelihood of large populations.[4]

The impacts of corporate decisions are not confined to the economic or envi-ronmental spheres—they also shape cultural and ideological values, resocializing each succeeding generation to regard its social world as natural and inevitable. Though audiences typically view television as entertainment interrupted by com-mercial announcements, from an economic viewpoint television entertainment is a lure designed to capture the attention of audiences to sell them the commodities advertised in commercials. The topics addressed in programming, ranging from situation comedies to news programs, must attract corporate sponsorship if the programs are to be commercially viable. With the partial exception of govern-ment-owned media, which do not accept advertisements (such as CBC Radio and educational television in some provinces), this reliance on corporate financing by media, which are themselves corporate structures, tends to reinforce a viewpoint that protects corporate power from critical examination.[5] Canadians watch an average of 23.8 hours of television per week, and media images of the world play an increasing role in everyday life.[6] The corporate media are engaged in an ongoing process of attempting to shape taste and fashion[7] and, ultimately, in defining what is important and valuable to its host culture. Most commonly, these values include a free-enterprise ethic of competitive individualism and the definition of personal satisfaction and fulfilment in terms of the acquisition of commodities.

Finally, it must be noted that the work of Harvey Brenner[8] and others has demonstrated a correlation between investment decisions and certain social problems. Every "one percent increase in the unemployment rate sustained over a period of six years" is associated with a demonstrable increase in rates of suicide, homicide, alcoholism, mental hospital admissions, imprisonment, family break-up, and homelessness in counties where the unemployment occurs. It is this kind of evidence that has convinced many social scientists of the importance of discovering in whose hands this degree of influence lies.

THE STATE AND CAPITAL

Wallace Clement's classic study, *The Canadian Corporate Elite*, inquired into the characteristics of the almost 1500 directors of the biggest 113 corporations in Canada who were resident in Canada.[9] (A further 301 directors resided elsewhere.) Clement found that the corporate elite was drawn overwhelmingly from people with privileged backgrounds. Forty-nine percent of them had parents, uncles, or spouses who were already in the corporate or state elites, compared to between 1 and 2 percent of the general Canadian population. Adding in corporate directors who had gone to private school or who had fathers in professional or managerial positions accounted for 68 percent of the corporate elite, compared with 15 percent of the general population. Only 6 percent came from parents who had more modest jobs, though this accounts for 85 percent of all Canadians. Clement also found that people of British ethnic background were overrepresented among elite corporate directors while every other ethnic group, with the exception of Jews, was underrepresented. The ethnic composition mirrors, not surprisingly, the religious breakdown of the directorships, with Anglicans predominating, members of the Presbyterian and United churches holding their own, and others falling behind in proportional representation. Only 0.6 percent of corporate directors were women.

Later work done by Jorge Niosi pointed out that Clement's definition of corporate power in Canada was too generous in that all corporate directors are not equal with one another.[10] Most corporate boards include directors appointed in an advisory capacity—most notably lawyers, financial advisors, and other technical experts—who do not have the power to make decisions contrary to the interests of the directors who actually own the largest blocks of shares in the corporation. If these advisors are taken out of the analysis, a much smaller set of very powerful families emerges as the effective stewards of Canadian capital. In William Carroll's words, "nine Canadian families control 46 per cent of the value of the three hundred most important companies on the Toronto Stock Exchange."[11] Among these are the billionaire families of Paul Desmarais, Conrad Black, the Bronfmans, the Westons, the Thomsons, the Irvings, the Eatons, and the Reichmanns.[12] A series of books by Peter Newman has given a glimpse into the lavish lifestyles of Canada's rich and (not always) famous. Included is a biography of Conrad Black, who took over one of Canada's largest financial empires, and a beautifully illustrated tour of the Palm Beach mansions and equestrian clubs of Canada's corporate elite.[13]

All of this raises the question of how corporate power relates to governmental power. This remains a hotly debated topic, with one school of thought contending that economic and political elites are separate, as governments remain responsible to the people through elections, and corporations are "private" entities preferring to do business without government interference. Opponents to this viewpoint hold that the role of the state in capitalist societies is to guarantee the conditions for capital accumulation. In other words, they claim that because governments depend on tax revenue, they primarily help corporations to make money and help "manage" the obstacles to this process, whether these obstacles are discontented workers, environmental destruction, or insufficient capital.

The answers to this debate have far-reaching implications for determining for whom laws are made, who gets taxed, how tax money is spent, and in whose interests policing is done. Dennis Olsen's study of *The State Elite* found that Cabinet ministers, Supreme Court judges, and senior civil servants typically share the social backgrounds of the corporate elite but that there was somewhat better representation of other ethnic groups, especially the French, in political positions. For example, Francophones made up 24 percent of the political elite but only 8 percent of the corporate elite; other ethnic groups made up 8 percent of the political elite compared with 5 percent of the corporate elite; and women accounted for 2 percent of the political elite versus under 1 percent of corporate directors.[14] Other work has examined circulation among elites, that is, the tendency of high-rank politicians to be drawn from or retire into corporate directorships when out of office, as well as more general personal and social connections between business and government leaders. Peter Newman, for example, notes that Brian Mulroney knew and "worked for" Conrad Black when Black had substantial holdings in the Iron Ore Company and that John Turner was a lawyer for Black's Argus Corporation.[15] Jean Chrétien came to the Liberal leadership from elite directorships with Consolidated Bathurst and the Toronto-Dominion Bank. Others have pointed out politicians' heavy reliance on corporate sponsors to finance election campaigns. Candidates who offend business interests are likely to be frozen out of the fund-raising battle.

GENDER AND SOCIAL CLASS

All of these studies reveal that Canada, like other advanced capitalist countries, draws most of its key decision makers from a relatively small group of citizens defined by their social class backgrounds, gender, and ethnicity. To talk about *social class* is a shorthand way of referring to the degree to which people are able to influence or control what happens to them in their own lives. Social class is the major determinant of people's *life-chances*. What this means is that social class restricts the scope of options and opportunities available to individuals in society. Most often measured in terms of income and occupational status, social-class position directly affects people's levels of material comfort and financial security, the quality of diet and living conditions, health and life expectancy, opportunities for education and personal development, job security, and job fulfilment.

One way of looking at the overall distribution of wealth in Canada is to look at income quintiles. If there were complete income equality, any group of 20 percent of Canadian income-earners would earn 20 percent of the total income of the nation. As it is, the wealthiest 20 percent of Canadians hold 38.9 percent of the national income, while the poorest 20 percent have 6.1 percent.[16]

Overrepresented in this poorest quintile are the people who have the hardest time maintaining a foothold in wage labour. Most notable in this category are old-age pensioners and households headed by females. Forty-nine percent of unattached men and 60 percent of unattached women over sixty-five, as well as 60 percent of women under sixty-five who are single parents, live on incomes below the poverty line as defined by Statistics Canada.[17]

In liberal democratic societies such as Canada, education has been assigned a central role in creating the conditions for equality of opportunity and in opening avenues to upward social mobility. Education holds out the promise that people originating from any class position can acquire the credentials necessary to secure employment that can guarantee an improved quality of life. Indeed, education does "pay off" with significantly higher income levels. In a country where barely 10 percent of the population acquires a university degree, higher education remains a meaningful route for upward mobility. Since the 1960s, the overall educational levels of Canadians in general and women in particular have increased considerably. While women have even begun to exceed men in earning bachelor degrees since the 1980s, they have yet to gain parity in professional and post-graduate education.[18]

Still, the educational system often succeeds only in duplicating and reaffirming the social inequality of society rather than offering the means to overcome it. Porter, Porter, and Blishen's study of 9000 high-school students found that social class background predicted university entrance better than did I.Q. scores. They conclude, "having a high self-concept of ability, which is associated with having high educational aspirations is very much related to the perceived parental aspirations and to the degree of parental influence, which in turn are largely a function of social class."[19] Since per-student expenditures for higher education have fallen steadily since the mid-1970s, colleges and universities fall back toward the pre-1960s norm, which guarantees an education only to those who can afford one, thus anointing the sons and daughters of the middle and upper classes with the credentials needed to retain their class status, while turning away working-class and aboriginal people from new opportunities. Indeed, some have argued that a primary function of the educational system is to legitimize class inequalities by convincing people that their class positions are deserved due to their failure to complete enough education.

Traditional studies of social class typically categorized women's status in terms of their husbands and fathers; yet women's growing participation in wage labour in this century has shown the degree to which gender has been used to limit women's life-chances apart from their social class origins. Despite some recent gains in the entry of women into the professions, Pat and Hugh Armstrong found that, overall, women are "still overwhelmingly slotted into specific industries and occupations characterized by low pay, low skill requirements, low productivity, and low prospects for advancement."[20] Women and minorities have long suffered from the "LIFO" phenomenon, that is, they are the "last in" and "first out" of jobs where a more senior white, male work force has gained job security and higher incomes. Women have typically made up a "reserve army of labour, taking paid jobs when new industries and occupations were being created, when men were off fighting wars, when the business cycle was peaking, [and] when seasonal or part-time work was available."[21] And as men have rarely taken up domestic work and child care as women have entered paid labour, women have often found themselves burdened with work both at home and on the job. The recent increase in enrolment of women in professional programs in universities is cause for optimism that women can become integrated into the social stratification system now occupied by men, but studies of political and economic elites suggest that women remain virtually shut out of the upper echelons of power.

DEMOCRACY AND SOCIAL MOVEMENTS

Social research into wealth and power in Canada has revealed that some social groups have a much greater say than others in law making, economic development, mass communication, and the distribution of rewards. It is hardly surprising, then, that various groups of people who are affected by these processes, but who remain outside of the decision-making centres, have organized themselves to resist or to change existing social arrangements. From the tension between the ideal of democracy, which holds that every person should have a say in the destiny of society, and the reality of democracy, arise social movements to improve the status of excluded peoples. Social groups blocked from the corridors of power make up the support base for organizations that seek to extend the promise of democracy. Not content with a democracy reduced to legal ideals and periodic elections, most social movements share the desire to give voice to a sub-ordinated segment of the population in order to influence the processes that impact upon their lives.[22]

Among the most historically significant Canadian social movements have been struggles organized around region, workplace, and household. Perhaps strongest of all have been the regional movements based on nationalist solidarities. Québécois nationalism has always been shaped by a sense among Francophones of being a beleaguered cultural island in an English-language ocean dependent for its survival on its provincial government. Characterized in the 1950s as a conservative, defensive movement, Québec nationalism found its greatest strength in rural areas, the Roman Catholic Church, and local elites—the heartland of Francophone culture. With increasing industrialization of the province through the 1960s, the cities, business, and labour became more serious contenders in the political arena. Through the Quiet Revolution of the 1960s, the political party of conservative nationalism, the Union Nationale, gave way to a government elected on the slogan *"Maîtres chez nous"* ("Masters in our own house"), which modernized the educational system and social services and embarked on a program of economic development. The Parti Québécois, reorganized in 1968, continues to appeal to a wide cross-section of Québécois who are drawn to nationalist programs promising self-determination through an independent nation-state that could defend its distinct cultural identity from a largely Anglophone federal government and corporate elite.

Native Indian organizations have tended to share nationalist convictions. Though composed of numerous culturally-distinct groups, 400 years of ongoing European conquest have brought indigenous peoples together to defend and attempt to reclaim lost land and cultural communities. Though British authorities once promised Indian peoples a nation in the Great Lakes region in return for their support in the War of 1812, they were dispossessed of the land from which they had survived for millennia in favour of small reserve lands. In British Columbia, the displacement of Indians from their traditional lands was never formalized by treaty and the process continues today as governments and industries seek to develop northern lands where Indians and Inuit continue to live on land still not "legally" recognized as theirs. When a joint corporate–government megaproject to build a gas pipeline through the Mackenzie Valley of the Northwest Territories was proposed in the 1960s, Frank T'Seleie, Chief of the Fort Good Hope Band, testified before the Berger Commission:

> There is a life and death struggle going on between us, between you and me. Somehow in your carpeted boardrooms, in your panelled office, you are plotting to take away my soul. . . . By plotting to invade my land you are invading me. If you ever dig a trench through my land, you are cutting through me. You are like the Pentagon, Mr. Blair [the corporate president], planning the slaughter of the innocent Vietnamese. Don't tell me you are not responsible for the destruction of my nation. . . . You are coming with your troops to slaughter us and steal land that is rightfully ours.[23]

In recent years, governments have begun to negotiate with native organizations usually with the intent of offering a cash settlement for land, as when the Cree agreed to cede a vast amount of territory for the James Bay hydro-electric project. But these have been very limited "solutions" for people who have never recovered from the invasion of their land and loss of their livelihood and who, as a consequence, have the highest unemployment rates, lowest educational levels, lowest life expectancy, and highest rates of imprisonment and suicide in the country. Public inquiries in the late 1980s in Nova Scotia and Manitoba have revealed that these statistics come about not only for historical reasons but because of continuing active racism in the application of criminal justice to native peoples. Indian movements continue to press for redress and increased self-determination to reclaim both an economic foundation and cultural autonomy.[24]

Other movements have centred around the effects of capitalist industrialization. Most central in bringing about the redistribution of income in Canada has been the labour movement. Workers organized into trade unions have been the single most important brake on the process in which industrial prosperity enriches corporate owners at the expense of workers.[25] In countries without the right to unionize or the right to strike, workers have frequently remained impoverished while owners of land and industry have enjoyed considerable luxury. The labour movement has been able to improve the standard of living of the one-third of the work force that is unionized and, as well, has been the primary force in the development of social programs that benefit everyone. In capitalist societies, the free market provides a wide range of goods and services—but at a price. While the wealthy are able to choose among them at will, the poor may be unable to afford the basic requirements of shelter and nutrition. A perennial political division of modern democracies concerns the policy of conservative parties to privatize certain goods and services in order to place them on the free market, while social democratic parties and the labour movement seek to remove goods and services from market considerations to make them available to everyone regardless of their ability to pay. Labour movement pressure has been critical in the development of such universal programs as health care, education, unemployment insurance, and pensions.

Like the labour movement, environmental groups might be thought of as citizens' defence groups against the effects of unrestrained capitalism. Local organizations press for workplace health and safety, monitor drinking water, oppose nuclear power because of the danger of contamination, push for recycling and energy conservation, ban smoking, and protest air pollution and acid rain. They are, in a sense, "mopping up after" and resisting the "side effects" of an industrial system with no incentive to solve these problems until profits are threatened by fines.

The women's movement has sought to increase women's control over their own lives, and a major part of its work has been to open the doors for career advancement, assure equal pay for equal work, and more recently, to revalue the work performed in female "job ghettos." As an equal-rights movement, the women's movement struggled for and won inclusion of sex in the 1982 Constitution as a prohibited ground for discrimination. Feminists work to resist harassment and violence directed toward women whether it comes from police, employers, husbands, or men in the streets. And in common with other groups such as activists for people of colour or the disabled, they challenge stereotypes presented by schools and the media and strive to project a diversity of experience and role models. Feminism also presses for a more thorough agenda that would change how people relate to one another at home, in the workplace, and in other interaction. Feminism contests the reliance of men and of the larger economic system upon the unpaid domestic work of women in taking care of family members. Abortion figures centrally in current debates (as did contraception before), because it asserts a right of women to control their own reproductive potential. Gaining control over one's life can mean not only the redistribution of wealth and power, but protection of the integrity of one's body.[26]

The gay and lesbian movement aspires, as well, to ban discrimination and has won the inclusion of "sexual orientation" in the human-rights codes of Québec, Ontario, Manitoba, Nova Scotia, and the Yukon. It offers defence against violence from numerous sources, and it works to allow homosexuals to speak for themselves against the many "experts"—religious leaders, educators, politicians, and assorted authorities—who perpetuate myths about homosexuality. Like feminism, gay and lesbian liberation presses for the freedom to express intimacy and sexuality without outside management by church or government. While the freedom to select religious and political beliefs according to one's own conscience is now an established right of democratic societies, the freedom to love and live with the person of one's own choice has yet to be fully recognized, and the gay and lesbian movement insists that the privileges and duties accorded to heterosexual relationships be extended to same-sex relationships.[27]

The legacy of social movements, then, has been to amplify the civil liberties of all. In recent years, Canada, along with the United States and the European Community, has witnessed a growth in new social movements that, despite their various particularities, have common interests in bringing about change in areas other than the economy. These movements seek to remedy problems of subordination in various spheres of life:

- at the workplace and in unions where racial and gender disadvantages have become set in wage scales, seniority, and "glass ceilings" to career advancement, in health and safety regulation, and in the distribution of family benefits;
- in the streets and public places where violence is perpetuated through rape, gaybashing, and predation of the poor and visible minorities;
- in households, with their own politics around who does the housework and who controls the "family" paycheck, and in housing controlled by landlords, insurance companies, municipal zoning, and social welfare bureaucracies;

- in the delivery of health and social services, with their patchwork response to women seeking abortions, people living with AIDS, those in non-"family" households, rural and aboriginal peoples;
- in churches that legitimize heterosexism, poverty, and the "place" of women in society;
- in the mass media, education, and the arts, where subordinated people find themselves talked to rather than speaking for themselves;
- and in the natural environment, where nuclear technology poses threats of total annihilation or slow poisoning, where acid rain threatens forest and fish, and air- and water-borne pollutants create new health risks.[28]

Social movements struggle to curb or modify the power of political and economic elites and, in their more radical moments, have sought to remove them altogether in favour of a more genuinely democratic social system.

CANADA IN THE WORLD SYSTEM

Until now, this chapter has treated social inequality as an issue *internal* to Canada, but Canada can also be examined in terms of an international economic order of rich and poor nations. Social analysts have differed in their views of Canada's place in the world economic system and the implications of that place for the future. Some see Canada as a *semi-peripheral nation* showing alarming signs of dependency upon forces beyond its control; others argue that Canada has the traits of other advanced capitalist nations.

Canada's dependency is most evident in the ownership patterns of the economy, with the majority of the largest corporations in most economic sectors being owned abroad. As Clement showed, the majority of fundamental industries such as mining, manufacturing, and the retail trade are owned by foreigners, especially US corporations.[29] Finance, communication, transportation, and utilities remain in Canadian hands, at least partly due to government regulations. For most of this century, banks and insurance companies were protected from foreign takeover by laws restricting foreign shareholding. Radio and television enjoy similar protection, while railways and airlines have had significant direct federal government ownership through Crown corporations, and hydro power has, in most instances, been managed by provincial governments.

The dependency school in Canadian studies argues that this ownership pattern has a number of important consequences. First, any analysis of Canadian elites reveals only part of the picture because so much of the economic direction of the nation comes from head offices in New York, Houston, and Chicago, which are even less accessible to the concerns and needs of Canadians. Second, this ownership pattern enriches foreign elites with profits generated in Canada but lost to it. Canada tends to remain "underdeveloped," being heavily dependent on resource extraction, that is, oil, minerals, forests, and grains, while research and innovation in manufacturing and high technology go on at corporate headquarters outside the country. Foreign corporations set up shop in Canada to sell to the domestic market but have little interest in creating new products for export since this can be done at the parent corporation. A consequence of this is fewer jobs for Canadian scientists and professionals. Whereas 22 percent of the US labour force is engaged in highly qualified occupations, only 17 percent of the Canadian labour force is similarly employed.[30] The manufacturing sector employs 17 percent of professional and technical workers in the United States, but only 8 percent in Canada, and thus the balance must rely on the Canadian-owned sector and government for employment.

This assessment of Canadian dependency has stimulated a nationalist movement critical of Canadian governments, which it sees as compliant with US interests in foreign policy, military control, and economic development. Nationalists interpret free trade with the United States as a further capitulation to US domination, as trends toward the privatization of Crown corporations and the removal of Canadian ownership laws leave the nation open to an accelerated buy-out by foreign capital, and leave Canadians with declining control over economic and cultural development. The result is that Canadian workers become more directly exposed to the forces of the global economy with fewer safeguards to limit the accelerated movement of capital, which can devastate cities and regions.

Others deny the fears of nationalists, pointing out that Canada has the socio-economic profile of a rich nation with a small agricultural sector, large service sector, and high per capita income. Foreign investment in Canada, they argue, is matched by extensive Canadian investment elsewhere. Both foreign investment and free trade are indicative of a growing internationalization of capital in which investors—at least among the advanced, capitalist nations of western Europe, North America, and Japan—move capital without regard to national boundaries, and multinational corporate trading blocs are sidelining national governments.[31] Like other capitalist powers, Canada has its own dependencies with significant holdings in the Caribbean and other Third World countries.[32] Free trade, in this view, may allow Canadian entrepreneurs access to larger markets, which will generate more wealth for Canada, more money for innovation, and more jobs. According to this argument, government supervision of capital movements results only in discouraging foreign investment and the creation of new jobs without doing anything about the distribution of wealth and power within Canada.

CONCLUSION

Social science has been illuminating patterns of wealth, status, and power in Canada, and has also considered Canada's place in the world system. Behind the facade of formal democracy and equality are discernable sets of people with an immense capacity to shape the destiny of the nation in terms of its economic development, cultural and ideological reconstruction, and natural environment.

Social movements have mobilized many Canadians from time to time to challenge that power and to extend rights and freedoms to more and more people. At its best, the study of Canadian society may allow people to reflect upon their place in the scheme of things and to decide how current social arrangements might be improved.

Notes

[1] M. Parenti, *Power and the Powerless* (New York: St Martin's Press, 1978).

[2] Before his election to the leadership of the Progressive Conservative Party, Prime Minister Brian Mulroney presided over the closure of the Schefferville mine as president of the Iron Ore Company, a subsidiary of an Ohio-based corporation.

[3] W. Clement, *Hard-Rock Mining* (Toronto: McClelland & Stewart, 1981).

[4] W. Leiss, ed., *Ecology versus Politics in Canada* (Toronto: University of Toronto Press, 1979).

[5] See E. Herman and N. Chomsky, *Manufacturing Consent* (New York: Pantheon, 1988). Canada, Kent Commission, *Royal Commission on Newspapers* (Ottawa: Supply and Services Canada, 1981).

[6] G. Mori, "Religious Affiliation in Canada," *Canadian Social Trends* (Autumn 1987): 15, and A. Young, "Television Viewing," *Canadian Social Trends* (Autumn 1989): 14.

[7] See S. Ewen and E. Ewen, *Channels of Desire* (New York: McGraw-Hill, 1982).

[8] H. Brenner, *Estimating the Social Costs of National Economic Policy* (Washington, DC: Joint Economic Committee, United States Government Printing Office, 1976).

[9] W. Clement, *The Canadian Corporate Elite* (Toronto: McClelland & Stewart, 1975).

[10] J. Niosi, *Canadian Capitalism* (Toronto: Lorimer, 1981).

[11] W. Carroll, *Corporate Power and Canadian Capitalism* (Vancouver: University of British Columbia Press, 1986), 182.

[12] D. Francis, *Controlling Interests* (Toronto: Macmillan, 1986), 182.

[13] P. Newman, *The Establishment Man* (Toronto: McClelland & Stewart, 1982); P. Newman, *Debrett's Illustrated Guide to the Canadian Establishment* (Toronto: Methuen, 1983).

[14] D. Olsen, *The State Elite* (Toronto: McClelland & Stewart, 1980).

[15] Newman, *The Establishment Man.*

[16] A. Himelfarb and C.J. Richardson, *Sociology for Canadians* (Toronto: McGraw-Hill Ryerson, 1982), 277.

[17] National Council on Welfare, "Poverty in Canada," and "Sixty-five and Older," in J. Curtis et al., eds., *Social Inequality in Canada* (Scarborough: Prentice-Hall, 1988).

[18] S. Gilbert and N. Guppy, "Trends in Participation in Higher Education by Gender," in Curtis et al., *Social Inequality in Canada.*

[19] J. Porter, M. Porter, and B. Blishen, *Stations and Callings* (Toronto: Methuen, 1982), 312.

[20] P. Armstrong and H. Armstrong, *The Double Ghetto* (Toronto: McClelland & Stewart, 1984), 18.

[21] Ibid., 21.

[22] S. Bowles and H. Gintis, *Democracy and Capitalism* (New York: Basic, 1987).

[23] Canada, Berger Commission, *Northern Frontier, Northern Homeland* (Ottawa: Supply and Services Canada, 1977).

[24] See M. Hedley, chapter 4 in this volume.

[25] A. Hunter, *Class Tells*, 2nd ed. (Toronto: Butterworths, 1986).

[26] A. Miles and G. Finn, eds., *Feminism* (Montreal: Black Rose, 1986).

[27] B.D. Adam, *The Rise of a Gay and Lesbian Movement* (Boston: G.K. Hall, 1987).

[28] B.D. Adam, "(Post) Marxism and the New Social Movements" (Plenary address to the Society for the Study of Social Movements, Cincinnati, Ohio, 1991).

[29] W. Clement, *Continental Corporate Power* (Toronto: McClelland & Stewart, 1977).

[30] J. Novek, "University–industry Interaction," *Social Science Federation of Canada Bulletin* (Dec. 1983): 8.

[31] Carroll, *Corporate Power and Canadian Capitalism*.

[32] J. Niosi, *Canadian Multinationals* (Toronto: Between the Lines, 1985).

Bibliography

Adam, B.D. "(Post) Marxism and the New Social Movements." Plenary address to the Society for the Study of Social Problems, Cincinnati, Ohio, 1991.

Adam, B.D. *The Rise of a Gay and Lesbian Movement*. Boston: G.K. Hall, 1987.

Berger Commission (Canada). *Northern Frontier, Northern Homeland*. Ottawa: Supply and Services Canada, 1977.

Bowles, S., and H. Gintis. *Democracy and Capitalism*. New York: Basic Books, 1987.

Brenner, H. *Estimating the Social Costs of National Economic Policy*. Washington, DC: Joint Economic Committee, United States Government Printing Office, 1976.

Carroll, W. *Corporate Power and Canadian Capitalism*. Vancouver: University of British Columbia Press, 1986.

Clement, W. *The Canadian Corporate Elite*. Toronto: McClelland & Stewart, 1975.

Clement, W. *Continental Corporate Power*. Toronto: McClelland & Stewart, 1977.

Clement, W. *Hard-Rock Mining*. Toronto: McClelland and Stewart, 1981.

Curtis, J., E. Grabb, N. Guppy, and S. Gilbert, eds. *Social Inequality in Canada*. Scarborough: Prentice-Hall, 1986.

Ewen, S., and E. Ewen. *Channels of Desire*. New York: McGraw-Hill, 1982.

Francis, D. *Controlling Interests*. Toronto: Macmillan, 1986.

Herman, E., and N. Chomsky. *Manufacturing Consent*. New York: Pantheon, 1988.

Himelfarb, A., and C.J. Richardson. *Sociology for Canadians*. Toronto: McGraw Hill Ryerson, 1982.

Hunter, A. *Class Tells*. 2nd ed. Toronto: Butterworths, 1986.

Kent Commission (Canada). *Royal Commission on Newspapers*. Ottawa: Supply and Services Canada, 1981.

Leiss, W. *Ecology versus Politics in Canada*. Toronto: University of Toronto Press, 1979.

Miles, A., and G. Finn, eds. *Feminism*. Montreal: Black Rose, 1988.

Newman, P. *Debrett's Illustrated Guide to the Canadian Establishment*. Toronto: Methuen, 1983.

Newman, P. *The Establishment Man*. Toronto: McClelland & Stewart, 1982.

Mori, G. "Religious Affiliation in Canada," *Canadian Social Trends* (Autumn 1987): 12–16.

Niosi, J. *Canadian Capitalism*. Toronto: Lorimer, 1981.

Niosi, J. *Canadian Multinationals*. Toronto: Between the Lines, 1985.

Novek, J. "University-industry Interaction," *Social Science Federation of Canada Bulletin* (Dec. 1983).

Olsen, D. *The State Elite*. Toronto: McClelland & Stewart, 1980.

Parenti, M. *Power and the Powerless*. New York: St. Martin's Press, 1978.

Porter, J., M. Porter and B. Blishen. *Stations and Callings*. Toronto: Methuen, 1982.

Young, A. "Television Viewing," *Canadian Social Trends* (Autumn 1989): 13–15.

Native Peoples in Canada*

Max J. Hedley

INTRODUCTION

T he prevailing imagery of aboriginal peoples in Canada rests on a radical distinction drawn between "them" and "us." This is most commonly expressed in an opposition between "Indian" and "white," though the meanings ("stereotypes" would be a better term) that are associated with these words vary considerably. In this view, native peoples are seen to possess a common cultural heritage that not only makes them distinct, but that sets them apart because they are understood as being outside of Canadian society. More negatively, they are represented as a people bound by traditions that prevent them from becoming part of the modern world. It was such a perspective that informed and justified government policies that sought to destroy traditional ways of life and assimilate (the older term was "civilize") aboriginal peoples into the beliefs and practices of western society. This process is vividly captured by the phrase "cultural genocide."

Alternatively, the position of native peoples is seen to be a reminder not only of past injustices and present inequalities, but also of the inequalities and problems that beset industrial society generally. Cast in this more favourable light, their culture has been incorporated into a critique of civilization. In this view, transgressions of the workplace, environmental degradation, excessive levels of

*The author would like to acknowledge the support of the Institute of Social and Economic Research, Memorial University of Newfoundland, and the Social Science and Humanities Research Council of Canada (Award No. 410-89-1559). Maps drawn by Margaret Lawrence.

consumption, and the possessiveness of western culture are held in stark contrast to the more natural and harmonious representation of native culture.

Whatever the attraction of these ideas, they do not offer a reliable means of understanding the position of aboriginal peoples in Canadian society. Both views, negative or positive, share the assumption that native peoples exist outside of society. When we adopt this view, we tend to down-play the significance of the many ways in which native peoples have become part of Canadian society, and that this involvement has long historical roots. Such views also contain the assumption that aboriginal peoples are the same in their "otherness." This easily leads us to ignore the range of current and past diversity in that we simply think in terms of a single Native Culture.[1] In fact, this diversity should serve to remind us that the terms *Indian* and *native* are the "gifts" of an ethnocentric European world view, which showed little appreciation of cultural diversity other than as an indicator of cultural distance from the achievement of civilization in the grand evolutionary schemes of the nineteenth century. A third erroneous assumption is that white society itself is characterized by social and economic equality. This allows us to lose sight of the significance of differences in such social characteristics as wealth, power, ethnicity, and gender, which separate the interests and life experiences of different groups and individuals within Canadian society.[2]

Starting from the foregoing premises, we are easily led to see the problems confronting native peoples today as stemming from a refusal to change and become part of Canadian society. Thus, we are but a short step from concluding that this perceived failure to enter white society is rooted in their own traditions or backwardness and, from this, advocating a policy of assimilation. In other words, we are led to the view that it is only when aboriginal cultures give way to white culture (the process of assimilation) that their social and economic difficulties will be resolved. By working with such a model, we fail to recognize the many ways in which the lives of aboriginal peoples are incorporated into the institutional structures of Canadian society. Consequently, we are unable to appreciate the extent to which the mode of incorporation has shaped the social, cultural, and economic problems that confront them.

This chapter is structured around two interlocking themes. The first theme develops the idea that native peoples, despite their continuing cultural distinctiveness, are very much part of the modern world. In discussing this, some of the ways in which their incorporation into Canadian society is distinct from that of other social groups will be highlighted. This will entail a brief discussion of unique aspects of their legal rights and their relationship with the federal government. The second theme provides a clear indication of the considerable diversity found in the situations of different native communities. This will be obtained through a brief examination of a group of northern hunter-trappers and a reserve community in southern Ontario.

ABORIGINAL AND TREATY RIGHTS

One major outcome of a long process of colonization was the erosion of the territorial and political independence of native peoples. As recently as 1969, the federal government was prepared to assert that this loss was total and that aboriginal rights would not be recognized.[3] This was in stark contrast to the native perspective. According to this view, aboriginal rights had not been irrevocably lost, but could be reclaimed through the legal framework that had been imposed upon them by the colonizing powers. A little more than a decade later it was the native view that was confirmed, for the same Liberal government recognized aboriginal rights and the binding nature of treaties by enshrining them in the new Canadian Constitution. Section 35 of the 1982 Constitution Act "recognizes and affirms" the "existing aboriginal and treaty rights" of Indian, Inuit, and Metis of Canada.[4] It may be noted that the nature of these rights, and a delineation of who falls into the categories of Indian, Inuit, and Metis remains undecided.[5]

An important precursor to this change was the ruling of the Supreme Court of Canada (1972) in a case concerning the Nishga people of British Columbia. The Nishga sought to establish aboriginal title to land that they and their ancestors had occupied and used from time immemorial, which had not been ceded by treaty.[6] The Nishga claim was lost on the basis of a technicality. It was ruled that legal action concerning the Crown's title to the land could not be pursued without the lieutenant governor's consent. The Nishga had not obtained this consent.[7] However, the ruling of the court clearly suggested that prior occupancy of the land did provide a basis for the existence of aboriginal title,[8] providing that this had not been extinguished by subsequent legislation. This ruling was of broader significance because it opened the possibility that aboriginal peoples throughout Canada, at least those who had not signed treaties extinguishing their claims, may well retain legal title to their land.[9]

In addition to aboriginal rights based on occupancy, native peoples also possess rights that derive from the treaties that were entered into with the British Imperial or federal governments. While the provisions of treaties can be overruled by federal legislation, those that remain are legally enforceable.[10] A recent and important confirmation of this occurred in 1986 when the Supreme Court of Canada overturned the conviction of a Micmac Indian for violating provincial hunting regulations in Nova Scotia. In doing this, the court ruled that provincial legislation had not superseded the rights derived from a treaty signed by a Micmac chief in 1752.[11] More recently, an Ontario Provincial Court judge ruled that the hunting rights specified in a treaty signed in 1701 at Albany, New York with the Iroquois "cannot be restricted by provincial fish and game legislation."[12] In other words, the court was prepared to override provincial legislation in favour of a 300-year-old treaty that predates the formation of the Canadian state. As with the delineation of aboriginal rights mentioned above, it is not possible to offer a precise legal definition of treaty rights or the extent to which they are enforceable in the courts. Any legal delineation of these rights involves a number of complex issues. These include the problem of interpreting the meaning and provisions of written documents, the significance of promises that were made but not incorporated into treaty documents, the determination of the extent to which specific provisions have been overridden by federal legislation, and the problem of determining the level of compensation in situations in which the provisions of treaties have been broken.

The federal government's response to the legal recognition of aboriginal rights and the demands by native peoples to have their concerns addressed was the creation in 1973 of "comprehensive" and "specific" claims processes. Comprehensive claims concern those areas of Canada in which aboriginal rights to the land were never extinguished by treaty or superseded by law.[13] The areas potentially open to these claims include British Columbia, the Yukon, Northwest Territories, northern Québec, and eastern Canada. Specific claims are those that have arisen from the federal government's failure to fulfil its lawful treaty obligations. The procedures involved in the claims process have been consistently criticized by native leaders because of the power they bestow on one party to the negotiations. It is the government that decides whether or not a claim against the government is acceptable.[14] Also, the government is in a position to determine the framework of negotiations. An indication of the latter is the government's insistence that land-claims settlements must include the total extinction of aboriginal rights.[15] The importance of this issue can be seen in the recent rejection of a proposed agreement between the federal government (July 1990) and the Dene Nation of the Northwest Territories.[16] The Dene rejected the proposed agreement because they were not prepared to extinguish aboriginal rights for themselves or for future generations.[17] A further indication of the aboriginal people's lack of power is the government's readiness to sanction the use of resources in contested areas without the agreement of those who continue to live off the land. Finally, there are inordinate delays in the resolution of both comprehensive and specific claims. Over an eighteen-year period, only two comprehensive claims have been settled (the James Bay and Northern Québec Agreement 1975, and the Inuvialuit Agreement 1984, which covers the Mackenzie Delta region of the Northwest Territories), six are in the process of negotiation, and nineteen await the initiation of negotiations.[18]

Issues associated with aboriginal rights, particularly land claims and political sovereignty, are the focus of some of the major legal and political struggles of the native peoples. The successful resolution of land claims offers the possibility of gaining a measure of independence from the federal government and gaining the resources by which pressing issues of social and economic development can be addressed. Thus, it is not surprising to find that native peoples have responded to the threats to their rights and the limitations of the claims process in many different ways. They have developed local, regional, national, and international associations that pursue land and treaty claims through litigation or negotiation and lobby for their rights in provincial, national, and international arenas.[19] The latter include forays to the International Court, the United Nations, and the British Parliament.[20] When all else fails, or there is an immediacy to the threats to their communities, they turn to blockades and other forms of civil disobedience.

NATIVE PEOPLES AND THE FEDERAL GOVERNMENT

A unique feature of the position of native peoples in Canadian society, and a focal point of considerable conflict, is their relationship, with the federal government. To fully understand this relationship, one must go back to the earliest days of colonization.[21] While this is not possible here, a brief explanation is in order. Prior to Confederation, policies were generally concerned with establishing military alliances during periods of war, and peaceful co-existence at other times. This changed in the early nineteenth century, when native peoples had ceased to be valuable allies, for by the 1850s the dominant objectives were "protection" from the disreputable elements among the colonizers, "protection" of Indian lands (these could be alienated only through the Crown), and the transmission of the virtues of civilization and Christianity (i.e., assimilation). Of course, it was through the regulation of relationships with native peoples that the political and territorial ambitions of colonial governments could be realized. These general concerns continued to shape Indian policy after Confederation.

At Confederation the federal government assumed the exclusive responsibility for native peoples. Since then a considerable amount of legislation has been passed by Parliament to regulate their affairs. Consolidated into the Indian Act, this legislation is of paramount importance to the lives of native peoples. At different times, these regulations have allowed the government to control the expropriation of Indian land, determine the way the resources of reserves and band trust funds were to be used, and regulate the movement of goods and people on reserves. The regulations provided the legal basis for a system of education in which government and missions conspired to deny new generations any knowledge of their cultural heritage. Where education proved insufficient to dampen the enthusiasm for traditional cultural practices, further legislation was readily introduced. In 1884 a law was introduced to prohibit the potlatch celebrations of West Coast tribes. In 1914 legislation was introduced that required native people to obtain the Indian agent's permission before they could participate in traditional dances or perform at rodeos and exhibitions. This was explicitly designed to control native peoples in the western provinces and the territories.[22] It was not only the suppression of tradition that was sought, for the Indian Act also made it an offence for native people to raise the funds required for the pursuit of treaty or land claims in the courts. This provision remained in place until 1950. Moreover—and this is hard to believe in a democratic society—they were denied the right to vote in a federal election until 1961.

An important question to ask is: To whom do the provisions of the Indian Act apply? If you answered this question by suggesting that it applies to any person of aboriginal ancestry, you would be incorrect. For the purposes of the Indian

Act, an Indian is defined as one of the descendants of those individuals considered or entitled to be registered as Indians at the time of the first Indian Act (1876).[23] Those who are covered by this definition are referred to as registered or status Indians. Difficulties arise when it is recognized that not all people of native ancestry were registered. Most notably in this respect was the exclusion of the Inuit and Metis. Further complicating the issue is the fact that Indian status, as we will see below, could be lost. In other words, the category of people described as registered or status Indians is identified in strictly legal terms. Expressed differently, an individual could be of any degree of aboriginal ancestry and culturally in every respect a native person, yet be excluded from the provisions of the Indian Act. This has important implications, for it is only registered Indians who are entitled to the services provided under the terms of the act.

As mentioned above, registered status could be lost. This occurred through voluntary or involuntary disenfranchisement. The possibility of the latter points to one of the more oppressive and discriminatory provisions of the Indian Act. Prior to an amendment of the act in 1985, an Indian woman who married a non-Indian, including a nonregistered person of Indian ancestry, automatically lost registered status for herself and her descendants. This was not returned upon divorce, separation, or the death of her husband. Indian males, on the other hand, did not lose their registered status upon marriage to a non-Indian. In fact, the non-Indian wife and her descendants automatically received Indian status and came within the jurisdiction of the act. The consequences of this provision of the act for women were considerable. Marriage to a non-Indian led to the loss of a woman's rights to receive federal services designated for status Indians, retain reserve property, or even to reside in her home community. It is not difficult to imagine that this could lead to considerable hardship.[24]

Changes to the Indian Act in 1985 removed this particular provision and allowed those who had lost their status to regain it. Despite the fact that this right does not extend back beyond one generation, by July 1988 there were 104 133 applicants for reinstatement.[25] It is, then, important to recognize that Indian status is a legal category that is determined independently of the degree of intermarriage or of cultural characteristics. With the foregoing in mind, the following comments concerning the relations with the federal government refer only to those defined as status Indians, who number approximately 500 000.

The responsibility for administering federal policy applicable to registered Indians lies with the Department of Indian Affairs.[26] It was Indian Affairs that administered the provisions of the Indian Act and implemented the policy of assimilation. Until the 1970s the department was a hierarchically organized bureaucracy that operated in a highly authoritarian manner.[27] At the base of the hierarchy was the Indian agent. Assigned to one or more reserves, the agent was responsible for implementing the directives of the department, and had the responsibility of upholding the provisions of the Indian Act. This paternalistic figure was the focal point of considerable power. Any decisions made by elected or traditional band governments could be implemented only with the agent's approval. The agent also had the power to both prosecute and sentence registered Indians for violations of the provisions of the Indian Act.[28] Moreover, it was a mere twenty-five years ago that the process of withdrawing Indian agents from the reserves was initiated. The pervasiveness of federal control over reserves led many observers to describe the relationship as paternalistic and colonial in nature,[29] and even to liken it to a system of apartheid.[30]

A century after Confederation, it was clear that Indian policy had failed. Despite extensive intervention into the affairs of registered Indians, the policy of assimilation had not brought about the expected results. Not only did identifiable native groups persist, but they remained committed to maintaining their distinctiveness. Of course, colonization had taken its toll, for the economic basis of their lives had been transformed, resources had been lost, and their cultural traditions had suffered the impact of policies designed for their eradication.[31] Compounding these injustices, reserve populations were left in a state of poverty. Without meaningful consultation, the government's response to this failure (the 1969 White Paper) was to propose that special status under the Indian Act be abolished, Indian Affairs terminated, and that the responsibility for services be transferred to the provinces. In other words, the reserve system and the special status of registered Indians were identified as the problem. Native leaders from across the country quickly voiced their opposition to these proposals.[32] This seemingly contradictory stand, given a history of past resistance to government control, resulted from the recognition that the proposed changes would more likely lead to a deterioration of their condition than to an improvement. In fact, the policy came to be seen as but another variant in the government's long-standing policy of assimilation.

As a policy initiative, the White Paper failed. Yet it gained considerable symbolic significance as a crucial point in the struggle of native peoples to regain control over their own affairs. It marked the beginning of a powerful resurgence of Indian political organizations, which have sought to address past wrongs and to bring about changes that are meaningful in terms of the goals of native communities rather than those of the federal government. While the Indian Act and Indian Affairs remain in place, there has been a devolution of administrative responsibility during the last thirty years. The Indian agent has disappeared, and bands have increasingly assumed greater responsibility for the administration of their own affairs. Despite such changes, the dominant role of Indian Affairs continues. Consequently, it is not surprising that Indian communities and organizations have continued to press for greater powers of self-government.

CONTEMPORARY DIVERSITY

Throughout their prolonged engagement with the agents of colonization, native peoples have been drawn into national and international processes of economic change. Not only have their resources been lost or threatened, but they have contributed their own labour to the Canadian economy in many different ways. To further our understanding of the diverse situations and concerns of native peoples, some appreciation of the interplay of economic, political, and cultural interests is necessary. It is with this in mind that we now turn our attention to an examination of two contrasting situations. The first concerns northern hunter-trappers in Québec who have long been incorporated into the international economy through their involvement in the fur trade. The second concerns a reserve in southern Ontario with a long history of both political, economic, and cultural incorporation into the institutions of the colonizing society.

❑ NORTHERN HUNTER-TRAPPERS

The importance of the resources of land and water have been well established by many studies that have sought to identify past and present patterns of land use by Indian and Inuit peoples in northern Canada.[33] The phrase "our land is our life" takes on particular significance for aboriginal peoples who continue to draw heavily on the land to produce commodities for both exchange and consumption. Despite their incorporation into the institutional structures of Canadian society, we find distinctive forms of social organization, territorial rights, and cultural traditions.[34] To illustrate this, we now turn to the eastern James Bay region of Québec, where the Cree have been involved in the fur trade for over 300 years. The economy of the region is divided into settlement and bush sectors. While the two are intertwined, it is the latter sector that is of specific interest here.

When we think of trapping, we are likely to recall an image of the lone pioneer spending days or even months alone on a trapline, while other members of the household remain at home pursuing the many domestic tasks required for their survival. While this model can be found among native peoples, they also work under very different cultural arrangements. In the James Bay region of Québec, groups of native people such as the Mistassini and the Wemendji Cree trap in the context of hunting groups and family hunting territories. The system is very old, for it seems that its basic elements were in place in the region during the eighteenth century and that the presence of some may predate European contact.[35] Hunting groups consist of from two to five families who form co-residential groups for part or all of the winter season (approximately nine or ten months). While some provisions are taken into the bush camp, the bulk of the food consumed is provided through hunting (beaver, moose, caribou, black bear, goose, small game) and fishing.[36] Unlike the model of the white trapper, or native trappers in areas where game is scarce, groups like the Mistassini and Wemendji Cree became involved in the fur trade without developing an overwhelming reliance on store-purchased food.[37] They are not simply engaged in the pursuit of profit when they are procuring furs, but have integrated this activity into the pursuit of a distinctive way of life. In other words, the production of commodities (furs) remains subordinate to the production of a distinct and desirable way of life.[38]

A glimpse of the cultural distinctiveness of the eastern James Bay Cree can be seen in the particular way the hunting group is organized, and in the relationship

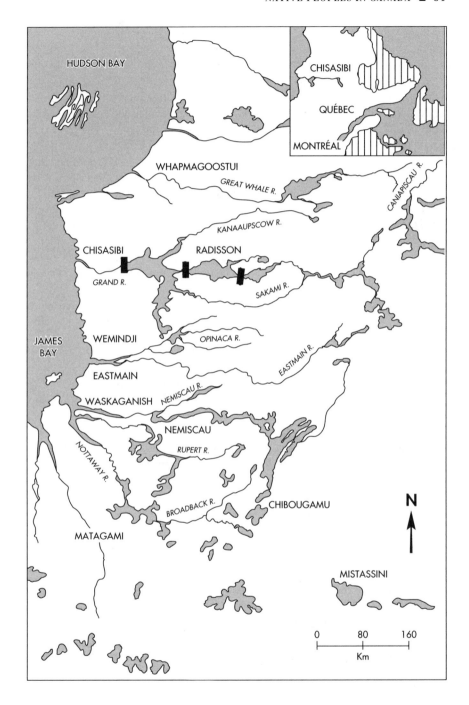

Figure 1 Region of Eastern James Bay Cree

of these groups to the territories they harvest. Hunting areas within the Cree region are divided into about 300 territories ranging in size from 230 to 1200 square kilometres.[39] The rights to hunt in a particular territory are controlled by an individual who is seen as the custodian of the land. These territories are not what we think of as private property, for they cannot be purchased or sold. An individual's relationship with a territory is normally established through inheritance, a gift, or in recognition of the prolonged use of the land.[40] The rights are conditional on the continuous use of the area, though this does not have to be on a yearly basis. Moreover, the custodian is expected to act in a manner that ensures the conservation of the area by deciding when an area should be hunted, and to decide when a species should be hunted and the quantity to be hunted. Also, the custodian has the authority to determine which households will be invited to form the hunting group, but cannot prevent those with a long-term right to an area from using it. This authority is supported by traditional spiritual sanctions and by the special relationship, revealed in dreams and signs, that the custodian has with animals.[41] Once part of a hunting group, households acquire access to all the resources of the territory, including fur-bearing animals required for the maintainance of its members. Despite the co-residential nature of the group, households are largely responsible for meeting their own needs, though co-operation on specific tasks routinely occurs. Thus, those who find a lair or kill or cripple an animal are considered to have "ownership." However, this does not necessarily entail an exclusive right in a context marked by a strong tradition of sharing subsistence resources and provisions with those in need,[42] and in which collective activities invoke obligations regardless of who makes the actual kill.

These observations are insufficient to convey the cultural richness of the Cree way of life in their bush camps. Yet, perhaps enough has been said to help us begin to appreciate the meaning of the expression "our land is our life" for the James Bay Cree and for other aboriginal peoples who continue to rely on the land. Anything that threatens access to the resources of the land is a threat not only to a source of cash income, but also to control over the continuity of patterns of authority, values, religion, and social relations, that is, control over cultural life and the cultural identity that flows from this. The consequences of a rapid break-down of established ways of life, associated with a lack of power to control the process of change, can be devastating. These may include unemployment and welfare dependence, drug abuse, high suicide rates, malnutrition, and many other social ills.[43] Thus, it is hardly surprising that we find native peoples across Canada engaged in many different forms of protest as they seek to gain control over the direction of their own lives.

The threats to hunting-trapping ways of life come from many different directions: changes in the demand for furs (the influence of the anti-fur lobby for example),[44] changes in the cost of production (new trapping methods), destructive patterns of resource exploitation (clear-cutting of forests, pollution of lakes and streams by pulp-and-paper and mining operations), and government policies (relocation, and the centralization of communities). Returning to the James Bay Cree, we find a clear example of a threat to the way of life of trappers as well as the importance of control over the land in the development of the James Bay Project. Initiated in 1970, the first stage of this vast hydro-electric project involved the construction of dams and the flooding of an area of 10 500 square kilometres.[45] The consequence of this on the Cree families who were hunting and trapping in this area are not difficult to imagine. Yet the initiation of the project did not involve any consultation with the Cree or any recognition of their aboriginal rights. Following the initiation of legal proceedings against the Québec government and an injunction that briefly delayed work on the project in 1974, the federal and provincial governments acknowledged native interest in the land and entered a process of negotiation that lasted two years. Native groups involved in the negotiations included the Grand Council of the Cree (Québec); the Northern Québec Inuit Association; the Inuit of Québec; and the Inuit of Port Burwell.[46]

The complicated agreement that emerged included monetary compensation, increased powers of local government, control over education, increased jurisdiction over the administration of criminal justice, increased control over environmental management, and the implementation of programs of social and economic development. Considerable importance was attached to ensuring the continuing viability of the hunting-trapping way of life. This is reflected in the guaranteed rights for fishing, trapping, and hunting, in an income security program for hunter-trappers, and in the powers concerning environmental management. On the other hand, the Cree were clearly aware that support of the hunting economy was not enough to ensure the future social and economic viability of their communities. Consequently, we find that the agreement includes programs and services (training and job placement, assistance to new businesses) that would address the problems faced by those displaced from the traditional way of life as well as those of a newer generation who have had little experience of it. To put it simply, the Cree and the Inuit sought to enhance the strengths of traditional ways of life and to meaningfully benefit from resource development in the region.

However, the agreement, signed under duress, has been criticized because it does not seem to provide the resources to adequately realize these goals.[47] Moreover, following a long tradition, it is also apparent that the governments involved have failed to honour their commitment to implement the terms of the agreement.[48] With respect to this, Chief Billy Diamond, Grand Chief and the main Cree signatory at the time, has stated that he would have refused to sign the agreement if he had known how "solemn commitments" would become "twisted" in their interpretation and ignored.[49] At the present time the implementation of these commitments is critical because the Québec government has initiated Phase II of the project.[50] This poses a further threat to the people of the region for it will increase the area used for reservoirs from 14 000 to 25 835 square kilometres.[51]

It is now difficult to ignore the importance of the resources of land and water to the lives of native peoples. We find frequent expressions of their concern in the media, particularly when they are obliged to defend their interests in the land. From coast to coast we find voices raised in reaction to the destructive effects of such projects as low-level fighter training flights over hunting grounds, the construction of dams, the pollution of lakes and rivers, oil and gas exploration, and logging. From coast to coast we also find aboriginal peoples asserting their rights through comprehensive land claims as they seek to reclaim control over their own future. This opposition should not lead us to assume that native peoples are necessarily opposed to different patterns of resource use. More often it means that the idea of development should be broad enough to allow for the continuity of traditional patterns of land use, and to ensure that there is a meaningful place for native peoples and their communities in any industrialization that does occur.

❏ A SOUTHERN RESERVE

The discussion of hunters and trappers provides an example of one way in which native people are incorporated into the national and global economy, and an indication of some of the issues facing them in the Canadian North. To further appreciate the complex variations in their position, we will now turn our attention to the position of aboriginal peoples in the more settled regions of southern Canada. Here we also find considerable cultural and situational diversity. There are aboriginal peoples with or without registered status living in urban[52] and rural areas,[53] and registered Indians living on reserves[54] who fall within the terms of the Indian Act.

The effects of colonization were more pervasive in the more populated regions of southern Canada. Not only did native peoples have to contend with the problem that their settlements were on reserves under federal control, but they also lost access to the resources required to sustain a native way of life in areas where settlers surrounded their communities. Not only was there competition for resources, but the character of the landscape changed as cultivation destroyed the habitat of many of the species of wildlife upon which native peoples relied.[55] Moreover, these sedentary populations were more vulnerable to the policies of government and missionaries, which were directed toward the total transformation of native cultures.

Following Confederation, the Canadian government implemented a policy of assimilation. Supported by missionaries, this aim was to be achieved through the curtailment of nomadic patterns of land use through settlement, the development of agriculture, education, and the inculcation of Christian beliefs and practices. The objective was to fit the Indian into a particular vision of "civilized" life: this included "not only a scholastic education, but instruction in the means of gaining a livelihood from the soil or as a member of an industrial or mercantile community, and the substitution of Christian ideals of conduct and morals for aboriginal concepts of both."[56] The government's vision of agriculture was one in which independent households produced for their own consumption and for the market. Regardless of the wishes of native peoples, the government imposed the social organization of settler agriculture. The policy was to be financed through the management of funds derived from the sale of native land.[57] In other words, they were to pay for their own domination.

To help us appreciate the general legacy of government policy and the influence of changes in the economy, we will draw examples from the situation of Walpole Island First Nation. Located in southwestern Ontario and bordering the state of Michigan, the reserve occupies the Canadian portion of the delta of the St. Clair River. It covers an area of approximately 58 000 hectares, which is characterized by a mixture of high-quality agricultural land, forested land, and extensive wetlands. The latter is a major habitat for muskrat and large numbers of birds that migrate through the region. The current population of the reserve is approximately 2000 people whose tribal origins are Chippewa (primarily), Pottowattomie, and Ottawa. The reserve was established before the formation of the Canadian state. Its occupants came under the auspices of a superintendent of Indian Affairs during the 1830s and a resident Indian agent in 1883. A missionary presence was established on the island by the 1840s. By the end of the next decade (1858), it seems that 302 of the band's 522 members were reported as

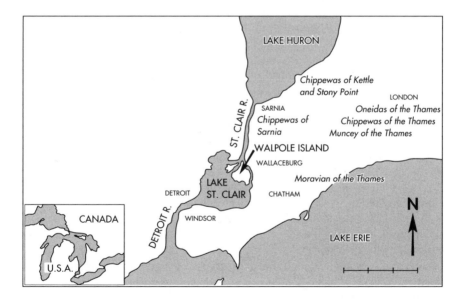

Figure 2   Reserves in Southwestern Ontario

having a religious affiliation with one of the Christian churches.[58] Both government officials and missionaries sought to establish a sedentary population, encourage the development of agriculture, and further the process of assimilation.

The earliest involvement in agriculture seems to have been in the 1830s. At this time farming methods were derived from tribal practice,[59] and were probably secondary to the direct use of the environment and the more nomadic practices associated with this. By the end of the century farming had become the major means of making a livelihood, though income was also generated through fishing, hunting, the sale of crafts, and casual wage labour. This transformation is not surprising, because access to the resources that supported more nomadic patterns had steadily declined with the settlement of the region. The new agrarian economy that had emerged was organized on a household basis and followed modern farming methods. Families grew wheat, oats, barley, sugar beets (early twentieth century), cherries, peaches, apples, and vegetables of all kinds, and raised cattle, hogs, sheep, chickens, and horses. Indian farmers were successfully competing with Euro-Canadians in agricultural fairs, and were organizing their own exhibitions on the reserve. Like their Euro-Canadian counterparts, Indian farmers obtained their livelihood from a blend of production for the market and for consumption, which was supplemented by off-farm work. This allowed Walpole households to readily meet their needs without external assistance.

Impelled by the loss of resources to settlers in the surrounding area and enjoined by agents and missionaries to adopt agriculture, the people of Walpole Island completed a notable transformation in their way of life. By the end of the century, nomadic patterns had been replaced by a style of farming that was no different from that of settlers in the surrounding area. Like other Indian communities in southern Ontario,[60] the people of Walpole had forged a place in the economy of the day that was perfectly modern. They were self-supporting, and though they were subject to federal control they had developed a stable way of life that did not depend on government funding in any way. This modernity in the context of the time should be stressed, for in observing the difficulties faced by reserve communities today, it is all too easy to think that the contemporary array of social and economic problems stem from a cultural inability to change. Moreover, it should also be noted that involvement in agriculture was but one of the many ways in which native peoples had become incorporated into the Canadian economy by the end of the nineteenth century.

As part of the Canadian economy, they were not insulated from changes occurring in the structure of agriculture generally or in the economy of the region. From approximately 1900, there was a decline in reserve agriculture in Ontario and a movement into other occupations. This general change was registered on Walpole Island, where by 1910 the majority of young men were working in factories or as agricultural labourers in the surrounding area. The pattern of subsistence and commercial agriculture was not totally abandoned, though output declined. Moreover, by the Depression years of the 1930s it seems that most households were again dependent on agriculture, at least in the form of a garden, as people were obliged to rely heavily on the resources of the reserve for their livelihood. At this time, households were deeply embroiled in a mixture of subsistence and commercial farming with extensive gardens. This was complemented by trapping, fishing, hunting, the production of crafts, and casual labour.

Despite these changes, households retained the capacity to secure a livelihood that was free of government support. Moreover, community life continued to be free of the social problems characteristic of many reserve populations today. During this time (1920–1940s) people felt that they had considerable control over everyday life. Community life was characterized by mutual aid, work bees, patterns of exchange, and an intense round of social activity that centred on household, church, and school. Dense patterns of local interaction were reflected in the influence that adults had over the young. The latter learned the values, patterns of authority, and conventional practices of the community through their everyday work and social routines in the household. This local organization and local control of community life was similar to that found in rural areas in other parts of Canada. The extent to which ideas, values, and practices from the distant past were incorporated into the emergent culture is not an issue that can be pursued here. However, we may observe that the way of life of this period, though forged under social conditions beyond local control, also constitute an important part of their cultural heritage.

Changes in the economy of the region during the Second World War and the early postwar years were associated with a high demand for labour. As they had four decades earlier, band members gradually abandoned household agrarian pursuits and entered the work force as wage labourers. This proved to be short-lived, for by the 1960s the reserve was characterized by high levels of unemployment, a dependence on transfer payments (associated with the extension of social services to native peoples), and the appearance of many of the social ills that came to beset reserve populations. Thus, the present character of unemployment and dependence are of very recent origin. It may be added that this type of experience has been repeated in many native communities based on reserves. Clearly, this has nothing to do with the persistence of traditional culture or a failure on the part of native people to enter Canadian society. This is hardly surprising, for unemployment and dependence on transfer payments are characteristics shared by many Canadians.

An analysis of the conditions that generate unemployment and dependence would take us beyond the parameters of this chapter. However, a brief comment is in order to allow us to appreciate the particular constraints facing reserve communities. Throughout this century, particularly since the Second World War, competitive forces were at work that underpinned a general movement out of agriculture. Particularly in the postwar years, a continuous cost-price squeeze was associated with the rapid application of new machinery to agricultural production, specialization, and a continuous increase in the land area required for an economically viable farm. This meant that there was a steady increase in the capital required to either maintain or increase a household's farm income. In coping with these changes, Indian farmers who wished to continue in agriculture were at a distinct disadvantage because reserve land, under the provisions of the Indian Act, could not be used as collateral to raise capital. Lacking alternative sources of funds, it is not entirely unexpected to find band members on Walpole Island leasing their land to Euro-Canadian farmers rather than farming it themselves. The constraints of the Indian Act, and an absence of federal policies to compensate for this, helped to ensure that farming was beyond the reach of individual band members. When Indian-controlled agriculture finally did return, it took the form of a large farm (currently over 4000 acres) operated by the band. However, many of the difficulties encountered in establishing the band farm continued to reflect the problems of raising capital under the terms of the Indian Act. The general point to appreciate is that not only do reserve populations have to cope with the vagaries of economic change, but also with problems emerging from the provisions of the Indian Act and the policies of the Department of Indian Affairs.

High unemployment, an increasing array of social problems, and the persistence of government policies that had failed to deliver the level of services found in contiguous areas were contributing factors to the emergence, in the 1960s, of opposition to the tutelage of Indian Affairs. Despite working with an elected council for over eighty years,[61] the Indian agent still controlled council meetings, retained a veto over council decisions, and imposed federal policy in an arbitrary manner. It was this array of problems that led the people of Walpole Island to eject the Indian agent. This was associated with modifications of the Indian Act, which allowed Walpole Island in 1965 to become the first Indian nation to obtain the powers of self-administration.[62] This change did not solve the many problems that faced the community. However, the changes that have occurred clearly indicate the advantages of increased local control.[63]

This experiment in self-administration was rapidly followed on other reserves. For the first time, Indian bands were in a position to pursue policies in which the reserve community was seen as a place to develop for the benefit of present and future generations. This contrasted with the thrust of federal policy in the past, in which reserves were regarded as little more than a place to control people until they had been assimilated into the population at large. Despite these changes, the overall control of reserve policy remains within the hands of the federal bureaucracy, while the powers of band governments continue to be circumscribed by the legal framework of the Indian Act. Moreover, reserve communities continue to experience a wide range of social and economic ills. These frequently include unemployment, poor housing, pollution,[64] and a general lack of services and infrastructure. It is in response to the persistence of local problems, and the continuing limitations on local powers of self-administration, that we find Indian bands throughout Canada seeking ways to increase their political, economic, social, and cultural autonomy. With such concerns in mind, it is easy to appreciate the significance of the many calls for self-government or sovereignty.

CONCLUSION

We began this chapter with a description of the prevailing imagery of aboriginal peoples, including the tendency to portray native peoples as though they exist outside of Canadian society, and the assumption that the culture of aboriginal peoples is everywhere the same. By now it should be clear that a recognition of the continuing distinctiveness of aboriginal peoples does not entail a denial of their incorporation into the structures of Canadian society. On the contrary, the issues that confront them reflect their colonial history and their mode of incorporation. Therefore, the resolution of the problems that beset aboriginal communities is not one of joining or leaving Canadian society, but of establishing the kind of political and economic relationships that would allow them to realize their collective aspirations, however these may be defined. With this in mind, we can readily see the importance attached to their efforts to reclaim control of land and water resources, and to develop their own forms of self-government. For aboriginal peoples, the acquisition of new political and economic powers would enhance their ability to protect the interests of their communities, and would allow them to pursue their own cultural aspirations.

Notes

[1] A useful account of the present and past diversity of native peoples can be found in R.B. Morrison and C.R. Wilson, eds., *Native Peoples: The Canadian Experience* (Toronto: McClelland & Stewart, 1986).

[2] See B. Adam, chapter 3 in this volume.

[3] See "Prime Minister Trudeau: Remarks on Aboriginal and Treaty Rights," in P. Cumming and N.H. Mickenberg, *Native Rights in Canada* (Toronto: Indian–Eskimo Association of Canada, 1972), 331–32.

[4] D.W. Elliott, "Aboriginal Title," in B.W. Morse, ed., *Aboriginal Peoples and the Law: Indian, Metis and Inuit Rights in Canada* (Ottawa: Carleton University Press, 1985), 48–121.

[5] It may be noted that the recognition of aboriginal rights in the Constitutional Act of 1982 was achieved only after extensive lobbying by native organizations in Canada, the United Kingdom, and to the United Nations. An account of this can be found in D. Sanders, "The Indian Lobby and the Canadian Constitution, 1978–1982," in N. Dyck, ed., *Indigenous Peoples and the Nation-State: Fourth World Politics in Canada, Australia and Norway.* Social and Economic Papers, no. 14. (St. John's: Institute of Social and Economic Research, Memorial University of Newfoundland, 1985), 150–89.

[6] With the exception of small areas on Vancouver Island and the Peace River area, there were no treaties involving land surrenders made with the native peoples of British Columbia. See R.H. Bartlett, "Reserve Lands," in B.W. Morse, ed., *Aboriginal Peoples and the Law,* 467–578.

[7] D. Elliott, "Aboriginal Title," in B. Morse, ed., *Aboriginal Peoples and the Law,* 7.

[8] Ibid., 75.

[9] Discussions of the complex legal issues concerning the position of native peoples can be found in P. Cumming and N.H. Mickenberg, *Native Rights in Canada* , and in B. Morse, ed., *Aboriginal Peoples and the Law.* See also M. Asch, *Home and Native Land: Aboriginal Rights and the Canadian Constitution* (Toronto: Methuen, 1984).

[10] B.H. Wildsmith, "Pre-Confederation Treaties," in B.W. Morse, ed., *Aboriginal Peoples and the Law,* 127.

[11] D. Jones, "An Abused Treaty's Revenge," *Atlantic Insight* (Feb. 1986): 15.

[12] *Globe and Mail* (4 April 1990), 8.

[13] B.W. Morse, "The Resolution of Land Claims," in B. W. Morse, ed., *Aboriginal Peoples and the Law,* 630.

[14] The recent armed blockade by the Mohawks of Oka (1990) was linked to the failure of the claims process or the courts to offer any recognition of their land claims.

[15] G. Erasmus, "The Solution We Favour for Change," in B. Richardson, ed., *Drum Beat: Anger and Renewal in Indian Country* (Toronto: Summerhill Press, Assembly of First Nations, 1989), 295–302.

[16] The Dene Nation consists of a number of different groupings, such as the Dogrib, Slavey, Kutchin, and Chipeweyan, who occupy an area of 1 186 800 square kilometres in the Mackenzie River region of the Northwest Territories.

[17] *Globe and Mail* (20 July 1990), A4. Since the rejection of the agreement, the federal government has initiated negotiations with two of the groups in the region who had previously pursued their claims as part of the Dene Nation.

[18] K.J. Crowe, "Claims on the Land," *Arctic Circle* 1, 3 (1990): 14–23.

[19] The opposition to the Meech Lake Accord by Elijah Harper in the Manitoba Legislature (1990) is an example of this. The opposition to the accord was based on its failure to recognize natives as founding peoples of Canada, to address their desire to be recognized as distinct societies, and to include them in the constitutional process.

[20] See Sanders, "The Indian Lobby."

[21] For an overview of Canadian native history, see E.P. Patterson, *The Canadian Indians: A History Since 1500* (Toronto: Collier Macmillan, 1972).

[22] For further examples and a discussion of Indian policy, see B. Titley, *A Narrow Vision: Duncan Campbell Scott and the Administration of Indian Affairs in Canada* (Vancouver: University of British Columbia Press, 1986).

[23] The definition (Section 11 of the Indian Act) refers to the descendants of a person who ". . . was considered (by statute of May 26, 1874) to be entitled to use and enjoy lands belonging to the various tribes and bands of Indians in Canada; (b) is a member of a band (i) for whose use and benefit, in common, lands have been set apart or, since the 26th day of May, 1874, have been agreed by treaty to be set apart, or (ii) that has been declared by the Governor-in-Council to be a band for the purposes of this Act;" P. Cumming and N.H. Mickenberg, *Native Rights in Canada*, 6.

[24] See K. Jamieson, *Indian Women and the Law in Canada: Citizens Minus* (Ottawa: Advisory Council on the Status of Women, 1978).

[25] R. Ponting, "Public Opinion on Aboriginal Peoples' Issues in Canada," in C. Mckie and K. Thompson, eds. *Canadian Social Trends* (Ottawa: Minister of Supply and Services, Thompson Educational Publishing, 1990), 21. For a discussion of these changes, see J. Frideres, *Native Peoples in Canada: Contemporary Conflicts* (Scarborough: Prentice-Hall, 1988), 12–15.

[26] The agency concerned with the administration of native peoples is currently the Department of Indian Affairs and Northern Development. Prior to this, Indian Affairs had been located in such departments as the Secretary of State for the Provinces, the Department of the Interior, Mines and Resources, and the Department of Citizenship and Immigration. See Treaties and Historical Research Centre, *The Historical Development of the Indian Act* (Ottawa: Indian and Northern Affairs, 1978), v–xi.

[27] See Titley, *A Narrow Vision*.

[28] Ibid., 14.

[29] See H. Cardinal, *The Unjust Society* (Edmonton: Hurtig Publishers, 1969), and H.B. Hawthorne, *A Survey of the Contemporary Indians of Canada—A Report on Economic, Political, Educational Needs and Policies* vols. 1 and 2 (Ottawa: The Indian Affairs Branch, 1966, 1967).

[30] P. Carstens, "Coercion and Change," in R. Ossenberg, ed., *Canadian Society: Pluralism, Change and Conflict* (Scarborough: Prentice-Hall, 1971).

[31] It may be noted that, while the Inuit were not subject to the provisions of the Indian Act, the character of their relationship with the federal government seems to have developed along essentially similar lines. See H. Brody, *The People's Land: Eskimos and Whites in the Eastern Arctic* (Middlesex: Penguin Books, 1983), and R. Paine, ed., *The White Arctic* (St. John's: Institute of Social and Economic Research, Memorial University of Newfoundland, 1977).

[32] See Cardinal, *The Unjust Society.*

[33] See Asch, *Home and Native Land*; T. Berger, *Northern Frontier Northern Homeland: The Report of the Mackenzie Valley Pipeline Inquiry*, vol. 1 (Ottawa: Minister of Supply and Services, 1977); H. Brody, *Maps and Dreams: Indians and the British Columbia Frontier* (England: Pelican Books, 1983).

[34] Asch, *Home and Native Land*, 14–25; Brody, *Maps and Dreams*, 83–148; A. Tanner, *Bringing Home Animals: Religious Ideology and the Mode of Production of the Mistassini Cree Hunters* (St. John's: Institute of Social and Economic Research, Memorial University of Newfoundland, 1979).

[35] T. Morantz, "Historical Perspectives on Family Hunting Territories in Eastern James Bay," *Anthropologica, N.S.* 28, 1–2 (1986): 64–91.

[36] From the 1950s, the value of subsistence hunting to the household has far exceeded that received for the sale of furs. See C. Scott, "Production and Exchange Among Wemindji Cree: Egalitarian Ideology and Economic Base," *Culture* 2, 3 (1982): 54.

[37] Tanner, *Bringing Home Animals*, 22–23.

[38] Scott, *"Production and Exchange,"* 56.

[39] H. Feit, "Legitimation and Autonomy in James Bay Cree Responses to Hydro-Electric Development," in N. Dyck, ed., *Indigenous Peoples and the Nation-State*, 32.

[40] Tanner, *Bringing Home Animals*, 22.

[41] Feit, "Legitimation and Autonomy," 32.

[42] Tanner, *Bringing Home Animals*, 67.

[43] Brody, *The People's Land*; G. Henriksen, *Hunters in the Barrens: The Naskapi on the Edge of the White Man's World* (St. John's: Institute of Social and Economic Research, Memorial University of Newfoundland, 1973); A. Shkilnyk, *A Poison Stronger than Love: The Destruction of an Ojibwa Community* (New Haven: Yale University Press, 1984).

[44] A detailed discussion of the effects of the animal rights movement on native ways of life can be found in G. Wenzel, *Animal Rights, Human Rights: Ecology, Economy and Ideology in the Canadian Arctic* (Toronto: University of Toronto Press, 1991).

[45] B. Diamond, "Villages of the Dammed," *Arctic Circle* 1, 3 (1990): 26.

[46] W. Moss, "The Implementation of the James Bay and Northern Québec Agreement," in B.W. Morse, ed., *Aboriginal Peoples and the Law*, 685.

[47] P. Cumming, "Canada's North and Native Rights," in B.W. Morse, ed., *Aboriginal Peoples and the Law*, 724.

[48] Crowe, "Claims on the Land," 18; Moss, "The Implementation," 688–92.

[49] Diamond,"Villages of the Dammed," 28.

[50] The government of Québec initiated the construction of the project without the completion of an environmental review. Faced with native and international opposition, the Québec Minister of the Environment, Pierre Paradis, announced the delay of the project in the summer of 1991. See the *Globe and Mail* (22 Aug. 1991). In addition, the Federal Court of Canada has ordered the federal government to launch a new and independent review that would not circumvent the terms of the 1975 agreement. The *Globe and Mail* (11 Sept. 1991).

[51] Diamond, "Villages of the Dammed," 26.

[52] E.J. Dosman, *Indians: The Urban Dilemma* (Toronto: McClelland & Stewart, 1972).

[53] E.J. Hedican, *The Ogoki River Guides: Emergent Leadership Among the Northern Ojibwa* (Waterloo: Wilfrid Laurier University Press, 1986).

[54] G.Y. Lithman, *The Community Apart: A Case Study of a Canadian Indian Reserve Community* (Winnipeg: University of Manitoba Press, 1984). See also P. Carstens, *The Queen's People: A Study of Hegemony, Coercion, and Accommodation among the Okanagan of Canada* (Toronto: University of Toronto Press, 1991).

[55] I. Spry, "The Great Transformation: The Disappearance of the Commons in Western Canada," in R. Allen ed., *Man and Nature on the Prairies* (Regina: Canadian Plains Research Centre, 1976).

[56] Superintendent of Education, *Sessional Papers* 1911.

[57] L.F.S. Upton, "The Origins of Canadian Indian Policy," *Journal of Canadian Studies* 8 (Nov. 1973): 51–61.

[58] Church of England 230, Methodist 53, Roman Catholic 19. *Walpole Island: The Soul of Indian Territory* (Walpole Island, ON: Nin.Da.Waab.Jig, 1987).

[59] Ibid., 34.

[60] R. Knight, *Indians at Work: An Informal History of Native Indian Labour in British Columbia, 1858–1930* (Vancouver: New Star Books, 1978).

[61] There were initially two councils formed on Walpole Island in the 1880s (Ottawa and Pottawatomi). These were amalgamated in 1940.

[62] See J.L. Taylor, *Indian Self-Government in the 1960s: A Case Study of Walpole Island* (Ottawa: Department of Indian and Northern Affairs, 1984).

[63] These include the construction of roads, housing, a water filtration plant, and a bridge that allowed better access to the island, a new school (run by the band since 1990), and an old people's home. In addition, the band developed a 4000-acre farm, a corn-drying facility, and a tool-and-die plant.

[64] Walpole Island is exposed to a wide range of pollutants. Its water is continuously subject to spills from Canada's major petrochemical and refining industry in Sarnia, pesticide and fertilizer run-off from farms, and discharges from merchant vessels and pleasure craft. The extent to which these affect wildlife and the health of the population are of considerable concern.

Bibliography

Asch, M. *Home and Native Land: Aboriginal Rights and the Canadian Constitution.* Toronto: Methuen, 1984.

Bartlett, R.H. "Reserve Lands." In B.W. Morse, ed. *Aboriginal Peoples and the Law: Indian, Metis and Inuit Rights in Canada.* Ottawa: Carleton University Press, 1985.

Berger, T. *Northern Frontier Northern Homeland: The Report of the Mackenzie Valley Pipeline Inquiry.* Vol. 1. Ottawa: Minister of Supply and Services,1977.

Brody, H. *Maps and Dreams: Indians and the British Columbia Frontier.* England: Pelican Books, 1983.

Brody, H. *The People's Land: Eskimos and Whites in the Eastern Arctic.* Middlesex: Penguin Books Ltd., 1975.

Cardinal, H. *The Unjust Society.* Edmonton: Hurtig Publishers, 1969.

Carstens, P. "Coercion and Change." In R.J. Ossenberg, ed. *Canadian Society: Pluralism, Change and Conflict.* Scarborough: Prentice-Hall, 1971.

Carstens, P. *The Queen's People: A Study of Hegemony, Coercion, and Accommodation among the Okanagan of Canada.* Toronto: University of Toronto Press, 1991.

Crowe, K.J. "Claims on the Land," *Arctic Circle* 1, 3 (1990): 14–23.

Cumming, P. "Canada's North and Native Rights." In B.W. Morse, ed. *Aboriginal Peoples and the Law.*

Cumming, P., and N.H. Mickenberg. *Native Rights in Canada.* 2nd ed. Toronto: Indian–Eskimo Association of Canada, 1972.

Davis, M. "Aspects of Aboriginal Rights in International Law." In B.W. Morse, ed. *Aboriginal Peoples and the Law.*

Diamond, B. "Villages of the Dammed." *Arctic Circle* 1, 3 (1990): 24–34.

Dosman, E.J. *Indians: The Urban Dilemma.* Toronto: McClelland & Stewart, 1972.

Dyck, N. ed. *Indigenous Peoples and the Nation-State: Fourth World Politics in Canada, Australia and Norway.* Social and Economic Papers No. 14. St. John's: Institute of Social and Economic Research, Memorial University of Newfoundland, 1985.

Elliott, D.W. "Aboriginal Title." In B.W. Morse, ed. *Aboriginal Peoples and the Law.*

Erasmus, G. "The Solution We Favour for Change." In B. Richardson, ed. *Drum Beat: Anger and Renewal in Indian Country.* Toronto: Summerhill Press, Assembly of First Nations, 1989.

Feit, H. "Legitimation and Autonomy in James Bay Cree Responses to Hydro-Electric Development." In N. Dyck, ed. *Indigenous Peoples and the Nation-State.*

Fenge, T. "The Animal Rights Movement: A Case of Evangelical Imperialism," *Alternatives* 15, 3 (1988): 69–71.

Frideres, J. *Native Peoples in Canada: Contemporary Conflicts.* Scarborough: Prentice-Hall, 1988.

Government of Canada. *Indian Self-Government.* Report of the Special Committee on Indian Self-Government. Ottawa: Queen's Printer, 1983.

Hawthorne, H.B. *A Survey of the Contemporary Indians of Canada—A Report on Economic, Political, Educational Needs and Policies*. Vols. 1 & 2. Ottawa: Indian Affairs Branch, 1966, 1967.

Hedican, E.J. *The Ogoki River Guides: Emergent Leadership Among the Northern Ojibwa*. Waterloo: Wilfrid Laurier University Press, 1986.

Henriksen, G. *Hunters in the Barrens: The Naskapi on the Edge of the White Man's World*. St. John's: Institute of Social and Economic Research, Memorial University of Newfoundland, 1973.

Inglis, G. "Canadian Indian Reserve Populations: Some Problems of Conceptualization," *Northwest Anthropological Research Notes* 5, 1 (1971): 23–36.

Jamieson, K. *Indian Women and the Law in Canada: Citizens Minus*. Ottawa: Advisory Council on the Status of Women, 1978.

Jamieson, K. "Multiple Jeopardy: The Evolution of a Native Women's Movement," *Atlantis* 4, 2 (part 2) (1979): 157–88.

Jones, D. "An Abused Treaty's Revenge." *Atlantic Insight* (Feb. 1986): 15.

Knight, R. *Indians at Work: An Informal History of Native Indian Labour in British Columbia, 1858–1930*. Vancouver: New Star Books, 1978.

Lithman, Y.G. *The Community Apart: A Case Study of a Canadian Indian Reserve Community*. Winnipeg: University of Manitoba Press, 1984.

Morantz, T. "Historical Perspectives on Family Hunting Territories in Eastern James Bay." *Anthropologica, N.S.* 28, 1–2 (1986): 64–91.

Morrison, R.B., and C.R. Wilson, eds. *Native Peoples: The Canadian Experience*. Toronto: McClelland & Stewart, 1986.

Morse, B.W., ed. *Aboriginal Peoples and the Law: Indian, Metis and Inuit Rights in Canada*. Ottawa: Carleton University Press, 1985.

Morse, B.W. "The Resolution of Land Claims." In B.W. Morse, ed. *Aboriginal Peoples and the Law*.

Moss, W. "The Implementation of the James Bay and Northern Québec Agreement." In B.W. Morse, ed. *Aboriginal Peoples and the Law*.

Nin.Da.Waab.Jig. *Walpole Island: The Soul of Indian Territory*. Walpole Island, ON: Nin.Da.Waab.Jig, 1987.

Paine, R., ed. *The White Arctic*. St. John's: Institute of Social and Economic Research, Memorial University of Newfoundland, 1977.

Patterson, E.P. *The Canadian Indians: A History Since 1500*. Toronto: Collier-Macmillan, 1972.

Ponting, R.J. "Public Opinion on Aboriginal Peoples' Issues in Canada." In C. Mckie and K. Thompson, eds. *Canadian Social Trends*. Ottawa: Minister of Supply and Services and Thompson Educational Publishing, 1990, 19–27.

Richardson, B., ed. *Drum Beat: Anger and Renewal in Indian Country*. Toronto: Summerhill Press, Assembly of First Nations, 1989.

Rogers, E.S., and F. Tobobondung. *Parry Island Farmers: A Period of Change in the Way of Life of the Algonkians of Southern Ontario*. Mercury Series, Canadian Ethnological Service, Paper No. 31. Ottawa: National Museum of Man, 1975.

Ross, D., and P. Usher. *From the Roots Up: Economic Development as if Community Mattered*. The Canadian Council of Social Development Series. Toronto: Lorimer, 1986.

Ross, D., and P. Usher. "The Informal Economy: Has Public Policy Neglected it?" *Transition* (March 1983): 9–12.

Sanders, D.E. "The Indian Lobby and the Canadian Constitution, 1978–1982." In N. Dyck, ed. *Indigenous Peoples and the Nation-State.*

Scott, C. "Production And Exchange among Wemindji Cree: Egalitarian Ideology and Economic Base," *Culture* 2, 3 (1982): 51–64.

Shkilnyk, A. *A Poison Stronger than Love: The Destruction of an Ojibwa Community.* New Haven: Yale University Press, 1984.

Spry, I. "The Great Transformation: The Disappearance of the Commons in Western Canada." In R. Allen, ed. *Man and Nature on the Prairies.* Canadian Plains Studies 6. Regina: Canadian Plains Research Centre, 1976.

Tanner, A. *Bringing Home Animals: Religious Ideology and the Mode of Production of the Mistassini Cree Hunters.* Social and Economic Studies No. 23. St John's: Institute of Social and Economic Research, Memorial University of Newfoundland, 1979.

Taylor, J.L. *Indian Self-Government in the 1960s: A Case Study of Walpole Island.* Ottawa: Department of Indian and Northern Affairs, 1984.

Titley, B. *A Narrow Vision: Duncan Campbell Scott and the Administration of Indian Affairs in Canada.* Vancouver: University of British Columbia Press, 1986.

Treaties and Historical Research Centre. *The Historical Development of the Indian Act.* Ottawa: Indian and Northern Affairs, 1978.

Upton, L.F.S. "The Origins of Canadian Indian Policy." *Journal of Canadian Studies*, 8 (Nov. 1973): 51–61.

Wagner, M.W. "Domestic Hunting and Fishing by Manitoba Indians: Magnitude, Composition and Implications for Management." *The Canadian Journal of Native Studies* 6, 2 (1986): 333–49.

Wenzel, G. *Animal Rights, Human Rights: Ecology, Economy and Ideology in the Canadian Arctic.* Toronto: University of Toronto Press, 1991.

Wildsmith, B.H. "Pre-Confederation Treaties." In B.W. Morse, ed., *Aboriginal Peoples and the Law.*

York, G. *The Dispossessed: Life and Death in Native Canada.* London: Vintage, 1990.

The Institutions
of the
Canadian State

Ronald H. Wagenberg

INTRODUCTION

I n Canada, as elsewhere, a variety of mechanisms has been developed to perform the three functions required by the state to govern society: the legislative, or law-making; the executive, or administrative; and the judicial, or interpretation of law. These are often called the three branches of government. The Constitution Acts (1867–1982) are the basis for the structure of the Canadian state, setting forth essentials of the legislative, executive, and judicial organs and providing the authority to create governing mechanisms through law, and to change them through an amendment process. Beyond that, certain constitutional conventions, or customary ways of doing things, that are not described specifically in the constitution are regarded as having constitutional status and are essential rules of the game of the Canadian state.

The constitution provides Canada with a federal system, which means that the governing authority has been divided between a central government (usually called the federal government) and ten provincial governments, each of which has legislative, executive, and judicial organs. In addition to carrying out their jurisdiction over provincial institutions, the provinces have created municipalities to perform state functions, although these municipalities do not have sovereign status as do the senior governments under the constitution. Thus, the Canadian state and its institutions do not mean a monolithic structure centred in Ottawa, but, rather, a multiplicity of structures manifested all over the country.

This chapter covers the major mechanisms of the state in Canada—institutions operated by people imbued with the norms and values of Canadian society. Thus, while Canadian institutions may look very much like the British ones after which they were modelled, the political development and processes described by Krause and Soderlund in chapter 7 have endowed those Canadian institutions with unique Canadian characteristics. Certainly the relationships between the central government and the provinces have affected the institutional frameworks of both jurisdictions and have given rise to the mechanisms of "executive federalism," as Donald Smiley has referred to them.[1] One may liken the institutional structures of the Canadian state to its skeleton and vital organs. The processes that make the state work—parties, interest groups, the media, and the dynamics of federal–provincial relationships—are the central nervous system, the circulatory system, and the muscle structure—the flesh and blood of the political system. Therefore, a description of the institutions of the Canadian state is only the beginning of a study of how Canada is governed.

THE FEDERAL SYSTEM IN CANADA

While many states have adopted the federal system of government, in few has the debate about how that system should work been as continuous or intense as it has been in Canada in recent decades. Federalism divides the constitutional power to make laws between a central government for the entire country and a number of smaller units (in Canada, ten provinces) inside their own particular borders. When exercising their legislative authority within their jurisdiction, each government is supreme if this system operates in its classic form. The federal system has been adopted in countries like Canada to allow territories to unite into a larger state with a central government to achieve a variety of goals, while retaining a degree of self-government to preserve their own identities. In Canada this was crucial to the establishment of the country, since Québec insisted on an arrangement that would allow it to protect its culture by its own means. At the same time, Nova Scotia and New Brunswick, with their own histories of separate government, were equally unwilling to cede all legislative powers to a central government. Beyond that, attracting other British North American colonies to join eventually might have been impossible if they had been required to yield all constitutional power to Ottawa.

In constructing their federal state, the Fathers of Confederation were influenced by two major factors. First, their experience with government and the model they held in highest esteem was the British parliamentary system. In Great Britain there was a unitary system, that is, all constitutional power resided in one Parliament. The second influence was the experience of the United States, a federal system in which a civil war was being fought. Thus, by temperament the leading drafters of the British North America Act inclined towards one powerful central government, and their preference was confirmed by their judgment of the danger of too much regional power as demonstrated in the United States. The division of legislative powers that was adopted, therefore, sought to give the central government the most important jurisdictions—the ones that would allow a strong country to be built. The provinces, on the other hand, were given powers sufficient to maintain their local cultural identities. However, the Fathers of Confederation went even further from the classic model of federalism and gave the central government authority to interfere with the provinces, most notably by disallowing their legislation. Such provisions prompted a noted scholar of federalism to define the British North America Act, 1867 as a "quasi-federal" constitution.[2] Without doubt, Canada was meant to have a highly centralized, rather than decentralized, form of federalism.

Sections 91 and 92 of the Constitution Act 1867 (as the BNA Act was renamed in 1982) define the legislative powers of the Parliament of Canada and the legislatures of the provinces, respectively. Section 91 gave Parliament power to make laws "for the Peace, Order and good government of Canada" in all matters not assigned to the provinces in Section 92. This grant of "residual" powers to Parliament was the opposite strategy to that followed in the United States Constitution, where residual powers were granted to the states. Section 91 goes on to enumerate twenty-nine powers of the federal Parliament. When one groups these powers it is evident that they were meant to direct trade and commerce, the financial system, transportation, and military defence of the entire country in the federal sphere of competence. Parliament was also empowered to raise revenue by any means of taxation. Criminal law was made a subject of central jurisdiction, as was responsibility for Indians and lands reserved for them, a matter of major concern in the late-twentieth century. In general, Parliament was endowed with jurisdiction over those matters that seemed crucial in an era when there was much less government involvement in the lives of people.

On the other hand, Section 92 gave provincial legislatures jurisdiction over matters considered more local in nature, which would allow the continuance of their unique characteristics. These included incorporation of companies doing business in the province, as well as "property and civil rights," which were viewed as encompassing essentially business and family law. Judicial interpretation later enhanced the importance of that power. Responsibility for health and welfare and for municipal government, neither of which were of the great significance they are today, was given to the provinces. The provincial power to tax, unlike the federal power, was restricted to direct taxation. In Section 93, education was made the exclusive responsibility of the provinces, although the federal government was given the power to intervene should a province violate the educational rights of a religious minority. Section 95 provided for so-called concurrent jurisdiction of both Parliament and the provincial legislatures over agriculture and immigration, with the laws of Parliament taking precedence should there be any conflict in the provisions of those laws.

Thus, the initial terms of the federal bargain clearly sought to give the federal government the powers to build a strong country and to avoid the problems perceived in the United States. Nonetheless, these terms of Confederation were adopted for a country that even then was far-flung and populated by people who in one province had a different language than the others, and in all provinces were governed by provincial leaders who were convinced that they should have an important role in making public policy. These problems became ever more apparent as Canada grew to ten provinces; as judicial decisions enthroned provincial powers; and as the constitutional responsibilities of provinces in education, health, welfare, and municipal government came to be important and expensive priorities. By the 1990s, provincial leaders, and most especially those in Québec, were asking fundamental questions about federalism in Canada.

As a linguistic and ethnic minority, the French population of Québec has always been confronted with the historical reality that its association with English Canada resulted from the Conquest of 1759. The goal of Francophone leaders for much of Canadian history was survival. With the coming of the Quiet Revolution of 1960, equality rather than mere survival became the objective. This was expressed in a variety of ways in the next thirty years: "*maîtres chez nous*," "*égalité ou indépendance*," "sovereignty-association," and "distinct society." Provincial leaders used these phrases to assert a special role for the province of Québec. Others, primarily Pierre Trudeau, sought to base the equality of Francophones not on their province but on their status as Canadians in a country where French was an official language with equal status, where linguistic rights had constitutional protection, and where French-speaking people could aspire to an equal share in the running of the country. There can be little doubt that at the beginning of the 1990s the dominant view within Québec was that equality should be pursued as a community, either in or out of Canada, rather than as individual Canadian citizens.

The Quiet Revolution of 1960 was characterized by Quebeckers accepting a major role for the state in the direction of their society.[3] It was the state in its provincial guise that was chosen as an instrument of change. Predictably, then, an era was ushered in that witnessed a continuous struggle for power, with the Québec government demanding the jurisdiction necessary to carry out its newly adopted role. By the 1970s other provinces were also aggressively pursuing the capacity to direct their own policies with less, or no, input from Ottawa. This was true of Alberta and Saskatchewan with regard to their resources, and later, Newfoundland with regard to its offshore oil and fisheries. But it was in Québec where the ultimate question of adherence to the Canadian state was raised by the Parti Québécois (PQ), which won an election in 1976. Although in 1980 the PQ could not win a referendum that asked for a mandate to negotiate sovereignty-association (an independent Québec with economic ties to Canada), it did win reelection. It was thus in a position to refuse to sign the agreement that led to the Constitution Act 1982, a constitutional package that adopted an amendment process for Canada as well as the Canadian Charter of Rights and Freedoms. While Québec was subject to the Canadian Constitution, the refusal of its government to voice its approval of the 1982 changes provided the backdrop for the unsuccessful Meech Lake Accord signed in 1987, but aborted in 1990.

The process of constitutional amendment is especially critical in a federal state because neither of the constituent parts (provinces nor the central government) would accept that their respective powers could be changed except by substantial agreement by both sides. The difficult challenge of finding an acceptable amendment formula was side-stepped by the Fathers of Confederation by simply not having one. In 1867 the rationale for this seemingly glaring omission was that Canada was at the time only a self-governing colony, not an independent state, and the entire constitution was, in fact, a piece of British legislation that could be amended by the British Parliament when necessary. As Canada achieved its independence over time, the continuing involvement of Britain in the Canadian constitutional process became a concern for many, but not all, Canadians. Beginning in 1927, therefore, periodic attempts were made to agree on an amendment process.

In the meantime, however, when amendments were needed, the federal Parliament would ask the British Parliament to do so, and the latter would comply without question. Almost always the federal Parliament would ask the British for an amendment only when there was unanimous consent with the provinces. In Québec, the so-called Compact Theory, which in essence held that Confederation was a treaty that could be changed only with the consent of all parties, had wide currency. Indeed, in other provinces, as well, the idea of a constitutional convention requiring unanimity had evolved.

By 1960, a number of factors created a growing pressure to find an acceptable amendment process. The Quiet Revolution in Québec meant that the Québécois were no longer interested in defending the constitutional status quo. Canadian nationalism became more evident and the continued role of Britain in the constitutional process became unacceptable. Provinces other than Québec were also interested in seeing their jurisdictions expanded in areas of particular interest to them, such as natural resources for Alberta or fisheries for Newfoundland. Thus, there emerged the unsuccessful Fulton-Favreau formula of 1964, the close-to-successful Victoria Charter of 1971, and finally, the successful but controversial Constitution Act of 1982, which patriated the constitution by adopting an amendment process and ending Britain's involvement.

The controversy stemmed from the fact that the federal government under Pierre Trudeau threatened to proceed unilaterally if it did not get provincial approval. Only Ontario and New Brunswick sided with the federal government. The others formed the so-called Gang of Eight to fight the federal government. Among other developments, Québec agreed to give up its veto as a part of its efforts to maintain solidarity with the noncompliant provinces. Legal challenges ultimately led to a Supreme Court judgment that a constitutional convention regarding unanimity did not exist, but that, nonetheless, the federal Parliament had to have substantial agreement from the provincial legislatures before an amendment could be sought. Ultimately, a complicated amendment formula emerged, based on ideas developed by Alberta, which stressed the equality of the provinces and therefore gave none of them a veto. Québec was outraged and denounced the Constitution Act of 1982 as a betrayal of its interests. It refused to sign the document, which while having no legal significance, obviously had major political import. This set the stage for Prime Minister Mulroney's efforts to have Québec rejoin the fold.

The Meech Lake Accord sought to accommodate five demands that Premier Bourassa considered to be minimal for Québec to willingly accept the federal bargain.[4] These conditions were: (1) that Québec be defined as a distinct society within Canada and the constitution be interpreted accordingly; (2) that Québec's entitlement to three Supreme Court justices be entrenched in the constitution and that Québec have the right to provide a list of nominees from which the prime minister would choose; (3) that Québec have a veto on constitutional amendments; (4) that the spending power, i.e., the right of the federal government to spend in areas of provincial jurisdiction, be subject to provisions that would allow provinces to stay out of federal–provincial programs without any loss of money; and (5) that Québec have a greater role in controlling immigration to the province. These demands were met to some large degree, in some cases by extending the new provisions to all provinces. In addition, promises were made to explore Senate reform, which western provinces, especially, felt was a key to more equal treatment in the federation.

Critics of the accord concentrated on the "distinct society" clause as giving a special legislative status to Québec. In addition, spokespersons of women's groups, as well as others, expressed concern that the protection of the Charter of Rights and Freedoms might be diluted by the distinct society clause. Native peoples argued that they were certainly deserving of distinct status and that their constitutional concerns had been ignored. People in the Northwest Territories and the Yukon were upset that they could never become provinces without unanimous consent of the other provinces. When elections created new circumstances in New Brunswick, Manitoba, and Newfoundland, the process of ratification in the provincial legislatures was derailed. Renewed negotiations in June of 1990 were ultimately proven to be unable to save the accord, when Elijah Harper (a native MLA in Manitoba) used procedural tactics to prevent its adoption before 23 June, the deadline for passage. In light of this, Premier Clyde Wells of Newfoundland decided that his legislature need not vote on the matter.

Thus, by the summer of 1990, the terms under which Québec would remain a province within the Canadian federal state were very much in question. Indeed, whether Québec would become an independent state was an option that was seriously debated by Quebeckers. Other provinces, as well, had to consider what would be their circumstances and legislative powers in a restructured federal state. In these circumstances it was unfortunately too easy to ignore how successful the Canadian state had been since 1867 in providing its citizens with freedom, law and order, economic prosperity, a widespread network of social services, and an honoured place in international society.

THE EXECUTIVE BRANCH

Section 9 of the Constitution Act, 1867 states that "Executive Government and Authority of and over Canada is hereby declared to continue and be vested in the Queen." Hence, Canada is a constitutional monarchy and the Constitution

Act, 1982 provides in Section 41(a) that it will require the unanimous consent of Parliament and all provincial legislatures to change the office of the Queen or her representative, the governor general. Sections 10 through 16 of the Constitution Act, 1867 prescribe the Queen's role as "head of state," which in almost all instances is carried out by her representative, the governor general. Section 11 provides for a Queen's Privy Council for Canada to "aid and advise in the Government of Canada." The governor general is to appoint and remove these people. This is a classic example in which the words of the written constitution do not instruct us in the true operation of our system of government. Rather, it is a "constitutional convention" that we must understand, for the governor general must take her or his advice from those who have the confidence of the House of Commons. To have the confidence of the House of Commons means to be capable of achieving a majority of votes in the House.

Elections that determine who wins a seat in the House are contested by people nominated by political parties. The leader of the political party that either wins a majority of the 295 seats (as of 1992), or that wins enough seats that with the support of another smaller party it can expect to pass legislation, is asked by the governor general to become prime minister. The prime minister, in turn, chooses other members of his party to form a Cabinet. It is these people who are sworn in as privy councillors, and it is they who are entitled "to aid and advise in the Government of Canada." The title of privy councillor may be given to others as a form of honour, and Cabinet ministers retain the title even after they lose power or retire. Nonetheless, only those privy councillors who are members of the Cabinet of the day and who are commonly referred to as "The Government" are able to advise the governor general; that is, are allowed to conduct executive government.

THE PRIME MINISTER AND CABINET

The terms "prime minister" and "Cabinet" do not appear in the constitutional sections discussed above, nor is the relationship between elections to the House of Commons and who becomes the government described. The system of responsible government that developed in Canada based on the British model was one that was already well understood in the 1860s, and the Fathers of Confederation felt no need to describe it in the constitution. The expectations of Canadian citizens and those who govern them, however, are framed by what is well understood to be the conventional practice of government. Thus, the governor general carries out the symbolic and ceremonial role as head of state, while real political power rests with the prime minister as head of government and the Cabinet ministers who individually and collectively direct the administrative functions of the Canadian state.

The prime minister and Cabinet dominate the Canadian system of government.[5] They have responsibility for executing the laws of the land and in doing so must construct policies to implement the intent of those laws. The modern state in Canada and elsewhere is fundamentally involved in the economy, and thus its fiscal policy (the management of government expenditures on one hand and the levels of taxation and borrowing on the other) and monetary policy (the regulation of interest rates, the amount of money in circulation, the foreign exchange rate of the dollar) have a major impact on society. Canadian relations with foreign states, its foreign policy, is essentially a matter of prime ministerial and Cabinet direction. In other vital concerns of the Canadian public—the environment, for instance—the Cabinet occupies the crucial decision-making role.

Not only does the Cabinet dominate the administration of laws, but it also plays the key role in proposing changes to existing laws and introducing new legislation. Almost all of the legislation that is discussed by the House of Commons is initiated by Cabinet ministers. Only Cabinet ministers are constitutionally empowered to introduce measures to spend or tax. Since our system of responsible government fuses the executive and legislative branches rather than separating them, a prime minister and Cabinet who have the support of a majority party whose members practise strict party discipline can expect to see their proposals accepted. Even in so-called minority-government situations in which the government depends on support from a party other than its own, the advantages of the government allow it to dominate the legislative process.

The prime minister (advised by his minister of justice) also determines who will sit as judges. Even the failed Meech Lake Accord, which would have allowed provinces to nominate potential Supreme Court judges, would have left the final decision to the prime minister. The growing importance of the judiciary after the adoption of the Charter of Rights and Freedoms in 1982 could make the power of appointment that the prime minister possesses an even more important instrument of power. However, the independence of the judiciary from the executive and legislative branches in Canada is a fundamental principle of our system and the prime minister cannot direct the work of judges once they have been appointed. Nonetheless, one must conclude that prime ministers, when considering senior judicial appointments, will prefer to choose people whose philosophy is similar to their own.

Because the prime minister and Cabinet are so central to the operation of the Canadian state, a brief review of how their functions are organized is appropriate at this point. The constitution provides no specific instructions about the structure of the political executive, and thus each prime minister has considerable latitude in organizing the Cabinet according to personal style and philosophy as well as in reaction to major contemporary issues. The size of the Cabinet, for instance, has grown over recent decades and the Mulroney government in 1992 had about forty ministers. In addition to ministers for each of the twenty-four departments (e.g., Finance, External Affairs, Agriculture, Environment, etc.) there are ministers who have important roles but no department (e.g., Minister for International Trade, President of the Privy Council, Leader of the Government in the Senate) and ministers of state for a variety of concerns (Fitness and Amateur Sport, Youth, Multiculturalism, Small Business, Tourism).

Each of these ministers is individually responsible to Parliament for the efficient carrying out of the legislation that their department administrates. Together, however, they have collective responsibility. All members of Cabinet must publicly defend all of the policies of their colleagues. If they are unable to do this, they must resign. The secrecy of Cabinet meetings (minutes are not released for thirty years) is based on the sensitivity of matters under discussion and the need to allow ministers to argue their differences in private if they are to defend their decisions collectively in public. Should the prime minister decide that political circumstances require that he or she resign, then the whole Cabinet must do so. Again, it is the convention of responsible government rather than written constitutional provisions that requires this.

The prime minister is unchallenged in importance in the structure of the state. As leader of the political party that has won the latest election, the prime minister can lay claim to a democratic mandate to govern. Even if the margin of victory is slim, representing a plurality rather than a majority, and whether or not another party seems to be more popular between elections, the prime minister's authority is unassailable. Unless defeated in the House of Commons, a prime minister is free to determine the date of an election restricted only by the requirement to call one within five years of the last one. The prime minister chooses who will be in the Cabinet; what portfolios they will fill; when they will be promoted to more important ones, demoted, or indeed, dropped from the Cabinet. The appointment of senators, judges, deputy ministers, and chairpersons and members of important boards gives the prime minister important leverage in the entire structure of the state.

It is no surprise, then, that the prime minister has become the focus of the system of government in the eyes of the citizenry and the media. To help in the exercise of these wide powers, a large Prime Minister's Office (PMO) has emerged. While previously the leading figure in this office was the principal secretary, under Prime Minister Mulroney the position of Chief of Staff has become preeminent. The PMO is staffed by political appointees of the prime minister rather than by public servants, although career public servants may be brought in as was the case with Derek Burney, who was for a time Mulroney's chief of staff. Partisan political activities, as well as policy advice, are required of the PMO, and thus its members include media relations experts, policy advisors, assistants who recommend who should be appointed to the various positions that the prime minister can fill, legislative assistants to aid the prime minister in his relations with members of Parliament, and staff to organize the meetings, travel, speeches, and correspondence of the prime minister.

The Privy Council Office (PCO) organizes the work of the Cabinet. The PCO has become increasingly important as governing Canada has become more complex. Along with the Department of Finance and the Treasury Board, the PCO is considered one of the central agencies that attempts to bring coherence to the making of policy in so many different issue areas. The Clerk of the Privy Council heads the PCO and is regarded as the leading career public servant of the state.

The PCO performs the organizational function for the Cabinet by bringing to it the material necessary for decision making, recording the decisions, and transmitting those decisions to the public service to be implemented. Since there are so many departments and agencies seeking to have their policies accepted by Cabinet and its committees, in acting as a traffic director the PCO can have considerable influence over what Cabinet deals with and when. Beyond that, since the proposals of one department may have an impact on the activity of others, the Privy Council Office must organize attempts to assure, if possible, that consistent rather than conflicting recommendations reach Cabinet for decision. The PCO is responsible for the security of Cabinet documents, that is, to maintain Cabinet secrecy. The Federal–Provincial Relations Office is within the PCO structure and is responsible for organizing the federal government's extensive interaction with the provinces and the scores of meetings, most notably the First Minister Conferences. These crucial roles mean that the PCO occupies a strategic position in carrying out the business of the Canadian state.

Since the 1950s the operation of the Cabinet has become progressively more complex. Before that time, ministers appeared to be freer to develop departmental policies and their relations were more directly with the prime minister than with one another. Cabinet meetings involving all ministers were able to deal with the flow of business, to iron out conflicts when they arose, and to deal with partisan political matters. The only important committee was the Treasury Board, a Cabinet committee chaired by the Minister of Finance with five other ministers. It was mandated by the Financial Administration Act to deal with preparation of estimates (the yearly requests for expenditures by departments), to authorize contracts for expenditure, to manage the organization of the public service, and to set pay scales for public servants. In the 1960s the Treasury Board got its own minister, known as the President of the Treasury Board, and the public servants who worked for it were separated from the Finance Department into a department called the Treasury Board Secretariat. While its role remained in expenditure development and control and public service organization, it also became the government's bargaining agent with the newly-empowered public service unions that had gained the right to bargain collectively.

A fully developed Cabinet committee system evolved during the Pearson government of the 1960s and continued to be refined by each succeeding prime minister. The most important committee is the Priorities and Planning Committee, which is chaired by the prime minister. As its name indicates, this committee decides the overall direction of government and the policy and legislative ideas of ministers must conform to it. This committee is sometimes thought of as an inner Cabinet, and membership on it is taken as a sign of the influence that a Cabinet minister has. Priorities and Planning, along with the Treasury Board and the Operations Committee, which oversees the weekly business agenda of government and co-ordinates other committees, were the three key committees as of 1992. The Legislative and House Planning Committee, which is responsible for decisions regarding Cabinet's legislative agenda in the House of

Commons, the Federal–Provincial Relations Committee, the Special Committee of Council, and Communications are the other committees that provide major co-ordinating functions for Cabinet.

In Mulroney's set-up there are eight standing Cabinet committees that deal with substantive issue areas—for example, Economic Policy, Foreign Affairs and Defence, and Environment. These include the ministers of departments whose policies fall within these areas and are chaired by the minister with the most important role in the policy issue group. The chairs of these committees are members of the Priorities and Planning Committee as well. Policy matters and legislative proposals are to some large degree decided in these committees rather than being dealt with by Cabinet as a whole. The full Cabinet has become a forum for settling questions that cannot be resolved by the committees, as well as the forum for debate about major party political questions.

THE BUREAUCRACY

The prime minister and Cabinet constitute the political executive, which is drawn almost exclusively from the House of Commons and is responsible to it for the operation of the bureaucracy that administers the laws and policies of the Canadian state. The bureaucracy has grown into a vast organization in response to societal demands that had led to the development of a variety of government programs. This growth in state intervention, and the number of public servants needed to carry out these functions, created a backlash that contributed to neo-conservative demands for a reduction in government activity, for deregulation, and for the privatization of state-owned enterprises. The Mulroney government, elected in 1984, implemented a number of measures that reflected these demands. Thus, calculation of the number of federal public servants and employ-ees of publicly owned enterprises made in 1990 will need adjustment as long as deregulation and privatization remain the policy of the government in office.

With this qualification in mind, it can be reported that in 1992 approximately 570 000 people were employed by the federal government and its enterprises. That figure included about 215 000 employees who worked under the terms of the Public Service Act and were most directly regulated by the Treasury Board. The armed forces numbered about 89 000 and RCMP uniformed personnel about 19 000. There were thousands of employees who worked on a contract basis and others who worked part-time. About 200 000 worked for enterprises such as Canada Post, Canadian National Railways, Via Rail, the Canadian Broadcasting Corporation, and Petro-Canada. The latter had been designated for privatization and so its employees, like those of Air Canada, which had earlier been sold, will no longer be members of the federal work force. Despite the will to diminish the size of the federal payroll, the bureaucracy remains a significant portion of the Canadian work force. However, the provinces and municipalities have even more employees in their bureaucracies and public enterprises (Ontario Hydro, Hydro-Québec). These number around 900 000 and this figure does not include school teachers, professors and community college instructors, or hospital personnel, whose salaries come essentially from the state. Government employment constitutes upwards of 12 percent of the Canadian working population.

The organization of the public service and its procedures forms the basis for a branch of political science known as public administration. Public servants are found in departments (there were twenty-seven in 1992) such as Finance, National Health and Welfare, External Affairs, and National Defence, to name only a few. They also work in a variety of other agencies, whose various categories are defined in the Financial Administration Act. There are scores of these various commissions, boards, and councils. A few examples are the Unemployment Insurance Commission, the Atomic Energy Control Board, the Canadian Wheat Board, the Economic Council of Canada, and the Bank of Canada. Departments are the direct responsibility of the ministers who head them, while the other kinds of agencies have varying degrees of independence from direct ministerial control.

Within the public service the Privy Council Office, the Treasury Board Secretariat, and the Department of Finance are known as central agencies. The Privy Council Office, which organizes the work of the Cabinet and its committees, plays a key role in co-ordinating the movement of legislative and policy proposals to the decision-making stage. The Treasury Board Secretariat organizes the development of the expenditure plans of the various departments and in addition has the responsibility for the organizational development and personnel policies of the public service. The Department of Finance, which is responsible for the fiscal policy of the government, exercises influence over all matters that involve significant expenditures.

Most departments carry out a "line function"; that is, they carry out some purpose that is directly related to the public or some part of the public. The Department of National Revenue, for instance, is the tax-collecting organization, although perhaps this is a service many Canadians find a mixed blessing at best. The programs carried out by the Department of Veterans Affairs might be of more general appeal, at least to its particular client group. Other departments have a primary role in the carrying out of functions that help the line departments perform their roles. The Supply and Services Department, for instance, is in effect the purchasing department of the federal government. The Public Works Department operates the federal buildings in which the other departments are housed. These kinds of functions are known as "staff functions," and the central agencies described above perform this kind of role as well.

The bureaucracy is huge and there is a constant attempt to refine its techniques to make it efficient. Canadians, like the citizens of most modern states, do not have much difficulty in finding cause to criticize the bureaucracy as being overly large, expensive, wasteful, and inefficient. While some of this criticism may be based on personal experience, very little is the product of intensive study. It is hard to imagine an overhaul of the public service that could satisfy the critics but would not involve a significant reduction in service. Canadians do not appear to wish that the goods and services they get from the state be reduced dramatically, and thus they will have to continue to abide a large and expensive (but, one hopes, efficient) bureaucracy.

THE LEGISLATIVE BRANCH

In the Canadian state the legislative function is exercised by Parliament for federal matters and the ten provincial legislative assemblies (known by various names) for provincial matters. Municipal councils legislate on local matters, but only to the degree and in the manner they are mandated by their provincial legislature. Section 17 of the Constitution Act, 1867 states "There shall be One Parliament for Canada, consisting of the Queen, an Upper House styled the Senate, and the House of Commons." For a bill to become a law, therefore, it must pass the House of Commons and the Senate in exactly the same form and be given royal assent by the governor general acting on behalf of the Queen. By convention, royal assent is never denied. In addition, for most of Canadian history the Senate has played the secondary role of recommending only changes that do not affect the main principles of a bill and has rarely challenged the will of the House of Commons. The change in this behaviour, which emerged in the late 1980s and early 1990s, is discussed below, as are suggestions for Senate reform. Most Canadians have grown to look at Parliament as being synonymous with the House of Commons because it has been that body that has wielded parliamentary authority, and it is to that House that the prime minister and Cabinet are responsible.

The membership of the House of Commons is determined by periodic elections that can be no more than five years apart according to the constitution. However, convention dictates that election dates are determined by the prime minister, who advises the governor general to dissolve the House of Commons so that a general election may take place. Elections therefore usually occur about four years apart, although the conditions of minority government or a rare defeat of the government in the House may make them more frequent. The members of the House of Commons, known as members of Parliament (MPs), are elected from constituencies whose number and boundaries are determined after each decennial census and are incorporated into a Representation Act passed under the terms of Section 51 of the constitution. There were 295 members of the House of Commons in 1992, divided among the provinces basically in proportion to their population, although there are some minimum guarantees for the less populous provinces. By province and territory the allocations were: Newfoundland 7, Nova Scotia 11, New Brunswick 10, Prince Edward Island 4, Québec 75, Ontario 99, Manitoba 14, Saskatchewan 14, Alberta 26, British Columbia 32, Northwest Territories 2, Yukon 1. Within each province the boundaries of the constituencies are determined by an Electoral Boundaries Commission.

Election is determined by plurality, that is, the person who gets the most votes (not necessarily a majority) among a number of candidates wins the election.

Because several candidates (most representing political parties) contest each election, it is common to have an MP elected with less than 50 percent of the vote and for a government to get a majority of the 295 seats with about 42 percent of the national vote. While this type of result concerns some critics, it does produce a government and opposition, and thus the legitimacy of the system has not been seriously challenged by the citizens. Nevertheless, it is undeniable that national political parties have been underrepresented in some regions of the country and this has had its impact on the federal system.

The passage of legislation is the most obvious function of the House of Commons. Nonetheless, it has other important roles.[6] It provides the pool of talent from which the Cabinet is drawn. Its members represent their constituents in a variety of ways and, indeed, they spend most of their time on constituency service. The House of Commons is expected to monitor the executive function, and the daily question period is only one of the techniques it uses to exercise that role. The House of Commons is expected to be the focal point for important national debates. For instance, during the 1990 confrontation between the Mohawk Nation and the Québec Provincial Police, both the native people and opposition members of Parliament demanded that Parliament be recalled from its summer recess. This demand was voiced even though the solution to the problem was not a matter of legislation but rather of government policy.

The passage of legislation, however, remains the central responsibility of Parliament. A complex procedure has been developed to deal with bills, as the draft proposals are known. The bills, which are almost all prepared by the government (private members' bills being the exceptions), and must be if they are bills to tax or spend, are introduced by a Cabinet minister who moves *first reading*. This stage gets the process moving and copies of the bill are printed for all members. Days, weeks, or perhaps even months later, the bill comes back to the House for *second reading*, the stage at which the principles of the bill are debated. After it is debated in these general terms it is sent to an appropriate standing committee for detailed clause-by-clause investigation, during which amendments can be proposed. The committee, some time later, will transmit its conclusions on the bill back to the House where the committee's work will be debated in report stage. The final phase, *third reading,* will be voted upon soon thereafter, at which time the House of Commons has completed the legislative work and the bill goes to the Senate to undergo the same process.

As indicated above, the Senate has rarely taken an aggressive role in law making despite the fact that it has constitutional powers spelled out in the constitution. The Senate was developed to act as a check on the popularly elected House of Commons, and its members are appointed by the prime minister to serve until age seventy-five. While in 1867 this concern over possible democratic excess was considered justified in some circles, in the 1990s the unelected status of senators denies them the popular legitimacy to take, and play, an equal role in law making with the House of Commons. The other role assigned to the Senate was to represent more equally the views of the provinces in the central organs of the state than the population-based House of Commons might do. This is a function commonly assigned to a second legislative chamber in a federal state.

The failure of the Senate to perform adequately its role as a regional representative body has prompted calls for its reform. The less populous provinces of Atlantic Canada and the West have had, for obvious reasons, a greater interest in reform than have Ontario and Québec. It has been Alberta in the 1980s and 1990s that provided the most widely discussed proposal for change: the Triple E Senate.[7] The three Es stand for equal, elected, and effective. The hope is that a Senate constructed on these principles can play a legitimate role in ensuring that policies adopted in Ottawa take into consideration the needs and aspirations of the less populous provinces, which have historically felt their interests to be ignored. To this point there have not been detailed assessments of how this type of Senate would affect the legislative function of Parliament or, indeed, what its impact would be on Canada's Cabinet system of government.

THE JUDICIAL BRANCH

A system of courts has been set up in which the laws of the Canadian state can be interpreted and applied. Criminal law falls under the jurisdiction of Parliament and is thus uniform across the country. Civil law, on the other hand, is within the competence of the provincial legislatures and thus may vary from province to province. The biggest difference is that the *civil code* based on the French model prevails in Québec while the *common law* based on the English system holds sway in the other provinces. Each province administers a system of courts that deals with both civil and criminal matters. There is a Supreme Court of Canada to which appeals may be directed from the provincial systems. At the federal level there is a court called the Federal Court of Canada that deals with a specialized range of matters, as well as a Tax Court, which is limited to that concern.

While the system of courts varies with each province, the systems are similar in their broad outlines. At the bottom are justices of the peace, whose duties may involve procedural matters such as issuing warrants, setting bail, or settling minor cases, especially regarding municipal by-laws. On the next level of the system are the provincial courts, which have responsibilities in a wide range of civil and criminal matters. In fact, these courts, whose judges are appointed by the provincial governments, handle a large percentage of the judicial work in Canada. The next level of court is one whose judges are appointed by the federal government, as are all judges in higher courts. At one time these courts were designated as county or district courts and were responsible for civil cases involving larger amounts of money and more serious criminal cases as defined in the criminal code. Judges in these courts might decide cases alone or there might be a jury, depending on the type of case and the decision of the accused. More recently, however, these courts and their jurisdictions have been merged with the superior courts in most provinces. These superior courts are often called the Supreme Court in a province, although other designations exist, and their jurisdiction relates to even higher sums of money in civil cases and the most serious aspects of criminal law. They also have an important role in hearing appeals from lower courts. Finally, at the apex of each provincial system is a group of judges who constitute an appeals court and whose only function is to review cases already tried in a lower court. Cases may be appealed to the Supreme Court of Canada, which decides which cases it wants to hear. The role of the Supreme Court of Canada is to interpret and clarify the law so that such law will be uniformly applied across the country.

The adoption of the Canadian Charter of Right and Freedoms in 1982 has given the courts the basis for an expanded role.[8] Until that time the concept of parliamentary supremacy encouraged the practice of judicial restraint. The courts were prone to uphold the laws of Parliament or the provincial legislatures unless those laws could be found to be outside the jurisdiction (*ultra vires*) of the body that passed them. The charter, however, limited the concept of parliamentary supremacy by spelling out a variety of rights that were not to be violated by any law. This new situation provided the basis for judicial activism, and some critics were worried about the possibility of judicial supremacy. Section 33 of the Constitution Act 1982, the so-called notwithstanding clause, provided for Parliament or the provincial legislatures to assert their parliamentary supremacy despite the rulings of courts on Section 2 (the fundamental freedoms) or 7-15 (democratic, mobility, legal or equality rights). Proponents of a strong charter have decried this clause as potentially making the charter meaningless.

There is no doubt that the Charter of Rights and Freedoms has created a new situation. Individuals and interest groups may challenge the legislation and policies of governments before the courts on grounds that were not possible before. The courts, on their part, have a broader basis on which to interpret law than was the case previously. The experience of courts with the charter is still in its early years and thus a judgment on the impact of its adoption must await the passage of time. It is possible to say at this stage, however, that the courts have not shown that they wish to challenge legislation to the point where government by elected representatives no longer exists. Neither have governments indicated that they intend an assault on the rights of Canadians through the use of the notwithstanding clause. It is safe to assert that the courts now have a more prominent role in the structure of the Canadian state than was the case before 1982.

CONCLUSION

What has been described in the previous pages is the bare outline of the structure of the Canadian state. Its essential features are that it has a federal constitution and is a constitutional monarchy that operates with a parliamentary system. The Cabinet is drawn from the House of Commons, which thus provides for the responsibility of the executive to the legislature. The judiciary is independent of the other two branches and has an enhanced role since the adoption of the Canadian Charter of Rights and Freedoms in 1982.

It should be borne in mind that other states have similar institutions. The physical circumstances of the land and the societal characteristics of the people who inhabit the land have interacted to imbue the Canadian state with its own distinctive characteristics. On the whole, however, and especially when compared to the records of other states in international society, the Canadian state has admirably achieved its stated goals of "peace, order and good government."

Notes

[1] D.V. Smiley, *The Federal Condition in Canada* (Toronto: McGraw-Hill Ryerson, 1987), 83–99.

[2] K.C. Wheare, *Federal Government*, 4th ed. (New York: Oxford University Press, 1969), 19.

[3] K. McRoberts, *Québec: Social Change and Political Crisis*, 3rd ed. (Toronto: McClelland & Stewart, 1988), 128–72.

[4] R.M. Campbell and L.A. Pal, *The Real Worlds of Canadian Politics* (Peterborough: Broadview Press, 1989), 227–314.

[5] W.L. White, R.H. Wagenberg, R.C. Nelson, *Introduction to Canadian Politics and Government*, 5th ed. (Toronto: Holt, Rinehart and Winston, 1990), 135–49.

[6] C.E.S. Franks, *The Parliament of Canada* (Toronto: University of Toronto Press, 1987).

[7] The Alberta Select Special Committee on Upper House Reform, *Strengthening Canada, Reform of Canada's Senate* (Edmonton: Alberta Legislative Assembly, 1985).

[8] R.I. Cheffins and R.A. Johnson, *The Revised Canadian Constitution, Politics and Law* (Toronto: McGraw-Hill Ryerson, 1986).

Bibliography

Alberta Select Special Committee on Upper House Reform. *Strengthening Canada, Reform of Canada's Senate.* Edmonton: Alberta Legislative Assembly, 1985.

Campbell, R.M., and L.A. Pal. *The Real Worlds of Canadian Politics.* Peterborough: Broadview Press, 1989.

Cheffins, R.I., and R.A. Johnson. *The Revised Canadian Constitution, Politics and Law.* Toronto: McGraw-Hill Ryerson, 1986.

Franks, C.E.S. *The Parliament of Canada.* Toronto: University of Toronto Press, 1987.

Jackson, R.J., D. Jackson, and N. Baxter-Moore. *Politics in Canada.* Scarborough: Prentice-Hall, 1986.

Krause, R.M., and R.H. Wagenberg, eds. *Introductory Readings in Canadian Government and Politics.* Toronto: Copp Clark Pitman, 1991.

McRoberts, K. *Québec: Social Change and Political Crisis.* 3rd ed. Toronto: McClelland and Stewart, 1988.

Smiley, D.V. *The Federal Condition in Canada.* Toronto: McGraw-Hill Ryerson, 1987.

Van Loon, R., and M.S. Wittington. *The Canadian Political System.* 4th ed. McGraw-Hill Ryerson, 1987.

Wheare, K.C. *Federal Government.* 4th ed. New York: Oxford University Press, 1969.

White, W.L., R.H. Wagenberg, and R.C. Nelson. *Introduction to Canadian Politics and Government.* 5th ed. Toronto: Holt, Rinehart and Winston, 1990.

6

❏ ❏ ❏ ❏ ❏ ❏ ❏

Canadian
Economic Affairs

Ian M. Drummond

INTRODUCTION

Most North American and British academic economists would probably argue that economics is a scientific subject whose aim is to make and test general hypotheses about economic affairs. Therefore, Canadian economics makes no more sense than Canadian chemistry or Canadian astronomy, so far as the subject matter of the discipline is concerned. Nevertheless, there are some economic topics, distinctly Canadian, that do merit special study. The first is a factual description of the national economy, which we address in this chapter. We also point to some of the peculiarities, from the Canadian studies perspective, in economists' ways looking at things Canadian. Equally interesting, although not surveyed here, are the study of Canada's economic history—the history of economic development—and the examination of economic thought in Canada. There is a large literature on the former topic, and some on the latter.[1] It is also possible to study both national and provincial policy; here there is a vast literature.[2]

Canadian governments have tended to be interventionist, and Canadian economists devote much of their time to analysing their activities. However, economists commonly work within the intellectual framework peculiar to economics, virtually ensuring that the interested public cannot, or will not, read what they write. Where fields overlap, as for instance on many legal topics, it is necessary for economists to retrain their would-be collaborators—never a popular process. A similar difficulty has arisen with respect to the policy studies that are increasingly popular among political scientists. These on occasion have been called "economics without economics," or at least without economists.

Like other specialists, economists tend to be critical when anyone else dares to tread upon their professional turf. As we shall see, this has been very apparent in connection with the question of foreign investment. Many Canadians, especially those in the arts community, believe that foreign investment is a problem. Over the years they have generated a considerable literature dealing with the possibility of harm stemming from foreign investment. People in the arts community, in particular, frequently talk as if harm has really been demonstrated. But this is not so, and mere repetition cannot prove the charge or demonstrate it. Hence the tendency of most, though not all, Canadian economists, when asked about the problem of foreign investment, to shrug and ask, "What problem?"[3] Indeed, since the outbreak of World War II, Canada's economic performance has been sufficiently good to make one wonder why anyone would think there is, or was, a serious problem. And if economists are told, as a media person recently told a colleague, that today's Hong Kong investment is "good" whereas US foreign investment is "bad," they are likely to become quite shrill, or at least demand an explanation.[4]

Parallel problems arise when Canada's trading patterns are under discussion. Even among scholars, it is still widely believed that in international trade Canada is a country of "hewers of wood and drawers of water"—that is, an exporter of primary products and an importer of manufactures. But at present, and for a good many years in the past, things are, and have been, quite different. Even though some students, no doubt influenced by courses in history and political science, indicate in their essays that Canada has a natural affinity with those Third World countries that live by exporting one or two raw materials, this is not so.

In fact, according to most indices of economic organization, the Canadian economy is rather like those of other prosperous countries in western Europe and around the Pacific rim. In most respects, it also resembles the US economy, although it is smaller and it exports a much larger proportion of its output. For this reason we say that Canada is a comparatively export-oriented economy, more resembling some of the economies of western Europe. Canada's regional disparities are a source of worry. But several European states, including the United Kingdom, also exhibit such disparities. Also, for nearly fifty years the Canadian economy has delivered a rising level of employment and a strong upward trend in living standards, while since 1945 the regional disparities have tended to diminish. Admittedly there have been regional unhappinesses, especially in those areas that depend on the export of fish or wheat.[5]

Because Canada exports about one-third of its output, our prosperity is intertwined with conditions in the industrial states that buy most of our exports. Thus, a slump in Japan, western Europe, or especially the United States, which takes about 70 percent of our exports, tends to produce a slump in Canada. Export dependence is commonplace nowadays, especially in western Europe. Even the comparatively shock-proof United States is far more vulnerable to such developments than it was in the 1950s or 1960s. The shock of any economic downturn is transmitted both directly, because exports will be depressed, and indirectly, because the resultant export slump will tend to depress new investment and consumer spending in Canada. Indeed, that is what happened in the early 1980s when Canada experienced its first real recession since the 1930s. As there was a recession in the United States and western Europe in the early 1980s, Canada could not hope to be spared.

CHARACTERISTICS OF ECONOMIC GROWTH

Modern economic growth displays certain strong regularities and these are evident in Canada's experience. Perhaps the most interesting is the shift in the labour force. Everywhere, agriculture and other "primary" industries and occupations comprise a diminishing share of the total, while "tertiary" occupations—the white-collar trades—become ever more important. At present, more than 60 percent of Canada's workers are employed in white-collar occupations. In general, the reasons are clear enough: with rising prosperity comes a shift in demand towards the products of secondary and tertiary activity, which until recently, because such services did not lend themselves to mechanization, could only be met by employing more labour. Economic growth, therefore, involved a major structural change in Canada's pattern of employment. Urbanization followed naturally from this,[6] not only in Canada, but in western Europe and the United States as well.

The structure of Canadian work and earning patterns is very similar to the American one. Most people are wage earners. Self-employment is widespread, but most of it is urban. The sturdy yeoman of the mythic past is now hard to find, whether in Québec or elsewhere in the country. By the time of the 1981 census, for every three farm workers there was one in "sport, recreation, and culture."[7] The cultural industries, therefore, emerged as an important lobbying, interest, and pressure group.

❑ REGIONALISM

Canada's most populated area lies close to the nation's boundary with the United States, and even within this ribbon, the various kinds of economic activity are not evenly spread. Manufacturing is concentrated in the larger cities, especially in the St. Lawrence basin, as are many tertiary industries. The federal government has enacted elaborate and expensive programs that are meant to spread industry and finance more widely, especially to Atlantic Canada. These do not appear to have been very successful and it remains the case that Atlantic Canada does not have the share of manufacturing that might have been predicted, either by its nineteenth-century economic status or by its share of Canada's twentieth-century population. The reasons for this are much debated. Some observers say the main trouble is location; the distance from major North American markets is too great.

Others blame the resource base, held to be deficient in quantity or quality of one or more key industrial materials. Still others blame local management, provincial government policies, or even the federal government's efforts to be helpful. The study of "Atlantic retardation" has become a considerable regional industry, supported, like so many other Atlantic activities, by federal money.

❑ AGRICULTURE

Agriculture, also, is spread unevenly across the country, although mixed farming and livestock can be found in all the provinces and territories. Cultivated areas lie comparatively close to the US border, and crop marketing has traditionally been heavily dependent on the railway system, which, in turn, depended heavily on capital subsidies, not only from Ottawa, but from the provinces as well. Prairie wheat exports, which used to flow to Britain and western Europe, have been displaced by European Community subsidies; they now go chiefly to eastern Europe, China, and what was the Soviet Union, states where ill-advised government policies have done much damage to domestic farming. The Prairie provinces also produce large amounts of coarse grains and of rapeseed (now better known as canola). In the Okanagan Valley of British Columbia and the Niagara Peninsula of Ontario, there are many fruit growers, including 3500 growers of grapes. Tobacco comes mostly from southwestern Ontario.

Agricultural marketing is now very largely collectivized. Since the middle of World War II, the prairie wheat crop has been marketed by the Canadian Wheat Board. The board's policy is to export the wheat for the best price it can get, dividing the proceeds, after the fact, among the farmers. Most other agricultural products are marketed through or by provincial marketing boards, which try to manage sales and production on the domestic market. For some products, as for chickens, there is federally sponsored co-operation among the provincial boards. There is also a wide-ranging system of agricultural price support, operated and financed by Ottawa. For wheat, there is a two-price system, whereby the domestic price is considerably higher than the export price.

❑ MANUFACTURING

Canada's industrial array is a reasonably comprehensive one. Table 1 summarizes some recent data. At times we are told that Canada lacks, or has lacked, "strategic goods." This phrase does not appear to be related to defence production, but rather to capital goods—industrial equipment, heavy transport equipment, and iron and steel.

The data, however, show that, in fact, the nation is a sizable producer of capital goods, and even exports some, such as locomotives and combine harvesters. This kind of production has a long history. Well before 1914, for instance, Canada produced motor cars, locomotives, other rolling stock, street cars, iron and steel, agricultural implements, electrical generating equipment, and ships, among

Table 1   Summary Data on Canadian Manufacturing (1985)

	Employment (thousand)	Shipment of Goods of Own Manufacture (million dollars)
Food Industries	192.0	32.8
Beverage Industries	31.9	4.8
Tobacco Products Industries	7.1	1.6
Rubber Products Industries	25.9	2.5
Plastic Products Industries	38.2	3.9
Leather and Allied Products Industries	23.1	1.3
Primary Textile Industries	26.8	2.7
Textile Products Industries	31.1	2.7
Clothing Industries	110.9	5.5
Wood Industries	107.6	11.1
Furniture and Fixtures Industries	49.9	3.4
Paper and Allied Products Industries	114.2	18.1
Printing, Publishing, and Allied Industries	117.2	8.5
* Primary Metal Industries	106.8	17.0
* Fabricated Metal Products	139.7	14.0
* Machinery Industries	74.7	7.5
* Transportation Equipment Industries	211.0	43.2
* Electric/Electronic Products Industries	137.2	13.5
Non-metallic Mineral Industries	50.6	5.9
Refined Petroleum and Coal Products Industries	16.7	24.4
Chemical and Chemical Products Industries	87.2	18.3
Other Manufacturing Industries	67.7	5.1
TOTAL, CANADA	1766.8	248.8

Source: *Canada Year Book*, 1990, pp.16-18 to 16-20, reproducing findings from the
annual *Census of Manufacturing* (Statistics Canada reference number 47-250).

many other kinds of capital goods. To show just how important this sector is, in Table 1 we have starred the capital goods industries. The grouping is not logically impeccable: many industry groups produce both consumer and capital goods, while some also produce inputs for other industries. Nevertheless, we can work out a broad impression of the sector's contribution, imperfect though it may be.

After thirty-five years of intense debate on the subject, most Canadians know that a good deal of the Canadian manufacturing industry is foreign owned. Indeed, it is likely that many Canadians exaggerate the extent of that foreign ownership. Table 2 presents some recent data on the question.

Statisticians class an entire firm as "foreign owned" so long as foreigners own over half of its shares. Similarly, a firm may be classed as "foreign-controlled" so long as statisticians believe that foreigners actually do control major decisions, no matter who owns the shares. No one considers the fact that Canadians may own many shares in the parent firms. Thus GM Canada is treated as a foreign-owned and foreign-controlled firm because there is substantially no Canadian shareholding in it. So is Ford Canada, because Americans are believed to control the business, even though for many decades there was Canadian management

Table 2   Non-financial Corporations, Canada, 1987, by Country of Control

	Foreign-controlled	Canadian-controlled	Total
Total			
Corporations (number)	3 146	445 111	450 119
Sales ($ million)	252 152	667 061	919 213
Mining including oil and gas			
Corporations (number)	387	7 864	8 251
Sales ($ million)	15 364	22 903	38 257
Manufacturing			
Corporations (number)	1 831	42 493	44 324
Sales ($ million)	153 169	161 814	314 983
Construction			
Corporations (number)	159	66 060	66 219
Sales ($ million)	3 015	53 279	56 294
Utilities			
Corporations (number)	245	27 445	27 690
Sales ($ million)	4 720	82 775	87 495
Wholesale Trade			
Corporations (number)	1 482	51 544	53 026
Sales ($million)	51 169	138 060	189 230
Retail Trade			
Corporations (number)	183	90 189	90 372
Sales ($ million)	17 891	136 900	154 791
Services			
Corporations (number)	657	134 725	135 262
Sales ($ million)	6 588	60 267	66 856

Source: *Annual Report of the Minister of Industry, Science and Technology under the Corporations and Labour Relations Returns Act*, Part I, 1987 (catalogue no. 61-210; published March 1990).

and substantial Canadian minority shareholding. Small shifts in shareholding have been enough to move companies such as Alcan, Inco, and Bell Canada from the foreign-controlled to the Canadian-controlled category.

Most economists maintain that there is no special magic or special opprobrium attached to the category of foreign ownership. Nor is it altogether clear just how foreign ownership became so widespread in Canada. One important element is believed to be Canada's protective tariff. Canada's National Policy of 1879 certainly did attract some US-owned branch plants, which would produce for Canada's newly protected domestic market. Other foreign-owned firms exploited Canadian natural resources, largely, but not entirely, for the US market. These firms were especially noticeable in forest products, in mining, and more recently in oil and gas. A few firms, most obviously in the automobile industry, used Canadian plants as the bases for exports to the British Empire. Here the early attraction was the system of imperial preferential tariffs, which emerged in many parts of the empire before 1914. Until the recent past it was often difficult or impossible to sell in the United States. American tariffs were so high as to be prohibitive. Only when there was no US tariff, as with newsprint paper in and after 1914, did Canadian manufacturers readily export to the United States. Some of these exporters were Canadian owned; some were not.[8]

Finally, in certain periods US firms bought up Canadian firms, apparently to consolidate markets and to manage the transfer of technical knowledge. There were some of these purchases before 1914, rather more during the 1920s, and many more in the 1950s, when the practice attracted adverse comment. From 1974 until 1985, most foreign acquisitions, whether in manufacturing or in other sectors, were screened by Ottawa's Foreign Investment Review Agency (FIRA). On the assumption that FIRA was discouraging foreign investment (surely its main purpose), the Mulroney government replaced it with Investment Canada, announcing that "Canada is open for business again." Already by 1985, however, the Canadian business community had become a major actor on the American corporate stage. By 1990, it was clear that, so far as entrepreneurship and financing were concerned, the national boundary mattered much less than the concerned non-economist thought. Nor, for that matter, had most economists managed to involve themselves with the whole issue. One produced a serious scholarly study of the phenomenon: so far as one can tell, only economists read it.[9] Another enrolled as a polemicist, eventually publishing a tract with the seductive title *Getting It Back*.[10] Still others worked with concerned citizens, groups of Indians and Inuit and others who "cared deeply." But among most economists, there was considerable, though not universal, agreement with the words of C.D. Howe: in the mid-1950s, the federal Cabinet minister had explained that since the firms were subject to Canadian law and regulation, he did not care who owned them.[11]

For decades Canada's patterns of regional specialization have caused political trouble. The four western provinces specialize in primary production, much of which is exported. The same is true of the Atlantic provinces, though less so. Manufacturing, however, is concentrated in the St. Lawrence basin. The primary producers complain that although they have to pay tariff-protected prices for their manufactures, they have to sell on the international free market. They therefore press for federal government help and for international commodity agreements that would raise the prices they receive. As a consequence, Canada has been a strong supporter of the various international wheat agreements, and is energetically opposed to wheat subsidization policies in the US and the European community.

THE INTERNATIONAL ENVIRONMENT

Because so many Canadian areas rely heavily on export markets, the federal government tends to support the international bargaining sessions whose main purpose is tariff reduction, although like other governments, it is more anxious to receive concessions than to give them. Nowadays this bargaining is sponsored largely by the General Agreement on Tariffs and Trade (GATT), an international organization that periodically arranges for rounds of bargaining, partly for tariff reduction and partly for the better regulation of international commerce. Because it has a small population, Canada carries relatively little weight in the GATT forum. Nevertheless, by working together with other like-minded countries, whether in the Commonwealth or in the North Atlantic area, Canada is sometimes able to do something. Furthermore, thanks to over forty years of GATT bargaining rounds, Canada has won new markets for many goods, and has opened its own markets somewhat to the exports of other countries. Protectionism in international trade is always a danger. But in fact, both for exports and for imports, in the past forty-five years a great deal has been done to keep it at bay.

There is also tariff-bargaining outside GATT. This is called bilateral bargaining (as contrasted with GATT-style multilateral negotiations). At one extreme, bilateral bargaining can produce bilateral free trade. The 1988 Canada–US Free Trade Agreement is an example of such negotiation. The GATT rules prevent member countries from extending new preferential concessions to other members (except to certain poor countries), but they do permit free-trade areas—a somewhat illogical concession that can be explained only by examining the trading patterns of the 1930s and 1940s. But bilateral bargaining can, and usually does, aim lower. Thus, Canada made various bilateral trade agreements with the USSR, China, and some of the smaller socialist countries. Since the late 1950s, these have provided the legal framework for Canada's massive West to East wheat trade, which began in a small way in the 1920s, lapsed for almost thirty years, resumed and boomed in and after 1963.

These overseas arrangements are interesting and important, but for the Canadian economy as a whole, the US has long been the most important external influence, both as buyer and as supplier. In the recent past over 70 percent of Canadian exports have been going to the United States, and over 70 percent of imports come from there. Canadians used to think of the nation's trade as a "North Atlantic triangle."[12] Traditionally, Canada sold a great deal to Britain but bought little there. The pattern with respect to the United States was reversed; much more was bought than was sold. The surplus of Canadian transatlantic trade thus covered, or partly covered, the deficit on North American dealings. This pattern began to crumble in the 1920s, when the US became an important buyer of Canadian pulp, paper, and metals, and an important supplier of cars and parts. The triangle reappeared in the 1930s and during World War II, but then began to fade again. Thus, by the late 1970s, Britain was supplying barely 3 percent of Canada's imports, and taking less than 4 percent of exports. Japan, once absolutely insignificant, was now more important than Britain under both headings. As for the Canada–United States trade balance, by 1980 Canada was running a trade surplus with the United States, a phenomenon that has continued.

There has also been pressure, both internal and external, for trade sanctions against South Africa. For Canada, there was something unreal about the resulting controversy. It was difficult to believe that Canada's actions could really induce the South African government to change its ways, if only because the two countries had so little to do with one another. There had certainly been some private lending to South Africa, but the trade flows were tiny. In 1978, for instance, South Africa took 0.2 percent of Canada's exports and supplied only 0.3 percent of imports. Sanctions, therefore, probably could not hurt Canadians: there were bound to be alternative markets and other sources of supply. This perhaps accounts for the speed with which provincial liquor monopolies began to drop South African wines and spirits from their lists. By 1990, South Africa had begun the process of dismantling the system of apartheid and was trying to devise a more equitable political system. It does not seem likely that Canada's sanctions deserved the credit.

ENERGY

❑ OIL AND GAS

By 1980, in the world of international economic affairs, Canada's oil and natural gas had become much more important than they had been in the past. Even before 1945, some oil and gas were produced in Ontario, New Brunswick, and Alberta. But output was very small relative to domestic demand, which was met chiefly by imports—partly from the United States, and partly from Mexico, Venezuela, and Trinidad. Things changed quickly in the late 1940s, however, when major discoveries were made first in Alberta, then in Saskatchewan, and then in British Columbia. During the 1950s, oil and gas pipelines were laid, connecting the western fields with major markets in Ontario and the United States. Much politicking was needed to open and maintain the US market. Ottawa required Ontario to use the comparatively costly Canadian crude, but the poorer regions of Québec and Atlantic Canada were allowed to rely on cheap imported oil from overseas. Oil pipelines, therefore, did not reach Québec, nor did gas pipelines reach the Maritime provinces. Thus, though Canada produced more oil than it consumed, some regions were oil importers while others were exporters.

When the overseas oil-producing countries quadrupled the world price of oil late in 1973, the situation presented problems for Canada. The government responded by subsidizing imports for the East, taxing exports from the West, and trying to maintain a domestic made-in-Canada price that was below world levels.[13] It also tried to aim at a long-run self-sufficiency by expanding the domestic pipeline system and by encouraging exploration in the Northwest Territories.

The oil and gas problem was especially complicated because of arrangements that had been made decades before, when conditions were different. For one thing, most oil and gas were provincial property, because when Crown land had been disposed of, subsoil rights had commonly been retained. Thus, in western Canada, the provincial governments were the main oil landlords; and the higher the price of oil, the higher the oil royalties they could charge. Ottawa's made-in-Canada price was an attack on the pocketbooks of the provincial treasuries, especially that of Alberta, which had most of the oil and gas—hence the slogan often seen in Alberta during the 1970s: "let the bastards freeze in the dark."

A factor causing further problems is that since 1957, Ottawa had been committed to equalization—a system of unconditional grants to provinces meant to ensure national standards of service in each province. Therefore, because additional oil and gas royalties made the Alberta government more prosperous, Ottawa was required to pay more equalization to the poorer regions of the country, especially to Québec and the Atlantic provinces.

The result, for more than a decade, was a depressing tale of federal–provincial wrangling.[14] Meanwhile, Ottawa tried to encourage oil and gas development in the so-called "Canada lands." These lay in the Northwest Territories and off the Arctic shores; in these districts there were no provincial governments, and for the time being—until the emergence of Indian and Inuit self-government—Ottawa would own the subsoil rights. Most of the exploration was undertaken by private companies, both Canadian and foreign. But some part belonged to Petro-Canada (the national state-owned oil company that had been formed in 1975), as well as to Suncor, in which the Ontario government had bought a share.

Oil and gas were certainly found along the Arctic shore and under the offshore waters, but by 1991 none had been marketed: the transportation problems were too great. In 1990 it seemed likely that, at long last, a gas pipeline would be built through the Mackenzie River Valley. Meanwhile, during the mid-1980s, Ottawa had acted to deregulate oil and gas: although many rules and regulations remained in force, the tangle of the 1970s was largely swept away, and with it the made-in-Canada pricing structure. Petro-Canada, however, survived as a Crown corporation, having bought several refineries and chains of retail stations.

❑ ELECTRICITY

Fortunately for everybody, electric power has not been manipulated as oil and gas have been. Most of the generating capacity is in the hands of provincial governments. Because of regional resource peculiarities, the generating systems are very different across the country. In Canada as a whole, some 70 percent of all electricity is generated by hydro-electric installations, such as the ones at Niagara Falls. In the 1970s, nuclear power provided almost 10 percent of total power, but almost all of this capacity was in Ontario, which derived nearly one-third of its electricity from nuclear plants. Beyond hydro and nuclear power there is thermal power, supplying just over 20 percent for Canada as a whole, but far more in some provinces and far less in others. Thus, in British Columbia, 96 percent of all generation is hydro-fuelled, and the remainder comes from oil. In Québec, almost 100 percent of electricity comes from hydro, and there are plans for further massive development with an eye to export. In Newfoundland the figures are similar, but at the other extreme, the only power generated in Prince Edward Island is oil-fuelled. Nova Scotia and New Brunswick have little hydro-electricity—13 and 26 percent respectively—and their thermal systems are mostly or entirely oil-fired. Consequently, when world oil prices quadrupled following 1973, these provinces were especially exposed. Ontario, however, was comparatively secure: nearly 40 percent of its output came from hydro, another 30 percent from nuclear plants, and of the remainder, little was fuelled by oil or gas. Understandably, some other provinces have been anxious to emulate Ontario: since the mid-1970s, both Québec and New Brunswick have begun to build nuclear power plants, while Québec has been anxious to expand further its immense hydro installations at James Bay.[15]

Since Canada is a very large country that stretches over many time zones, it would seem sensible to connect the provincial power systems into a national grid. This has been slow to develop, but there are some interconnections. Hydro-Québec, for instance, supplies power to Ontario, which in turn has elaborate arrangements for international interchange with the US at Niagara Falls and elsewhere. Newfoundland supplies Hydro-Québec, which transmits much of this power to the United States. New Brunswick has similar hopes. Indeed, the anxious consumers of New York and New England seem to favour Canadian power as a clean alternative to local thermal or nuclear plants. And for Canada's power authorities, exports can be helpful. As yet, however, they produce less than 1 percent of Canada's total export receipts. Furthermore, and largely because of Ontario Hydro's load-sharing schemes, Canada imports some power, though imports are small in relation to exports.

❑ COAL

In many countries industrialization was based on local coal. The mineral was needed not just to run railways and gas works, but to fuel steam engines, thus providing the basic energy for new industries. This was not the case in Canada, because manufacturing developed in Central Canada, which had most of the population, while the country's coal was thousands of miles away in Nova Scotia, Alberta, and British Columbia. Central Canada, then, imported coal—a little from Britain, and a lot from the United States. In addition to water power, Canada's early industrialization was based on imported coal, and the locally fuelled industry, as in Nova Scotia, was a small part of the picture. With the growth of the electrical system, coal lost much of its central position as an industrial fuel, and conversion to diesel fuel cost it the railway market. In the recent past there has been some revival of demand: oil is now a comparatively costly fuel, and export demand for coal, chiefly from Japan, has grown greatly. British Columbia, therefore, ships a great deal of coal to Japan; new railways and ports have been built to move the coal quickly and cheaply.

FISHING

Fishing is chiefly a matter for the two ocean coasts, and although few people earn their living by fishing in the nation as a whole, for the ocean provinces the health of the fishery is a matter of great importance. Constitutionally, the care of the fishery is a federal responsibility; economically, however, Canadian fishermen have to share the fish with those of other countries. Ottawa, therefore, has busied itself in international discussions meant to conserve the fish population, and in 1977, it extended Canada's fishing frontier far out to sea—360 kilometres, in fact. The fishery is in part a matter of small family boats, and in part a matter of large corporate enterprises; fish processing is an affair for a few very large businesses. Fishing is a seasonal activity, and for many of the fishermen there are really no alternative out-of-season jobs. Ottawa has extended the unemployment insurance system so that the fishermen can draw benefits. This is an illogical arrangement: many or most of the fishermen are self-employed, and wage earners cannot properly be said to be unemployed by the regular and predictable seasonal shutdown. But no one has been able to find any alternative. Ottawa has also tried to deal with the long-run problem of fish conservation. In principle, this might be managed by international co-operation, but in practice it has had to be done unilaterally—by the fixing and restricting of annual catch quotas. This device is meant to conserve fish stocks, and one has trouble thinking of any alternative. But naturally enough, the quotas anger the fishermen.

MANUFACTURING

In 1978 there were almost 32 000 manufacturing establishments in the country, employing 1.8 million women and men—just under 20 percent of the labour force. Value added was $52 billion, just under 23 percent of gross national product. Half of the manufacturing activity was in Ontario, another 26 percent was in Québec, while 9 percent was in British Columbia. The remaining 15 percent was spread among the other seven provinces. For thirty years or more, Ottawa and the provinces have been working to try to encourage more manufacturers to establish in Atlantic Canada and the Prairies. There have been some successes: for example, petrochemicals in Alberta, fertilizer in Saskatchewan, and bluejeans and buses in Manitoba. But there have also been some embarrassing failures: for example, oil refineries and heavy-water installations in Atlantic Canada. Furthermore, some old industries seem to stagger onward towards extinction. That may well be the fate of the Sydney iron and steel complex, which has been government owned for several years now. Ottawa spends money on these kinds of industries in the hope of equalizing rates of unemployment and real incomes in the several regions of the country. In Québec and Atlantic Canada, unemployment is usually higher and earned incomes are always lower than in Ontario. Sad to say, it is hard to see much result from such regional development assistance. The main beneficiaries, perhaps, are the professionals—economists and others—who design the schemes.

Many Canadians seem to think that the country's manufacturing industry is entirely artificial, the product of Canada's protective tariff. It is for this reason that people react so negatively when Ottawa proposes to reduce or remove these tariffs. Economists, however, see the situation differently.[16] Much of Canada's manufacturing relies on cheap local materials and exporting its product easily and without drama. However, much manufacturing does not have this kind of advantage, and it naturally looks more exposed. But many such industries do enjoy cost advantages that suggest that in a free-trade environment they could, and would, grow. For some industries, too, location provides some protection. For over thirty years such questions have been studied, and the verdicts are unequivocal: by reducing its protective tariffs, Canada could raise output and living standards, though not by much.

It is sometimes suggested that much of Canada's production and exportation of manufactures does not count because it results from the further processing of Canadian raw materials, or from some special international arrangement such as the Canada–US Auto Pact. Most economists would find such assertions specious. Why is it wrong to process one's own raw materials, or for that matter, to import raw materials and process imports? In this respect, what is the difference between Britain's nineteenth-century cotton-textile industry, and Canada's twentieth-century aluminum industry? Both employ imported raw materials and domestic inputs to produce a commodity that is largely exported in a semifinished state for further processing in other countries. The cotton-textile industry, everyone agrees, was a mainspring of Britain's Industrial Revolution; might not the same be true of Canada's aluminum industry? If not, why not? As for the Auto Pact and similar arrangements, economists have been interested chiefly in the results, not the reasons for seeking or concluding them.

FINANCE

The Canadian financial system has always resembled the systems that we find in other countries of new settlement, such as Australia or New Zealand. It also bears a strong resemblance to the British system, although in some respects the US model has also been influential. In Canada the number of banking firms is comparatively few, and consequently, branch banking is common. A few bank names, therefore, appear all over the country. This is like the British pattern, and very unlike the American. In the late 1970s, there were only eleven banks with over 7400 offices in Canada and almost 300 offices abroad. Because at one time each bank had been incorporated by a special act of Parliament, the commercial banks are called "chartered banks." Besides the six big banks, there are a few small regional banks and several dozen specialized small banks—recent entrants, having appeared under the new regulations enacted in the 1980s. Many of these new entrants are foreign-owned, but their role in the financial system is a limited one. The large branch banks are very long-lived indeed: the oldest dates from 1817, and the system of nation-wide branching had taken shape by 1914. Although there have sometimes been foreign-owned banks among the chartered banks, the industry is overwhelmingly Canadian-owned. By 1914 the larger chartered banks had extended their activities abroad—to the

United States, Mexico, London, the British West Indies, Cuba, and Latin America. From 1923 until 1985, no bank in Canada failed, although at certain times, some were saved only by merger with larger and stronger banks.

The system was capped in 1934 when Parliament provided for a new central bank, the Bank of Canada, which could do all the things that central banks do. It began to operate in 1935. Because the public almost always wants inexpensive and plentiful credit, when the Bank of Canada presses the system in the opposite direction it generally becomes an object of controversy. Economists have a different set of more profound reasons for being somewhat nervous about the Bank of Canada. For one thing, there is some suspicion that the Bank of Canada, like central banks in other countries, sometimes gets its timing wrong, thus making booms "boomier" and slumps "slumpier." As well, there is now some doubt about the actual efficacy of its policies. Since Canadians can and do borrow and lend money internationally, just what is the effect of managing our domestic credit system? International lending will certainly be affected, and so will our foreign exchange reserves, the price of our currency, or both. These changes will affect the domestic economy, but both the routes and the impacts will be different from the ones that Canadian economists would have stressed forty years ago. The difference reflects the fact that Canada's financial system is now quite closely integrated with the world economy: there is little point in developing models that assume that capital funds do not move, or that imports and exports can be neglected.

Meanwhile, Canadian business has found ways to behave like a bank without calling itself one. Constitutionally, only federal authorities can incorporate a bank, and a very elaborate federal Bank Act (a regulatory code that is revised every decade or so) regulates their activities. However, what is the case with trust companies, mortgage-loan companies, and credit unions? By 1914 the answer was clear. Trust and mortgage companies could incorporate either provincially or federally; their behaviour would be regulated by the incorporating government, either through a special incorporating act or under general legislation. Credit unions would operate under provincial regulation.

Besides all these banks and bank-like businesses, there are some 900 insurance companies—Canadian, British, and foreign—operating in the country. Although 100 years ago the Canadian life insurance companies were few and weak, they now do about 80 percent of the Canadian business. They have also long since extended their businesses to the US, Britain, and other Commonwealth markets, so that during the 1980s, about 20 percent of their total business was non-Canadian. Among sellers of insurance, Canadians are known to be notoriously thrift prone.

Canadians are offered a full range of financial services by such firms as bond houses, brokerage firms, pension consultants, and investment trusts of various sorts.[17] Such businesses tend to cluster in Montreal and Toronto, especially the latter, but there are active firms in many other centres as well. For a long time it has been illegal for a bank or a federally incorporated insurance company to spread its business into all these fields, although the life insurance companies have long been major actors in the field of pensions and annuities. By 1990, Ottawa had said that it would remove the barriers to competition in finance, but as yet (July 1991) few steps have been taken.

It has been argued that the banks were responsible for the growth of foreign direct investment. The argument begins with an assertion that the banks were too committed to short-term credit, to commercial credit, or to both. The result, it was said, was to starve the manufacturing industry of long-term capital, opening the way for foreign, direct investment.[18] As evidence accumulates,[19] this hypothesis looks less and less tenable: the banks do not seem to have abstained from industrial lending, nor was long-term industrial capital particularly scarce. Nowadays, of course, Canada's banks behave much like those of other developed industrial countries: they have proliferated various kinds of medium-term loans, including loans to the Third World, and no one would now claim that they starve any particular sector or activity, although naturally no region or sector is happy with the amount of credit that it gets.

MARXISM AND KEYNESIANISM

A problem for many Canadian economists has been the semi-Marxist framework that has conditioned the thinking of many critics of the current economic system. Few Canadians are comfortable with this view of the world. But if one starts with the idea that in a capitalist state, the government is a sort of committee of the capitalist class, then it obviously matters who the capitalists are. The bigger the foreign component among the capitalists, the less truly autonomous will be the nation's policies, whether these be domestic or external. Furthermore, it will be harder for the nation to "ripen" towards socialist revolution: the domestic stresses and tensions that Marx described will become a part of a much larger international context. Further, the Canadian pattern of development is interpreted, explicitly or implicitly, as some sort of departure from the Marxist model. Just why have foreigners invested so much? What has given them the chance? Obviously, because something has gone wrong, or has been wrong with Canadian capitalism. The banks, perhaps, have been reluctant to lend to industry. Or perhaps they have lent to the wrong industrialists. While few economists agreed with these hypotheses, no one could dispose of them quickly. In any event, a good deal of research proved to be necessary; and the weight of the evidence produced does not confirm the semi-Marxist framework.

A great deal of modern economics concerns itself with fiscal policy: the management of tax rates and spending programs so as to reduce inflationary pressure and to moderate slumps. This is the "Keynesian fiscal policy" that descends from the work of the great British economist, John Maynard Keynes. During the 1940s and 1950s, Canadian economists and Canadian economic management worked on these topics, and by the mid-1970s the standard professional rhetoric—cut taxes in slumps but raise tax rates in booms; raise spending in slumps but cut spending in booms—had become the national political rhetoric as well, especially on the part of the left. Sad to say, during the seventies the results of these policies were not impressive. In Canada as elsewhere, many economists became somewhat sceptical about this kind of fiscal policy. In the 1940s, federal authorities dominated the fiscal scene. Their tax and spending programs therefore could, and did, have real leverage on the whole national economy. But gradually this has ceased to be so. Provincial spending came to matter much more, and larger shares of critical revenues were transferred to the provinces, while Ottawa became involved in a large number of shared-cost programs—medicare, higher education, and various welfare schemes—that were hard to cut. By 1990, some economists were talking and writing as if the most important fiscal problem was the distressing federal government deficit; others clung to the old faith in Keynesian fiscal management, while wondering if Canada would ever be able to employ it again. The same attitudinal changes have occurred in the United States and in western Europe, especially in the United Kingdom. In this respect, as in so many others, Canadian ways have become less distinctive. During the 1940s, taxing and spending were managed in accordance with Keynesian precepts; indeed, from time to time the annual budget speeches were used for lectures on rational fiscal policy. By 1990, these times were gone.

CONCLUSION

I have tried to suggest how economics can help us understand Canada. This is partly a matter of facts about the economic structure—patterns of production, trade, unemployment and employment, living standards, and consumption. It is partly a matter of information about important economic structures—everything from labour and banking law to competition policy. I have suggested that such facts and information are by no means widely known; indeed, with respect to economic reality many are ill-informed. Economics is less satisfactory in explaining why things are the way they are; here the historian, the student of diplomacy, and the political scientist have much to contribute.

Economics can also help with the design and evaluation of government policy in many fields: agriculture, fisheries, energy, mining, banking, regional development, intergovernmental financial transfers, trade, and foreign ownership, as well as many other areas. In considering such matters, economists, like other specialists, will inevitably be influenced by their own desires—in the professional jargon, "preferences" or "utility functions." But self-awareness is some protection against this influence, and most economists really do try to guard against it. Another guard is the professional methodology: "If you do *this*, then *that* will follow, other things being equal."

In this kind of policy analysis, economists can and often do work along with other specialists, generally political scientists, but sometimes sociologists, lawyers, and historians; especially with respect to evaluation, these groups may make a larger and more telling contribution than the economists. In this kind of work, many economists would probably agree that although there may be no clear, right answer, it is important at least to identify the wrong ones. Rent control is often thought to be one example; so is agricultural price support, whether local or international.

Sad to say, there are problems in the relations between economics and other subjects. Economists themselves are somewhat to blame. They often write and talk in a private jargon, at least as impenetrable as the jargons of some other disciplines. They sometimes extend their professional methodology into areas where it has little or nothing to contribute. This has sometimes been called the "imperial tendency of economics." The result is sometimes nonsensical, and it is always annoying. On the other hand, some problems arise from the other side of the relationship.

A surprising number of scholars seem to believe that economists are committed to an economic interpretation of events. Disliking such interpretations, they decide to dislike economists, thereby protecting their own ignorance. There is also the suspicion that because economists choose to study economic affairs (a "low and degrading topic"), they are low and degrading people. This can be connected with a dislike of our present economic order. An eminent Canadian professor of divinity, a lifelong social democrat, once told a gathering, "Economics is the theology of capitalism." Naturally he would not discuss anything with economists, or read their writings. But he knew. Finally, there are problems arising from media handling of the subject. Certain facts—unemployment, national output, the balance of imports and exports—are reported and the media ask economists to comment on the data, explain them, and forecast their movement. The comments are inevitably casual and unscientific, reflecting only a tiny part of modern economic work, and giving very little sense of what the discipline can do. Yet for some people they serve as a definition. I know an eminent Canadian historian who really does believe that this media-babble defines modern economics. I have corresponded with an eminent Canadian zoologist and ecologist who believes the same thing. When there is so much misunderstanding, dialogue is bound to be difficult, and sometimes it is impossible.

Notes

[1] General surveys of Canadian economic history and economic thought that may prove of interest to students are: W.T. Easterbrook and H. Aitken, *Canadian Economic History* (Toronto: Macmillan, 1956; reissued University of Toronto Press, 1988); R. Pomfret, *The Economic Development of Canada* (Toronto: Methuen, 1981); R. Bothwell, I.M. Drummond, and J. English, *Canada 1900–1945* (Toronto: University of Toronto Press, 1988) and *Canada since 1945* (Toronto: University of Toronto Press, 1989). All of the above works can be read and understood by non-economists. A more technical approach is found in W. Marr and D. Paterson, *Canada: An Economic History* (Toronto: Macmillan, 1980). Also useful are the seventy-two *Research Studies of the Royal Commission on the Economic Union and Development Prospects for Canada* (Toronto: University of Toronto Press, 1986). For specific works dealing with Canadian economic thought, see R. Neill, *A New Theory of Value: The Canadian Economics of Harold Innis* (Toronto: University of Toronto Press, 1972) and C. Goodwin, *Canadian Economic Thought* (Durham, NC: Duke University Press, 1961).

[2] Useful introductions to these topics can be found in the policy chapters of any introductory textbook on economics, such as R.G. Lipsey, D. Purvis, and P.O. Steiner, *Economics*, 6th ed. (New York: Harper and Row, 1988).

[3] For Canada, the classical texts are the *Reports of the Royal Commission on Canada's Economic Prospects* (1957) (The Gordon Report); *The Task Force on the Structure of Canadian Industry* (1967) (The Watkins Report); and *The Gray Report* (1971). The latter was originally a memorandum to Cabinet, "Domestic Control of the National Economic Environment: The Problem of Foreign Ownership" (May 1971). For an abridged version, see Editors of the *Canadian Forum*, *A Citizen's Guide to the Gray Report* (Toronto: New Press, 1971).

[4] A.E. Safarian, *Foreign Ownership of Canadian Industry* (Toronto: McGraw-Hill, 1966).

[5] Surveyed in Bothwell et al., *Canada 1900–1945*.

[6] Treated by S. Kuznets, *Modern Economic Growth: Rate, Structure and Spread* (New Haven: Yale University Press, 1966).

[7] Surveyed by I.M. Drummond, in J. Sargent, Research Co-ordinator, *Postwar Macroeconomic Developments*, vol. 20 in the *Research Studies of the Royal Commission on the Economic Union and Development Prospects for Canada* (Toronto: University of Toronto Press, 1986).

[8] Exemplified at a time when it was already passing from the scene in *Report of the Royal Commission on Canada's Economic Prospects* (1957); see also J.B. Brebner, *North Atlantic Triangle* (New Haven: Yale University Press, 1945; reissued Toronto: McClelland & Stewart, 1966).

[9] See Safarian, *Foreign Ownership*.

[10] A. Rotstein and G. Lax, *Getting It Back* (Toronto: Clarke, Irwin, 1974).

[11] R. Bothwell and W. Kilbourn, *C.D. Howe* (Toronto: McClelland & Stewart, 1979), chs. 17 and 18.

[12] See note 8.

[13] The arrangements were surveyed each year in the *Canadian Annual Review*.

[14] Ibid.

[15] Basic data are from *Canada Year Book*; annual updates from *Canadian Annual Review*.

[16] The pioneering study was that of J. Young, *Canadian Commercial Policy* (Ottawa: Queen's Printer, 1957). More recent work has been done for the Economic Council of Canada and for the Royal Commission on the Economic Union and Development Prospects for Canada (the Macdonald Commission).

[17] E.P. Neufeld, *The Financial System of Canada* (Toronto: Macmillan, 1972).

[18] W.T. Naylor, *The Business History of Canada* (Toronto: Lorimer, 1975).

[19] M. Bliss, *Northern Enterprise* (Toronto: McClelland & Stewart, 1987).

Bibliography

Bliss, M. *Northern Enterprise: Five Centuries of Canadian Business*. Toronto: McClelland & Stewart, 1987.

Bothwell, R., I. Drummond, and J. English. *Canada: 1900–1945*. Toronto: University of Toronto Press, 1988.

Bothwell, R., I. Drummond, and J. English. *Canada since 1945*. 2nd ed. Toronto: University of Toronto Press, 1989.

Bothwell, R., and W. Kilbourn. *C.D. Howe*. Toronto: McClelland & Stewart, 1979.

Brebner, J.B. *North Atlantic Triangle*. New Haven: Yale University Press, 1945.

Canadian Annual Review. Toronto: University of Toronto Press, annual.

The Canada Yearbook. Ottawa: Ministry of Supply and Services, annual.

Easterbrook, W.T., and H.G.J. Aitken. *Canadian Economic History*. Toronto: Macmillan, 1956; reissued, Toronto: University of Toronto Press, 1988.

Editors of the *Canadian Forum*. *A Citizen's Guide to the Gray Report*. Toronto: New Press, 1961.

Goodwin, C. *Canadian Economic Thought*. Durham, NC: Duke University Press, 1961.

Kuznets, S. *Modern Economic Growth: Rate, Structure and Spread*. New Haven: Yale University Press, 1966.

Marr, W., and D. Patterson. *Canada: An Economic History*. Toronto: Macmillan, 1980.

Naylor, W.T. *The Business History of Canada*. Toronto: James Lorimer, 1975.

Neill, R. *A New Theory of Value: The Canadian Economics of Harold Innis*. Toronto: University of Toronto Press, 1972.

Neufeld, E.P. *The Financial System of Canada*. Toronto: Macmillan, 1972.

Pomfret, R. *The Economic Development of Canada*. Toronto: Methuen, 1981.

Royal Commission on Canada's Economic Prospects. *Report*. Ottawa: Queen's Printer, 1987.

Royal Commission on the Economic Union and Development Prospects for Canada. Vol. 20. *Research Studies*. Toronto: University of Toronto Press, 1986.

Rotstein, A., and G. Lax. *Getting It Back*. Toronto: Clarke, Irwin, 1974.

Safarian, A.E. *Foreign Ownership of Canadian Industry*. Toronto: McGraw-Hill, 1966.

Task Force on the Structure of Canadian Industry. *Report*. Ottawa: Queen's Printer, 1967.

Young, J. *Canadian Commercial Policy*. Ottawa: Queen's Printer, 1957.

Policy
Process

Canadian Politics

Robert M. Krause
Walter C. Soderlund

INTRODUCTION

Canadian politics, in most of its dimensions, fits squarely into the Anglo-American democratic tradition. This tradition is characterized by features such as constitutional government, a competitive party system, mass participation, and a free press. However, particular historical circumstances, combined with geographic, economic, and cultural cleavages, modified this broad framework of Anglo-American democracy within which Canadian politics functions, and adapted it in unique ways. It is these peculiarities that are stressed in this treatment of Canadian politics: specifically, the process of political integration leading to Confederation in 1867; the nature of Canadian federalism and the subsequent two-tiered party system; and a parliamentary system affected by features of the American presidential system, as well as models of judicial review. Finally, a number of key contemporary political issues within Canada will be discussed in light of the unique features of the Canadian political system.

POLITICAL INTEGRATION AND CONFEDERATION

The circumstances surrounding the founding of a country are important in understanding the context in which subsequent political decisions are made. Two points respecting Canadian Confederation are of crucial importance in this regard. First, Confederation, which was not a movement for political independence, was not the end product of an ongoing process of economic and social integration; rather, it was a response to a number of perceived military, economic, and political crises, which affected British North America in the early

1860s. Second, the federal character of the political system was not adopted as a result of profound theoretical reflection, but as a pragmatic response to dealing with a specific set of serious and seemingly intractable problems. The union of the provinces of Canada (East and West) with those of Nova Scotia and New Brunswick in 1867 clearly was not the result of the type of social and economic integration that Karl Deutsch, among others, posits as key to securing political integration.[1] In fact, there was extremely limited movement of people between the provinces, both at the mass and the elite level, and trade tended to be either transatlantic or trans-border with the United States, rather than interprovincial.[2] As well, attitudes held by political elites (especially among those in the Maritime provinces) were non-supportive of political union.[3]

Political unification occurred, therefore, in spite of economic and social barriers and in response to a number of coincident international and domestic forces. The international forces were the American Civil War (1861–1865) and the consequent deterioration in relations between Great Britain and the United States; the American decision to abrogate the Reciprocity Treaty, which since 1854 had provided the basis for economic prosperity in all of British North America save Newfoundland; and the introduction of the "Irish Question" to the shores of British North America in the form of the Fenian Movement.[4] Finally, on the domestic side, not the least of the problems was the political deadlock that had paralyzed the largest and most politically powerful province, the Province of Canada. This deadlock reflected the reality of English–French political power and the consequent futility of the strategy of French assimilation.[5]

If Confederation itself was the result of an unplanned set of factors, so, too, was the federal system that emerged as a solution to the problems inherent in a scheme of political integration. The choice of federalism as a system of government was without doubt the result of pragmatic considerations grounded in the problems of the day, as opposed to the sophisticated application of an abstract political theory. From a reading of the Confederation debates, it is evident that few politicians of the day exhibited either much interest in, or knowledge of, the finer points of federal theory. Nevertheless, they were acutely aware of the perceived failure of the American federal system. Sir John A. Macdonald believed, in fact, that the provincial governments would quickly lose their appeal and that Canada would come to approximate a unitary state along the British model.[6] Federalism was thus seen as a compromise. It was necessary to reconcile the fears of the French Canadians regarding cultural assimilation, and those of Maritimers, who thought they would be politically overwhelmed under rules of the game calling for representation by population (in which the population factor worked to the advantage of the Province of Canada), with the pressures for union created by the set of factors discussed above.

It is ironic that, while federalism was a simple expedient, neither well respected nor well understood, it was the underlying reality of Canada as a "federal society" that necessitated a political system that recognized regional and cultural diversity. It is this underlying reality rather than constitutional mechanisms written into the British North America Act (Canada's original constitution) that determined, at various points in Canada's historical development, the interplay between provincial and federal governments. This reality also forms the legacy of Canadian federalism.

FEDERALISM

Federalism entails a division of power between two levels of government. The constitution, which specifies the division of powers between the central and sub-units of government within the federation, may be either centralist or decentralist in its allocation of powers between the two levels of government. In a centralized federation, the national or central government (which in Canada is referred to as the federal government) dominates the component parts of the federation (the provinces), while in a decentralized federation the subunits either dominate or encroach upon the federal government's powers.

In spite of the lack of agreement among the architects of Confederation as to precisely what the concept of federalism entailed, the Canadian Constitution gave the federal government a predominant position in the new state. Sections 91 and 92 of the British North America Act, which outline the legislative powers of the federal and provincial governments, allocated to the federal government twenty-nine enumerated areas of constitutional jurisdiction, which gave it power over the most important substantive functions of government: defence, trade, and economy. Conversely, the sixteen enumerated powers allocated to the provinces were those that were considered in the 1800s to be either relatively unimportant or of a local nature: health, welfare, education. So that there would be no doubt on the matter of the predominance of federal power, the central government was given an additional general area of legislative authority "to make Laws for Peace, Order, and good Government of Canada, in relation to all matters not coming within the Classes of subjects by this Act assigned exclusively to the Legislatures of the Provinces."[7] Additionally, the federal government was assigned the powers of "reservation" and "disallowance," which in essence gave the federal government veto power over legislation passed by a provincial legislature. To further buttress the role of the federal government in the performance of its legislative tasks, the British North America Act gave to that government the ability to pay for those responsibilities by "The raising of Money by any Mode or System of Taxation."[8] At the same time, the provinces were restricted to direct taxation, which was then considered to be both a minor and an unpopular taxing power. However, in spite of the strong centralist thrust of the constitution, the actual evolution of the federation was not in the direction that a literal reading of the constitution would suggest. Rather than becoming a centralized federation, the Canadian federation has swung on a pendulum between periods of centralism and decentralism.

Only infrequently has the pendulum come to rest in a centralist position. While strong proponents of provincial rights might disagree, there have been only three historical periods during which the Canadian federation was highly centralized: the immediate decades following Confederation (1867–1883), the First World War period (1914–1918), and the period immediately preceding and following the Second World War (1937–1955). The swings in power between the two levels of government can be attributed to political, economic, and social factors that emerged over time. The consequent changes in the direction of the Canadian federation (centralist/decentralist) have been accompanied by competing images of the nature of federalism in Canada.

While Canada began to operate as a quasi-federal state under strong national direction, the federal government's role depended to a great extent upon two conditions: first, an acceptance by the provinces of its leading role; second, a recognition by the Canadian populace that such a federal role was legitimate. Soon after Confederation, both conditions weakened. Strong provincial premiers began to emerge and grow restless as their laws and enactments were either reserved or disallowed by the federal government. The primacy of the federal government in setting national policy was also questioned by the Canadian people as the country entered into a period of economic stagnation and depression in the decades following Confederation. As a result, the centralist vision of Canadian federalism was challenged by two competing conceptions of the nature of federalism: the compact and the co-ordinate.[9]

The compact perception of federalism emphasized the role of the provinces in the creation of the new nation. To provincial proponents of this theory, the federal government was a creation of the provinces, and thus they advocated a subservient role for that government and a leadership role for the provinces in the federation. Another interpretation, the co-ordinate view, also argued for an emphasis on increased provincial powers by stating that the enumerated legislative powers given to both the federal and provincial governments were proof that both levels of government were equal within their respective legislative fields of competence. Thus, no one level of government was paramount over the other, but rather, both levels should remain in their own areas of legislative jurisdiction.

The early proponents of a more decentralized Canadian federation found support for their contentions in the constitutional interpretations made by the Judicial Committee of the British Privy Council, which gradually began to whittle away the powers of the federal government.[10] For example, the general legislative grant of power given to the federal government to make laws for "peace, order, and good government" was interpreted by the British Court of Appeal in such a manner that by 1896 that power had been placed in a position subordinate and secondary to the enumerated legislative powers given to both the federal and provincial governments.[11]

The erosion of federal power was accelerated by the nature of unequal economic development among the Canadian provinces, which had surfaced by the end of the nineteenth century. Three distinct economic sectors had developed in Canada: secondary manufacturing, export-oriented agriculture, and export-oriented resource industries. Each of these sectors was located primarily in different provinces and regions of the country. Consequently, provinces developed distinct views on the nature of federalism. As federal economic policy would impact differently on the provinces, economic self-interest of various provinces would produce positions on policy areas that were at odds with those of the federal government and other provincial governments.[12]

The balance of power between the federal and provincial governments had gradually begun to shift away from the centralist dominance of early decades into an era when the provinces had increased their salience. At the same time, it was not long before the pendulum began to move once more towards enhanced federal power. While the powers of reservation and disallowance were not employed as frequently as they had been in the past, the federal government was able to assert a degree of influence over the provinces. The opening of the Canadian West and the wheat boom gave the federal government a greater national policy-making role. By the beginning of the First World War the federal government was still the dominant power in the federation. Its paramount role was enhanced by the war, when for all practical purposes, the country was run as a unitary state. To meet the financial requirements of a war effort, however, the federal government found it necessary to introduce a "temporary" personal income tax. As income taxes are a direct tax, one over which the provinces have constitutional jurisdiction, provincial co-operation was sought and achieved.

The wartime co-operation and taxing experience saw the emergence of a new variety of federalism—administrative federalism. As Edwin Black notes, "Its advocates assume the long term continuance of the provincial governments, but emphasize the necessity and desirability of expanding the tradition of intergovernmental co-operation without the antagonistic flaunting of sovereign rights and privileges."[13]

While all four competing visions of federalism (centralist, compact, co-ordinative, administrative) had both proponents and detractors, the Depression of the 1930s and the Second World War lessened the attractiveness and practical utility of the co-ordinative and compact views. By 1955, the centralist and administrative perceptions remained as alternatives for the operation of the Canadian federal system. But even here the economic difficulties of the Depression and the security concerns of the war tended to produce a system in which the federal government had more prominence than it had during the inter-war period.

The period of federal predominance, however, soon came to an end with the growth of a "new" Québec and the resurrection of provincial powers facilitated by the growth of the welfare state, which followed the end of World War II. For nationalists in Québec, the old compact version of federalism with its defensive overtones gave way to a more aggressive and expansionist "dual alliance" concept of the nature of Canadian federalism. Here it was argued that the essence of federalism was not found in the compact between the provinces and the national government, but in a bargain entered into between two cultural communities— French and English. While this version of federalism gave the single province of

Québec enhanced status, Québec was not the only provincial voice arguing for greater provincial rights. Other provinces argued forcefully for the co-ordinative and administrative positions with respect to federalism. Their position emerged as a direct result of the federal government's growing involvement in their fields of jurisdiction and in its consequent expanding use of conditional grants.[14] The onslaught by Québec and the other provinces against federal preeminence was such that in the 1960s the most recent centralist period of dominance gradually came to end. Provincial rights and provincial powers became the dominant elements within a highly decentralized Canadian federation. Yet, the nature of Canadian federalism remained open to change.

While the administrative version of federalism buttressed by co-ordinate arguments had been a feature of Canadian federalism for a great many years, the operation of the concepts gradually shaded into the present era of "executive federalism."[15] In executive federalism, provincial premiers and the prime minister of Canada, together with the support of their executives, determine much of public policy in Canada. The instrument by which the new shared power is implemented is an elaborate machinery of inter-governmental committees and conferences, with the plenary conference of first ministers being the most important feature.

POLITICAL PARTY SYSTEM

The contemporary Canadian party system is multi-competitive, with three major parties (Liberal, Progressive Conservative, and New Democratic) electing members to the Canadian Parliament. Of the parties represented in the Canadian Parliament, two have their origins in the pre-Confederation period—Liberal and Progressive Conservative—while the New Democratic Party (NDP) is of more recent vintage. These three parties have not been the only ones to have elected members to Parliament. Rather, with the breakdown of the original two-party system (Liberal/Conservative) in 1921, the Canadian Parliament has had representation from a wide variety of third parties. At the same time, Canada does not have a true three-party system, but rather a two-and-a-half party system in which the Liberals and Progressive Conservatives receive approximately 80 percent of the national popular vote and third parties obtain the remainder. Thus, Canada has a multi-competitive party system, but one in which only the Progressive Conservatives and Liberals have had the necessary plurality of electoral support across the country to form national governments.

While only two parties have been successful in forming governments at the federal level in Canada, all but the Atlantic provinces have had a provincial government that was neither Progressive Conservative nor Liberal. Further, three provinces have had governments formed by parties that do not contest elections at the national level (e.g., the Parti Québécois in Québec). In addition, the NDP has been able to form, at one time or another, governments in three of Canada's western provinces (Saskatchewan, British Columbia, and Manitoba), and in Ontario (1990).[16] Canadian federal parties, thus, do not enjoy a monopoly on governmental power, nor do they find the same degree of electoral support at the federal and provincial levels.

One of the reasons for the different party systems at the provincial and federal levels relates to how seats are distributed in the national Parliament. The two most populous provinces, Ontario and Québec, send over 60 percent of the elected members to the House of Commons. As a consequence, successful federal parties have crafted their electoral policies to garner support in this core region of the country. The "peripheral" regions of the country (Atlantic Canada and the West), have thus not received the same degree of policy attention as the "core" region. While voters in Atlantic Canada, the poorest region of the country, have not stopped supporting the two older parties at the federal or provincial levels of government, such was not the case in the Canadian West. Here, third parties such as the Co-operative Commonwealth Federation (CCF),[17] and its predecessor the Progressive Party, rose in part to protest the core orientation in policy making of the two original national political parties.

Canada's single-member plurality electoral system has also contributed to the fragmentation and dual nature of the Canadian party system(s). This voting system tends to overrepresent the party receiving the largest percentage of votes in the House of Commons, which has led to a situation whereby "relatively small swings in votes between parties often result in a large number of seats changing hands." As a consequence, national parties have tended to emphasize "regional and more particularly ethnic differences in order to get elected."[18]

The result has been a national party system within which brokerage politics, rather than ideological or programmatic politics, has been practised extensively. By acting as brokers, the Liberals and Progressive Conservatives have attempted to balance and trade competing interests across the country by appealing "to many narrow interests based on short term views of specific issues."[19] In short, parties seeking electoral success have become pragmatic in issue orientation.

The effect of the brokerage nature of politics practised by the two original Canadian national parties has been twofold. First, as the nation grew more diverse economically and culturally, the older parties found it more difficult to broker the diverse interests arising across the country. As they have been successful in forming national governments, they have not often felt the need to offer more principled or programmatic policies. On the other hand, as many of the same divisions in opinions found across the country cannot be fully articulated and aggregated by the parties, third parties with more programmatic appeals have arisen at the national and provincial level. As well, provincial wings of national parties have become more regionally oriented to protect and enhance their distinct provincial interests and legislative responsibilities.

Sectional appeals by Canadian parties have dramatically affected the degree of organizational centralization found within Canadian federal political parties. Where parties of the same name at both the provincial and national levels of government were once basically "integrated" in their organizational structure, more recently they have become highly decentralized or "confederal." This holds true for Canadian parties in general, but the present three parties do vary slightly in the degree of decentralization between their federal and provincial wings, by both regional and internal levels of party organization. As Donald Smiley notes,

> The Progressive Conservatives and the NDP are slightly less confederal than the Liberals. The organizational separation of the federal and provincial wings of the two major parties [Liberals and Conservatives] has progressed less far in the Atlantic provinces than elsewhere in Canada. Confederalism is most marked at the higher levels of party organization, and in the constituencies, the same persons often carry out both federal and provincial party activity. With these caveats, the Canadian party system is significantly more confederal than that of any other federation.[20]

THE PARLIAMENTARY SYSTEM

As colonies of Great Britain, the provinces that united to become Canada were the beneficiaries of a number of crucial democratic traditions—among the most important were traditions of a free press and constitutional government.[21] A key component of British constitutional practice was the idea of a parliamentary system based on "responsible government," meaning that the legislature holds the executive responsible, mainly through control of the raising and disbursement of money.

Parliamentary structures were in place in all British North American colonies prior to Confederation, and the practice of responsible government had begun to be established in the 1840s. In all colonies, Parliaments consisted of two Houses (an Upper and a Lower), which are now called the Senate and the House of Commons, respectively. Prior to Confederation, all Lower Houses were elected and one Upper House was also partially elected. As a result of the Confederation agreement, the House of Commons was designated an elective body based on the principle of representation by population, while the Senate was to be appointed by the governor general in council, i.e., the prime minister and Cabinet.

Analogous in function to the British House of Lords, the Senate was to be a chamber of "sober second thought." However, as Canada was also a federal system, the Senate was to serve another important function, that of regional representation. Thus, as in the United States, representation in the Senate was not based on population. Rather, each region of the country was allocated a specific number of Senate seats.

The mid-nineteenth century represented a transition period in democratic practice from old to new principles of legitimacy. As the legitimacy of the House of Commons was based on popular election, while the Senate's was based on appointment, over the years the Lower House emerged as the dominant structure in Canadian politics.

In contrast to the doctrine of "separation of powers" characteristic of a presidential system, a parliamentary system of government is based on the principle of "fusion of power." This means that the executive (the prime minister and

Cabinet) must be members of the legislature, i.e., either the House or Senate, although most Cabinet members are elected members of the House of Commons. The theory of "responsible government" suggests logically that there be some means whereby members of the House are organized. Although not mentioned in the British North America Act, the structure through which this organization occurred was the political party. Thus, the prime minister, again through convention rather than constitutional designation, emerged as the leader of the party that obtained the largest number of seats in the House of Commons. If this number of seats constituted an absolute majority, the practice of party discipline whereby party members are expected to vote as a bloc enabled a prime minister to serve a constitutional term limited to five years on the basis of a majority government. If, on the other hand, a party received less than an absolute majority of seats, the prime minister's position was tenuous, dependent on support from other political parties, i.e., a minority government. If he were not able to maintain the "confidence of the House" (50 percent or more of the membership), the government would fall and the governor general (the Queen's representative and titular head of state), would either call on another party leader to form a government that would enjoy the confidence of the House, or failing that, call an election.

While the theory of parliamentary democracy holds the legislature supreme in power over the executive, over the years the reality of government based on party cohesion has led to a situation in which the prime minister and Cabinet have become the dominant power within the parliamentary system.[22] This power has been enhanced further by development of a television-oriented, American campaign style that places great emphasis on leadership attributes.[23] Also contributing to this growth in executive dominance has been the development of a bureaucracy, necessitated by the increasing number of functions falling under the jurisdiction of the state: health, education, welfare, and economic growth. The result of these two trends is that policy making is not primarily in the hands of elected members of Parliament, but has shifted to the executive-bureaucratic arena.[24] Another factor that has led to the decline of Parliament is growth of provincial power, which resulted in the executive federalism described earlier. National decisions are increasingly made outside of the confines of Parliament, in plenary conferences and through other agreements between the provinces and the federal government. Thus, the House of Commons has become, in many instances, the ratifier of decisions made elsewhere.

CONTEMPORARY POLITICAL ISSUES

There tends to be an enduring quality to political issues in Canada. As identified by the late Donald Smiley, one of Canada's premier political scientists, these coalesce along three axes: the influence of the United States on Canadian politics; the tension between French and English founding cultures; and relations between the "core" and "peripheral" regions of the country.[25]

Due in large measure to the animosity between Great Britain and the United States resulting from the US Civil War, Canadian Confederation was not the outcome of a movement for independence, but was seen as a means of buttressing British power against the perceived aggressive neighbouring republic. Throughout its history, Canada has always been aware of the neighbour to the South, both as an example of what to avoid and what to borrow. A resolution to this love/hate relationship does not seem likely.

While it has been argued that Canada is ideologically more conservative than the United States as a result of its counter-revolutionary origins,[26] the simple fact that the United States is ten times larger in population than Canada is enough to account for Canadian fears of either being assimilated into or seen as an appendage of the United States. This defensive posture is evident both in the economic and cultural spheres. As is argued by Romanow in chapter 8, cultural preservation and promotion are consciously seen as legitimate concerns of government policy. In spite of this, American cultural penetration has been immense, particularly in areas of mass popular culture: television, film, and magazines.

In the economic area, policy has fluctuated between nationalist and continentalist directions. The 1854 Reciprocity Treaty served as a model for Canadian continentalists. Its rejection by the United States in the mid-1860s was one of the factors leading to Confederation. Free trade surfaced again in 1911, to be rejected by Canadian voters, and reemerged successfully as the Free Trade Agreement, solidified by the 1988 election. This Free Trade Agreement between Canada and the United States, which came into effect in January 1989, is seen by some Canadians as a positive development, while for others it signifies the final step in the Americanization of Canada.

The area of French–English relations likewise has its roots deep in history. The "French fact" in North America was established some 200 years before Confederation. However, since the defeat of the French forces on the Plains of Abraham in 1759, French culture has had to survive in an environment reflecting the reality of English-speaking political power.

The initial decade of Québec's existence under British rule saw the testing of the extent to which British control could be exercised. After rather draconian beginnings, British policy gradually recognized that Québec was indeed a "distinct society." The Québec Act of 1774 acknowledged that distinctiveness as it gave the Catholic Church the right to collect tithes; recognized French civil law and the seigneurial system; eliminated the Test Act (which demanded the renunciation of the Pope); and opened the civil service to French-Canadian participation. The Constitutional Act of 1791, which split the province of Québec into Upper and Lower Canada (now Ontario and Québec), solidified French-Canadian control in the newly created province.[27]

A more hostile environment was evidenced prior to Confederation in the Durham Report (1839), which responded to the Rebellions of 1837 and 1838 and outlined an assimilative solution to the English–French dichotomy.

Confederation was testament to the failure of Lord Durham's solution, and since that day, the status of the French-speaking community in Canada has been the subject of political negotiation.

At times relationships between the two founding cultural groups have been relatively cordial, while at other times they have been extremely contentious. For example, the drafting of soldiers leading to the conscription crises, which occurred in Québec during both world wars, presented very serious threats to Canadian national unity. Moreover, beginning in the 1960s, with the growth of the Quiet Revolution in Québec, new demands for Francophone equality (primarily linguistic) provided the impetus for the political organization of separatism, culminating in the electoral victory of the Parti Québécois in 1976. A major test of national unity was successfully met in 1980, as the pro-federal forces won the day in the Québec Referendum on the question of sovereignty association with the rest of Canada.[28]

As the federal government had promised if separatism were defeated, there would be a new Canadian Constitution, patriating the amendment provisions from Great Britain, where they had remained since Confederation; providing Canadians with a constitutionally entrenched Charter of Rights and Freedoms; and establishing a new division of powers between the two levels of government. The first two of these were accomplished. However, the division of powers between the two levels of government proved to be highly controversial. In fact, controversy was so high that Québec did not ratify the total package of constitutional revisions made in 1982. The process of constitutional reform was thus incomplete, as it lacked moral legitimacy in the province of Québec. It was this problem that the failed Meech Lake Accord was fashioned to solve.

The entrenchment of a Charter of Rights and Freedoms in the Canadian Constitution is potentially the most significant constitutional change made in Canadian history. This is so because it undermines the British tradition of parliamentary supremacy (there is no power greater than that of Parliament). While its full impact will not be evident for at least another decade, it may be argued that the judiciary will become a major political force, analogous to that of the Supreme Court in the United States. As a consequence, political issues will increasingly become legal issues. Such a change implies an Americanization of Canadian political processes far more significant than foreseen by critics of the Free Trade Agreement.

In no small measure, the difficulty in accommodating Québec's demands on constitutional reform can be attributed to the third of Smiley's three axes: core–periphery relations. Who benefits from decisions in a political system is more or less a direct function of the distribution of political power. At the time of Confederation, political elites in the Maritime provinces were fully aware that in a Rep by Pop system they would have less influence in the new Confederation than the more populous regions of the country—Ontario and Québec. The first manifestation of dissatisfaction with the financial terms of union in Canada followed immediately upon Confederation, as Joseph Howe of Nova Scotia successfully sought and received better terms for his province.[29] Despite this, the overwhelming realities of political power resulted in a series of policies (the National Policy of Sir John A. Macdonald), which were designed to protect and enhance the manufacturing and industrial interests of Central Canada. Over time, these led to the de-industrialization of the Maritimes and migration of population to Central Canada and the United States.[30]

Provinces comprising the West were not partners in the initial formation of the country. Thus the circumstances of their admission were dependent upon whether they were "created" (Alberta, Manitoba, and Saskatchewan) or were a pre-existing former British colony (British Columbia). Joining Confederation in 1949, Newfoundland received more favourable terms than the provinces that joined earlier. The conditions of and terms for joining Confederation varied among the provinces, giving a historical basis for tensions among the new provinces. As well, the new provinces as a group did not enjoy the same status as the original partners; for example, the control of natural resources in the new provinces created in western Canada remained under federal control until 1930. Since the economies of the West were largely resource-based, and these provinces have a small population relative to the central Canadian provinces, western grievances have persisted. At various times this alienation has led to the formation of third parties, most recently the Reform Party. In the early 1980s, due to different perceptions of what direction Canada's energy policy should take, there was even talk of Western separation.

To further complicate the matter, the core region experienced the rise of Québec separatism, which, while initially defeated, entailed perceived concessions to the province of Québec. Many in the western provinces did not hold these concessions in high esteem, as they were seen as confirming the greater importance of the policy concerns of the core regions.

This interrelated and difficult set of circumstances explains the failure encountered in the ratification of the Meech Lake Accord. In 1987 Prime Minister Mulroney had forged this compromise, which, by granting Québec designation as a "distinct society," sought to reconcile Québec with the Constitutional Agreement. Opponents to Meech Lake argued primarily that the price paid for Québec's inclusion was too high. It was feared that the resulting diminution of federal political power, coupled with the Free Trade Agreement with the United States, would weaken the power of the federal government to help the peripheries.

CONCLUSION

In a comparative perspective, the problems that Canada has had to face are certainly not among the most serious in the world. This said, however, current problems appear to be formidable. Canadian politics can best be described as the institutionalization of successful compromise; compromises necessitated by geographical location and configuration, historical events, and diversity of populations, combined with pressures resulting from industrialization and societal modernization. In the past, significant compromises have been worked out in each of the three policy areas: Canadian–American, French–English, and core–periphery relations. As is evidenced in the recent history of the Free Trade Agreement, constitutional reform, and Meech Lake, these policy areas are interrelated, and decisions taken to deal with one set of problems spill over to affect the others.

The current challenge to Canada's survival as a nation is as serious a one as the country has ever faced. Goodwill and mutual trust seem in extremely short supply, while cultural and regional self-interest abound. In short, the future for a united Canada including Québec seems problematic. What is unique about Canada's political process has been its continuing ability to cope with problems of political integration within a workable political framework in which federalism has seen centralized and decentralized configurations. Canadian federalism is dynamic rather than static, and there is some hope at least that a model can be agreed upon to satisfy the demands for further radical decentralization. What should be clear to all, however, is that measured by standards involving quality of life, Canadian federalism cannot be judged to have failed. The result of the persistent process of accommodation, practised by generations of Canadian politicians of all political persuasions, is a country that rivals any other in terms of being a desirable place to live. This is no mean achievement.

Notes

[1] K.W. Deutsch, S.A. Burrell, R.A. Kann, M. Lee Jr., M. Lichterman, R. Lindgren, F.L. Loewenheim, and R.W. Van Wagenen, *Political Community and the North Atlantic Area: International Organization in Light of Historical Experience* (Princeton: Princeton University Press, 1957).

[2] The data on which these observations are made are found in R.C. Nelson, W.C. Soderlund, R.H. Wagenberg, and E.D. Briggs, "Canadian Confederation as a Case Study in Community Formation," in G. Martin, ed., *The Causes of Canadian Confederation: Cantilever or Coincidence?* (Fredericton: Acadiensis Press, 1990), 50–85; and R.H. Wagenberg, W.C. Soderlund, R.C. Nelson, and E.D. Briggs, "Federal Societies and the Founding of Federal States," in *Canadian Federalism: Past, Present, and Future*, ed. M. Burgess (Leicester: Leicester University Press, 1990), 7–39.

[3] W.C. Soderlund, R.C. Nelson, E.D. Briggs, and R.H. Wagenberg, "Attitudes Toward Community Formation: The Atlantic Provinces and the Province of Canada Compared," *British Journal of Canadian Studies* 5 (1990): 57–77.

[4] The standard work on the interplay between social and political factors involved in Confederation is P.B. Waite's *The Life and Times of Confederation* (Toronto: University of Toronto Press, 1962).

[5] Following unsuccessful rebellions in both Upper and Lower Canada in 1837, Lord Durham was sent from Britain to assess the situation. His solution, French assimilation, was incorporated in the report bearing his name. See G. Martin, *The Durham Report and British Policy* (Cambridge: Cambridge University Press, 1972).

[6] Waite, *The Life and Times*, 123.

[7] *Canada Act*, sec. 91 (3).

[8] Ibid., sec. 91 (3).

[9] The five concepts of federalism (centralist, co-ordinate, administrative, compact, and dual alliance) discussed in this chapter are found in E.R. Black, *Divided Loyalties: Canadian Concepts of Federalism* (Montreal: McGill-Queen's University Press, 1975).

[10] Canada was the first federal system established in the British Empire. Prior to Confederation, the Judicial Committee of the Privy Council had served as the highest court of appeal for colonial legislation. As the British North America Act was an imperial statute, creating a Dominion, not an independent nation, it was thought that the prior arrangement would cover all areas of jurisdiction between the two levels of government and do so in a manner of "absolute impartiality and disinterestedness" (p. 377). It served as the highest court of appeal for Canada until 1949. For a description of the Judicial Committee of the Privy Council and its role in interpreting the Canadian Constitution, see, J.R. Mallory, *The Structure of Canadian Government*, rev. ed. (Toronto: Gage, 1984), 377–91.

[11] R.J. Van Loon and M.S. Whittington, *The Canadian Political System: Environment, Structure and Process*, 4th ed. (Toronto: McGraw-Hill Ryerson, 1987), 249.

[12] See G. Stevenson, *Unfulfilled Union*, 3rd ed. (Toronto: Gage, 1989), 77–81.

[13] Black, *Divided Loyalties*, 16.

[14] Conditional grants are closely linked to shared-cost programs between the federal and provincial governments. As Adie and Thomas note, "Under such arrangements the federal government provided financial assistance, either in the form of a lump sum or a fixed ratio of the cost of a program, on the condition that the provincial governments provide certain services. While the B.N.A. Act makes no explicit provision for the use of conditional grants, over the years the federal government has used them to involve itself in virtually all areas of provincial jurisdiction." R.F. Adie and P.G. Thomas, *Canadian Public Administration: Problematical Perspectives*, 2nd ed. (Scarborough: Prentice-Hall, 1987), 435.

[15] For a discussion of executive federalism, see D.V. Smiley, *The Federal Condition in Canada* (Toronto: McGraw-Hill Ryerson, 1987), 83–99.

[16] For those interested in pursuing at greater length the subject of party systems at the provincial level, see M. Robin, ed., *Canadian Provincial Politics: The Party Systems of the Ten Provinces*, 2nd ed. (Scarborough: Prentice-Hall, 1978).

[17] The rise of third parties in Canada has been a subject of considerable theoretical speculation. See C.B. McPherson, *Democracy in Alberta: The Theory and Practice of a Quasi-party System* (Toronto: University of Toronto Press, 1953); and M. Pinard, "One Party Dominance and Third Parties," *Canadian Journal of Economics and Political Science* 33 (1967): 358–73.

[18] Van Loon and Whittington, *The Canadian Political System*, 395. For a discussion on the impact of the Canadian electoral system on Canadian political parties, see A.C. Cairns, "The Electoral System and the Party System in Canada, 1921–1965," *Canadian Journal of Political Science* 1 (1968): 55–80; and W.P. Irvine, "Reforming the Electoral System," in H.G. Thorburn, ed., *Party Politics in Canada,* 5th ed. (Scarborough: Prentice-Hall, 1985): 128–39.

[19] See Van Loon and Whittington, *The Canadian Political System*, 309. The authors outline the principle characteristics of brokerage and non-brokerage party systems.

[20] Smiley, *The Federal Condition*, 117. See also R. Dyck, "Relations Between Federal and Provincial Parties," in A.G. Gagnon and A.B. Tanguay, eds., *Canadian Parties in Transition* (Scarborough: Nelson, 1989): 186–219.

[21] A. Siegel, *Politics and the Mass Media in Canada* (Toronto: McGraw-Hill Ryerson, 1983), 92.

[22] C.E.S. Franks, *The Parliament of Canada* (Toronto: University of Toronto Press, 1987), 6.

[23] W.C. Soderlund, W.I. Romanow, E.D. Briggs, R.H. Wagenberg, *Media and Elections in Canada* (Toronto: Holt, Rinehart and Winston, 1984), 127–30.

[24] See G.B. Doern and P. Aucoin, eds., *The Structures of Policy-Making in Canada* (Toronto: Macmillan, 1971), 39–75; and V.S. Wilson, *Canadian Public Policy and Administration: Theory and Environment* (Toronto: McGraw-Hill Ryerson, 1981), 214.

[25] D.V. Smiley, *Canada in Question: Federalism in the Eighties,* 3rd ed. (Toronto: McGraw-Hill Ryerson, 1980), viii.

[26] S.M. Lipset, *Continental Divide: The Values and Institutions of the United States and Canada* (New York: Routledge, Chapman and Hall, 1990), 42–56, 172–92.

[27] M. Brunet, "Changing of the Guard," in *Horizon Canada* 12 (Québec: Centre of the Study of Teaching Canada, 1987), 433–39.

[28] Sovereignty-association is the term used by the Parti-Québécois for its proposed association between a sovereign Québec and Canada. K. McRoberts points out that "the proposed association closely reflected the conviction of the PQ leadership that Québec's accession to independence should not constitute radical change or 'rupture.' In fact, the preamble of *D'égal à égal* declared that the good of Québec, as well as the interest of Canada, doubtlessly necessitates that 'in the measure compatible with our collective interests, the nation accede to sovereignty in a perspective of economic continuity.' Thus, Québec would formally assume the powers of a state and it would acquire its share of federal assets and debts. But it would maintain a relatively high level of economic integration with the rest of Canada." (300–301) For many Canadians outside of Québec, however, sovereignty-association meant separatism or independence for Québec and the disintegration of Canada as a viable political entity. See K. McRoberts, *Québec: Social Change and Political Crisis*, 3rd ed. (Toronto: McClelland & Stewart, 1988).

[29] K.G. Pryke, *Nova Scotia and Confederation, 1864–74* (Toronto: University of Toronto Press, 1979), 80–97.

[30] T.W. Acheson, "The National Policy and the Industrialization of the Maritimes," *Acadiensis* 1 (Spring 1972): 2–32; and E.R. Forbes, "Misguided Symmetry: The Destruction of Regional Transportation Policy for the Maritimes," in D.J. Bercuson, ed., *Canada and the Burden of Unity* (Toronto: Macmillan, 1977), 60–86.

Bibliography

Acheson, T.W. "The National Policy and the Industrialization of the Maritimes,"
Acadiensis 1 (Spring 1972) 2–32.

Adie, R.F., and P.G. Thomas. *Canadian Public Administration: Problematical
Perspectives.* 2nd ed. Scarborough: Prentice-Hall, 1987.

Bercuson, D.J., ed. *Canada and the Burden of Unity.* Toronto: Macmillan, 1977.

Black, E.R. *Divided Loyalties: Canadian Concepts of Federalism.* Montreal: McGill-Queen's
University Press, 1975.

Burgess, M., ed. *Canadian Federalism: Past, Present and Future.* Leicester: University of
Leicester Press, 1990.

Cairns, A.C. "The Electoral System and the Party System in Canada, 1921–1965,"
Canadian Journal of Political Science 1 (1968): 55–80.

Deutsch, K.W., S.A. Burrell, R.A. Kann, M. Lee Jr., M. Lichterman, R. Lindgren, F.A.
Lowenheim, and R.W. Van Wagenen. *Political Community and the North Atlantic
Area: International Organization in Light of Historical Experience.* Princeton: Princeton
University Press, 1957.

Doern, G.B. and P. Aucoin, eds. *The Structures of Policy-Making in Canada.* Toronto:
Macmillan, 1971.

Dyck, R. "Relations Between Federal and Provincial Parties." In A.G. Gagnon and A.B.
Tanguay, eds. *Canadian Parties in Transition.* Scarborough: Nelson, 1989.

Forbes, E.R. "Misguided Symmetry: The Destruction of Regional Transportation Policy for
the Maritimes." In D.J. Bercuson, ed. *Canada and the Burden of Unity.* Toronto:
Macmillan, 1977.

Franks, C.E.S. *The Parliament of Canada.* Toronto: University of Toronto Press, 1987.

Gagnon, A.G., and A.B. Tanguay, eds. *Canadian Parties in Transition.* Scarborough:
Nelson, 1989.

Irvine, W.P. "Reforming the Electoral System." in H. Thorburn, ed. *Party Politics in
Canada.* 5th ed. Scarborough: Prentice-Hall, 1985.

Jackson, R.J., D. Jackson, N. Baxter-Moore. *Politics in Canada: Culture, Institutions,
Behaviour and Public Policy.* Scarborough: Prentice-Hall, 1987.

Landes, R.G. *The Canadian Polity: A Comparative Introduction.* 2nd ed. Scarborough:
Prentice-Hall, 1987.

Lipset, S.M. *Continental Divide: The Values and Institutions of the United States and
Canada.* New York: Routledge, Chapman and Hall, 1990.

Mallory, J.R. *The Structure of Canadian Government.* Rev. ed. Toronto: Gage, 1984.

Martin G., ed. *The Causes of Canadian Confederation.* Fredericton Acadiensis Press, 1990.

Martin, G. *The Durham Report and British Policy.* Cambridge: Cambridge University Press,
1972.

McPherson, C.B. *Democracy in Alberta: The Theory and Practice of a Quasi-party System.* Toronto: University of Toronto Press, 1953.

McRoberts, K. *Québec: Social Change and Political Crisis.* 3rd ed. Toronto: McClelland & Stewart, 1988.

Nelson, R.C., W.C. Soderlund, R.H. Wagenberg, and E.D. Briggs. "Canadian Confederation as a Case Study in Community Formation," In G. Martin, ed. *The Causes of Canadian Confederation.* Fredericton: Acadiensis Press, 1990.

Pinard, M. "One Party Dominance and Third Parties," *Canadian Journal of Economics and Political Science* 33 (1967): 358–73.

Pryke, K.G. *Nova Scotia and Confederation, 1864–74.* Toronto: University of Toronto Press, 1979.

Robin, M., ed. *Canadian Provincial Politics: The Party Systems of the Ten Provinces.* 2nd ed. Scarborough: Prentice-Hall, 1978.

Siegel, A. *Politics and the Mass Media in Canada.* Toronto: McGraw-Hill Ryerson, 1983.

Smiley, D.V. *Canada in Question: Federalism in the Eighties.* 3rd ed. Toronto: McGraw-Hill Ryerson, 1980.

Smiley, D.V. *The Federal Condition in Canada.* Toronto: McGraw-Hill Ryerson, 1987.

Soderlund, W.C., R.C. Nelson, E.D. Briggs, and R.H. Wagenberg. "Attitudes Toward Community Formation: The Atlantic Provinces and the Province of Canada Compared." *British Journal of Canadian Studies* 5 (1990): 57–77.

Soderlund, W.C., W.I. Romanow, E.D. Briggs, and R.H. Wagenberg. *Media and Elections in Canada.* Toronto: Holt, Rinehart and Winston, 1984.

Stevenson, G. *Unfulfilled Union.* 3rd ed. Toronto: Gage, 1989.

Thorburn, H., ed. *Party Politics in Canada.* 5th ed. Scarborough: Nelson, 1989.

Van Loon, R.J., and M.S. Whittington. *The Canadian Political System: Environment, Structure and Process.* 4th ed. Toronto: McGraw-Hill Ryerson, 1987.

Wagenberg, R.H., W.C. Soderlund, R.C. Nelson, and E.D. Briggs. "Federal Societies and the Founding of Federal States." In M. Burgess, ed. *Canadian Federalism: Past, Present and Future.* Leicester: University of Leicester Press, 1990.

Waite, P.B. *The Life and Times of Confederation*: Toronto: University of Toronto Press, 1962.

White, W.L., R.H. Wagenberg, and R.C. Nelson. *Introduction to Canadian Politics and Government.* 5th ed. Toronto: Holt, Rinehart and Winston, 1989.

Wilson, V S. *Canadian Public Policy and Administration: Theory and Environment.* Toronto: McGraw-Hill Ryerson, 1981.

8

❏   ❏   ❏   ❏   ❏   ❏   ❏

Communication Policy and Canadian Society

Walter I. Romanow

INTRODUCTION

The term "nation-building," as used in the literature of journalism and communication studies, has normally referred to the task assigned to the mass media for their developmental–supportive role in the political–cultural structure of a society. As well, since the 1940s the term has been applicable to the harnessing of mass media in Third World nations as these societies began to shed colonial ties and struggled to become politically self-sustaining communities. Given this developing nation orientation, some Canadians were surprised to read that the central mission of Canada's federal Department of Communication was described as "Nation Building; helping Canadians share their ideas, information and dreams."[1] Other Canadians were ready to concede that the implied designation of Canada as a "developing society" might not be out of order, given Canada's proximity to the United States and the daily bombardment of the informational products of US media industries. Thus, Canadians might legitimately profess the same problem as Third World societies: having taken a number of years to proclaim its independence as a nation, Canada could very well have become linked to the United States as part of its "electric colony."

The condition of Canada's population, living in a recognizable First World country with a considerable degree of economic and cultural sophistication, is obviously advantaged over populations in less developed Third World societies. Nevertheless, in terms of cultural and national identity, Canada's media have played strategic roles that might be termed defensive in the face of US information systems. For, as has been the case in many Third World nations, Canadians have attributed to their mass media, in differing ways, some degree of responsibility for maintaining the integrity of their nation as a distinct society, in political, economic, sociological, and cultural dimensions.

The purpose of this chapter is to present an overview of some of the regulatory strategies that Canadians have introduced for their mass media to fulfill what the 1968 Broadcasting Act has described as a central responsibility ". . . to safeguard, enrich and strengthen the cultural, political, social and economic fabric of Canada."[2]

While this responsibility was articulated in the 1968 Broadcasting Act and reiterated in the 1991 Act, it has been implicit from the earliest days of regulatory activity by the federal government that such behaviour for broadcasting was inherent in the matter of licensing logic—that is, in return for the privilege of using a broadcasting licence, broadcasters were expected to behave in a socially responsible manner.

In the mandate cited above, the words used are not idly inserted into the phraseology: to "safeguard" implies one sort of behaviour on the part of broadcasters; to "strengthen and enrich" implies quite another. On the one hand, to safeguard has meant a strategy to prevent the entry of foreign information, while, on the other hand, to enrich and to strengthen have meant the development of Canada's own resources with respect to the products of media and cultural industries.

Neither dimension of this overall strategy has been easy to implement, either by regulatory bodies or by the media industries, even though the importance of the strategy cannot be overestimated. A variety of problems inherent in Canada's geographical, political, and social contexts have been difficult to overcome satisfactorily so as to permit operation of the overall safeguard-enrich-strengthen regulatory approaches taken.

PROBLEMS OF THE REGULATORY STRATEGY

While various regulations have been enacted, modified, and replaced, the problems that have affected the regulatory process have been constant and unchanging. To understand Canada's communication systems properly, one must see them in the light of the factors that mitigate against the systems functioning in the way Canadians would prefer.[3]

❑ GEOGRAPHY

Canada is a huge territorial mass, now the largest country in the world. In a country as vast as Canada, the shared community experiences that are central to the concept of nationhood are difficult to achieve because of distances that separate individuals and groups. Sociologists and anthropologists have emphasized that to be a nation the conditions should permit people to share commonalities—their desires, aspirations, beliefs, ideals, and values—with one another, over distances, wherever they may live. It is in this sense that we expect communication systems to provide such needed links whereby people can "converse" with one another.[4] But the concept of distance has two dimensions, the geographical and the cultural. Whereas communication systems, physically, might provide links between groups of people scattered around a huge geographical territory, the content of those physical links—the radio or television program, the newspaper story, the film-video narrative—might be culturally foreign from one area to another.

A successful act of communication assumes that the senders and receivers of messages share some large degree of commonality—language, lifestyle, experience. In a country as vast as is Canada, the lifestyles of Maritimers, for example, vary considerably from those of Prairie farmers. The one group might be experiencing a bountiful fishing harvest, while the other might be experiencing an economically crippling drought, with all of the attendant human suffering associated with such climatic conditions. The geographical context, then, is such that it intervenes in the most fundamental of human environments—the basic living condition. Further, it is more likely that the Prairie farmer would have a more sympathetic relationship with those who farm the adjacent agricultural areas in the US than with fellow Canadians in the East.

❏ PROVINCIAL POLITICAL STRENGTHS

Canadian provinces and territories possess a great deal of independent political powers flowing from the Canadian Constitution.[5] Thus, if provincial governments are politically and philosophically different from the federal government in Ottawa, the norm can be a relationship of day-to-day bargaining (some observers would call it "haggling"). National unity and harmony often are not a first-level consideration when provincial premiers meet with the prime minister to discuss mutual problems. If the media are to report faithfully on events in their society, they focus on the dramatic differences that characterize such political affairs, and thus, information provided does not foster national unity. Rather, audiences are more likely to remember the reality of disunity projected by the media.

❏ REGIONALISM

Canadian sociologists advance the idea that Canada is characterized by five clearly identifiable regions: the West Coast, the Prairies, Central Canada (Ontario), Québec, and the Maritimes.[6] Such regions differ from one another according to peculiarities of economic–industrial employment behaviour of residents, differing degrees of urbanization, differences of ethnic-group settlements, and in the case of Québec, primarily, by linguistic differences. The task of national media to find commonalities amidst such differences is a difficult one indeed.

❏ MASS MEDIA TECHNOLOGY

More than half of Canada's population (about one-tenth of that of the United States) lives along a narrow strip bordering the 49th parallel. What this has meant, of course, is that historically there has been a natural and constant flow and interchange of people, goods, and ideas between the two nations. Given the current global economic environment, which is focused on expanded trade arrangements, such interchanges between the US and Canada are constantly increasing in kind and quantity. In the midst of such free-and-easy exchanges has been the ready flow of the content products of media technologies. In the earlier days of radio broadcasting, and later television broadcasting, Canadians became quite accustomed to accepting such programming, more often than not in preference to the product of their own broadcasting media.

Such declarations of preferences have not changed to this day, and with the exception of some news and sports programs produced and broadcast in Canada, Canadians, when offered a choice, prefer US broadcasting content over their own. A typical A.C. Nielsen-rated week of Canadian TV viewing preferences is likely to indicate that eight of the top ten rated programs will be US in origin. The two Canadian programs that normally are found in such ratings, depending in this instance on the season, are "Hockey Night in Canada" and CBCs "The National."[7] The role of Canadian mass media in fulfilling the nation-building strategies discussed earlier becomes more and more challenging, given the ready availability of CATV and satellite program delivery systems in a constantly increasing spectrum of programs from the US and other parts of the globe.

HISTORICAL EMPHASIS OF "NATION BUILDING"

While the 1968 Broadcasting Act articulated a philosophical mandate for broadcasting, such emphasis was neither the first nor the last in Canada's history. Canada's earliest broadcasting royal commission (called the Aird Commission, for its chair) in 1929 recognized the impact that US radio was having on Canadian society. The commission stressed that the destiny of Canada was directly linked to the resolve Canadians needed if they were to control and utilize their communication systems to fulfil Canadian purposes.[8]

Reference to selected other studies in the matter of media responsibility in the Canadian context will offer readers some insight, first of all, into the frequency with which Canadians consider that the issue should be reviewed, and second, the importance that Canadians place on the particular topic. Finally, this brief overview of formal studies will also reveal the need for a strategy for mass media discussed earlier (to "safeguard, enrich and strengthen"):

- 1951

  The national system, however, has constantly kept in view three objectives for broadcasting in Canada: an adequate coverage of the entire population, opportunities for Canadian talent and Canadian self-expression generally, *and successful resistance to the absorption of Canada into the general cultural pattern of the United States.*[9]

• 1957

But as a nation we cannot accept in these powerful and persuasive media, the natural and complete flow of *another nation's culture without danger to our national identity.* . . . If we want to have radio and television contribute to a Canadian consciousness and sense of identity, if we wish to make some part of the trade in ideas and culture move east and west across the country, *if we seek to avoid engulfment by American cultural forces, we must regulate such matters as importation of programs.*[10]

• 1961

In these functions it may be claimed—claimed without much challenge—*that the communications of a nation are as vital to its life as its defences, and should receive at least as great a measure of national protection.*[11]

• 1965

Left to operate freely, economic factors would quickly tend to make Canadian television stations mere extensions of the American networks. . . . *The Canadian broadcasting system must never become a mere agency for transmitting foreign programs, however excellent they may be.*[12]

• 1973

[Technological developments] are of specially urgent concern for Canada because of its proximity to the United States, where the generation of information and entertainment is on a scale that threatens to overwhelm Canadian cultural resources, creative capacity, and sources of information, and to constrict the means of access to them.[13]

• 1979

We urge the Government of Canada and the governments of the provinces to take immediate action to establish a rational structure for telecommunications in Canada as a defence against the further loss of sovereignty in all its economic, social, cultural and political aspects[14]

Thus, over the years Canada has turned to its mass media as instruments of social support and as links between Canada's scattered population and differing linguistic and cultural groups. Occasionally analogies have been drawn between such functional roles for transportation and communication systems: since the railroads, for example, in the late 1800s and in the early 1900s were performing this social role, so, too, could the concept of unification be a priority task for media-communication systems.[15] Historically, then, Canada's mass media, in differing ways, have been central to a social aspiration that emphasizes a need for Canada to be a fully identifiable cultural and social entity.

PUBLISHING

The development of Canadian newspapers and magazines occurred in a manner very similar to that in the United States. Journalism in Canada, as historian Wilfred Kesterton points out, was a transplant industry.[16] As well, the battles for the principles of a free press already were won, even if there were few opportunities to practise them in the early colonial settlements, given the need for the community printing establishment to depend upon the monarch's representative for sustenance. The early news sheets filled the governor's requirements for distributing news and information needed by the settlements. As the possibility developed for news-sheet editors to gain revenue from subscriptions and advertising, these editors found it possible to become more self-sustaining with respect to writing and editing within the parameters of free expression and within a new spirit of independence.[17]

The press in both countries experienced a similar form of development, particularly in the late 1800s when the forces of free and competitive market systems made possible what continues to this day—the concentration and consolidation of media ownership into fewer and fewer hands. Attempts to stem this trend have been made in Canada, and two studies, in particular, stand out for the recommendations they have made regarding the role of print media in Canadian society.

The first of the two, the *Report of the Special Senate Committee on Mass Media* (the Davey Report, named for its chair)[18] examined problems consequent to centralization of print ownership in the country. The committee, in its concern for constrictions on social freedom of expression due to the lack of newspaper competition, enunciated several recommendations that were intended to halt the concentration trend. The committee used the analogy of the existence of regulations over broadcasting to justify its recommendations for extending government regulation over the print industry.

> The principle is now well established that the state has the right to safeguard the public's right to information by approving, disapproving, or disallowing various property transactions within the broadcasting industry. The Committee believes it is time for this principle to be extended to include the print media.[19]

While the committee's full slate of recommendations was not acted upon, two consequences of the committee's report stand out in the context of the discussion here about mass media and nation building. First, the committee revealed that while Canadian newspapers devoted about a third of their news content to news from countries other than Canada, not all of that was the result of reports written by Canadians. The committee's reaction is noteworthy. Discussing the operation of Canadian Press wire service (CP) in utilizing international news from US Associated Press sources, the committee noted:

> We do not suggest that the Associated Press, for example, is not a fine news service. It is. But it is an American news service. . . . An American reporter,

writing for an American audience, writes in the American idiom, which is not yet the Canadian idiom. He writes from a background of American experience and American national interest, which are not the Canadian experience and the Canadian interest.[20]

While it is impossible to determine whether the Davey Committee's concern about the lack of international affairs being reported for Canadians by Canadian reporters has had a direct effect on recent developments, changes in this regard are apparent. For example, following Thomson Newspapers' 1980 acquisition of the properties of FP Limited (including the prestigious *Globe and Mail* and the *Winnipeg Free Press*), international press bureaus in the organization increased from three to eight,[21] matching Southam News in number of international news bureaus. Other Canadian media organizations are following suit. While he indicates that no complete figures are available, media specialist George Bain of *Maclean's* magazine observed, "it is certain that more Canadians have been assigned abroad in the past year than ever before, two world wars included." Recent dramatic political events in the global community may have triggered such a reporting interest, or, it may well be, as Bain speculates, "that Canadian journalism has jumped the fence and finally, irrevocably, discovered the great abroad."[22]

Second, the Davey Committee deplored the financially weak positions of Canada's magazine press, primarily due to the openly competitive situation enjoyed in Canada by US *Time* and *Reader's Digest* magazines. These two, the committee pointed out, accounted for over half of all magazine advertising revenues in the country.[23] This factor, combined with the massive overflow of other US publications into Canada, threatened the future of the Canadian magazine industry. For example, the committee's research revealed that Canadians annually spent about as much money on US *Playboy* as they did on Canada's seventeen largest English-language consumer magazines; and they spent more money buying US comic books than they did on seventeen leading Canadian publications.[24] In the opinion of the committee, Canadian magazines, "in terms of cultural survival," could "potentially be as important as railroads, airlines, national broadcasting networks, and national hockey leagues."[25]

Seven years later, the Canadian Parliament introduced amendments to the Income Tax Act, which offered some of the protection to Canadian magazines asked for by the Davey Committee. Henceforth, the amendment stated, if Canadian advertising accounts wanted to calculate their magazine advertising costs as business expenses, the publications bearing their advertising were required to have a majority Canadian content (no less than 80 percent) as well as having a majority Canadian ownership (no less than 75 percent).[26] This amendment concerning Canadian ownership extended to all publications, including newspapers: the effect, in this instance, was to discourage acquisition of Canadian magazines and newspapers by foreign firms.

The second newspaper study, the 1981 *Report of the Royal Commission on Newspapers*, was less nationalistic in its overall assessment of ownership consolidation than was the Davey Committee a decade earlier. Nevertheless, the commission concluded that the heavy measure of newspaper ownership concentration had become detrimental to what one of the commission's terms of reference described as "the political, economic, social and intellectual vitality and *cohesion of the nation as a whole.*"[27] Because massive corporate structures are obliged to heed the demands of business concerns, such extraneous interests "are the chains that today limit the freedom of the press." Consequently, the expressions of freedom that are essential to the functioning of open democratic societies, concluded the commission, are threatened.

The majority of the commission's recommendations were aimed at preventing any further concentration of ownership and at reducing the detrimental effects of the worst cases of concentration as they existed at the time. Nevertheless, the commission also made a recommendation pertinent to the point of this chapter—media and nationhood. Very little international news is reported through Canadian eyes, indicated the commission, echoing a concern of the Davey Committee. To remedy such a fault, it would be important for the government, under a proposed Canadian Newspaper Act, to offer tax incentives to Canadian wire services or news organizations that made a substantial commitment to correct the lack of Canadian foreign news bureaus.[28]

Neither a newspaper act nor the recommendation cited above have been acted upon. As has been pointed out above, however, several news organizations in Canada have taken initiatives to bolster their foreign reporting services with Canadian journalists who are either stationed or who travel abroad.

But a greater measure of responsibility for national identity has been placed on the broadcasting industry, with its public and private ownership sectors, than on the publishing industry.

BROADCASTING

The regulatory history of Canadian broadcasting has not been smooth, primarily because the broadcasting system has dual components of private corporate ownership, as well as public ownership (the publicly owned Canadian Broadcasting Corporation, for example). At times the degree of co-operation between the two disparate systems—one operating for profit, the second operating with a view to providing needed public-service broadcasting—has been excellent; at other times considerably less than that. Canadian Parliament, reacting to complaints about the dominant role the CBC had gained as broadcaster and as regulator of the entire system, struck a Royal Commission in 1955 to review the matter, as well as to prepare an overview of future directions which broadcasting should take. Television had arrived in Canada as it did in the US as a popularized medium in 1951, and the question of national identity in the light of the new medium again presented itself to Canadian society. The Royal Commission presented its report in 1957, with several pertinent and far-reaching consequences.

First, the commission recommended the establishment of an independent regulatory body for broadcasting (the Board of Broadcast Governors, or BBG) in lieu of government agencies or the Crown corporation CBC, as had been the case before. Second, the commission recommended the enactment of a new Broadcasting Act, which contained several important changes to the previous act; none, however, was as significant in intent or as far-reaching in result as the revised statement of "Objects and Purposes" of the board with respect to Canadian broadcasting. The new act emphasized that the BBG had the responsibility to ensure the continuing existence and efficient operation of a national, comprehensive service of "a high standard *that is basically Canadian in content and character.*"[29]

The new board wasted little time in offering its interpretation to the changed direction that broadcasting would take and in the kind of content broadcasters would be expected to schedule. Within two years of the passage of the new act, the BBG announced that, henceforth, television broadcasting stations and networks in Canada would be expected to schedule no less than 55 percent of their overall programming with Canadian content.[30]

Reaction by broadcasters, particularly from the private sector, was immediate, and comments from broadcasters focused on such predictions that Canadian TV programming would prove to be inferior to imported materials; the cost to stations in conforming to the regulations would threaten stations' ability to exist; and in the light of increasing US television competition, the regulation, if fully enforced, would drive Canadian viewers away in droves from Canadian stations. The chairman of the BBG on a number of occasions at the time acknowledged that producing content in specified amounts and of the quality that would attract Canadian viewers was not going to be an easy task. Nevertheless, he emphasized that the new regulations were intended to result in greater use of Canada's own resources and the linking of Canadians from sea to sea to permit them to communicate with one another. Thus, he affirmed, the basic intentions of the regulations "are the strengthening of Canadian unity and the development of a Canadian way of life."[31]

At the same time, the chairman identified some of the realistic problems the board had encountered in effecting the objects and purposes cited in the Broadcasting Act; namely, while the vast majority of Canadians indicated their support to the intent of the regulations, when offered a choice they selected programs that were not Canadian. Thus, while Canadians as citizens supported the work of the board in fulfilling the intent of the Broadcasting Act, "as audience, they cast their votes against it."[32]

Some regulatory difficulties for the BBG caused it to be replaced by a strengthened independent body, the Canadian Radio-Television Commission (CRTC), in 1968. The CRTC was quick to carry on with the policies that had been established earlier by the BBG with respect to Canadian content. While the quota system for television had become a way of life for broadcasters and regulators, there were still some very apparent problems, one of them being, as one critic was to point out, "wall-to-wall Hollywood in prime time."[33] Indeed, broadcasters were quick to learn that if they scheduled Canadian programming either in "ghetto" hours, or on the fringes of prime time (then calculated from 6 PM to midnight), they could still schedule popular, commercially rewarding US programming in peak viewing hours. The CRTC took to heart an observation made by the Royal Commission (which had recommended its establishment) that economic factors, left to operate freely, would quickly tend to make Canadian private television stations mere extensions of American networks.[34]

Moving quickly, the CRTC began in 1970 to introduce changes for broadcasters that would continue the work begun by the BBG concerning the nation-building role assigned to broadcasters. First, the content quota for television was boosted from 55 percent to 60 percent. Second, a quota for AM radio was introduced, which would make it mandatory for AM radio stations to schedule no less than 30 percent Canadian music of all music broadcast. Two of the following four criteria qualified as Canadian music for AM and FM radio: music composed by a Canadian; lyrics written by a Canadian; performance by a Canadian; music performed or recorded in Canada. For FM radio, Canadian quotas were set from 20 percent to 30 percent of all music played, the quota depending upon the classification of music. Also, Community Antennae Television (CATV) systems were required to distribute programming on a Canadian-priority basis. Third, so as to be consistent with the new act's demand that the broadcasting system be "effectively" owned by Canadians, the CRTC introduced an ownership quota of no less than 80 percent Canadian for each broadcasting unit. As a matter of interest, such a proportion of 80/20 is precisely the ratio that had been established many years earlier in the United States by the Federal Communications Commission. Finally, to permit the development of Canadian human and industrial programming resources (independent producers, for example, or Canadian producers in collaboration with producers in other nations), the CRTC in co-operation with the Canadian Film and Videotape Certification Office designed and operationalized an elaborate point scale whereby productions, to be classified as "Canadian," needed to fulfil a rather involved and cumbersome point-earning system. While at first glance the system appears to be awkward to regulate, it offers fair credit to producers who employ Canadians and Canadian technical resources in key, creative production functions.[35]

More recently, the CRTC has modified its stance with respect to a broadcasting-quota system based on quantification alone. In the spring of 1989 the CRTC, in granting licence-renewal applications for 75 stations, stipulated that as a condition of receiving the licence renewal, stations would be expected to spend an increased amount of their revenues in program production. Such increases, according to the CRTC, were expected to inject at least $2 billion into the Canadian production industry in the years 1989–1994.[36] As well, in an attempt to encourage the production of programming that is notably underrepresented in Canadian production schedules—drama, children's programs, documentaries, and variety programs, for example—the CRTC offered to increase the Canadian content value of such programs by 50 percent. Rather than calculating such programs as 100 percent in fulfilling a content quota, stations would be permitted to evaluate such content, which is more demanding in production time and cost, at 150 percent.[37] The effect of such a change in calculation of content would be to reduce the overall 60 percent quota to something less in a specified reporting period.

In the midst of these far-reaching changes in broadcasting aimed at enhancing the cultural identity of the nation, the CBC as a publicly-owned system has had a special role. From its earliest days when it was established as a Crown corporation in 1936, the CBC has been regarded as functioning in the forefront of strategies to develop a sense of Canadian nationhood. Given its budget (currently in excess of $1 billion annually, about 75 percent of which comes from taxpayers and the remainder from advertising), the CBC has been expected, at different times, to function as a public broadcaster in the style of the British Broadcasting Corporation; as a service to all taxpayers; as a financially self-sustaining institution; and as a system that would accommodate any or all promising Canadian talent into its ranks or under a contract. All of this was to be done, whenever possible, in both official languages.

Given the massive amount of direct competition from the US and from the private broadcasting sector in Canada, this responsibility of the CBC as a public broadcaster has not been easy to fulfil. In the 1968 Broadcasting Act a highly demanding and questionable mandate—questionable in terms of whether the mandate could be accommodated—was imposed on the CBC. That mandate specified that the CBC as a national broadcasting service should "contribute to the development of national unity and provide for a continuing expression of Canadian identity."[38] The contribution to the development of national unity has been more difficult to fulfil than the second part. Consistently, from the days in 1960 when the Canadian content quotas came into effect, the CBC has been a pace-setter with respect to the production of Canadian programming, including those that the CRTC has identified as being underrepresented by the private broadcasting sector—the more difficult and more costly categories of content to produce. In discussions with the minister of communications in 1988, as he was planning for the introduction of a new Broadcasting Act, the CBC indicated its preparedness, given appropriate budgetary support, to increase its Canadian content up to 90 percent overall, and up to 95 percent in English-language television prime time.[39] It is in this sense, assuming a leadership role with respect to fulfilling regulatory expectations, that the CBC has consistently been the principal instrument of Canadian broadcasting policy. However, to what extent the CBC has been successful in its mandate to contribute to the development of national unity is a contentious question. For example, budgetary reductions in the winter of 1991 have caused the CBC to reduce significantly its production and programming in eleven communities.

At the same time, in the late 1980s and in the early 1990s in particular, Canada has shown itself to be more disunified than at any previous time in its history. If the quality of federal–provincial relations is to be used as a yardstick, inter-governmental relations have been considerably less than harmonious, particularly during the abortive Meech Lake constitutional debates in the spring and summer of 1990. Further, the CBC mandate specifies that the corporation was expected to be a *contributor* to, rather than the sole agent of national unity. Suggested here, of course, is that other social forces have a role to play in such a mandate as national unity; for example, the private broadcasting industry.

Nevertheless, in the broad sphere of national endeavours towards national identity, the broadcasting industries have consistently been saddled with heavy measures of responsibilities. In its *Annual Report 1987–1988*, the CRTC, in commenting on foreign influences acting on the Canadian community, reminds readers that in 1967 the Parliamentary Committee for Broadcasting, Film and Assistance to the Arts stated that broadcasting would become "the central nervous system of Canadian nationhood."[40] This is seen in changes brought about in the functioning and purposes of the Canadian Film Development Corporation (Telefilm) in recent years (the development of a feature film industry in Canada), and particularly with the establishment of a funding component under the aegis of Telefilm (the Broadcast Program Development Fund).

CENSORSHIP AND CULTURAL IDENTITY

The question of government censorship over the content of mass media arises—particularly over broadcasting—when the efforts of government to regulate content are examined. Indeed, if examined in the light of the US First Amendment ("Congress shall make no law respecting an establishment of religion, or prohibiting the free exercise thereof; or abridging the freedom of speech or of the press"), Canadian policies would long ago have been challenged in the courts. In light of Canada's new constitution ("Everyone has the following fundamental freedoms . . . freedom of thought, belief, opinion and expression, including freedom of the press and other media of communication"), the question of whether broadcasting regulations constitute censorship is one begging to be tested. Broadcasting regulatory bodies, however, have responded to the question by indicating that it would be censorship of Canada's own resources if Canadian materials were to be crowded from the airwaves because of an economic preference by broadcasters to schedule less expensive, popular, imported programs. The response of the CRTC was that the Canadian content regulations were a "paradox," in that quotas needed to be established to ensure that accomplishments of Canadians "have their rightful place on our airwaves."[41]

As well, in discussions with broadcasters' groups, the argument of the "higher imperative" has been used on occasion; that is, the need for a national identity and the avoidance of acculturation by the United States are presently of greater importance to Canadian society than are philosophical demands for freedom of expression. In this sense, the argument claims that freedoms are not absolute, and the claims of censorship might well be countered with the statement in the Canadian Charter of Rights and Freedoms that indicates that rights and freedoms are guaranteed, "subject only to such reasonable limits prescribed by law as can be demonstrably justified in a free and democratic society."

THE IMPACT OF US CULTURE

While broadcasting, and print, to some degree, are in the forefront of a defensive posture against intrusion by US cultural content, other sorts of culture-laden products continue to move into Canada unhindered, as they have for many years. A recently concluded Free Trade Agreement between Canada and the US will only increase that cultural flow into Canada. The cars Canadians drive, the fast-food outlets they patronize, the clothes they wear, and many other products embossed liberally with a "US" cultural stamp continue to be used by Canadians as if they were their own. And, perhaps more to the point, these products are readily imported into Canada because Canadians demand them. In sum, the Canadian posture concerning "Canadiana" is not consistent in the entire society. To expect broadcasters to fulfil some ideal goal about national unity in the face of the daily onslaught of culture-loaded materials from the US might well be an unrealistic expectation.

Similarly, Canadian choices for media content from the US in preference to their own continue without much change from the time that the Aird Commission in 1929 identified the problem. While in some instances Canadian viewing of Canadian TV *channels* might be going up, the choice of *programming* is not much affected. While such a change in viewing of channels might appear as a paradox, it isn't. Canadians view American programs irrespective of their distribution sources: this source might be a Canadian over-the-air TV station, or it might be a US program delivered to a Canadian home via a Canadian cable distribution system.

Earlier, it was explained that the Davey Committee in its 1970 Report deplored the imbalance of Canadian–US magazine sales in Canada. If Canadians at that time were spending as much on *Playboy* as they were on the leading seventeen Canadian consumer magazines, it was not because the American product was being force-fed to Canadians. Canadians then, as now, make their preferences for media content known, and suppliers of that product (in most cases US producers) are happy enough to make the product readily available. With respect to television and to Canada–US border radio contexts, program-rating services continue to reveal such preferences by Canadians. A 1987 public opinion survey, which claimed to have been the most comprehensive study done since the one conducted by the Davey Committee for its 1970 report, indicated that "most Canadians do not care if their radio, newspapers and magazines fail to reflect a Canadian point of view." And while Canadians tend to agree that American television may be exerting an influence on the Canadian way of life, "most . . . apparently oppose any form of cultural nationalism that would deprive them of their favourite US shows."[42]

Whether preference changes are to occur in the future in a manner that will favour Canadian content is unknown, and is not predictable. What appears to be happening, however, is that the depiction of a purely Canadian consciousness and lifestyle is an elusive program production quality, primarily because of a perceived difficulty in distinguishing clearly between US and Canadian cultural value systems. While such a desirable Canadian production quality might be an expectation of some federal government funding agencies (for example, Telefilm),[43] it is not always sought after by those who produce programs in Canada for commercial sale to stations or theatres. A harsh reality is that a program produced in Canada by, say, an independent producer is not likely to recover its production costs from Canadian sales alone.[44] Thus, producers are forced to resort to (or are happy to) make their products available to other national markets. To recoup their investments, then, producers tend to shape the quality of their productions so as to make them attractive to out-of-Canada buyers, and in most cases, this would mean Hollywood-style production values.

On occasion, it might even be preferred to emulate the Hollywood flavour for Canadian productions geared to Canadian audiences. When it was pointed out to a Canadian TV network executive that one of the network's home-grown successes tended to have a distinct Hollywood flavour, the executive responded, "You bet. What's wrong with that? It's what the public wants."[45] Nevertheless, while such an attitude might well express a hard-core commercial orientation, it isn't the only prevalent attitude. There continue to be those hardy Canadian souls who profess, strongly, that a Canadian consciousness is discoverable and can well become an attractive production value for viewers in the Canadian society.[46]

OWNERSHIP

As in other Western nations, Canadian media industries have also been characterized by growth and concentration of ownership, phenomena that have been regarded as antithetical to the democratic principle of a need for multiple and diverse voices and opinions in society. In two cases, the CRTC has been contributory to such ownership growth despite its own recognition that excessive concentration of ownership is not desirable in the media industries.

In the first instance, a Cabinet directive in 1968 for the CRTC to regulate the transfer of the titles of US-owned Canadian broadcasting outlets into Canadian hands resulted in a situation in which those who bought out previous US owners were those who could well afford to do so. Rogers Communications (CATV systems) and Baton Broadcasting (radio and televison stations), are only two examples of growth attributable to the directive regarding Canadian ownership.

Second, following the 1960 introduction of Canadian content regulations for television, the CRTC recognized the logic in the argument of some broadcasters that a sound and expanded financial base was prerequisite to produce competitive quality television programming. Thus, on several occasions, such growth was encouraged, and large broadcasting companies were permitted to buy out other independently owned radio, television, or cable operations, in spite of the fact that such growth has been contrary to the "local" ownership concept that the CRTC has favoured in its licensing practices.

To what extent such growth has resulted in the desired quality of content has not been determined. Nevertheless, despite an expanded industrial production base in the country, with a few exceptions it is recognized that the privately-owned broadcasting industry has not been contributing sufficiently to fulfilment of national broadcasting objectives. For example, in 1986 a federal Task Force on Broadcasting Policy, after careful study of both the public and private industries, concluded that "most viewing of private Canadian stations in English television is of foreign programs. . . . The contribution of private broadcasters to Canadian performance programming has been less than impressive over the past 25 years."[47] The divestiture process of US ownership in Canadian broadcasting and the efforts made to strengthen the economic bases of broadcasters could have been effective strategies in supporting the quality of content required by Canadian society, but they apparently did not succeed.

❑ GOVERNMENT–MEDIA RELATIONS

The intrusive role the government has had in the nation's media and cultural industries introduces the question about a state-run cultural environment. A brief recitation of the component parts of the empire that the Ministry of Communications and Culture regulates will offer the reader an important insight into such intrusive powers. The federal minister's portfolio includes jurisdiction over sixteen separate media–cultural groups, including, among others: the CRTC; the CBC; the National Film Board; the Canada Council; Telefilm Canada; the National Art Centre; the National Archives of Canada; and the Canadian Museum of Civilization.[48] It is obvious that Canada would be poorly-off as a modern society were it not for the federal government's initiatives (as well as supplementary initiatives by most of the provincial governments) in developing and providing for a future for each of the media–cultural groups by guaranteed patterns of funding support. And, in this sense, Canadians generally applaud such thoughtful and socially beneficial initiatives. However, what gives many Canadians some concern is when the ministry identifies its mission statement as "nation-building." The pertinent and core question, of course, is *whose view* of the nation will prevail: that of the minister? the ministry employees? the Cabinet? the government of the day? the CBC? the CRTC? the NFB? Added to that list could be many more persons or groups, including those who own and are responsible for the content of privately owned media industries.

Certainly there is little unanimity in Canada about what should be the relationship (influence) between the government and media–cultural agencies: opinions vary from too much government involvement to not enough government involvement. Indeed, some advocate full nationalization of the media industries. Studies, formal and informal, have grappled with the question and little agreement has resulted. For example, a Federal Cultural Policy Review Committee in 1982 strongly advocated an arm's-length relationship between the government of the day and the media–cultural industries. Yet, about forty of the committee's 101 recommendations concerning cultural activities in the nation asked for continued funding, increased funding, or start-up funding by the government.[49]

CONCLUSION

The questions being asked today about Canadian identity and about the status of the country and its distinctiveness are little different from those that were being asked in Parliament at the time of the submission of the 1929 *Report of the Royal Commission on Radio Broadcasting*. Yet, some progress towards that goal of distinctiveness has been made despite the increasing strength of the pull of continentalism in the powerful US information systems. A study of the effects of the Canadian content regulations after their establishment for about a dozen years of broadcasting revealed at least two positive results: first, new production facilities were created—very few existed before the regulations; second, Canadians are more involved than ever before in making decisions regarding their own media content.[50] To what extent that content is accurate in reflecting the nation's cultural identity and consciousness might be a moot point: the *decisions* about that content are at least mainly Canadian.

The apparent success of such overall efforts that Canada has made in defending its own identity may have triggered other nations to emulate the Canadian experience. Shortly before his retirement as chair of the CRTC, André Bureau indicated to a group of broadcasters, "We have, over the years, developed a system which, thanks to our ingenuity, entrepreneurship and expertise, has become a model around the world. The French, Australians, New Zealanders, Koreans, and others are copying the structure, the regulatory framework and many of our policies to build or reorganize their own systems."[51] Such apparent recognition of Canada's achievements in defending against US "electronic colonialism" should be gratifying for Canadians. It is unclear whether the same can be said in the future, in the light of a rapidly growing and pervasive informational onslaught, not only from the US but from the global community at large.

Keith Spicer, who recently took over the reins as CRTC chairman, in one of his early public addresses commented on the Canadian experience and on the continuing challenge to be "ourselves in North America and the rest of the world." In putting all of our efforts together, he indicated we really need to be what a young Canadian girl on a radio contest stated about being Canadian—to be "as Canadian as possible, under the circumstances."[52]

And, realistically, certainly no more than that can be done.

Notes

[1] Canada, Communications Canada, *Annual Report 1988–1989* (Ottawa: Supply and Services, 1989), 4.

[2] Canada, *Broadcasting Act 1967–1968*, sec 3(b); also Canada, *Broadcasting Act 1991*, sec. 3(d)(i).

[3] For developed discussions concerning the Canadian regulatory environment, see A. Siegel, *Politics and the Media in Canada* (Toronto: McGraw-Hill Ryerson, 1983), 1–12. Also see W.I. Romanow and W.C. Soderlund, "The Canadian Media-Telecommunications Context," *Media Canada: An Introductory Analysis* (Toronto: Copp Clark Pitman, 1992).

[4] See K.W. Deutsch, *Nationalism and Social Communication: An Inquiry Into the Foundations of Nationality*, 2nd ed. (Cambridge: MIT Press, 1966), 96–100.

[5] For a discussion on the division of powers between the federal and provincial governments see W. White, R. Wagenberg, and R. Nelson, *Introduction to Canadian Government and Politics*, 5th ed. (Toronto: Holt, Rinehart and Winston 1990), 45–58.

[6] H.H. Hiller, *Canadian Society: A Sociological Analysis* (Scarborough: Prentice-Hall, 1976), 12.

[7] See P. Young, "The Numbers Game," *Maclean's* 103 (29 Jan. 1990), 65.

[8] Canada, *Report of the Royal Commission on Radio Broadcasting 1929* (Ottawa: King's Printer, 1929).

[9] Canada, *Report of the Royal Commission on National Development in the Arts, Letters and Sciences* (Ottawa: Queen's Printer, 1951), 40.1 (emphasis added). The serialization of extracts from various formal government-sponsored studies is a reporting style that has been used occasionally in Canadian literature to bring emphasis to a matter, and to demonstrate historical consistency in policy formulation. See W. Romanow, "A Developing Canadian Identity: A Consequence of a Defensive Regulatory Posture for Broadcasting," *Gazette* 22 (1976): 28. Also see Canada, CRTC, *Public Announcement: The Improvement and Development of Canadian Broadcasting and the Extension of US Television Coverage in Canada by CATV* (Ottawa: CRTC, 3 Dec. 1969).

[10] Canada, *Report of the Royal Commission on Broadcasting 1957* (Ottawa: The Queen's Printer, 1957), 8 (emphasis added).

[11] Canada, *Report of the Royal Commission on Publications 1961* (Ottawa: Queen's Printer, 1961), 5 (emphasis added).

[12] Canada, *Report of the Royal Committee on Broadcasting 1965* (Ottawa: Queen's Printer, 1965), 45 (emphasis added).

[13] Canada, Department of Communications, *Proposals for a Communications Policy for Canada* (Ottawa: Information Canada, 1973), 8.

[14] Canada, *Report of the Consultative Committee on the Implications of Telecommunications for Canadian Sovereignty, Telecommunications in Canada* (Ottawa: Supply and Services, 1979), 76.

[15] For a discussion concerning the views of Sir Henry Thornton, President of the Canadian National Railways and the railroad–broadcasting analogy, see F.W. Peers, *The Politics of Canadian Broadcasting 1920–1951* (Toronto: University of Toronto Press, 1969), 22–27.

[16] W.H. Kesterton, *A History of Journalism in Canada* (Toronto: McClelland & Stewart, 1967), 1.

[17] Ibid., 20.

[18] Canada, Canadian Senate, *Report of the Special Senate Committee on Mass Media*, 3 vols. (Ottawa: Information Canada, 1970).

[19] Canada, Canadian Senate, vol. 1, *The Uncertain Mirror*, 68.

[20] Ibid., 233.

[21] W. Romanow and W. Soderlund, "Thomson Newspapers' Acquisition of *The Globe and Mail*," *Gazette* 41 (1988): 11.

[22] G. Bain, "Discovering the Great Abroad," *Maclean's* 103 (22 Jan. 1990), 42.

[23] Canada, Canadian Senate, vol. 1, *The Uncertain Mirror*, 157.

[24] Ibid., 156.

[25] Ibid., 153.

[26] Canada, *Canadian Income Tax Act with Income Tax Regulations Consolidated to October 23, 1990* (Don Mills, ON: Commerce Clearinghouse, 1990), 35530–33.

[27] Canada, *Report of the Royal Commission on Newspapers* (Ottawa: Supply and Services, 1981), 237 (emphasis added).

[28] Ibid., 254–55.

[29] Canada, *Broadcasting Act 1958*, sec. 10 (emphasis added).

[30] Canada, Board of Broadcast Governors, *BBG Announcement Regarding Radio (TV) Broadcasting Regulations 18 November 1959* (Ottawa: BBG, 1959), 7.

[31] Dr. A. Stewart, Chairman of the Board of Broadcast Governors, address to the Canadian Club of Ottawa, 18 April 1962.

[32] Ibid.

[33] T. Green, *The Universal Eye* (New York: Stein and Day, 1972), 44.

[34] Canada, *Report of the Royal Commission on Broadcasting* (Ottawa: Queen's Printer, 1965), 45.

[35] For a detailed discussion of the point system as it operates, see Canada, *Report of the Task Force on Broadcasting Policy* (Ottawa: Supply and Services, 1986): 113.

[36] "CRTC Renews Broadcast Licences of 75 TV Stations," *Globe and Mail* (7 April 1959): B3.

[37] Conditions for receiving this unusual Canadian content credit included the following: that the production be in the drama category; that the production qualify as Canadian under the specified point-credit schedule; and that the program be scheduled so that it begins between 7 PM and 10 PM. See Canada, CRTC, *Appendix to Public Notice CRTC 1984–94 Dated 15 April 1984: Recognition for Canadian Programs* (Ottawa: CRTC, 1984), sec. ix.

[38] *Broadcasting Act 1967–68*, sec. 3(g)(iv). The 1991 act modifies this particular expectation concerning "unity" to read "Should . . . contribute to shared national consciousness and identity." See Canada, *Broacasting Act 1991*, sec. 3.1(m)(vi).

[39] Canada, Department of Communications, *Canadian Voices: Canadian Choices, A New Broadcasting Policy for Canada* (Ottawa: Supply and Services, 1988), 25.

[40] Canada, CRTC, *Annual Report 1987–88* (Ottawa: CRTC, 1988), 31.

[41] Canada, CRTC, *Radio Frequencies Are Public Property: Public Announcement and Decisions of the Commission on the Application for Renewal of the Canadian Broadcasting Corporation's Television and Radio Licences 31 March 1974* (Ottawa: CRTC, 1974), 28.

[42] J. Wong, "Nationalism Not Key Issue for TV Fans, Survey Says," *Globe and Mail* (26 March 1987): A8.

[43] For an examination of what should be the expectations of Canadian producers who apply for public funding see Canada, *Report of the Task Force on Broadcasting Policy*, 371.

[44] C. Hoskins and S. McFadyen, "The Canadian Broadcast Program Development Fund: An Evaluation and Some Recommendations," *Canadian Public Policy* 12, 1 (March 1986): 230.

[45] J. Stockhouse, "Izzyism: Canada's Newest Media Mogul Has Thrown the Tight Little Television Industry into Conniptions," *Globe and Mail Report on Business Magazine* 6, 11 (May 1990): 78.

[46] In recommending that the CBC continue to be the "centrepiece of Canadian broadcasting," the Department of Communications stressed that the CBC mandate, rather than focusing on national unity, should be contributing to "shared national consciousness and identity." See Canada, *Canadian Voices: Canadian Choices*, 25.

[47] Canada, *Task Force on Broadcasting Policy*, 417.

[48] Canada, Ministry of Communications and Culture, *Annual Report 1988–1989* (Ottawa: Supply and Services, 1989), 4–5.

[49] Canada, Department of Communications, *Report of the Federal Cultural Policy Review Committee* (Ottawa: Supply and Services, 1982), 343–58.

[50] W. Romanow, "The Canadian Content Regulations in Canadian Broadcasting: An Historical and Critical Study" (Ph.D. dissertation, Wayne State University, 1974).

[51] A. Bureau, chair of the CRTC, an address to the Atlantic Association of Broadcasters, Charlottetown, PEI, 26 Sept. 1987.

[52] Keith Spicer, chair of the CRTC, "Change in the Air: The CRTC and the New World of Broadcasting," an address to the Canadian Association of Broadcasters, Montreal, PQ, 13 Nov. 1989.

Bibliography

Canada. *Broadcasting Act 1958*. Ottawa: Queen's Printer, 1958.

Canada. *Broadcasting Act 1967–1968*. Ottawa: Queen's Printer, 1968.

Canada. *Broadcasting Act 1991*. Ottawa: Supply and Services, 1991.

Canada. *Report of the Consultative Committee on the Implications of Telecommunications for Canadian Sovereignty, Telecommunications in Canada*. Ottawa: Supply and Services, 1979.

Canada. *Report of the Royal Commission on Broadcasting 1957*. Ottawa: Queen's Printer, 1957.

Canada. *Report of the Royal Committee on Broadcasting 1965*. Ottawa: Queen's Printer, 1965.

Canada. *Report of the Royal Commission on National Development in the Arts, Letters and Sciences*. Ottawa: Queen's Printer, 1951.

Canada. *Report of the Royal Commission on Newspapers*. Ottawa: Supply and Services, 1981.

Canada. *Report of the Royal Commission on Publications 1961*. Ottawa: Queen's Printer, 1961.

Canada. *Report of the Royal Commission on Radio Broadcasting 1929*. Ottawa: King's Printer, 1929.

Canada. *Report of the Task Force on Broadcasting Policy*. Ottawa: Supply and Services, 1986.

Canada. Department of Communications. *Canadian Voices: Canadian Choices, A New Broadcasting Policy for Canada*. Ottawa: Supply and Services, 1988.

Canada. Department of Communications. *Proposals for a Communications Policy for Canada*. Ottawa: Information Canada, 1973.

Canada. Department of Communications. *Report of the Federal Cultural Policy Review Committee*. Ottawa: Supply and Services, 1982.

Canada. Senate. *Report of the Special Senate Committee on Mass Media*. 3 vols. Ottawa: Information Canada, 1970.

Deutsch, K. *Nationalism and Social Communication: An Inquiry into the Foundations of Nationality*. 2nd ed. Cambridge: MIT Press, 1966.

Green, Timothy. *The Universal Eye*. New York: Stein and Day, 1972.

Hiller, H.H. *Canadian Society: A Sociological Analysis*. Scarborough: Prentice-Hall, 1976.

Hoskins, C., and S. McFadyen. "The Canadian Broadcast Program Development Fund: An Evaluation and Some Recommendations," *Canadian Public Policy* 12, 1 (March 1986); 227–35.

Kesterton, W. *A History of Journalism in Canada*. Toronto: McClelland & Stewart, 1967.

Peers, F.W. *The Politics of Canadian Broadcasting 1920–1951*. Toronto: University of Toronto Press, 1969.

Romanow, W. "The Canadian Content Regulations in Canadian Broadcasting: An Historical and Critical Study." Ph.D. dissertation, Wayne State University, 1974.

Romanow, W. "A Developing Canadian Identity: A Consequence of a Defensive Regulatory Posture for Broadcasting," *Gazette* 22 (1976): 26–37.

Romanow, W., and W. Soderlund. *Media Canada: An Introductory Analysis.* Toronto: Copp Clark Pitman, 1992.

Romanow, W., and W. Soderlund. "Thomson Newspapers' Acquisition of *The Globe and Mail*: A Case Study of Content Change," *Gazette* 41 (1988): 5–17.

Siegel, A. *Politics and the Media in Canada.* Toronto: McGraw-Hill Ryerson, 1983.

White, W., R. Wagenberg, and R. Nelson. *Introduction to Canadian Government and Politics.* 5th ed. Toronto: Holt, Rinehart and Winston, 1990.

Social Policy
in Canada

Robert G. Chandler

INTRODUCTION

Not a day goes by without an issue of social policy receiving significant, if not headline, coverage in almost every daily newspaper in Canada. Federal, provincial, and municipal governments spend much time debating these issues, and large amounts of public and private funds are devoted to the maintenance and development of social programs. Moreover, every resident of Canada is a beneficiary of these programs from the cradle to the grave. Since social policies occupy such a prominent place in Canadian life it is important for anyone studying Canada to acquire an understanding of the nature of these policies, the philosophies that give rise to them, and how they have developed over time to meet changing human needs.

After reviewing a number of definitions of social policy, S.A. Yelaga concludes that it is

> concerned with the public administration of welfare services, that is, the formulation, development and management of specific services of government at all levels, such as health, education, income maintenance, and welfare services. Social policy is formulated not only by government but also by institutions such as voluntary organizations, business, labour, industry, professional groups, public interest groups and churches.[1]

Social policies, then, are concerned with the establishment and delivery of services designed to maintain and promote the psycho-social well-being of citizens. It is assumed that in a modern industrial society such as Canada, certain needs can no longer be adequately met by individuals and families through their own efforts alone or through the market economy system. It is therefore necessary for the state to augment individual and family resources with a range of social programs. While this assumption is accepted by most Canadians, there is by no means total agreement as to the extent to which the state should intervene, nor what the objectives should be for such intervention. Views on the objectives of Canadian social policy range from social control (the prevention of social unrest), through efficient delivery of necessary services such as health and education, to the achievement of humanistic values.[2]

PHILOSOPHICAL DIFFERENCES

Richard Titmuss, a British pioneer in the field of social policy, describes three conceptual models for social policy. In the "residual welfare model" the state should respond with social policies and programs only when there is a break-down in the ability of the private market and the family to meet needs, and then only temporarily. "The true object of the Welfare State is to teach people how to do without it." The "industrial achievement-performance model" is based on incentives and rewards for "merit, work performance and productivity." This model is designed primarily to support the functioning of the market economy system and, while it assists people in need, it is also intended to maintain social control.

Finally, the "institutional redistributive model of social policy" is one which

> sees social welfare as a major integrated institution in society, providing universalist services outside the market on the principle of need. It is in part based on theories about the multiple effects of social change and the economic system, and in part on the principle of social equality. It is basically a model incorporating systems of redistribution in command-over-resources-through-time.[3]

While there are other theories of social policy, these three probably reflect the range of values held by Canadians through the years, and elements of all three can be found in Canada's present social policies. Four concepts arising out of these models merit further discussion.

❑ RESIDUAL VS. INSTITUTIONAL POLICIES

Those programs that are commonly referred to as "welfare," namely those that give assistance to persons who are unemployed and have exhausted all other financial resources, are examples of residual programs—those that are provided when normal functioning has broken down. At the other end of the spectrum are institutional programs, such as education and public-health services, which are available to all and address normal, day-to-day needs.

❑ THE DESERVING VS. THE UNDESERVING

The idea that people who require welfare should be divided into those who come to be in need through circumstances beyond their control and those who come to be in need through their own fault has been perpetuated to some degree in social policies and social-services delivery since at least the nineteenth century. This philosophy has resulted in giving greater benefits to disabled persons unable to work than to unemployed persons who are deemed employable, even though their needs may be the same, regardless that the employable may be out of work because of lack of jobs. This philosophy arises out of the fear that meeting needs too generously may act as disincentives to participation in the market economy.

❑ UNIVERSAL VS. SELECTIVE PROGRAMS

Canada's social policies reflect a mix of both kinds of programs. Examples of universal programs made available to all without regard to individual need are Old Age Security and Family Allowances. On the other hand, selective programs, which target persons in special need, are those such as the Child Tax Credit to low-income parents and the Guaranteed Income Supplement to low-income elderly. Because everyone benefits from universal programs, they are politically popular and hence more secure than selective programs.

❑ REDISTRIBUTION OF RESOURCES

This principle, as an underlying objective of social policy, is perhaps among the most controversial as it involves "taking from the rich and giving to the poor" in the minds of many. Nevertheless, many of Canada's policies such as refundable tax credits and income supplements have redistributive effects. Many believe that such policies are the most efficient means of eliminating chronic poverty.

❑ PURPOSES OF SOCIAL POLICY

If the fundamental purpose of social policy is to enable society to respond to human needs that individuals and families are unable to meet through normal interaction within the market economy, then it is useful to consider these needs and the kinds of policies required to respond to them. L.C. Johnson and C.L. Schwartz define such needs as food, clothing, and shelter; protection from illness and accidents; interpersonal relationships; emotional, intellectual, and spiritual growth; and social participation.[4] Social policies, then, need to be evaluated in terms of their effectiveness and efficiency in responding adequately to such needs. Canada's universal and selective income maintenance programs are designed to meet basic needs, while health insurance and workers' compensation respond to the need for protection in the event of illness or accident. The need for nurturing relationships is served by recreational and sports programs. Educational programs, public libraries, and religious institutions respond to the need for emotional, intellectual, and spiritual growth, while rehabilitation and training programs are designed to enable people to participate fully in society.

Because human needs are wide-ranging, Canada's social policies are correspondingly diverse in nature. Before examining the organization and nature of those policies as they exist today, it is useful to trace their historical development and to examine some major evolutionary themes. The following discussion will focus primarily on the role of the federal government since it is not possible in the space available to cover adequately the historical development in each of the provinces.

❑ HISTORICAL BACKGROUND

The historical study of Canadian social policy begins in New France in the seventeenth century with the early missionaries of the Roman Catholic Church who "assumed unquestioned authority to care for the sick, the aged, and the abandoned or orphaned child."[5] Indeed, the church had had a long history of caring for the needy in Europe and this experience made it the logical organization to assume such responsibilities in New France. Religious orders such as the Congregation of Notre Dame were founded specifically to respond to growing social needs in the new colony. Its founder, St. Marguerite Bourgeoys, has frequently been referred to as Canada's first social worker.

In British North America, however, the poor and the weak who were not cared for by their families were left to the mercy of charitable neighbours since there were not significant numbers of English missionaries among the early settlers to found similar institutions in Ontario and the Maritimes. Nor did local governments consider it their responsibility to relieve poverty, except in cases of dire necessity. It was not until the late eighteenth century that the English Poor Law was adopted in the Maritimes and local governments began to make meagre provision for the poor out of public funds.[6]

After the formation of Upper and Lower Canada (now the provinces of Ontario and Québec) in 1791, the population grew rapidly with immigration from both Europe and the United States. Many immigrants arrived in the country poor and quite ill, hence taxing the resources of religious orders to the point where they were unable to meet growing needs adequately without assistance. By the beginning of the nineteenth century the provincial government in Québec began to provide the religious orders with public funds to assist them in their work. In Ontario, which never enacted the English Poor Law, responsibility for the destitute continued to be left largely to individual and private philanthropy.

The passage of the British North America Act, Canada's constitution of 1867, had profound implications for the development of a national social policy. At the time of Confederation, social issues such as health and welfare were relatively unimportant compared to the more pressing issues of nation building. Hence the British North America Act relegated powers in this area primarily to the provinces. As the need for social policies and programs has grown, this reality has made it difficult to establish national social policy and to fund and develop national social programs. As will be seen later, some creative solutions have been required.

Late in the nineteenth century the concern of Ontario citizens was focused on the needs of children for care and protection, largely through the efforts of

J.J. Kelso, a Toronto journalist. "It was Kelso's contention that all children should be protected from ill treatment, reformed if delinquent, and cared for if dependent."[7] Kelso was instrumental in establishing the Toronto Children's Aid Society in 1891. This agency became a model for the foundation of child-welfare services throughout Ontario and in other parts of Canada. An Act for the Prevention of Cruelty to and Better Protection of Children, passed in 1893, established the principle of public intervention to protect children. In addition to child-welfare legislation, workers' compensation legislation first appeared in 1886 to support workers who were injured on the job.

In the period prior to 1900 there was a very limited response to persons in need. Public intervention by local authorities took place only after all individual and family resources had been exhausted, and the response was then often punitive in nature. Voluntary organizations began to provide more humanitarian social programs.

The early years of the twentieth century were marked by considerable growth in major voluntary social agencies such as Children's Aid Societies, the Toronto Family Service Agency (1914), the Canadian Mental Health Association (1918), and the Canadian National Institute for the Blind (1918), indicating increased recognition of needs other than purely economic ones.[8] The Canadian Council on Child Welfare (now the Canadian Council on Social Development), was established in 1920 for the purpose of advocating the establishment of social policy in response to a wide variety of human need. The founding of the first school of social work at the University of Toronto in 1914 is an indication of the growing need for trained professionals to staff the emerging social services. Only six years later the Canadian Association of Social Workers was established.

The federal Juvenile Delinquents Act (1908) firmly established principles for treating youthful offenders differently from adult offenders. Mothers' allowance legislation was passed in Manitoba in 1916, "providing for payments by the province to morally upright women with dependent children."[9] This marked the beginning of the shift of primary responsibility for economic relief from the local municipality to the provincial government, a responsibility that has ultimately come to be shared by all three levels of government.

The passage of the Old Age Pension Act in 1927 marked the first significant involvement of the federal government in the social-welfare arena. This act provided for the federal government to share costs with the provinces for assisting needy elderly people. Such shared-costs agreements have been the primary means of federal involvement in health, education, and social welfare, all constitutional responsibilities of the provinces.

The Great Depression of the 1930s made painfully evident how vulnerable individuals and families could be in a market economy system. However,

> unlike the United States which revolutionized its public welfare services in 1935 and Great Britain which laid the foundations for its later achievements in social security, Canada made do with stopgap measures and failed to come to grips with any major social welfare issues until much later.[10]

This was due at least in part to the previously mentioned constitutional impediment to the development of national social policy. The problem of devastating unemployment was addressed in 1935 with the passage of an unemployment insurance act, but this legislation was referred to the courts to decide whether it fell within Parliament's jurisdiction. The Judicial Committee of the Privy Council was the first court of appeal with respect to constitutional decisions until passage of the Canada Act in 1982.[11] It required an amendment of the act by the British Parliament to bring into effect the Unemployment Insurance Act of 1940. While it came too late to assist the victims of the Great Depression, it has certainly been instrumental in preventing suffering in recessions that have followed.

The next major piece of federal legislation came in 1944 with the passage of the Family Allowances Act, the first example of a "universal demogrant,"[12] payable to mothers for each of their children. The 1950s brought an expansion of income-security programs with the passage of the Old Age Security Act (1951) providing universal payments to all at age seventy (now at age sixty-five); a revised Old Age Assistance Act (1951) providing selective assistance to elderly persons in need; an allowance for blind persons (1951) and disabled persons (1955); and an Unemployment Assistance Act (1956) providing selective assistance to unemployed persons in need.[13] With the exception of the old age security universal demogrant, these pieces of legislation provided for cost-sharing with the provinces, which administered the programs. The 1950s also brought the beginning of public hospital care with the passage of the Hospital Insurance Act (1956), also establishing a cost-sharing arrangement with provinces that instituted hospital insurance programs.

The decade of the 1960s saw major expansion of social policies in the areas of low-income public housing, health care, and income security. While Saskatchewan introduced health insurance in 1962, it was not until 1968 that the federal government stimulated the development of nation-wide health care by passing the Medical Services Act and sharing costs with those provinces that established plans. By 1971 all provinces had done so.

The next piece of social insurance was the Canada Pension Plan (1966), which provided compulsory pensions for a wide spectrum of Canadian workers and was financed by employees, employers, and the federal government. The Québec Pension Plan provided similar coverage in the province of Québec. In the same year the government provided a minimum monthly income for all elderly Canadians through the Guaranteed Income Supplement (1966), which supplemented old age security payments. This act was particularly significant in that it marked the first use of the guaranteed income concept in Canadian social policy. Further, the Canada Assistance Plan (1966) extended cost-sharing arrangements with the provinces, enabling the federal government to fund 50 percent of the cost of a wide range of provincial social-welfare programs.

Another significant feature of the 1960s was the "rediscovery of poverty" in both Canada and the United States.[14] In 1968 the Special Senate Committee on Poverty began extensive nation-wide hearings under the chairmanship of Senator

David Croll. The committee published its report, *Poverty in Canada* in 1971, the most comprehensive study of poverty ever conducted in the country.[15] However, there was substantial disagreement about its findings and the committee's staff published *The Real Poverty Report*.[16] Together, these two volumes reveal a fascinating debate about the nature of poverty, not only among the chronically unemployed, but among those who are fully employed but underpaid in relation to family size. The working poor were thus "rediscovered."

The period of the 1970s was one of building upon the groundwork laid by the social policies established in the 1960s. The Croll Report made extensive recommendations for the restructuring of income security, including the establishment of a universal guaranteed annual income, a concept that is still being debated with little consensus emerging. The Unemployment Insurance Act was amended in 1971 to extend its coverage to all employed persons; in addition, sickness and maternity leave were added. In 1977, after extensive consultation and negotiation with the provinces, the Established Programs Financing Act was passed, revising federal–provincial cost-sharing arrangements for both health and post-secondary education.

Finally, the decade of the 1980s, beginning as it did with widespread recession and crippling inflation followed by increasing concern about the mounting federal deficit and calls for fiscal restraint, brought new social-policy dilemmas. While the federal government has assured Canadians that the country's social programs would remain secure, a number of cutbacks have taken place. Old age security and family allowance payments are now subject to "claw-back," or gradual reduction and elimination as family income rises. This is seen by many as destroying the universal nature of these programs. More recently, there have been significant revisions to the Unemployment Insurance Act, placing the entire burden of funding upon employees and employers and withdrawing the federal portion of the funding. There have also been revisions to eligibility and benefits, which have been criticized as weakening the economic safety net for the unemployed.

Major tax reform has also been a significant feature of the 1980s. The introduction of the refundable tax credit holds promise as a useful mechanism for redistribution of income, but the extent to which it will be used in this way remains to be seen. The goods and services tax applied to the purchase of almost everything except groceries is viewed by many as placing an inordinate burden upon low-income Canadians. However, the provision of a goods and services tax credit may mitigate this somewhat.

The decade has been dominated by the free trade debate and the subsequent signing of the Canada–US Free Trade Agreement. A significant component of the debate has been about the effect of free trade upon Canada's social policies, with speculation that our more liberal social programs and the cost of such programs may make Canadian industry less competitive or that some of our programs may be challenged as "unfair subsidies." The debate continues and it remains for the future to determine the impact of the agreement upon social policy.

In examining the historical evolution of Canadian social policy, D. Guest identifies five major themes.[17] The first is a gradual shift from purely residual assistance (as a last resort to persons in need) to institutional policies providing social security for all. The second is an increasing acceptance of a "social minimum,"[18] or minimum standards of health and decency below which no citizen should be allowed to fall. The third is a redefinition of the causes of poverty, with increasing acceptance of the fact that many people in an industrial society are poor through no fault of their own. Fourth, more and more members of the population are coming to be included in social programs as beneficiaries and as contributors through taxation and insurance contributions; therefore there has been a corresponding public interest and demand for participation in decision making. The final theme is the impact that constitutional realities have had from the very beginning of Confederation and continue to have today with the advent of the Charter of Rights and Freedoms and the problems of defining Québec's place in the constitution. Perhaps more than anything else, the British North America Act of 1867 and the more recent Canada Act have both complicated and stimulated the development of a unique system of social policy.

THE ORGANIZATION OF SOCIAL WELFARE

The separation of powers established in the British North America Act has resulted in each of the provinces developing and administering its social services in unique ways in response to regional needs. Nevertheless, the federal government, through constitutional amendments or through agreements with the provinces, has exercised a significant role in ensuring a reasonably uniform national social policy, either through cost sharing of programs or through direct administration of universal income-security programs. It is the residual assistance programs that provide both financial and personal assistance that vary most across the provinces since these programs need to be tailored to local conditions. This situation is complicated by the fact that those areas experiencing the greatest needs have the fewest resources. So, too, the extent of voluntary sector involvement in the delivery of social programs varies from province to province, with some provinces operating almost all social services and others entering into service agreements that allow voluntary agencies to deliver the services while the provincial government provides the funding.

Québec, while acknowledging the federal government's legislative role in income security, has insisted that provincial statutes should take precedence over federal ones and that when they do "the provincial government must receive the fiscal equivalent of whatever monies the federal government would have spent had its legislation applied."[19] Thus the Québec Pension Plan operates parallel to the Canada Pension Plan, which serves all other provinces.

Recently the long-standing criticism by native communities that social policies have been paternalistic and insensitive to native culture has resulted in a number of provinces transferring the administration of programs to Indian bands so that services can be increasingly delivered by indigenous personnel familiar with the culture. However, native groups insist that mere transfer of delivery does not go far enough.

> The Ontario Confederacy of First Nations has identified four principles for development of social and other community services. These services must be First Nation-specific, reflecting their culture in form and content; First Nation-determined, involving control over planning and development; community-based, with services developed and delivered within communities; and First Nation-controlled, with operations managed under the authority of First Nation councils and laws.[20]

MAJOR SOCIAL POLICY ISSUES

It is impossible to discuss all areas of Canadian social policy in this overview. Therefore it has been necessary to be selective in giving attention to such areas as income security, health, the elderly, women, and child welfare. Other components of social policy such as housing, immigration, education, and the needs of youth and disabled persons are equally important. It is hoped that the areas selected will serve to give an indication of the complex nature of Canadian social policy.

❏ INCOME SECURITY

The issue of income security has been an important component of Canadian social policy from its very beginning. A large number of programs have therefore been developed to respond to the problems of poverty and loss of income. Programs may be divided into universal demogrants, automatically payable to all eligible Canadians regardless of need; social insurance, with compulsory premiums being paid to guard against future risk; and social assistance, which is given selectively on the basis of established need and funded entirely through the tax system.

Canada has three universal demogrant programs: Family Allowances, Old Age Security, and Veterans' Pensions. These are payable monthly on behalf of all children under eighteen, to all persons sixty-five or over, and to disabled war veterans and their dependants. In theory those who do not need these allowances have them taxed back. The advantage of universal demogrant programs is their simplicity and economy of administration. Because they are payable to everyone, they do not carry the social stigma attached to some selective programs. However, critics point out that because they are universal, they do not significantly attack the problem of poverty. Not surprisingly, reductions in these programs are politically unpopular. A recent attempt to de-index Old Age Security payments[21] met with such widespread opposition that the government had to withdraw the proposal. An alternative strategy, the introduction of clawbacks to Family Allowances and Old Age Security, whereby the payment is gradually reduced to nothing as family income rises above a certain level, has been criticized as violating the principle of universality.

The most common type of program in the Canadian social policy system is social insurance. The federal government operates three such programs: Unemployment Insurance, Canada Pension Plan, and Guaranteed Income Supplement. These programs are funded primarily through premiums paid by employers and employees. Unemployment Insurance is paid to anyone who becomes unemployed after working long enough to qualify, and is paid for a limited period of time. Unemployment Insurance in Canada has undoubtedly cushioned the devastating effects of cyclical recession, but because benefits are paid for only a limited amount of time the program does not respond well to long periods of recession such as Canada experienced in the early 1980s and the beginning of the 1990s. Nor are the benefits adequate in the face of extreme inflation and runaway mortgage interest rates.

The Canada Pension Plan is payable to contributors sixty-five or over and is based on contributions of the employed. There is also a death benefit and survivor's allowance. The Guaranteed Income Supplement is paid to Old Age Security recipients who have no other income. The Canada (Québec) Pension Plan has certainly improved the income security of many retired persons but still is inadequate as a principal source of retirement income.

At the provincial level the only social insurance income-security program is that of Workers' Compensation, which is funded by employers' contributions. Benefits are paid to employees injured on the job and are based on a percentage of income up to a certain maximum. Workers' Compensation is the oldest of any kind of social-insurance program in Canada.

The last component of the income-security system is that of social assistance. The benefits of these programs are highly selective and are paid to those in need after the application of an "income test" determines them to be eligible. Persons in receipt of these programs are commonly referred to as being "on welfare," and are unfortunately stigmatized by large segments of society even though their condition is frequently not of their own making.

Social-assistance programs are cost-shared with the federal government under the Canada Assistance Plan, which provides for programs to be funded 50 percent by the province and 50 percent by the federal government. Some provinces require 20 percent of the costs of certain social-assistance programs to be borne by the local municipality, a remnant of the early concept of local responsibility for poverty relief.

Programs vary considerably from province to province and only Ontario's program will be briefly described here as an example. Ontario has two pieces of social-assistance legislation, the General Welfare Assistance Act and the Family Benefits Act. The General Welfare Assistance Act provides assistance to individuals and families considered to be in short-term need and currently "employable." This program has usually been administered by the municipality, which has also been responsible for 20 percent of the funding. General Welfare Assistance recipients have received smaller benefits than their Family Benefits counterparts in similar circumstances and have tended to be viewed with more stigma.

The Family Benefits Act is aimed at those individuals such as "sole support" mothers and disabled persons who are considered to be currently unemployable, and thus likely to be in need of assistance for longer periods of time. This program has been administered and funded by the province.

This division of funding and services and difference in benefits has been criticized as perpetuating the concept of the "worthy and unworthy poor," and a committee of inquiry has recently completed extensive hearings and made significant recommendations for revision and unification of the province's social-assistance program.[22]

Social-assistance programs are intended to provide a "safety net" whereby the needs of those persons who have exhausted the provisions of all other income-security programs are provided for. They are thus residual in nature. However, social-assistance programs have been woefully inadequate in that the levels of assistance leave recipients well below the poverty line. Moreover, little or no provision has been made in most provinces to assist the "working poor," who comprise 55 percent of those living below the poverty line in Canada.[23]

❑ HEALTH

The second major area of social policy in Canada is that of providing for the health-care needs of citizens. Some of the events leading to the establishment of Canada's health-care program have previously been discussed. Currently the federal government shares the costs of public medical care with the provinces through a system of grants under the Federal–Provincial Fiscal Arrangements and Federal–Provincial Post-Secondary Education and Health Contributions Act (1984), commonly referred to as the Established Programs Financing Act.[24] The Canada Health Act (1984) establishes certain conditions that must be met by provincial programs in order to qualify for funding. They must provide universal coverage to all residents, and coverage must be comprehensive, accessible, publicly administered, and portable. Extra billing and user charges are discouraged by the withholding of a portion of the funding by the federal government. There must be consultation with provincial medical associations in setting the fee schedule, together with the establishment of a process for settling disputes.[25] Thus, the federal government asserts control over standards of medicare programs, while leaving their development and administration to the provinces.

A variety of funding methods are employed at the federal level and may be carried out either through taxes or insurance premiums. The Ontario government, which had financed its plan largely through insurance contributions by subscribers with provision for premium assistance or exemption depending on income level, has recently replaced this method with an employer tax based on size of payroll.

Canada's medicare system has recently come under fire because of its inability to deliver adequate services when needed. Long waiting lists have developed for cardiac and transplant operations, and delays have proven life-threatening for some. Other criticisms have been levelled at patients and doctors for overusing the system and driving up costs. However, in spite of its limitations, the system provides outstanding protection against the potentially disastrous costs of illness and makes comprehensive medical care available to all citizens regardless of income.

❑ ELDERLY

Because of their rapidly growing proportion of the population, the elderly and their needs have increasingly become the subjects of social policy. Income-maintenance programs have already been discussed, but a number of other measures deserve attention here.

While the basic health needs of elderly Canadians are covered under medicare, their special needs have required additional programs such as nursing homes and chronic-care hospitals. As well, a variety of in-home services have been designed to enable increasingly dependent elderly persons to live at home for longer periods of time. Also, persons over the age of sixty-five receive free prescription drug services under medicare.

Another important area of social programming addressed at the provincial level is that designed to prevent social isolation through the establishment and funding of senior citizens' centres. Recently an innovative program to meet the housing needs of the elderly has been introduced in Ontario on an experimental basis through the Ministry of Housing. "Granny Flats . . . small, temporary and portable one-bedroom units are constructed in the backyards of existing single-family homes for occupancy by single elderly parents."[26] Critics of social policy for the elderly have pointed out that "no coherent, comprehensive national social policy . . . for the aged . . . exists to provide for their . . . economic security, psychological well-being, social integration and protected independence."[27]

A current issue in Canada is that of mandatory retirement, commonly at the age of sixty-five. It has been pointed out that such a policy deprives the elderly of the right to continue making a productive contribution to the economy and contributes to loss of self-esteem and marginalization on the part of those involuntarily retired. Critics on the other side have raised concerns about the possibility of persons remaining in employment for longer periods of time, thus restricting the availability of jobs for the young. However, the constitutionality of mandatory retirement has been upheld by the Supreme Court of Canada.

❑ WOMEN

As society has become increasingly sensitive to the unequal status of women, the need for public policies to redress these inequalities has become evident. Women comprise 85 percent of sole-support parents and more than 60 percent of the poor in Canada.[28] Women are paid significantly less than men for work of equal value and are underrepresented in many of the higher-paid positions. Increasing attention has been given to the physical and sexual abuse as well as the degradation of women. As a result there has been increased social-policy activity providing for family-law reform, pay equity, affirmative action in hiring, revision of sexual assault and pornography legislation, and the establishment of programs for the support and treatment of battered women and the prosecution and treatment of battering men.

❑ CHILD WELFARE

We have seen that some of the earliest social legislation in Canada was in the field of child welfare, and that field continues to occupy a prominent place in Canadian social policy. Current shifts in philosophy appear to be in the direction of accountability and children's rights.

At the federal level, the Young Offenders Act was passed in 1982, which substantially revised the Juvenile Delinquents Act of 1908. In the Juvenile Delinquents Act "a child . . . adjudged to have committed a delinquency. . . shall be dealt with, not as an offender, but as one in a condition of delinquency and therefore requiring help and guidance and proper supervision."[29] In the Young Offenders Act, on the other hand, young people must bear responsibility for their behaviour: "while young persons should not in all instances be held accountable in the same manner or suffer the same consequences for their behaviour as adults, young persons who commit offences should nonetheless bear responsibility for their contraventions."[30] Thus, while young people who break the law are to be treated differently from adult offenders, they are nevertheless to be considered offenders and the court is to balance the needs of the young offender with the interests of society. The new act established the uniform age for a young offender as between the ages of twelve and seventeen. Previously, the maximum age had varied between fifteen and seventeen from province to province and the minimum age was seven. There are a number of provisions to safeguard the rights of the young offender, which were absent in the Juvenile Delinquents Act. These changes providing young and old offenders with equal rights were largely precipitated by the Charter of Rights and Freedoms. While the Young Offenders Act is a federal statute, the responsibility for its administration rests with the provinces.

As with so much of Canada's social legislation, child-welfare legislation varies from province to province. A discussion of Ontario's legislation is presented here as an example of the changes that are occurring in the field of child welfare. Prior to 1984, Ontario had eight separate pieces of legislation pertaining to the care and protection of children: the Child Welfare Act, the Children's Residential Services Act, the Children's Mental Health Services Act, the Young Offenders Implementation Act, the Children's Institutions Act, the Developmental Services Act, the Homes for Retarded Persons Act, and the Charitable Institutions Act.[31]

The provisions dealing with children were consolidated into the Child and Family Services Act (1984). However, this new act did far more than tidy up existing legislation. It represented a shift from the "best interests of the child" to that of "children's rights." No longer can child-welfare authorities make arbitrary, though well-meaning, decisions on behalf of the child but are required to give due regard to a set of children's rights that are defined for the first time. The act declares that

> a child in care has the right to: reasonable privacy, uncensored mail, receive visits, personal property, religious instruction, education, recreation, food, clothing, medical and dental care and a plan of care; be free from corporal punishment; not be detained or locked up and not to be unduly restricted . . .; be informed of the rights under this Act; be informed of complaints procedures; be consulted and heard when major decisions affecting his or her life are being made; participate in the development of his or her plan of care and to be consulted and to express views when significant decisions are being made.[32]

Services are to be given that are the least restrictive and disruptive to the child's life. The act organizes services under six major categories: child welfare, child and family intervention, child treatment, child development, community support, and young offenders.[33]

CONCLUSION

As we enter the closing decade of the twentieth century, the future of social policy in Canada is uncertain. The threat of impending recession and mounting inflation, the growth of unemployment (particularly among the young), the increasing needs of the elderly, heightened recognition of the plight of the working poor, vexing, unsolved problems such as AIDS, and countless other issues all illustrate the fact that there will be a continuing demand for creative and progressive social policies to respond to increasing human needs. On the other hand, the growing federal deficit and the consequent need for fiscal restraint will make it increasingly difficult for federal and provincial governments to fund existing and new programs. Furthermore, the impact of free trade on the economy in general, and on social programs in particular, remains an unanswered question. Nevertheless, Canada has faced similar problems and dilemmas throughout the twentieth century and has managed to respond with enlightened social policies that have made its citizens among the most socially secure in the world. Canada has never ceased to wrestle creatively with "the historic problems of distributive justice (embracing) four well-known maxims: To each according to his need; to each according to his worth; to each according to his merit; to each according to his work."[34]

Notes

[1] S.A. Yelaga, ed., *Canadian Social Policy*, rev. ed. (Waterloo: Wilfrid Laurier University Press, 1987), 2.

[2] A. Armitage, *Social Welfare in Canada*, 2nd ed. (Toronto: McClelland & Stewart, 1988), 15.

[3] R.M. Titmuss, *Social Policy* (London: Allen and Unwin, 1974), 31.

[4] L.C. Johnson and C.L. Schwartz, *Social Welfare: A Response to Human Need* (Boston: Allyn and Bacon, 1988), 4.

[5] D. Bellamy, "Social Welfare in Canada," in *Encyclopedia of Social Work* (New York: National Association of Social Workers, 1965), 36.

[6] Ibid., 37.

[7] D. Bellamy and A. Irving, "Pioneers," in J.C. Turner and F.J. Turner, eds., *Canadian Social Welfare*, 2nd ed. (Don Mills: Collier Macmillan, 1986), 32.

[8] Armitage, *Social Welfare*, 271.

[9] Ibid.

[10] Bellamy, "Social Welfare," 42.

[11] P.H. Russell, ed., *Leading Constitutional Decisions: Cases on the British North America Act* (Toronto: McClelland & Stewart, 1965), 46–47.

[12] R.M. Jaco, "Social Agencies" in *Canadian Social Welfare*, 259.

[13] Armitage, *Social Welfare*, 275.

[14] D. Guest, *The Emergence of Social Security in Canada*, 2nd ed. (Vancouver: University of British Columbia Press, 1986), 166.

[15] Canada, Senate, Special Senate Committee on Poverty, *Poverty in Canada* (Ottawa: Information Canada, 1971).

[16] I. Adams, *The Real Poverty Report* (Edmonton: M.G. Hurtig, 1971).

[17] Guest, *The Emergence*, 3–4.

[18] Ibid., 3.

[19] Ibid., 184.

[20] Ontario, Social Assistance Review Committee, *Transitions*, summary (Toronto: Ministry of Community and Social Services, 1988), 83.

[21] National Council of Welfare, *The 1989 Budget and Social Policy* (Ottawa: Supply and Services Canada, 1989), 15.

[22] Ontario, Social Assistance Review Committee.

[23] D.P. Ross, "Income Security," in *Canadian Social Policy*, 36.

[24] Canada, Statutes, *Federal–Provincial Fiscal Arrangements and Federal–Provincial Post-Secondary Education and Health Contributions Act* (1984).

[25] C. Charles and R.F. Badgley, "Health and Inequality: Unresolved Policy Issues," in *Canadian Social Policy*, 47–64.

[26] Yelaga, *Canadian Social Policy*, 2.

[27] Ibid., 157, 169.

[28] R. Blaser, "The Feminine Face of Poverty," *The Presbyterian Record* (Oct. 1988):14–16.

[29] Canada, Statutes, *Juvenile Delinquents Act* (1971), R.S., c.160, s.1, sec. 3 (2).

[30] Canada, Statutes, *Young Offenders Act* (1982), sec. 3 (1).

[31] Ontario, Ministry of Community and Social Services, *Highlights of the Child and Family Services Act* (Toronto: Ontario Government, 1985), 2.

[32] Ibid., 23.

[33] Ibid., 9–10.

[34] Titmuss, *Social Policy,* 141.

Bibliography

Adams, I. *The Real Poverty Report*. Edmonton: M.G. Hurtig, 1971.

Armitage, A. *Social Welfare in Canada*. 2nd ed. Toronto: McClelland & Stewart, 1988.

Bellamy, D. "Social Welfare in Canada." *Encyclopedia of Social Work*. New York: National Association of Social Workers, 1965.

Bellamy, D., and A. Irving. "Pioneers." In J.C. Turner and F.J. Turner, eds. *Canadian Social Welfare*. 2nd ed. Don Mills: Collier Macmillan, 1986.

Blaser, R. "The Feminine Face of Poverty." *The Presbyterian Record*. (Oct. 1988): 14–16.

Charles, C. and R.F. Badgely. "Health and Inequality: Unresolved Policy Issues." In S.A. Yelaga, ed. *Canadian Social Policy*. Rev. ed. Waterloo: Wilfrid Laurier University Press, 1987.

Courchene, T.J. *Social Policy in the 1990s: Agenda for Reform*. Toronto: C.D. Howe Institute, 1987.

Drover, G., ed. *Free Trade and Social Policy*. Ottawa: Canadian Council on Social Development, 1988.

Guest, D. *The Emergence of Social Security in Canada*. 2nd ed. Vancouver: University of British Columbia Press, 1986.

Ismael, J.S., ed. *Canadian Social Welfare Policy*. Montreal: McGill-Queen's University Press, 1985.

Jaco, R.M. "Social Agencies." In J.C. Turner and F.J. Turner, eds. *Canadian Social Welfare*. 2nd ed. Don Mills: Collier Macmillan, 1986.

Johnson, L.C., and C.L. Schwartz. *Social Welfare: A Response to Human Need*. Boston: Allyn and Bacon, 1988.

Kahn, A.J. *Social Policy and Social Services*. New York: Random House, 1973.

Loney, M., D. Boswell, and J. Clarke, eds. *Social Policy and Social Welfare*. Milton Keynes: Open University Press, 1983.

Marsh, Leonard. *Report on Social Security for Canada*. Toronto: University of Toronto Press, 1975.

McGilly, F. *An Introduction to Canada's Public Social Services*. Toronto: McClelland & Stewart, 1990.

Morrow, H., ed. *Province of Ontario: Its Social Services*. 11th ed. Toronto: Ontario Social Development Council, 1983.

Moscovitch, A., and J. Albert, eds. *The Benevolent Welfare State: The Growth of Welfare in Canada*. Toronto: Garamond Press, 1987.

Naylor, C.D. *Private Practice: Canadian Medicine and the Politics of Health Insurance*. Montreal: McGill-Queen's University Press, 1986.

Ross, D.P. "Income Security." In S.A. Yelaga, ed. *Canadian Social Policy*. Rev. ed. Waterloo: Wilfrid Laurier University Press, 1987.

Russell, P.H., ed. *Leading Constitutional Decisions: Cases on the British North America Act*. Toronto: McClelland & Stewart, 1965.

Splane, R. *Social Welfare in Ontario, 1791–1893.* Toronto: University of Toronto Press, 1965.

Taylor, M.G. *Health Insurance and Canadian Public Policy: The Seven Decisions that Created the Canadian Health Insurance System.* Montreal: McGill-Queen's University Press, 1978.

Titmuss, R.M. *Social Policy.* London: Allen and Unwin, 1974.

Turner, J.C., and F.J. Turner, eds. *Canadian Social Welfare.* 2nd ed. Don Mills: Collier Macmillan, 1986.

Wharf, B., and N. Carter. *Planning for the Social Services: Canadian Experiences.* Ottawa: Canadian Council on Social Development, 1972.

Wilensky, H.L., and C.N. Lebeaux. *Industrial Society and Social Welfare.* New York: Free Press, 1965.

Willard, J.W. "Canadian Welfare Programs." *Encyclopedia of Social Work.* New York: National Association of Social Workers, 1965.

Yelaga, S.A., ed. *Canadian Social Policy.* Rev. ed. Waterloo: Wilfrid Laurier University Press, 1987.

10

❏   ❏   ❏   ❏   ❏   ❏   ❏

Canadian Foreign Policy

Terence A. Keenleyside

INTRODUCTION

F oreign policy has figured prominently in Canadian public affairs, especially since World War II. This phenomenon is an inevitable consequence of Canada's high dependence on foreign trade and investment for its economic well-being. It is also a product of Canada's vulnerability, as a modest power, to the actions of other actors, necessitating a vigilant and vigorous diplomacy to protect and enhance its interests in an increasingly complex international environment.

At the risk of simplification, Canadian foreign policy can be viewed as falling roughly into three periods, each of which has entailed different identifying characteristics and has prompted a particular perception of Canada's status in the international state system. Common to all three periods, however, has been a foreign policy shaped by the particular circumstances of Canada in each era and, hence, a policy with a distinct character of its own, different in nature from its mother countries, Britain and France, and from its closest neighbour and partner, the United States. This chapter surveys the principal features of foreign policy in each of these periods; identifies the recurring international preoccupations of Canada; and points to those elements of Canadian policy that lend a distinct identity to Canada's role in world affairs.

1867 TO 1939: DEPENDENCE AND NEO-ISOLATIONISM—CANADA AS A PERIPHERAL POWER

Prior to 1914, Canada was, in effect, a self-governing colony whose international relations were controlled, and in a formal sense conducted, by the imperial government in Great Britain. From late in the nineteenth century Canada did have its own agents serving abroad, largely as trade commissioners and immigration officials. However, these individuals did not enjoy diplomatic status with the attendant privileges and immunities, for Canada did not then possess the constitutional power to conduct diplomatic relations with other countries nor to enter into treaties of its own. To a gradually increasing degree in the late nineteenth and early twentieth centuries, the Canadian government did become involved in the shaping of policy on international matters of direct concern to Canada by providing its own personnel to participate in British delegations dealing with matters affecting Canada. Nevertheless, these delegations remained, at least nominally, under the control of the imperial power.

To facilitate the British conduct of Canadian foreign affairs, a Canadian Department of External Affairs was created in 1909, but it was an extremely modest operation in its early years. It was housed above a barber shop on Bank Street in Ottawa with an initial budget of $14 950. In 1913, it had only three professional officers, one of whom, Loring Christie, has been described as having been the "foreign office" of First World War Prime Minister Sir Robert Borden.[1]

Canada's subordinate international status was reflected in the fact that when World War I broke out it was automatically regarded as involved when Britain declared war against Germany. However, the war had a dramatic effect in transforming Canadian attitudes towards the empire connection and Canada's place in the wider international community. From a negligible military capability before the outbreak of fighting, Canada geared up to make a major wartime contribution that entailed the loss of some 60 000 lives. Considerable agricultural and industrial development during the course of the war also meant that Canada emerged at the end a more significant economic power. World War I thus contributed to a nascent sense of national identity and national self-confidence. Further, the sacrifices that Canada was called upon to make generated the feeling that it deserved to play a role in the shaping of empire defence and foreign policy in order to protect its own interests and prevent a recurrence of the bloodshed of World War I. This concern bore initial fruit in the creation in March 1917 of the Imperial War Cabinet and Imperial War Conference, with Canadian representation in each, and hence a voice in the determination of empire policy during the latter stages of the war. This was followed by agreement that Canada, like the other dominions (South Africa, Australia, and New Zealand) and India, should have a separate seat at the Peace Conference of 1918 and in the League of Nations, the international organization established at the end of the war with the principal aim of preventing major military conflicts in the future.

Canadian foreign policy over the ensuing inter-war period consisted principally of two interrelated themes: pursuit of the attainment of full autonomy in international affairs; and a policy of neo-isolationism and appeasement to avoid of commitments that might lead to involvement in another costly war.

The preoccupation with foreign policy independence was, in part, a natural by-product of the maturation process Canada had undergone during the war and the related sense of an emerging national identity. It was furthered by the dominance in Canadian politics over the inter-war years of the Liberal Party of Canada, whose leaders tended to be anti-imperial in outlook, decrying Downing Street domination of empire affairs, and who were at the same time favourably disposed towards continentalist ties with the United States. In particular, however, autonomy in international affairs was increasingly seen as important to prevent Canada's being sucked into fighting another war in Europe on behalf of British interests.

The 1920s and 1930s witnessed a number of landmark events on the path to full Canadian independence, but only three need to be mentioned. A 1926 Imperial Conference committee reached agreement on a report (commonly referred to as the Balfour Report) defining Britain and the dominions as "autonomous Communities within the British Empire, equal in status, in no way subordinate one to another in any respect of their domestic or external affairs, though united by common allegiance to the Crown, and freely associated as members of the British Commonwealth of Nations." Thereafter, Canada was clearly free to enter into its own international agreements and establish formal diplomatic relations with other countries. The latter commenced in 1927 with the appointment of Vincent Massey (later the first Canadian-born governor general of Canada) as minister plenipotentiary in Washington. The *de facto* autonomy that Canada achieved at the 1926 Imperial Conference acquired legal status in 1931 when the British Parliament passed the Statute of Westminster, which confirmed the political understanding that had been reached between Britain and the dominions in 1926. From that time on, at least from the standpoint of those who understood the constitutional evolution of the empire, Canada was a fully sovereign state.

However, the final achievement of autonomy in external affairs can be deemed to have occurred on 10 September 1939 when a separate Canadian proclamation of war against Germany was issued, a week after the British declaration. Ironically, in the context of Canada's long and tortuous struggle to make itself understood by the behemoth to its south, the United States was initially inclined to view Canada as at war with Germany with the British proclamation. Canadian intervention was required to set the Americans straight on Canada's new international status. With the capacity to take the ultimate foreign policy decision of peace or war on its own finally acknowledged by the United States, Canada's autonomy over its international affairs can be viewed as at last having been secured.

The neo-isolationist and appeasement orientation of Canadian foreign policy during the inter-war years reflected the concern of Canadian governments to avoid becoming entangled in another European conflict at tremendous human, economic, and political cost. Thus, the country would be free to get on with the task of building the new nation of Canada without interruption. The devastating political consequences for the two major political parties in introducing conscription during the First World War was a particular spur to the pursuit of a very cautious approach to international commitments. Conscription, intensely resented in Québec, had destroyed altogether the base of support for the Conservative Party in that province, since it was the coalition government of Conservative Prime Minister Sir Robert Borden that had introduced the dreaded scheme in 1917. At the same time, it had split the Liberal Party into two wings, with English-Canadian Liberals supporting conscription and Québec Liberals vehemently opposed. The lesson was clear: the building of national unity in Canada required that Canadian governments studiously avoid, at least until the outbreak of war, any commitment to become involved in support of Britain.

This cautious attitude towards international obligations was reinforced by a suspicion that the imperial powers of Europe were inherently belligerent and that their political machinations were bound to lead eventually to another ruinous war unrelated to any Canadian interests. Canadian delegates to the League of Nations even adopted the unfortunate habit—nauseating, no doubt, to their European counterparts—of referring to the long, undefended border between Canada and the United States as evidence of the peaceable manner in which North Americans handled their affairs in comparison with "the 'war drunk lunatics'. . . of Europe."[2] Canada's reluctance to undertake firm international obligations also stemmed from the mistaken view that it lived "in a fire-proof house, far from inflammable materials"[3] and that if another general war did occur in Europe it would not necessarily envelop North America. Thus, as Canadian officials saw it, Canada was being asked at the League to help ensure the security of other countries when Canada itself did not require any protective arrangements.

Finally, Canadian neo-isolationism and appeasement was a consequence of United States isolationism at this time, and thus an early indicator of American impact on the shaping of Canadian foreign policy. The failure of the United States to ratify the League of Nations Covenant and its consequent absence from the principal international organization of the inter-war period augmented the risks from a Canadian perspective of assuming any obligations, under the articles of the League or otherwise, to come to the assistance of states that were victims of aggression. Were the United States involved and committed to collective action, then Canada could more willingly have contemplated obligations of its own, confident that the responsibilities it would have to assume would be relatively modest. Moreover, the prospects for success of any initiatives taken by way of economic or military sanctions would also be greatly enhanced.

There are many examples of the negative foreign policy that Canada pursued during the inter-war years, but only two need be cited here as prominent illustrations. In 1931, when Japan launched an attack on the Chinese province of Manchuria in the first major conflict of the post-World War I period, the Canadian delegate to the League took the view that League members had to "distinguish between the rights of a case and the manner in which those rights are realized and enforced."[4] He thus implied that Japan had a good claim to Manchuria and had transgressed only by exercising its power inappropriately. Interestingly, in one of the few references to Canada in F.P. Walters' classic history of the League of Nations, this speech (together with milder ones by other delegates) is noted as having put "fresh heart into the Japanese delegation,"[5] with the ultimate result being the complete conquest of Manchuria and the establishment there of a Japanese puppet government.

In the autumn of 1935, when Italian forces rolled over a virtually defenceless Abyssinia (present-day Ethiopia), the Canadian delegation to the League was instructed to abstain in the vote on the League Council's report on Italian aggression and to avoid involvement in any initiative to apply economic sanctions against Italy. Contrary to instructions, the Canadian delegation accepted membership on a League committee of eighteen countries that was established to consider the imposition of sanctions; was instrumental in having nickel, a product largely produced in Canada at that time, placed on the initial list of embargoed products; and later proposed the extension of sanctions to include oil, coal, iron, and steel. For this final indiscretion, Walter Riddell, the leader of the Canadian delegation, was removed from his position and publicly repudiated by the government of Prime Minister Mackenzie King. The incident clearly reflected the unreadiness of Canada to play any sort of constructive role in the inter-war period in curbing aggression and thereby preventing, before it became inevitable, the Nazi aggression that precipitated World War II. For Lester Pearson, one of the principal architects of post-World War II Canadian foreign policy and the young diplomat who replaced Riddell on the Committee of Eighteen, Canadian policy making in the Abyssinian situation was a disillusioning experience. However, it was also one that had importance in shaping the approach he was to take to Canadian foreign policy after the war. In a reflective article published in 1967, then Prime Minister Lester Pearson wrote:

> I have always felt that World War II became not only unavoidable, but imminent, after the Fascist success against Ethiopia. . . . The lesson of this failure was very much in my own mind when later I became concerned with the organization of peace after the Second World War, the war which had been caused in large part by the failure to organize security effectively after World War I.[6]

In sum, Canada in this first period was very much on the periphery of international politics. Lacking full autonomy until the 1930s, a modest power in terms of economic, military, and diplomatic capability, and a state that opted for a limited, largely negative role in international affairs, it did not cut a wide or distinguished swath on the world stage. Its approach, however, reflected its leaders' perceptions of Canada's particular needs during this period and, accordingly, Canadian policy was distinguishable from the policies of those countries that principally influenced it at this time. The theme of acquiring and affirming Canada's autonomy over its international affairs stemmed from its own peculiar constitutional position and in this dimension, not surprisingly, its policy concerns most closely paralleled those of the other dominions, which were embarked on a similar evolutionary path. Canadian neo-isolationism bore some resemblance to the isolationism of the United States, but it was different in that Canada did not reject membership in the League of Nations, as that was important to its attainment of international recognition. Further, Canadian leaders were willing to collaborate in the League with other states in searching for pacific means of settling international disputes. It was only when it came to taking coercive action that Canada hesitated to commit itself, and even then its position was never categorical; it was a question of not making firm commitments prior to the outbreak of conflict.

Finally, Canada's support for appeasement was similar to the policy pursued by its European mother countries. Its reasons for taking this approach, however, differed as they pertained to the implications for Canadian unity of enmeshing itself in far-off entanglements and to the risks of doing so in the absence of US international involvement. And, finally, Canada's support for appeasement reflected a perhaps naive assumption that Britain and France never shared—that its own security was not directly threatened by conflict abroad. This was an assumption that the Second World War was to put to rest with major consequences for the future of Canadian foreign policy.

1940 TO 1967: THE "GOLDEN ERA" OF INTERNATIONALISM—CANADA AS A MIDDLE POWER

Like World War I, the Second World War had a profound effect on Canada, prompting almost a complete reversal of the approach to foreign policy of the inter-war period. In the end, Canada was unable to avoid involvement in a second costly conflict. Once again, it was called upon to build up its modest regular army to a force of 600 000 and its navy to play a leading convoy role in the North Atlantic. Once again, 42 000 of its citizens were obliged to pay the supreme sacrifice. Consequently, the policy of appeasing the fascist aggressors which Canada, along with the principal powers of Europe, had pursued in the 1930s was starkly revealed as a failure. Thus, abandoning its former neo-isolationism and appeasement orientation, Canada now adopted a posture of very active involvement in international affairs, determined to help put in place the international mechanisms necessary to ensure that any future territorial aggression was checked before there was a risk of escalation to another major war.

Canadian leaders also recognized that the rise of fascism in Germany, Italy, and Japan had been in part a consequence of the disruption caused by the economic depression of the 1930s. Preventing a recurrence of the economic chaos of that decade and the political turmoil it provoked clearly required an unprecedented degree of international co-operation. This involved the building of new economic institutions that would help to refurbish the war-torn economies of the European states and Japan, stabilize currencies, and encourage the general liberalization of trade. Canada's new active internationalism was thus also prompted in part by its interest in playing a constructive role in establishing those organizations that were put in place to deal with these issues—the International Bank for Reconstruction and Development (the World Bank), the International Monetary Fund, and the General Agreement on Tariffs and Trade (GATT). Moreover, as a country highly dependent on international trade for its own economic growth, Canada had a particular, vested interest in the development of these institutions, which would ensure the rapid reestablishment and preservation thereafter of an orderly, international trading environment.

It was, however, not only the lessons of the past that prompted a new internationalism on Canada's part, but new circumstances that confronted it and other states in the international system. The western European countries, allies and foes alike, lay in ruins after World War II, lacking the economic and military strength to check the similarly exhausted, but still powerful, Soviet Union. The latter, moving quickly after the war to consolidate its grip on the eastern European countries that the Red Army had occupied during the latter stages of the war, appeared poised to spread its physical and ideological control into western Europe. In effect, the historic balance of power in Europe that had in the past enabled United States isolationism was shattered, and North America—Canada and the United States together—was now required to restore it. The independence and vitality of the western European countries, so critical economically, politically, and culturally to the well-being of Canada and the United States, required a readiness on the part of Canada and the US to assume new international commitments. Consequently, Canada's surge of activism was accompanied by a similar trend in the United States, thereby eliminating one of the impediments to internationalism in the inter-war period.

At the same time, however, US involvement created new risks for Canada that added to the importance of its assuming international responsibilities. The Soviet Union and the United States were now the principal opposing powers in the international system, and the cold war that emerged between them meant that international politics had come to North America rather than being essentially a European affair. And Canada, sitting astride the shortest air route between the two super-powers, was placed in a vulnerable position should open hostilities arise between them. As Lester Pearson described the postwar situation, "Washington, not London, would determine, with Moscow, whether peace, progress, and even survival were possible. American policies, therefore, must be watched closely. From their consequences Canada could not escape."[7]

Under these new postwar circumstances, international involvement in terms of bilateral defence co-operation with the United States was inevitable, for North America was for all intents and purposes a single strategic area. However, beyond that, it was important that Canada be active on the diplomatic front, in both bilateral and multilateral forums, in order to influence to whatever modest degree it could the conduct of United States foreign policy, especially vis-à-vis the Soviet bloc. Any failures in the execution of US policy would have grave consequences for the security of Canada.

Finally, Canada's active internationalism after World War II can be seen as following logically from its evolution to autonomy in foreign affairs during the inter-war period. Since that process had been gradual and there was no clear, single moment when Canada attained full autonomy, there was arguably both a political and psychological need to assume a prominent international role as a means of affirming, for both foreign and domestic audiences, Canada's new constitutional status. Moreover, eternally preoccupied with the search for identity (the one assured identifying characteristic of Canada), Canadians perhaps began to see the potential for binding the country together that could be derived from national pride in winning accolades for its constructive role in fostering global peace, security, and prosperity. In fact, Canada's very lack of identity—the fact that it had no imperialist past and historic enmities, that it was a comparatively new and innocent kid on the block—seemed to equip it well for the mediating and peacekeeping roles that it was to be called upon to perform. In sum, then, there seemed some prospect of Canada's solving its identity problem by the very lack of one, and by assuming an internationalist image instead.

Determined to acquire a prominent place in the international organs that they envisaged would be established after the war, Canadian leaders in 1943 espoused the concept of middle powers and attempted to delineate a special institutional status for them. While their efforts met with only limited success, they did symbolize Canada's intent to be active in the new international order. Moreover, there was by now little question that, measured in terms of economic, military, and diplomatic capability, Canada was, indeed, a middle power. Further, its postwar international role was played out largely through its involvement in international organizations—the United Nations, the North Atlantic Treaty Organization, and the Commonwealth in particular—in which it frequently assumed mediatory functions that advanced the wider cause of international peace and security rather than any narrowly-defined Canadian interests. Thus, this type of diplomacy ("liberal internationalism," as it is sometimes called)[8] came to be particularly identified with middle powers like Canada.

One of the most prominent features of Canadian foreign policy during this second period was the country's strong commitment to the whole family of United Nations institutions. Hopeful that the United Nations could be used as a vehicle to deter aggression, the Canadian Parliament early on passed legislation granting the government at its discretion the power to put into effect immediately any economic sanctions called for by the UN Security Council, thus enabling Canada to respond quickly to international crises. Further, Canada indicated its willingness to enter into a special military agreement with the United Nations Security Council and the UN Military Staff Committee for the purpose of placing forces at the permanent disposal of the United Nations for collective security measures. Due to a deadlock between the super-powers in the Military Staff Committee, this aim was never accomplished. Nevertheless, in 1950, following an attack on South Korea by the communist forces of the North, the United Nations Security Council did establish a UN force composed predominantly of American troops to repel the attack. Canada, after initial hesitation, participated and some 27 000 Canadians served in Korea. The UN Korean operation was, however, an anomaly, made possible only by the absence of the Soviet Union from the Security Council when the force was established. The absence of the USSR was in protest over the UN's failure to replace the Chinese Nationalist government of Taiwan by the People's Republic of China in the Security Council and General Assembly following the successful conclusion of the Chinese communist revolution the preceding year. Thereafter, the friction between the Soviet

Union and the United States and the possession by the five "great powers" (the United States, Soviet Union, Britain, France, and China) of a veto in the Security Council rendered the collective application of either economic or military sanctions against almost any state virtually impossible.

Even before collective security via the United Nations proved stillborn, a new United Nations function related to peace and security emerged and Canada became particularly identified with it. This was the establishment of UN observer and peacekeeping forces in situations of regional strife. Intended, among other objectives, to monitor ceasefires in conflicts in the Third World in particular, these operations were (and remain) a means of preventing the renewal or escalation of fighting to the point where one or more major powers might be tempted to intervene to safeguard or advance their interests, thus risking a larger war. Accordingly, by their very nature, these are United Nations missions from which the great powers must be excluded. Yet, at the same time, UN observer and peacekeeping functions require well-trained forces capable of acting with restraint under circumstances of extreme provocation, and forces possessing specialized skills in such areas as signals, air and ground transport, air reconnaissance, engineering, medicine, administration, and languages. Canada was one of those middle powers whose forces possessed these characteristics and it was not surprising, therefore, given its willingness to assume such responsibilities, that Canada became closely associated with this important UN activity.

Probably the most famous UN operation from a Canadian standpoint was the United Nations Emergency Force (UNEF) dispatched to the Suez in 1956. Following a joint British, French, and Israeli assault on Egypt in response to the latter's nationalization of the Suez Canal, UNEF was designed to enter Egyptian territory, oversee the withdrawal of the invading forces, and maintain the peace thereafter. Because of Egyptian objections to Canadian infantry participating in the operation due to close association with Britain, Canada's direct contribution was relatively modest, although important, in that it provided many of the specialized services UNEF required, as well as the first commander of the force, General E.L.M. Burns. Most important, however, was the role that Lester Pearson, then Secretary of State for External Affairs in the Liberal government of Louis St. Laurent, played in conjunction with the Secretary-General of the United Nations in bringing this first-ever peacekeeping—as opposed to observer—force quickly into being. This occurred at a time when there was scepticism over the feasibility of the UN's launching such a sizable operation on short notice. For his efforts he was awarded the Nobel Peace Prize the following year, perhaps the high-water mark of the golden era of Canadian diplomacy.

Canada was involved in every such UN operation during this period, and at the peak in 1964, over 2000 Canadians were serving abroad under the UN flag. In that same year, the defence White Paper of the Pearson Liberal government set peacekeeping as the first priority for the armed forces of Canada and emphasized the development of flexible, mobile forces capable of being rapidly deployed abroad for such duties. Canada's enthusiastic support for UN observer and peacekeeping activities provided its foreign policy throughout this period with a distinct identity. At the same time, Canada was an ardent participant in the various economic and social programs of the United Nations and a generous contributor to its various specialized agencies and voluntary programs. Since much of this UN activity seemed unrelated to fulfilling any vested interests of its own—other than the goal of preserving international peace and stability so that all states, including Canada, might prosper—Canada's foreign policy appeared to some degree at least to reflect a selfless contribution to the betterment of the international community at large, the essence of liberal internationalism.

Another central dimension of Canadian foreign policy during this second period was its involvement in military alliances directed at containing the perceived threat of Soviet expansion. Most important in this respect was the North Atlantic Treaty Organization, which came into being in 1949. Born out of frustration at the failure of the United Nations to emerge as an effective instrument for collective security, NATO brought Canada and the United States together with several western European powers in an alliance under which the contracting parties pledged to come to the assistance of any member subject to attack. Since 1951, Canada has had troops stationed in Europe under the pact. From the outset—even when there were still reservations in the United States—Canada was a vigorous advocate of the importance of this treaty arrangement. Cognizant of Lenin's dictum, "If you strike steel, pull back; if you strike mush, keep going," Canada recognized that NATO could provide the evidence of resolve that would protect western Europe from Soviet aggression, thus enhancing the security of all Western countries.

However, apart from this strategic objective that it shared with the other members, Canada had its own particular reasons for favouring the alliance. A multilateral association, tying Canada together with the western European countries as well as with the United States, was preferable to an exclusively bilateral pact with the latter. Put bluntly, there was comfort for Canada in numbers, in view of its close proximity to the American giant. Moreover, a multilateral alliance offered the prospect of Canada's combining with other like-minded states in the pact in attempting to influence not only alliance policy, but also the approach to foreign affairs of the dominant member, the United States. Indeed, over the years Canada frequently combined with the other small NATO countries, such as Norway, Denmark, Belgium, and the Netherlands, in attempting to persuade the senior members, especially the United States, to adopt more forthcoming attitudes towards the nonaligned states and the Soviet bloc and towards fostering détente. Finally, Canada hoped that NATO could serve as the foundation for closer economic and political co-operation between western Europe and North America and the building of some form of North Atlantic Community, thereby helping to reduce future Canadian dependence upon the United States. Until the collapse in 1989 of the communist threat in Europe, the other members exhibited little interest in NATO as more than a military alliance. But, at Canada's insistence, Article 2, stressing economic and political co-operation, was inserted into the charter and it expresses in a general way the wider goals that Ottawa envisaged for the association. Often referred to as the Canadian article, it stands as a symbol of the somewhat different character of Canada's commitment to NATO from that of its allies.

Canada also became allied with the United States under bilateral arrangements during this period. Starting with the Ogdensburg Agreement of 1940 and the creation of the Permanent Joint Defence Board to plan the wartime defence of North America, the two countries bound themselves together militarily in recognition of the United States's dependence on Canadian territory and Canada's dependence on American hardware for their mutual defence against an extra-continental attack. Over the years this defence co-operation has been extended. It culminated in 1958 in the creation of the North American Air Defence Command, now known as the North American Aerospace Command, a pact designed essentially to protect the US nuclear deterrent against a manned bomber attack by the Soviet Union. NORAD provides an integrated command structure for the air defence of North America and under it Canada and the United States have co-operated in the establishment of radar warning systems in Canada and in developing the capacity to intercept Soviet bombers.

A final, central institutional dimension of Canadian foreign policy during this period was its membership in the Commonwealth, an informal, voluntary association comprised of Britain, the dominions, and most of the former colonies of the British Empire. The Commonwealth is a loose gathering of countries with a shared history that confer together on a wide range of international issues, exchange information, and assist one another through a number of projects, most of them today related to the development of Third World Commonwealth countries. For Canada, the Commonwealth was, and is, another important extra-continental link by which it can forge relations with other countries in the hope of reducing the dominance of the United States in its international affairs. More than that, in the context of the liberal internationalist character of Canadian foreign policy during this second period, the Commonwealth—its membership expanded in the 1950s and 1960s with the granting of independence to Britain's far-flung colonies in Asia, Africa, and the Caribbean—became a symbol of the capacity of vastly different states to work together harmoniously in a multiracial organization. It was thus seen as an important element in the building of a co-operative, and perhaps more just, world order.

On several occasions over the years, Canada has played a central role in Commonwealth deliberations on sensitive political issues, preventing splits along racial lines between the old white and new non-white members, splits that might otherwise have destroyed the organization. One of the most famous of these occasions occurred in 1961 when South Africa applied for continuing membership in the Commonwealth upon becoming a republic. In view of its apartheid policies, there was vigorous opposition among the non-white members to accepting this request, and the Canadian Conservative prime minister of the day, John Diefenbaker, was sympathetic to their position. At the 1961 conference, when the Commonwealth prime ministers failed to reach agreement on the issue of continued South African membership and on the language of the final communiqué of the conference, including a declaration on racial equality, which Diefenbaker favoured, South Africa withdrew its application. It was an incident that symbolized Canada's middle-power role of bridge building during this second period of internationalism.

An alternative, less positive perspective on Canadian foreign policy in this era also exists. It is one that sees, in effect, a continuation of the first period of dependence and peripheral status for Canada with the dominion now a client state of the United States rather than of Britain. From this standpoint, Canada's expanding trade and investment ties with the United States under the influence of the continentalist economic policies of the postwar King and St. Laurent governments, and Canada's dependence for its security on the armed might of the United States, left it no option but to function as a pliant, very junior partner of its southern neighbour. Looked at this way, Canada was in NATO to do the bidding of the United States and had no choice about co-operating with the Americans in NORAD, for the alternative would have been American disregard of Canadian sovereignty and the unilateral use of Canadian land and air space for its own protection.

Even Canadian observer and peacekeeping missions via the United Nations could be seen as possible only because the United States had a vested interest in their creation. Canada's non-recognition of the People's Republic of China throughout this period—despite the fact that this was incompatible with the inherited British tradition of recognizing governments with *de facto* power—was frequently pointed to as evidence of how Canada was obliged to subordinate its foreign policy to US interests and demands. However, perhaps nothing reflected Canada's dependent status more than its role in the International Commissions for Supervision and Control in Vietnam, Laos, and Cambodia. When the Geneva Conference of 1954 concluded a cease-fire in the protracted war in Indochina between the erstwhile colonial power, France, and the nationalist Viet Minh forces of Ho Chi Minh, Canada reluctantly accepted a role in the tripartite commissions responsible for supervising the accord. While the commissions had some early success in overseeing the withdrawal of troops, exchange of prisoners, and movement of civilian populations, fighting flared again, in particular in Vietnam between the communist North and non-communist South, which was increasingly aided militarily by the United States after the French departure. In time, Canada found itself isolated from the other commission members (Poland and India) in defending South Vietnam and the United States against charges of violating the Geneva agreement. As well, under its Defence Production Sharing Agreement with the United States, Canada profited substantially from US defence contracts related to fighting the war in Vietnam. To the defendants of Canadian foreign policy, Canada's role in Indochina was another example of middle-power diplomacy and liberal internationalism—of Canada's attempting to make a constructive, altruistic contribution to the preservation of international peace and security in trying circumstances. However, to the critics, it was a stark and depressing indication of Canada's status as a client state, there to help advance the counter-revolutionary interests of the United States.[9]

By the time the Conservative Diefenbaker government came to power in 1957, there was an emerging sense that perhaps Canada had, indeed, gone from the frying pan to the fire in its international dependence, and the administration witnessed some efforts—not always constructive—to assert Canadian autonomy vis-à-vis the United States. Thus, the Diefenbaker government continued normal commercial relations with Cuba despite a US economic boycott after Fidel Castro came to power in 1959. Canada hesitated at the outset in supporting the American naval quarantine of Cuba during the missile crisis of 1962 and resisted US pressure to join the Organization of American States. Canada also procrastinated on the question of accepting nuclear warheads from the United States for the Bomarc missiles with which it had agreed to equip itself under NORAD.[10]

Tension and disagreement have been endemic to the Canada–US relationship ever since the Diefenbaker years. It is true that from 1963 to 1968 the Pearson government took some steps to repair the bilateral rifts; most notably it reversed the Liberal Party's former position on nuclear warheads for the Bomarcs and accepted them. However, in 1967, Pearson angered US President Lyndon Johnson (to the point of a brief physical skirmish) by publicly calling for a pause in the US bombing of North Vietnam. Further, in 1963, in the first major attempt to do something about the steady drift to economic integration with the United States, the Liberals introduced a 30 percent takeover tax on the sale of Canadian companies to foreign shareholders. In the face of intense opposition from the North American corporate community, the measure was withdrawn. It was, however, a harbinger of the sustained friction to come in bilateral economic relations in the third period of Canadian foreign policy.

In sum, Canadian foreign policy in this era doubtless did to some degree resemble the initial period of dependence and peripheral status. However, as the Canada–US disagreements from 1957 onward attest, Canada had its own viewpoint on international developments and its own interests to defend, and it was prepared on occasion to tangle with the United States. Moreover, its prominent role in the United Nations and the Commonwealth as a peacemaker and bridger of differences lent a distinct character to its foreign policy, distinguishing it from both the United States and Britain. Indeed, even within NATO, while its role was more modest, Canada had interests of its own that it pursued, nudging the alliance towards accommodation with the Soviet bloc, in keeping with its middle-power role of attempting to advance the universal goals of international understanding, peace, and stability.

1968 TO THE PRESENT: THE AGE OF REALISM— CANADA AS A PRINCIPAL POWER?

When Pierre Elliott Trudeau succeeded Lester Pearson as prime minister in 1968, he launched a major review of Canadian foreign policy. It was prompted by the prime minister's conviction that several of the traditional elements of Canadian policy were of questionable contemporary relevance, and that existing foreign policy was not effectively serving Canada's own national interests. In particular, Canada's contributions in the areas of peace and security—the central core of its past internationalism—were re-evaluated. As a result, the government's review de-emphasized the function of United Nations peacekeeping. Ottawa was concerned with the financial difficulties and problems of authorization and control that had arisen with respect to past operations, and there was also a certain disillusionment because of the failure of peacekeeping to lead to a resolution of the underlying conflicts that had brought the UN missions into existence in the first place. Thus, Ottawa took the view that not only were such operations less likely to arise in the future, but that Canada would also have to be more cautious about assuming such responsibilities. Similarly, Canada signalled its reluctance, unless a number of specific conditions were met, to accept a new supervisory role in Indochina should an accord between North and South Vietnam and the United States lead to the creation of a reconstituted International Control Commission. Canada's traditional role in NATO was also questioned in light of the perceived diminished threat of Soviet territorial expansion in Europe and the revived capacity of the western European powers to defend themselves. Accordingly, in 1969, even before the government's foreign policy review was published, Canada cut in half the size of its NATO contingent based in Europe.

In short, the Trudeau era commenced with a turning away from the internationalism of the second period, derisively referred to as Canada's undue preoccupation with playing the role of the "helpful fixer." In its place was to be a preoccupation with advancing national interests. At home, Canada was confronted with challenges to national unity as a result of the political ferment in the province of Québec; to the environment from air and water pollution; to its jurisdictional claims in the Arctic and off its coasts from foreign encroachments; and above all, to its economic, cultural, and perhaps political autonomy by the rapid advance of continental integration. Foreign policy had to be reshaped to effectively meet these new circumstances. Realism was thus to be the defining principle in the future.

At the same time, it was widely held that the conditions were right for such a reorientation of Canadian foreign policy. The decline of US hegemony in an international system where power was increasingly diffuse—together with the waning of the cold war, which had imposed constraints on Canadian foreign-policy independence in the interests of alliance solidarity—meant that Canada was better able to pursue its own goals at the international level even when they differed from those of the United States. Further, whatever the government's own view of Canada's position in the international hierarchy of states, in this period many Canadians started to argue that given Canada's diplomatic prowess, its contribution to international security, commerce, and Third World development, and its leadership role in a range of international organizations, the country was now a "foremost nation," "principal," or "major" power.[11] With those appellations, purportedly, went an enhanced capacity to pursue its own interests rather than, as in the past, those of the international community at large. Starting in 1976, Canada's participation in the annual meetings of the Group of Seven leading industrial powers seemed to many to confirm its recent elevation. To the sceptical, however, this redefinition of Canada's international position was simply a contemporary manifestation of the country's age-old preoccupation with its status and identity, observable also in the first two periods. Nevertheless, whether or not Canada had really progressed from a middle power to some uncertain higher order, after 1968 its governments exhibited a new determination to root foreign policy, more narrowly defined, in the national interest. This did not mean avoiding an active international role, but fashioning a foreign policy that was less reactive to external developments and more initiatory in character in responding to the country's own needs.

One important dimension of the new approach has been an emphasis in the third period by both the Trudeau and Mulroney governments on relations with the Francophone states. Canada has become active in a host of Francophone organizations, principal among them being L'Agence de Coopération Culturelle et Technique. It is also a regular participant in summit meetings of the Francophone leaders—gatherings that parallel and balance Canada's historic association with the Commonwealth. Perhaps most important has been the establishment of a substantial development assistance program in the Francophone African countries. These initiatives represent a federal response to the international aspirations of Québec and are designed, in part, to demonstrate Ottawa's capacity to reflect through national foreign policy the bilingual and bicultural character of Canada, thus undercutting provincial sentiment in favour of control over at least some aspects of international relations. At the same time, Canada's generosity in aiding the Francophone African countries has served Canadian interests by undermining whatever proclivity they may have shown for supporting Québec's quest for international status on its own. Canada's leadership role today in la francophonie, as well as the Commonwealth, is one feature that lends distinctiveness to its foreign policy vis-à-vis other states.

Canadian foreign policy in this third period has also been preoccupied with a number of issues of direct concern to Canada from the simultaneous standpoints of sovereignty/jurisdiction and the environment.

In response to the voyage of the giant US tanker *Manhattan* through the Northwest Passage, in 1970 Canada passed the Arctic Waters Pollution Prevention Act, asserting its jurisdiction for purposes of controlling pollution 100 miles out to sea from the islands of the Arctic archipelago. It was a measure deemed illegal by the United States. At the same time, Canada adopted a twelve-mile territorial sea, asserting complete sovereignty within this zone and thus obliging any vessels attempting to traverse the Northwest Passage to enter Canadian waters. At this time, the United States recognized only a three-mile territorial sea. In 1977, Canada declared exclusive jurisdiction over a 200-mile fisheries zone off its coasts, asserting the right to set regulations governing catches.

Since countries like the United States and France adopted similar positions, another Canadian foreign policy concern involved reaching agreements with these states on the boundary between their zones where their claims overlapped—in areas such as the Gulf of Maine and off the French island possessions of St. Pierre and Miquelon. Negotiations with these and other fishing countries over the sizes of their annual catches in waters contiguous to Canada have been another ongoing foreign policy preoccupation during this third period as Canada attempts to conserve the ocean fisheries for future generations of Canadians.

Finally, in 1986, following the voyage of the US icebreaker *Polar Sea* through the Northwest Passage, Canada declared outright sovereignty over its entire Arctic archipelago, including the waters lying between the islands. This territorial assertion has not yet been accepted by the United States, although it has agreed in future to seek permission from Canada prior to its vessels using the Northwest Passage, but without prejudice to its position that this is an international waterway. To strengthen its Arctic claims, Canada announced a number of moves to demonstrate manifest occupation of the region, including a proposal to purchase a fleet of nuclear-powered submarines to patrol the area and monitor the movement of both American and Soviet submarines. This decision was greeted unenthusiastically by the two super-powers, but in 1989, for budgetary reasons, the proposed acquisition was cancelled. Nevertheless, the general thrust of Canadian Arctic and maritime policy has been indicative of Canada's tendency in the third period to pursue its own national interests even when they have been at variance with those of the major powers.

Other issues related to the environment, but without the sovereignty/jurisdictional connotations of the above, have also featured prominently in Canadian diplomacy in this third period, especially vis-à-vis the United States. These have included the negotiation of three Great Lakes Water Quality Agreements; the ultimately successful efforts to curb the Garrison Diversion project in North Dakota, with its negative environmental implications for the province of Manitoba; and protracted pressure, which met with little response until the Bush administration, to get the United States to treat seriously the problem of acid rain.

Canada has also risked friction with the United States during this third period by introducing new domestic measures designed to preserve and strengthen Canadian culture. Its purpose was to facilitate expression of the special character of Canada—its distinct regions and different ethnic and linguistic groups— through the arts and print and electronic media. These measures, which have embraced radio, television, film, and the periodicals industry in particular, have often been resented in the United States as unwarranted subsidies that impede the free flow of information and, more important, restrict access to the Canadian market for American cultural products.

Whether or not it was so intended at the outset, realism in the Trudeau years of this period, above all, took the form of economic policies designed simultaneously to enhance Canada's economic growth and reduce its dependence upon the United States. Two United States actions in particular precipitated this orientation.

In August 1971, because of its balance of payments difficulties, the United States imposed a 10 percent surcharge on a wide range of import items from other countries. While Canada sought a special exemption from the measure because of its potential devastating effect on vitally important exports to the United States, the Nixon administration refused the request. In the same year, the United States implemented the Domestic International Sales Corporation scheme, designed through tax incentives to induce multinational corporations to produce within the United States for export at the expense of their foreign subsidiaries. The two measures illustrated graphically Canada's vulnerability both to US restrictions on trade and to alterations in the flow of capital in view of its heavy dependence on trade with the United States and on US investment in Canada.

The Trudeau government responded with its "third option strategy." It was designed to reduce gradually Canadian dependence upon the United States by the diversification of economic and other relations, and by the adoption of interventionist economic policies that would bring about a higher level of Canadian ownership of the economy.

At the international level, "bilateralism" replaced Canada's past focus on international institutions to a certain degree, and efforts were made to cultivate relations with specific countries where there were deemed to be long-term prospects of developing commercial relations that would act as a counter to the preponderant weight of the United States in Canadian economic affairs. Even before the formal adoption of this new strategy, Canada announced its intention to seek diplomatic recognition of the People's Republic of China. These negotiations, undertaken at a time when the United States was still opposed to official relations, were successfully concluded in 1970. While the motivations for recognition were principally political (the necessity of involving China in world councils), the effect was, at the same time, to expand the commercial opportunities for Canada in a vast, potential market, and China today has become one of Canada's leading export destinations.

The early Trudeau years also saw the negotiation of a number of exchange agreements with the Soviet Union, including ones in the industrial area, and in absolute terms exports to this market expanded dramatically. At the same time, major trade missions were launched to Japan in an effort to secure better access for Canadian goods in what had long been viewed as a highly protected market. In 1973 Japan replaced Britain as Canada's second most important trading partner. Even in the Middle East, there was a subtle shift in Canadian policy to a more balanced position vis-à-vis the Arab–Israeli conflict as Canada sought to take advantage of the commercial opportunities that stemmed from expanding wealth based on oil in the Arab states, especially in Saudi Arabia. At the multilateral level, emphasis was placed on GATT negotiations to remove tariff and non-tariff barriers to trade with other countries, and in 1976 a contractual link was concluded with the European Economic Community, albeit a weak one, to foster commercial relations with a trading bloc of increased importance to Canada following British entry in 1973. Finally, in 1982 the Department of External

Affairs was reorganized, with the trade commissioners' service and trade policy administration being integrated into the ministry from the former Department of Industry, Trade and Commerce. It was a move that emphasized the government's intention to give particular attention to trade and other economic matters in its foreign policy in this age of hard-nosed business realism.

On the domestic front, a number of initiatives were taken in response to the American economic challenge, but two were especially noteworthy. In 1973, the Trudeau government established the Foreign Investment Review Agency to ensure that in future any takeovers of Canadian firms or new foreign investments were of "significant benefit" to Canada. Subsequently, in 1980, the Liberals adopted a National Energy Program that entailed provisions for Canadianization of the oil and gas industry, and an increased federal share in energy exploitation and revenues. Both measures were intensely disliked by the United States, especially during the Reagan administration, given that it launched a crusade for deregulation, including the elimination of obstacles to the free flow of capital, goods, and services.

Long before the Mulroney government came to power in 1984, it was already clear that the Liberals' third option strategy had met with only limited, if any, success. Despite substantial absolute increases in Canadian exports to many countries, especially in the Pacific region, in relative terms no real diversification of trade had been achieved. Indeed, a significantly higher proportion of Canadian trade was with the United States at the end of the Trudeau era than at the beginning. Currently, roughly three-quarters of Canada's total trade (exports and imports) is with the United States. The lack of competitiveness of many Canadian goods, the existence of regional trading blocs, and an international climate of protectionism had all conspired to render trade diversification ineffective. With respect to investment, a combination of government policies, together with changing patterns of international investment, did lead to a decline in foreign control of Canadian industry from a peak of 37 percent in 1971 to 24 percent by 1986. However, in the view of the Mulroney government, the concern for the future was not the undue presence of foreign investment in Canada, but the risk of disinvestment, and thus it was important for Canada to encourage new inflows of capital from the United States and abroad.

Conscious of the failure to achieve trade diversification, holding a more benign view about the implications of reliance on foreign capital, and anxious about a growing climate of protectionism in the United States, as well as the atmosphere of friction that had characterized bilateral relations over the preceding years, the Mulroney government set about changing the orientation of Canadian foreign policy. "Good relations, super relations with the United States will be the cornerstone of our foreign policy,"[12] the prime minister declared. In keeping with this outlook, his government successfully negotiated a Free Trade Agreement to ensure continued access to the United States market despite American protectionism. On 1 January 1989 the agreement went into effect, liberalizing economic intercourse between the two countries in a host of areas beyond the removal of remaining tariff barriers. At the outset of Mulroney's first term, the Foreign Investment Review Agency was replaced by Investment Canada, and the latter was assigned the new task of encouraging desirable foreign investment. Under the Free Trade Agreement its function of screening foreign investment has been further reduced so that since 1991 in most instances it only reviews takeovers above a value of $150 million. The Mulroney government also quickly set about dismantling much of the Liberals' National Energy Program, and under the Free Trade Agreement a type of continental energy market has been established with the United States. Canada negotiated assured access to the US for its energy and in return granted the United States a secure energy supply in periods of shortage.

Beyond bilateral economic matters, the Mulroney government also moved during the latter half of the 1980s to improve relations with the United States in other areas. In the context of NORAD, Ottawa committed itself to 40 percent of the costs of a major modernization of the North Warning System. In 1985, the government asserted that in its view research on the US Strategic Defence Initiative (SDI, President Reagan's so-called Star Wars program) was prudent and in conformity with the 1972 Anti-Ballistic Missile Treaty. The government's 1987 defence White Paper was replete with Reagan-style cold-war rhetoric and generally pledged Canada to increased military expenditures, something for which the United States had long been pressing. Further, over the last half of the decade, the Conservatives moved very cautiously in responding to the atmosphere of glasnost in the Soviet Union. Regarding Latin America, despite private reservations, Canada was reticent about criticizing the US application of an economic embargo against Nicaragua and its support for the anti-Sandinista Contras. In 1984 and 1987 respectively, Canada also restored bilateral aid to the American-supported governments of El Salvador and Guatemala—aid that had been terminated by the Trudeau government in part because of serious human rights violations in these two states. Finally, in 1989, the Mulroney government lent its support (albeit with reservations) to the American military intervention in Panama and, after decades of hesitation for fear membership might lead to a subordination of Canadian perspectives to US interests, Canada joined the Organization of American States.

The cumulative effect of these new directions in policy was to lead some observers to the view that Canada was reverting to the dependent status that characterized the first and, in the opinion of some, second periods of Canadian foreign policy. There is doubtless some truth to this position, but it is important to acknowledge that Ottawa has not meekly submitted to US demands in the area of free trade and elsewhere; the government is pursuing what it perceives, rightly or wrongly, to be the national interests of Canada. Further, significant foreign policy differences with the United States remain. Canada's assertion of Arctic sovereignty and its focus on surveillance of its own territory in its defence policy are examples. In addition, while initially endorsing research on SDI, Ottawa subsequently declined to participate in that research at the governmental level.

Just as Canadian policy in the third period has reflected some of the dependence that characterized the earlier periods so, too, has it continued to manifest to a certain degree the liberal internationalism of the second. Realism has not meant a full retreat from the policies of the past. In the end, Ottawa did not turn its back on United Nations peacekeeping, and over this last period it has been involved in several new operations in the Middle East, as well as ones in Afghanistan, Namibia, and Central America. Following a new cease-fire arrangement in Indochina in 1973, it also became involved briefly there in a reconstituted International Control Commission. Canada has dispatched more personnel abroad for UN peacekeeping duties than any other country, and has participated at some stage in virtually every peacekeeping mission launched by the UN, the only country that can make such a claim.

Despite its initial cutting of forces in Europe under NATO, during the 1970s the Trudeau government reequipped its troops there with new tanks, jet-fighter aircraft, and other equipment, reaffirming its commitment to the alliance. In part, this reflected a realization that support for NATO was a *quid pro quo* for strengthening its economic ties with the western European countries under the third option strategy. However, it also indicated an awareness that, at least until 1989, helping to maintain NATO's capacity to respond conventionally to any Soviet bloc provocation in Europe was an important contribution to preventing a rapid escalation to nuclear war. Finally, it demonstrated an appreciation that—dare one say it—for a middle power like Canada, NATO remained important in providing Canada with a seat at the table from which to influence modestly the shaping of US and alliance policy. Canada has also continued to play an active, if necessarily secondary, role in the field of arms control and disarmament, making a particularly valuable contribution in the ever-thorny area of verification of agreements.

Finally, in a stark departure from the professed new realism of Canadian policy, the Trudeau government launched a major expansion of Canada's developmental assistance activities in the Third World. From an annual program of only $300 million at the outset of the Trudeau years, Canadian aid expanded to $1.4 billion by the end of his era. At a time when other governments were in relative terms reducing their aid commitments, Canada was expanding its disbursements, making it one of the leading Western donors not only in the volume of its assistance but in the generosity of its terms. Until a retrenchment in 1989 due to the government's determination to cut the size of the Canadian deficit, Canadian aid continued to grow during the Mulroney years, reaching roughly $3 billion in 1988–89, and Canada has now also adopted a program consisting entirely of grants. Further, the last few years have also seen increased Canadian concern with the global question of human rights and some greater readiness on Canada's part to confront states guilty of gross and persistent violations of the basic rights of their citizens. South Africa stands out as one example; in 1985 and 1986 in particular, a series of limited sanctions were applied against the regime in response to its repressive policy of apartheid.

It is possible to make a variety of criticisms of the dimensions of Canadian foreign policy we have discussed that reflect a concern for social justice in keeping with the spirit of internationalism that was kindled after World War II. However, on balance they have been positive aspects of Canada's international role and have helped to give it a character distinct from many other countries, especially the United States and Britain.

CONCLUSION

In sum, responding to its own particular circumstances, Canada reflects in its foreign policy today elements of all three periods. Different observers may characterize Canadian policy as essentially dependent, internationalist, or realist. There are also differing perceptions of Canada's relative status in the hierarchy of states. Most, however, would agree that Canada has a foreign policy and diplomatic style that is peculiarly its own and that it has made, and continues to make, a significant and generally constructive contribution to world affairs.

Notes

[1] G. Smith, "Canadian External Affairs during World War I," in H.L. Keenleyside et al., *The Growth of Canadian Policies in External Affairs* (Durham, NC: Duke University Press, 1960), 48.

[2] The jurist, Archer Martin, in a letter to Prime Minister Mackenzie King. Quoted in J. Eayrs, *In Defence of Canada,: From the Great War to the Great Depression* (Toronto: University of Toronto Press, 1964), 5.

[3] Senator Raoul Dandurand in an address to the Fifth Assembly of the League of Nations, quoted in C.P. Stacey, *Canada and the Age of Conflict: A History of Canadian External Policies*, Vol. 2, *1921–1948, The Mackenzie King Era* (Toronto: University of Toronto Press, 1981), 61.

[4] Sir George Perley, quoted in G.P. de T. Glazebrook, *A History of Canadian External Relations*, Vol. 2, *In the Empire and the World, 1914–1939* (Toronto: McClelland & Stewart, 1966), 112.

[5] F.P. Walters, *A History of the League of Nations* (London: Oxford University Press, 1960), 493.

[6] L.B. Pearson, "Forty Years on: Reflections on Our Foreign Policy," *International Journal* 22 (Summer 1967): 359.

[7] L.B. Pearson, *Mike: The Memoirs of the Right Honourable Lester B. Pearson,* Vol. 1, *1897–1948* (Toronto: University of Toronto Press, 1972), 284.

[8] For a discussion of this concept, see D.B. Dewitt and J.J. Kirton, *Canada as a Principal Power: A Study in Foreign Policy and International Relations* (Toronto: John Wiley & Sons, 1983), 17–28.

[9] The principal studies exploring Canada's role in Indochina are: J. Eayrs, *In Defence of Canada, Indochina: Roots of Complicity* (Toronto: University of Toronto Press, 1983); D.A. Ross, *In the Interests of Peace: Canada and Vietnam 1954–1973* (Toronto: University of Toronto Press, 1984); and C. Taylor, *Snow Job: Canada, the United States and Vietnam (1954–1973)* (Toronto: House of Anansi Press, 1974).

[10] For a good, recent account of Canadian foreign policy in the Diefenbaker years, see H.B. Robinson, *Diefenbaker's World: A Populist in Foreign Affairs* (Toronto: University of Toronto Press, 1989).

[11] See in particular J. Eayrs, "Defining a New Place for Canada in the Hierarchy of World Power," *International Perspectives* (May/June 1975): 15–24; N. Hillmer, G. Stevenson, eds., *Foremost Nation: Canadian Foreign Policy and a Changing World* (Toronto: McClelland & Stewart, 1977), 2; P.V. Lyon, B.W. Tomlin, *Canada as an International Actor* (Toronto: Macmillan, 1979), 72; Dewitt and Kirton, *Canada as a Principal Power*, esp. 36–48; and A. Gotlieb, "Canada: A Nation Comes of Age," *Globe and Mail* (29 October 1987), A7.

[12] Quoted in S. Clarkson, *Canada and the Reagan Challenge: Crisis and Adjustment, 1981–85* (Toronto: James Lorimer, 1985), 358.

Bibliography

Clarkson, S. *Canada and the Reagan Challenge: Crisis and Adjustment, 1981–85.* Toronto: James Lorimer, 1985.

Dewitt, D.B. and J.J. Kirton. *Canada as a Principal Power: A Study in Foreign Policy and International Relations.* Toronto: John Wiley & Sons, 1983.

Eayrs, J. "Defining a New Place for Canada in the Hierarchy of World Power," *International Perspectives* (May/June 1975): 15–24.

Eayrs, J. *In Defence of Canada: From the Great War to the Great Depression.* Toronto: University of Toronto Press, 1964.

Eayrs, J. *In Defence of Canada, Indochina: Roots of Complicity.* Toronto: University of Toronto Press, 1983.

Glazebrook, G.P. de T. *A History of Canadian External Relations*, Vol. 2, *In the Empire and the World, 1914–1939.* Toronto: McClelland & Stewart, 1966.

Gotlieb, A. "Canada: A Nation Comes of Age," *Globe and Mail* (29 October 1987), A7.

Granatstein, J.L., ed. *Canadian Foreign Policy: Historical Readings.* Toronto: Copp Clark Pitman, 1986.

Granatstein, J.L., and R. Bothwell. *Pirouette: Pierre Trudeau and Canadian Foreign Policy.* Toronto: University of Toronto Press, 1990.

Hillmer, N., ed. *Partners Nevertheless: Canadian–American Relations in the Twentieth Century.* Toronto: Copp Clark Pitman, 1989.

Hillmer, N., and G. Stevenson, eds. *Foremost Nation: Canadian Foreign Policy and a Changing World.* Toronto: McClelland & Stewart, 1977.

Keenleyside, H.L., et al. *The Growth of Canadian Policies in External Affairs.* Durham, NC: Duke University Press, 1960.

Lyon, P.V., and B.W. Tomlin. *Canada as an International Actor.* Toronto: Macmillan, 1979.

Nossal, K.R. *The Politics of Canadian Foreign Policy.* Scarborough: Prentice-Hall, 1989.

Pearson, L.B. "Forty Years on: Reflections on Our Foreign Policy," *International Journal* 22 (Summer 1967): 357–363.

Pearson, L.B. *Mike: The Memoirs of the Right Honourable Lester B. Pearson*, Vol.1, *1897–1948.* Toronto: University of Toronto Press, 1972.

Robinson, H.B. *Diefenbaker's World: A Populist in Foreign Affairs.* Toronto: University of Toronto Press, 1989.

Ross, D.A. *In the Interests of Peace: Canada and Vietnam 1954–1973.* Toronto: University of Toronto Press, 1984.

Stacey, C.P. *Canada and the Age of Conflict: A History of Canadian External Policies*, Vol. 2, *1921–1948, The Mackenzie King Era.* Toronto: University of Toronto Press, 1981.

Taylor, C. *Snow Job: Canada, the United States and Vietnam (1954–1973).* Toronto: House of Anansi Press, 1974.

Tucker, M. *Canadian Foreign Policy: Contemporary Issues and Themes.* Toronto: McGraw-Hill Ryerson, 1980.

Walters, F.P. *A History of the League of Nations.* London: Oxford University Press, 1960.

Economic Policy
in Canada

Stephen Brooks

INTRODUCTION

Canadians enjoy the second highest standard of living in the world, surpassed only by Americans.[1] Physically, Canada is richly endowed with many of the natural resources that are vital to modern industry, and it has a water transportation system—the Great Lakes–St. Lawrence Seaway—that serves one of the world's most affluent markets. The labour force is highly educated and the social system is one of the most stable in the world. With all of these advantages, it might be expected that Canadians and their governments would be relatively complacent about their economy.

But they are not. In fact, the state of Canada's economy has been the subject of anguished hand-wringing for the last two decades, despite levels of economic growth and job creation that have out-performed those in most other advanced capitalist economies. Climbing inflation led the federal government to impose wage and price controls between 1975 and 1978, arguing that there was an economic crisis. A few years later the economy slipped into the deepest economic recession since the Depression of the 1930s. Economic growth ground to a stop (the economy actually shrank in 1982) and the unemployment rate reached 13 percent in 1983. This situation produced fears that Canada's postwar prosperity had been based on global circumstances that belonged to the past. Between 1985 and 1988 the political agenda was dominated by the issue of free trade with the United States, a policy that Canadians and their governments had rejected for more than a century. Those who favoured free trade and those who rejected it agreed on one thing: Canada's economy required new policy directions in order to compete in the changing world economy.

An uneasy sense that things could soon go seriously wrong seems to be a permanent feature of the Canadian economic scene. Why? Can a country with Canada's enviable record of prosperity really have much to worry about? To answer this question, we need to look more closely at the structure of the Canadian economy. Embedded in it are problems that explain why Canadians and their governments are not more complacent about the economy.

CANADIAN INDUSTRIAL STRUCTURE

The term *industrial structure* is used to describe the principal characteristics of economic production and distribution within a geographic area. These characteristics include the sectoral balance of economic activity, the pattern of international trade, the regional distribution of industry, the level of foreign ownership, and the degree of competition in an economy and in particular industries. A country's industrial structure plays a key role in determining the economic policy agenda of governments. The particular way economic problems are defined and the policy measures taken by governments will, however, depend on the specific configuration of political influence within industries, regions, society as a whole, and the state itself.

In this section we examine the main features of Canada's industrial structure and the economic policies associated with them.

❏ THE SECTORAL BALANCE

Only about 6 percent of Canadian workers and just under 10 percent of gross domestic product are accounted for by industries such as farming, fishing, forestry, and mining—the industries that make up the primary sector of the economy. Yet a stereotype of Canadians as "hewers of wood, drawers of water" persists. In fact, the sectoral distribution of industrial activity in Canada is not much different from that in the United States or in other major capitalist economies (the G-7). Canada has a somewhat smaller manufacturing sector compared to these other economies, but at the same time service industries account for a marginally greater share of total employment in Canada compared to the G-7 average. The overall message that emerges from the data is one of similarity, not difference, between Canada and other advanced capitalist economies.

Canada's sectoral balance of industrial activity resembles that of its G-7 partners in another important respect. The share of total employment accounted for by the manufacturing and primary sectors of the economy has declined over the last few decades, while the service sector has grown. This trend has been labelled "de-industrialization." Only in Japan has the share of total employment in manufacturing increased since 1960, and there only marginally (1964: 24.3 percent; regular type 1981: 24.9 percent).[2] But if instead of employment share we look at each sector's contribution to GDP, we find that manufacturing has held its ground in Canada as elsewhere among the G-7 economies. The only exception is the

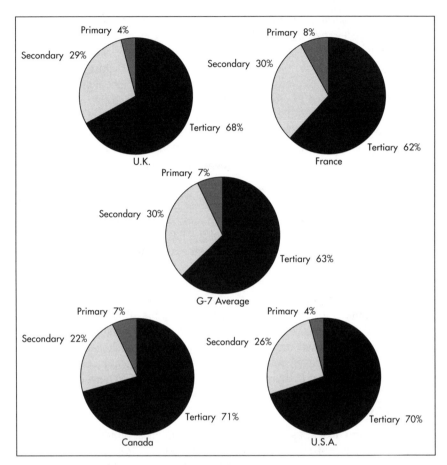

Figure 1   Employment by Sector—Various Countries, 1986

United Kingdom, where the contribution of manufacturing to GDP fell from 28.5 percent in 1960 to 24.2 percent in 1981. In Canada, manufacturing accounted for 19.6 percent of GDP in 1961 and 19.7 percent in 1987.[3]

In light of these similarities between the balance of industrial activity in Canada and in the other major capitalist economies, why does the image of Canada as a resource hinterland persist? The answer lies in particular features of Canadian manufacturing. Critics charge that this sector tends to be weak and internationally uncompetitive, with an extraordinary share of manufactured exports dependent on the Auto Pact with the United States. Too much of Canada's international trade, they argue, still depends on the export of raw materials. This resource dependence is particularly striking in the case of several provincial economies. British Columbia (forest products), Alberta (petroleum), Saskatchewan (grain and potash), and Québec (hydro-electric power) all fall into this category.

How have governments in Canada responded to this sectoral balance of economic activity? First of all, they have not always viewed reliance on natural resource industries as a disadvantage. There is a long history of state-subsidized megaprojects in Canada, based on the extraction and export of particular resources such as oil, gas, coal, and hydro-electric power. But there is an even longer history of efforts to promote activity in the manufacturing sector of the economy, efforts that date from the first tariffs imposed on imported manufactures in the mid-1800s.[4] Policies intended to shape the sectoral balance of industrial activity may be grouped under four major headings: tariffs, industrial subsidies, diversification, and research and development.

TARIFFS

High tariffs on manufactured goods coming into Canada were the centrepiece of the Conservative government's National Policy of 1879. Tariffs remained high for most of Canada's history, although today the average tariff level in Canada is about the same as it is in the other G-7 economies. The main purpose of tariffs has been to protect domestic producers from foreign competition in the Canadian market. Tariffs have certainly performed this function, making viable domestic industries that would not otherwise have been profitable. But tariffs have also contributed to the high level of foreign ownership in the Canadian economy, as foreign producers "jumped" the tariff wall by establishing branch plants in Canada. Moreover, high tariffs have encouraged the growth of inefficient industries, able to sell in the sheltered domestic market but incapable of competing abroad.

INDUSTRIAL SUBSIDIES

Governments in Canada, as in other capitalist economies, provide various direct and indirect forms of support for private industry. Some of this support is directed at primary industries such as agriculture, mining, and forestry. For example, a recent OECD study estimates that the cost of each farm job saved in Canada by production quotas, price floors, tax relief, and other public subsidies to agriculture is about $115 000, and that farm output would drop 17 percent if all forms of agricultural protection were eliminated.[5]

But much of the financial support that governments provide to private business is directed at manufacturing industries. The political explanation for these subsidies is fairly straightforward: an investment in manufacturing tends to generate more and (often) better-paying jobs than an equivalent investment in primary industry. Added to this is the fact that most people associate manufacturing with a modern, affluent economy, creating strong political pressures to subsidize such industries in regions where private businesses would not otherwise invest. In Canada's industrial heartland between Windsor and Montreal, the political pressures to subsidize manufacturing are even greater than in the peripheral regions of the country.

DIVERSIFICATION

Some of Canada's provincial governments have attempted to use their natural resource wealth to promote a more diversified industrial base. Québec, for example, has used its multibillion-dollar investments in hydro-electric power to promote provincial industries that supply the materials needed for these enormous capital projects. The lure of cheap, abundant electrical power has been used to attract some industries, notably aluminum smelting (even though Québec has no bauxite, the raw material for aluminum). Alberta governments have attempted to pump some of the revenue generated from that province's petroleum wealth into industrial diversification. In part, this has been done through investments of the Alberta Heritage Savings Trust Fund, the second largest pool of state investment capital in Canada, surpassed only by the *Caisse de dépôt et placement du Québec*.[6] Despite the fact that these efforts to broaden the industrial base date from the mid-1970s, Alberta's dependence on the petroleum industry remains undiminished.

Resource wealth is not the only fund that provinces draw on in attempting to diversify their economies. The provincially owned *Caisse de depôt et placement du Québec* has played an important role in channelling public savings into Québec-based corporations, including some of the province's major manufacturing and retail firms.[7] Three of Nova Scotia's most important private sector manufacturing establishments, Michelin Tire, Volvo, and Litton Industries, were attracted to the province partly on the strength of the public subsidies they received. Nova Scotia is also home to some of Canada's most celebrated industrial assistance failures, most notably the Glace Bay heavy water plant and the Sydney Steel Company. There is not much evidence from Nova Scotia or the other provinces that government efforts to diversify the industrial structure are enough.

RESEARCH AND DEVELOPMENT

Compared to its G-7 partners, and even to many smaller industrial economies, Canada spends little on research and development activity. This has long disturbed critics of Canada's industrial structure. They argue that this underinvestment in R & D is at the root of Canada's inability to produce internationally competitive manufacturing industries. In particular, these critics pin the blame on foreign-owned corporations whose Canadian subsidiaries tend to import R & D from their parent corporations.

Are the critics right? The evidence is unclear. Some argue that a low level of domestic R & D makes no difference, because a good deal of "invisible R & D" is imported into Canada through technology transfers between foreign corporations and their Canadian subsidiaries. Foreign ownership, they argue, actually increases the speed at which technological innovations are adopted in Canadian industry. Furthermore, the claim that foreign-owned firms spend less on R & D than their Canadian-owned counterparts is disputed by some studies.[8]

❑ INTERNATIONAL TRADE

Roughly one-quarter of Canada's national income is generated from export trade with other national economies. Compared to the other G-7 countries, only West Germany has depended more on exports (although German reunification, and the larger domestic market this has produced, is likely to reduce this dependence). About one-fifth of Canada's national income depends on trade with a single partner: the United States. No other advanced capitalist economy comes close to matching this level of dependency on trade with one other country. In 1989, exports to the United States amounted to three-quarters of total Canadian exports, and imports from the United States constituted about 70 percent of all imports. Canada's trade dependence on the United States has increased steadily since World War II.[9]

Trade consists of both merchandise and service transactions. Merchandise involves physical goods ranging from unprocessed resources to finished products. Services include such transactions as tourism, interest and dividend payments to foreigners, and business services such as patent and management fees. Since 1960, Canada has accumulated a surplus in its merchandise trade during every year except one (1975). On the other hand, Canada has registered a deficit in service transactions every year since 1950. The service transaction deficit is usually greater than the merchandise trade surplus, resulting in an overall balance-of-payments deficit during most years.

One of the long-standing criticisms of Canada's industrial structure is that our export trade is too dependent on natural resources. While this was once a fair observation, it no longer captures the reality of Canadian trade. Finished products accounted for only 7.7 percent of total exports in 1960, but comprised 42.7 percent of the total in 1987. This is not remarkably lower than the average for most advanced industrial economies (50–60 percent). Most of this growth in the export of manufactured goods has been in automobiles and automotive parts going to the United States under the Auto Pact. In fact, trade under the Auto Pact accounts for about 60 percent of the value of all Canadian manufactured exports and about one-quarter of total exports. The increasing importance of finished products in Canadian export trade has not produced a more diversified trading pattern. Automotive and wood products together account for about 40 percent of total Canadian exports. Not only is Canada extraordinarily dependent on a single foreign market, it is also highly dependent on a narrow range of products.

International trade is more important to some provincial economies than to others. Exports account for between one-quarter and one-third of provincial GDP in the most export-dependent provinces, and between 8 and 15 percent in the least trade-oriented provinces.[10] There are no clear regional divisions in dependence on international trade. For instance, over one-quarter of Ontario's GDP depends on exports compared to about 15 percent in Québec. In Atlantic Canada, exports account for about twice the share of New Brunswick's GDP as compared to Nova Scotia's, and about three times the share of that of PEI.

Regional divisions are clearer when it comes to manufactured exports. Most manufacturing is based in Ontario and Québec, and most manufactured exports originate from these provinces. Historically, the governments of these provinces have supported tariff barriers that primarily benefited producers in Central Canada, while the other provincial governments have tended to favour in varying degrees lower tariffs or even free trade with the United States (see figure 2).

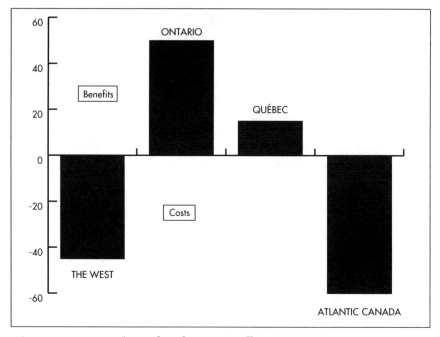

Figure 2   Costs and Benefits of Import Tariffs (per capita, 1983)

Source: The Economist, 15 Feb. 1986, p.16

Trade policy has been a vital and controversial cornerstone of Canadian economic policy since before Confederation. As we mentioned earlier in this chapter, high tariffs were one of the pillars of the National Policy of 1879. The 1879 tariffs have been described by historian A.R.M. Lower as "a frank creation of vested manufacturing interests living on the bounty of government."[11] The general level of tariffs on imports was increased sharply at the beginning of the Depression of the 1930s, but has declined steadily since World War II and is today at an all-time low of about 4 percent.

Although the overall thrust of Canadian trade policy has been strongly protectionist for most of this country's history, a counter-tendency favouring free trade with the United States has always existed. The Liberal government of Wilfrid Laurier actually negotiated a trade reciprocity treaty with the United States government in 1911, but lost the subsequent election which was fought, in part, on the free trade issue. Sectoral free trade between Canada and the United States was established by the 1959 Defence Production Sharing Agreement, a treaty that extended a 1941 agreement to establish free trade between the defence industries of the two countries, and by the 1965 Auto Pact.

Fears that Canada's growing dependence on the American market produced an unhealthy vulnerability to economic and policy shifts in the United States led to the adoption in the early 1970s of what was called the Third Option trade policy. The idea was simple enough: reduce Canada's exposure to events in the United States by increasing trade with other economies, particularly those of the Pacific rim and the European Economic Community (EEC).

Unfortunately the idea lacked realism. The Japanese market bristled with a variety of protectionist barriers and, in any case, Japanese manufacturers were so competitive at home and abroad that it was unlikely that Canada could sell Japan anything but a bit more coal, lumber, or newsprint. The EEC was chock-a-block with internal protectionism, and the idea of Canada's achieving some formal link with the community was a non-starter. Finally, the potential of developing countries as a market for Canadian exports was limited because of their inability to pay and because much of what Canada could export to them was produced more cheaply by their own companies (e.g., clothing, footwear) or could be purchased more cheaply from Japan, the United States, or the EEC. By the end of the 1970s, Canada's trade dependence on the United States was even greater than when the Third Option was launched, so that the policy was allowed to die an unceremonious death.

Canadian trade policy appeared to take a sharply different tack in 1985 when the Conservative government announced its intention to seek a free trade agreement with the United States. In fact, however, some tentative efforts in the direction of bilateral free trade had already been made in 1983. The previous Liberal government had been unsuccessful in its attempts to negotiate sectoral free trade deals for products such as steel, urban transit machinery, agricultural machinery, and informatics. Why were Canadian governments now converts to some form of free trade with the United States?

The answer is that changes in the global economy and in the political climate of the United States made the policy *status quo* untenable. The global economy had become a labyrinth of non-tariff barriers to trade. But whereas the members of the EEC had free access—or at least were heading in this direction—to the Community's market, and both Japan and the United States had large domestic markets, Canadian producers could count on free access to only a relatively small domestic market of 25 million people. Even more to the point, mounting protectionist sentiment in the American Congress erupted in a number of sectoral trade disputes between Canada and the United States during the 1980s. A bilateral free trade agreement, its advocates maintained, would insulate Canada from American hostility over that country's enormous trade deficit.

The Canada–United States Free Trade Agreement (FTA) came into force on 2 January 1989. It is a comprehensive trade agreement that not only eliminates all tariff barriers between the two economies—some immediately and others gradually—but also does the following:

- provides "national treatment" for American investors in Canada and vice versa;
- eliminates most federal government discrimination against the other country's suppliers in competitions for government contracts;
- commits Canada to maintaining energy supplies to the United States, even in the event of a Canadian shortage;
- establishes a bi-national tribunal with authority to decide whether one country's exports are unfairly dumped or subsidized in the other country, causing injury to the receiving country's industry;
- declares agreement to define, within 5–7 years, what constitutes unfair government subsidies.

The FTA goes well beyond tariffs into the realm of unfair government subsidies and non-tariff barriers to trade (NTBs). Canadian economic policy includes many examples of these, some of them obvious and others more discreet. Quotas on particular imports; voluntary restraint agreements by which a country agrees to limit its exports to Canada; government purchasing that discriminates in favour of Canadian suppliers; and countervailing duties against imports from a country whose government is judged to have unfairly subsidized exports are obvious NTBs. Investment incentives to business that have the effect of reducing the producer's costs and therefore making its products more competitive on export markets are also NTBs. In a celebrated case that transpired during the Canada–United States free trade negotiations, the American Department of Commerce ruled that Canada's softwood lumber industry was unfairly subsidized by government because the fee charged to companies for the right to chop down trees was too low. Canadian stumpage fees were considered to be export subsidies. Many of the FTA's critics claim that several of Canada's social programs, including medicare, public pensions, workers' compensation, and unemployment insurance, may ultimately be defined as unfair subsidies under the FTA. Time will tell.

❑ THE REGIONAL DISTRIBUTION OF INDUSTRY

In a country as physically vast as Canada, one would expect to find significant differences in the sorts of economic activities that predominate in different regions. The demands that different regional interests make on the government are often incompatible, giving rise to political conflict and even national disunity. There is a long history of such disputes in Canada, rooted in the claims of the western and eastern provinces that Ottawa's economic policies favour central Canadian interests.

Over 55 percent of Canada's population, over 60 percent of national income, and over 70 percent of manufacturing employment are concentrated in the narrow belt running from Windsor, Ontario to Québec City. Most of the country's largest corporations and financial institutions are located in this industrial heartland, particularly in Toronto and Montreal. Per capita earned income is higher in Ontario than in any other province. Québec is not as affluent as Ontario, but its significant manufacturing sector has provided the basis for shared interests with Ontario, often in opposition to the other provinces.

Resource industries tend to be more crucial to the health of the western and eastern provinces than to the economies of Ontario and Québec. Fisheries and forestry, as well as allied processing industries such as fish processing and pulp and paper, are key industries in Atlantic Canada. Unemployment rates there are the highest in Canada and personal incomes are the lowest (see figure 3).

In the three Prairie provinces of Manitoba, Saskatchewan, and Alberta, agriculture, petroleum, and mining are vital industries. Agriculture continues to account for about 10 percent of the Prairie work force (compared to about 4 percent for Canada as a whole), and over 20 percent of employment in Saskatchewan. Almost one-quarter of this region's exports are farm products. Petroleum is particularly important to Alberta's economy, while gas, uranium, and potash are major primary industries in Saskatchewan. Altogether, the primary sector accounts for over one-quarter of the region's GDP, and over one-third in both Alberta and Saskatchewan.

British Columbia's economy is, of all the provinces, the most dependent on natural resources. Forest products account for over 50 percent of BC's exports, and 85–90 percent of all exports are resource-based products. Over three-quarters of the province's manufacturing activity involves processing natural resources, including paper and wood products, food processing, refining petroleum and coal, and mineral processing.

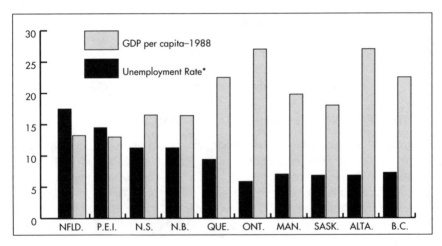

Figure 3   Regional Variations in Gross Domestic Product and Unemployment Rates

* Provincial unemployment rates as of May 1990.

Source: Statistics Canada, Canadian Economic Observer (Ottawa: Supply and Services, monthly).

In a broad sense, Canada has always had something that could be called a regional industrial policy. Tariffs and railway lines were hotly contested political issues in the post-Confederation period precisely because they were expected to have different economic consequences for different regions. The political weight of business interests in Central Canada, and the votes at stake in Ontario and Québec, have translated into federal economic policies that have tended to favour the industrial heartland at the expense of consumers and industries in the hinterland regions.

While Ottawa's economic policies have always had consequences for the pattern of regional industrial development in this country, the beginnings of regional industrial policy as a specialized field of economic policy with its own bureaucratic apparatus date from the late 1960s. The creation in 1968 of the Department of Regional Economic Expansion (DREE) raised the profile of regional industrial policy by giving it an institutional focus. DREE provided both a symbolic affirmation of Ottawa's commitment to assisting the economies of the have-not provinces and a channel through which this assistance would flow. Since then, Ottawa's regional economic policy has undergone several major reforms affecting the manner in which economic assistance decisions are made and implemented. Primary responsibility for this policy field currently rests with the Department of Regional Industrial Expansion (DRIE). The evolution of federal policy in this field has been extensively documented by others.[12]

Federal assistance from DREE to DRIE and business investment incentives available under the tax system have been geared towards encouraging the sort of industrial activity that characterizes Central Canada's industrial economy. This emphasis, economist Harvey Lithwick argues, may well run counter to an optimal strategy for national economic development. Lithwick suggests that if the well-being of the national economy is best promoted by specialization—which means in effect that different regions of the country will have different sectoral mixes, depending on their particular advantages—then a policy that encourages economic diversity within all regions is economically wrong-headed.[13] The federal Task Force on Program Review acknowledged this contradiction in its assessment of regional development programs. In the words of its report,

> Unfortunately national economic efficiency does not easily fit with interregional equity. . . . [F]or example, while the expansion of a plant may provide benefits for the region in which it is located, it could be adding capacity to an industry which on the whole is already suffering from an over-capacity situation.[14]

Of course, such a policy may carry political advantages. Controversy over the Conservative government's 1988 decision to award a multimillion-dollar service contract for the CF-18 fighter planes to Montréal-based Bombardier instead of to Winnipeg-based Bristol Aerospace—despite a bureaucratic recommendation that the Winnipeg company be chosen—just confirmed how important these political considerations are in Ottawa's decisions on where to locate job-creating investments. This and other procurement decisions constitute an important part of Ottawa's regional economic assistance. Indeed, the shipbuilding industry of eastern

Canada has been sustained for decades by federal purchases. New Brunswick's share of the Canadian Patrol Frigate contract awarded in 1984 caused the level of federal procurement dollars spent in that province to jump five-fold to about $1000 per capita (compared to $321 per capita for Canada as a whole in 1983–84).[15]

We should not conclude, however, that the economies of the have-not provinces have been the only (or even the main) beneficiaries of Ottawa's procurement policy. The Task Force on Program Review reported that the per capita level of spending by the federal government between 1979 and 1984 was higher in Ontario than in any other province.[16] Despite Ottawa's efforts to decentralize purchasing, the locational and industrial advantages of Ontario continue to give its economy a formidable edge in the competition for federal government contracts.

There is a consensus that the billions of dollars of economic assistance that successive federal governments have channelled into the economically weaker provinces has not promoted the ostensible goal of economic development. The economies of these provinces show no signs of having become less dependent on the public life-support system. Public sector investment accounts for close to half of all investment in Atlantic Canada. The investment incentives provided under DRIE and through the tax system have been accused of multiple sins: of encouraging an inefficient pattern of investment; of having a bias towards investment in new capital rather than job creation; and of transferring income to business that would have invested anyway, without producing new jobs in a self-sufficient private sector. But as Donald Savoie and John Chenier observe,

> The fact remains that no researcher has ever been able to state clearly the full impact of regional incentives either on slow-growth regions or on the location intentions of firms, even those that did receive a grant. About all that can be said is that things could have been worse for slow-growth regions if no regional incentives had been available.[17]

❑ FOREIGN INVESTMENT

Canada has always relied heavily on foreign capital for its economic development. Much of the money needed to construct the network of roads, railways, and canals that knit together the commercial economy of nineteenth-century Canada came from British investors. Canadian companies and governments actively sought to sell their bonds to foreign investors, particularly in London. Bonds pay interest to the creditor, but do not carry ownership rights. At Confederation, Canada was heavily in debt, although the level of foreign ownership of Canadian assets was not significant.

By the end of the nineteenth century, the pattern of foreign investment had started to swing towards greater dependence on *direct investment,* i.e., foreign investors actually owned productive assets in Canada. The largest proportion of direct investment came from the United States. The Canadian government was itself instrumental in promoting this influx of foreign ownership. The Patent Act of 1872 encouraged foreign companies to establish Canadian production facilities. In this way they would receive longer patent protection than if they served the Canadian market from abroad. Even more important, however, were the high tariffs of 1879. In order to avoid paying import duties that averaged about 28 percent, foreign companies often found it worthwhile to set up a subsidiary—sometimes called a branch plant—to serve the Canadian market. Historian Michael Bliss estimates that by 1913 about 450 American subsidiaries had been established in Canada. By the 1920s, American-based firms already dominated several of the fastest-growing industries in Canada's manufacturing sector, including automobiles, electrical products, drugs, and chemicals. It was during this decade that American investment surpassed British investment as the largest source of foreign capital in Canada.[18] Foreign investors controlled about one-fifth of the Canadian economy before World War II.

The level of foreign ownership increased significantly during the 1950s. Most of this increase was American investment. By the 1960s American capital accounted for over 60 percent of all investment in the petroleum and natural gas industries, over 50 percent of total investment in mining and smelting, and about 45 percent of all manufacturing investment.[19] The level of foreign ownership peaked in the early 1970s at about 37 percent of all economic assets. It has declined steadily since then, due mainly to Canadian takeovers of foreign-owned firms and the expansion of domestic capital. Today, foreign investors control less than one-quarter of all corporate assets in Canada (see figure 4).

When foreign investment first came to Canadian shores, no one imagined it to be harmful in any way. This benign attitude began to change in the 1950s. A series of major government studies in 1956, 1968, and 1972 all raised serious doubts about the effects of high levels of foreign ownership on the performance of Canada's economy. Public opinion polls taken during the 1960s showed that Canadians were becoming less favourable towards foreign investment, particularly from the United States.[20]

The chief criticisms levelled against foreign direct investment include the following:

- *Exports and Imports*. Foreign-owned manufacturing firms tend to produce only for the Canadian market. They also tend to import from their parent corporation, contributing to Canada's chronic trade deficit in service transactions (discussed earlier in this chapter).
- *R & D*. Foreign-owned firms add little to industrial innovation and new product development in Canada, because R & D activities are usually carried out at the parent corporation.
- *Balance of Payments*. Some of the profits generated by foreign-owned businesses leave Canada. These outflows take the form of dividends to foreign shareholders, income transfers from subsidiaries to their parent corporations, and various other payments such as licensing fees for the use of technology owned by the foreign parent corporation. According

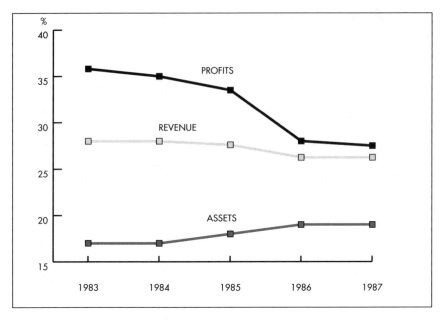

Figure 4   Foreign-Controlled Shares of Assets, Revenues, and Profits (all industries, 1938–87)

Source: Statistics Canada, Corporations and Labour Unions Returns Act (Ottawa: Supply and Services, March 1990, chart 1.1)

to one estimate, foreign-ownership-related payments amounted to $64 billion, or four-fifths of Canada's total service transaction deficit, between 1975 and 1982.[21]

- *Extra-territoriality.* The Canadian subsidiaries of foreign corporations are affected by the laws under which their parent corporations operate. This was particularly significant in the 1960s. In response to a large balance-of-payments deficit, the United States government passed legislation encouraging American-based multinationals to repatriate earnings made abroad rather than reinvesting them in the branch-plant economy. Other instances of the extra-territorial application of American laws to corporations operating in Canada have included the export sales retrictions imposed under the Trading with the Enemy Act, and demands by American courts and congressional committees for documents from the Canadian subsidiaries of US parent corporations in connection with anti-trust investigations. The extra-territoriality issue is rather dated, but it is still raised by nationalists to illustrate how Canada's political sovereignty may be compromised by extensive foreign ownership.

There is no consensus that foreign ownership, rather than other factors, is responsible for the low levels of Canadian R & D and manufactured exports.

Extra-territoriality is, if not a dead issue, no longer a serious cause for concern. The balance of payments problems caused by foreign ownership are, however, undeniable. Trade deficits that are due largely to foreign-ownership-related outflows put upward pressure on Canadian interest rates, simply because the Canadian economy must attract the foreign capital—mainly American—needed to make these payments to foreigners.

Canadian policy towards foreign investment has swung from being mildly restrictive in the 1970s to open armed in recent years. In 1973 the federal government established the Foreign Investment Review Agency (FIRA), a regulatory agency empowered to screen all new foreign investments. In 1975 FIRA's mandate was extended to cover expansion by existing foreign-owned businesses into new fields of activity. At the political level FIRA was an ongoing irritant in Canadian–American relations, especially after the Reagan administration came to power in 1980. But in terms of its actual effects, it is not clear that FIRA was a significant barrier to foreign investment. Critics of FIRA claim that it was a symbolic gesture intended to appease nationalist demands for some sort of controls. They argued that the approval rate of approximately 90 percent over FIRA's lifetime demonstrated that it was not a serious barrier to new foreign investment. Others have argued that the screening process may have discouraged potential foreign investors, so that the apparently high approval rate cannot be taken at face value. In addition, the fact that FIRA would bargain with applicants to ensure that their investment was of "significant benefit" to Canada is another reason for not drawing conclusions on the basis of the approval rate alone. In the end, FIRA satisfied neither the nationalists, who always viewed it as a paper tiger, nor those who felt that such a highly visible screening agency had adverse economic consequences.

FIRA was transformed into Investment Canada in 1985. The new agency's avowed function is to encourage investment. With the exception of screening and approval requirements for new foreign investments in cultural industries and for foreign takeovers above a certain value (gross assets above $5 million in the case of a direct takeover and above $50 million in the case of an indirect acquisition), foreign investment would no longer be reviewed.

The rules regulating foreign investment were relaxed even further by the Canada–United States Free Trade Agreement. Under the FTA, only direct acquisitions of assets valued at $150 million or more are subject to review by Investment Canada. This applies only to American investments, however. Other countries' investments are subject to lower review thresholds.

It is unlikely that FIRA merits much of the credit for declining levels of foreign ownership since the mid-1970s. By contrast, the National Energy Program, introduced in 1980, had a very clear impact on the balance of Canadian versus foreign ownership in the petroleum and gas industry. One of the main objectives of the NEP was to increase Canadian ownership in the oil and gas sectors to 50 percent by 1990. In fact, Canadian ownership increased from 28 to 34.7 percent during the NEP's first eighteen months,[22] but currently remains well below the 50 percent target. The NEP was eliminated by the Conservative government in

1985. Canadianization of the energy industry received a setback with the 1987 takeover of Dome Petroleum by Amoco of Chicago.

Although it is tempting to emphasize the fact that the level of foreign owner-ship in Canada continues to be higher than in any other advanced capitalist economy, this difference should not be allowed to overshadow an important similarity between Canada and these other economies. This involves the extent to which capital has become international. The fact that several of Canada's leading corporations are the subsidiaries of foreign parents has become less and less remarkable. For example, nine of the largest thirty-five industrial corpora-tions in Canada in 1987 were foreign-owned.[23] But in the UK, the presence of foreign capital among the largest industrial companies was about as strong, at seven of thirty firms.[24] Indeed, the UK and US economies have been the major recipients of the increasing worldwide volume of foreign investment.

❏ CORPORATE CONCENTRATION

Canada's economy is characterized by high levels of corporate concentration. As of 1987, about two-thirds of corporate assets, 60 percent of business profits, and over half of total sales were accounted for by the 500 largest companies in this country. These 500 represented less than 1 percent of all non-financial compa-nies in the country. The leading twenty-five enterprises alone accounted for about 40 percent of all corporate assets, a quarter of profits, and over one-fifth of sales (see figure 5).

These big businesses are not distributed evenly across sectors of the econ-omy. Instead, corporate concentration is greatest in the financial and utilities sec-tors, and is also high in some manufacturing industries such as tobacco products, automobiles, rubber and primary metals, and in many mining and extractive industries such as gold, nickel, and petroleum.

How does corporate concentration in Canada compare to levels in other advanced capitalist economies? Various studies comparing Canada to the United States all reach the same conclusion: concentration is significantly greater in the Canadian economy. Concentration levels in Canada also appear to be higher than in most other advanced capitalist economies. The Royal Commission on Corporate Concentration (1978) found that when Canada was compared to the United States, West Germany, France, Japan, and Sweden, only Japan came close to having the level of corporate concentration found in Canada.[25]

One needs to approach such comparisons with caution. They do not take into account the fact that competition in an industry may be provided by imports. Nor should one conclude that a high level of concentration in an industry is nec-essarily bad from either an economic or a political point of view.

From the economic point of view, the defenders of corporate concentration argue that size is an important advantage if a firm is to compete internationally. A corporation may dominate in the relatively small domestic market, and yet be dwarfed by its foreign competitors. In fact, only three of the capitalist world's

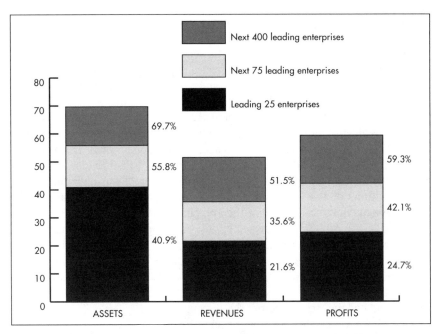

Figure 5   Cummulative Share of Total Assets, Revenues, and Profits
            Accounted for by Canada's Largest 500 Companies, 1985

Source: Based on Statistics Canada, Corporations and Labour Unions Returns Act, Report for 1987,
           part 1—Corporations, cat. 61-210 Annual (Ottawa: Supply and Services, March 1990), 71,
           table 4.1.

100 largest industrial companies are Canadian (General Motors of Canada, Ford
Motor of Canada, and Canadian Pacific).[26] Following the logic of this argument,
the size of Canadian firms should not be measured against the domestic market,
but against the international marketplace. If this is the standard, the "problem"
of corporate concentration disappears. It becomes, in fact, a virtue.

The takeover of one corporation by another has often been the occasion for
expressions of concern over the power of business. For example, the attempted
takeover of Argus Corporation by Power Corporation in the mid-1970s led to the
appointment of the Royal Commission on Corporate Concentration. More
recently, the 1986 takeover of Hiram Walker's by Allied Lyons of Britain, the
1987 purchase of Dome Petroleum by Chicago-based Amoco, the 1989 purchase
of Carling-O'Keefe by Molson's, and the takeover of Texaco Canada by Imperial
Oil were corporate mergers that received much attention in the business press.
These high-profile mergers represent only the tip of an iceberg of takeover activity that grows and shrinks over time, and which has been growing significantly
since the mid-1980s.

The extent of corporate concentration and its effects on competition have
moved in and out of the political spotlight over the last century, attracting most

attention when a major corporate takeover occurs. From its origins in the first competition law passed in 1889, the principal goal of competition policy has been to prevent the abuse of economic power. An important part of competition policy—that dealing with mergers—is directed at preventing corporate concentration that "is likely to prevent or lessen competition, substantially."[27]

The enforcement record of the merger provisions in the Combines Investigation Act, Canada's main competition law from 1910 to 1986, was abysmal. William Stanbury notes that only eight merger cases were taken to court from the law's passage, and not a single conviction resulted. The main reason for the apparent weakness of the law on mergers was that cases had to be tried under the criminal law in which the standard of proof was high and judges' interpretations of the law tended to be unsympathetic to the prosecution. Successive attempts to strengthen the Combines Investigation Act (Bill C-256, 1971; Bill C-42, 1977) were greeted by a hostile response from business.[28] The legislation introduced by the Liberal government in 1984, and that introduced by the Conservatives in 1985, were the products of extensive negotiation with major business organizations (including the Canadian Chamber of Commerce, the Canadian Manufacturers' Association, and the National Council on Business Issues) and had the tacit support of these groups.

One of the major reforms brought about by the new Competition Act and Competition Tribunal Act, passed in 1986, is that mergers are now reviewed under the civil law by a tribunal composed of federal court judges and appointed laypersons. Although it is too early to know whether the 1986 reforms have the teeth that the Combines Investigation Act lacked, there are a number of reasons for thinking that these changes will have only modest effects. Stanbury notes that the new merger provisions apply only to mergers of firms within the same industry or to firms that have a supplier–customer relationship. The new law could not have been used to review a merger such as occurred in 1986 between two of Canada's largest conglomerates, Imasco (ranked fifteenth among Canadian industrials in 1985) and Genstar (ranked seventeenth). And yet there was widespread concern expressed by the media and the federal government over this concentration of economic power. Moreover, for a merger to be prevented or dissolved, the competition law requires that a "substantial lessening of competition" be shown and that this lessening of competition not be offset by efficiency gains from the merger. In other words, the new Competition Act provides corporations with an "efficiency defence." Several large mergers of firms operating in the same industry have occurred since the act came into force. Not a single takeover has been prevented or seriously impeded.

CONCLUSION: "NO PLACE TO HIDE"[29]

This chapter began with the question of whether the structural features of Canada's economy justify anguished hand-wringing over the country's economic future. The answer is perhaps best left to seers, economists, and fools.

The aim of this conclusion is more modest. It is to speculate in very broad terms about the impact of changes in the world economy and the Canada–United States Free Trade Agreement on economic policy making in Canada. The greater formal integration of the Canadian and American economies brought about by the FTA is, in a sense, the political culmination of economic changes that have been underway for years now. These changes involve the growing internationalization of investment and production, which tended to strengthen the political hand of business interests while at the same time weakening the political strength of organized labour and those interests most committed to the Keynesian welfare state. Governments are more exposed to international economic forces that they cannot control, but that affect their ability to regulate the domestic economy and to finance existing state programs.

As capital becomes increasingly mobile and international competitive pressures intensify, many corporations and industries are forced to restructure their production activities or succumb to competition. Relocation to areas where production costs are lower becomes an increasingly attractive option. This process has already been underway for some time, and many large firms have shifted their production to cheap wage areas such as the *maquiladoras* in Mexico, where labour can be bought for as little as a dollar per hour. The movement of capital has also been taking place within the United States, where many companies have retreated from the higher wage, northern "rust belt" to the lower wage, less unionized "sun belt" of the American South and West. While capital is able to move around the world with relatively few impediments, workers obviously are much less mobile and the state cannot move at all. This permits business to use the threat of relocation to extract concessions from both labour and government in countries such as Canada.

Governments are not the only ones affected by international economic restructuring. Businesses also find that their ability to compete for markets and investment capital is influenced by economic developments beyond their national borders. Some of these businesses lose, unable to compete with their foreign rivals without hefty state subsidies. Their demands for protection often receive a sympathetic hearing from governments that are keen to preserve jobs, and that see no politically acceptable way of avoiding the subsidies bidding game that internationally mobile business investors are able to work to their advantage. Organized labour usually supports these subsidies, valuing the jobs associated with any new investment—no matter how it is attracted—more than the costs that paying for the investment may impose on taxpayers, consumers, and the overall economy.

It is easy, however, to exaggerate the degree to which business investment is free to cross national borders. Some sectors of the economy, like insurance, banking, and communications, typically are hedged in with all sorts of restrictions that limit foreign entry into the domestic market. Moreover, the world economy continues to bristle with a staggering array of protectionist measures that have thus far eluded GATT's efforts to lower barriers to international trade.

Nevertheless, by any measure, the world economy has become a more interdependent place and the icon of the current economic era is the trans-national corporation.

For those businesses whose markets are international and that are able to shift production between countries with relative ease in response to economic incentives (cheaper wages, weaker unions, government subsidies), the new economic order presents enormous opportunities. Other businesses require greater and greater protection just to hold onto their existing domestic market in the face of tough foreign competition. The internationalization of capital produces winners and losers in the business community. But its impact on governments is more uniform. To oversimplify matters, governments in advanced capitalist societies have two options. They can respond to intense foreign competition and mobile business investment by offering various forms of protection to domestic producers. The more dependent an economy is on international trade, the less viable this option will be. Alternatively, they can choose to provide a business environment that attracts capital investment because of its competitive advantages. Deregulation of industry, lower corporate taxation, and downward pressure on wages are ways in which this may be done.

Both of these options strengthen the political hand of business. The increased protectionism route benefits the vested corporate interests that see in state protection the best hope (sometimes the only hope) for survival. The competitive-advantage route benefits business by reducing the costs of producing in a particular country. Governments do not consciously choose between these options: the policy-making process is far messier than that. And there is nothing to prevent governments from moving simultaneously in both of these directions: protecting domestic producers from foreign competition at the same time as they bring the costs of doing business more into line with those in countries jostling for the same investment capital. Whether a government leans more towards the increased protectionism or the lower business-costs option depends largely on the particular mix of domestic politics and ideologies in a country.

The Canada–United States Free Trade Agreement is a response to the restructuring under way in the world economy. Corporate supporters of free trade see in it the promise of improved access to the huge American market (which is also a springboard to other international markets), as well as a possible lever for bringing production costs in Canada more into line with the level of our major trading partner. On the political side, both the business advocates of free trade and the governments that support it have argued that there is no alternative; that Canada's trade dependence on the United States and our vulnerability to protectionist American laws, combined with the intensity of global competition, mean that there literally is "no place to hide." And in any case, the economists remind us, most of our trade with the United States is already either "free" or subject to very low tariffs.

Free trade shifts the balance of social forces towards those whose interests lie primarily with the market and not with the state. When we think about who opposed and who supported the FTA, it is clear that most of free trade's opponents were groups who counted on government interference with the market—most of Canada's cultural community; farmers in marketing board sectors of agriculture; environmentalists; heavily regulated/protected industries such as banking and food processing; supporters of Canadian social programs—or, in the case of labour, who feared the effects that unleashing market forces might have on jobs and wages in Canada. For these groups, the FTA appeared to be more a menace than a blessing. On the other hand, the support of all the major business associations in this country was based on their expectation that a freer North American market would be to their advantage. The division between the defenders and the detractors of the FTA, therefore, came down to a fundamental difference of attitude towards the market.

As Canada approaches the twenty-first century and the concrete ramifications of the FTA are felt, controversy is almost certain to continue over who wins and who loses from free trade. But hardly anyone will dispute that the political victory of the FTA required the momentum that its powerful corporate backers provided, and that free trade reinforces at the formal, political level the economic interests of the North American-oriented segment of the Canadian business community.

Notes

[1] This ranking is based on what economists call "purchasing power parities," a cross-national measure of real purchasing power.

[2] M. Charette et al., "The Evolution of the Canadian Industrial Structure: An International Perspective," in D. McFetridge (research co-ordinator), *Canadian Industry in Transition* (Toronto: University of Toronto Press, 1985): 74–75.

[3] Statistics Canada, *Canadian Economic Observer*, quarterly, 1989.

[4] R. Pomfret, *The Economic Development of Canada* (Toronto: Methuen, 1981), 69.

[5] "Canada's Shame," *The Economist* (31 March 1990): 67–68.

[6] S. Brooks, "The State as Financier: A Comparison of the Caisse de dépôt et placement du Québec and the Alberta Heritage Savings Trust Fund," *Canadian Public Policy* 13, 3 (September 1987): 318–29.

[7] S. Brooks and A.B. Tanguay, "Québec's Caisse de dépôt et placement: Tool of Nationalism?" *Canadian Public Administration* 28, 1 (Spring 1985): 99–119.

[8] A review of studies on both sides of this controversy is found in S. Brooks, *Public Policy in Canada* (Toronto: McClelland & Stewart, 1989), 203–05.

[9] The percentage of Canadian exports going to the US stood at 38.9 percent in 1946. This increased to 55.8 percent in 1960, to 64.7 percent in 1975, and to about 75 percent at present.

[10] Statistics Canada, 13–213P and 65–202, 1988.

[11] A.R.M. Lower, *Colony to Nation*, 4th ed. (Don Mills: Longmans, 1964): 373–74.

[12] See D. Savoie, *Federal–Provincial Collaboration* (Montreal: McGill-Queen's University Press, 1981); Savoie, *Regional Economic Development: Canada's Search for Solutions* (Toronto: University of Toronto Press, 1986); W. Coffey and M. Polese, eds., *Still Living Together: Recent Trends and Future Directions in Canadian Regional Development* (Montreal: Institute for Research on Public Policy, 1987); and H. Lithwick, "Federal Government Regional Economic Development Policies: An Evaluation Survey," in L. Norrie, research co-ordinator, *Disparities and Interregional Adjustment*, vol. 64 for the Royal Commission on the Economic Union and Development Prospects for Canada, 1986.

[13] Lithwick, "Federal Government," 110–11.

[14] Canada, Task Force on Program Review, *Economic Growth: Services and Subsidies to Business* (Ottawa: Supply and Services, 1985), 108.

[15] Canada, Task Force on Program Review, *Management of Government: Procurement* (Ottawa: Supply and Services, 1985), 201, 205.

[16] This is based on contracts awarded through the Department of Supply and Services, and does not include purchases by federal Crown corporations.

[17] D. Savoie and J. Chenier, "The State and Development: The Politics of Regional Development Policy" in Coffey and Polese, eds., *Still Living Together,* 416.

[18] In 1920 British capital accounted for 52.9 percent of all foreign investment in Canada, compared to American investment's share of 43.7 percent. By 1930, American investment was 61.2 percent of the total and British investment was down to 36.3 percent.

[19] Canada, *Historical Statistics of Canada*, 2nd ed., Series G291–302 (Ottawa: Supply and Services, 1983).

[20] Gallup polls showed that the percentage of Canadians who thought that there was enough American investment in Canada rose from 46 percent in 1964 to 67 percent in 1972.

[21] M.A. Molot and G. Williams, "The Political Economy of Continentalism," in M. Whittington and G. Williams, eds., *Canadian Politics in the 1980s*, 2nd ed. (Toronto: Methuen, 1984), 95.

[22] Figures cited in S. Clarkson, *Canada and the Reagan Challenge*, 2nd ed. (Toronto: James Lorimer, 1985), 81.

[23] *Financial Post 500* (Summer 1988), 64–65.

[24] *Times 1000* (London) (1987–8): 26–27.

[25] Canada, Royal Commission on Corporate Concentration, *Report* (Ottawa: Supply and Services, 1978), 40–42.

[26] *Fortune* (1 August 1988), D3–D9.

[27] Competition Tribunal Act, 1986, s. 64.

[28] See the discussion in P.K. Gorecki and W.T. Stanbury, *The Objectives of Canadian Competition Policy: 1888–1983* (Montreal: Institute for Research on Public Policy, 1984), 92–100.

[29] The phrase "no place to hide" was used in the 1985 *Final Report* of the Royal Commission on the Economic Union and Development Prospects for Canada. It referred to the commission's belief that Canadian governments, as governments elsewhere, have become increasingly unable to shelter their producers and workers from the forces of global competition.

Bibliography

Banting, K. (research co-ordinator). *The State and Economic Interests*. Toronto: University of Toronto Press, 1986.

Bliss, M. *Northern Enterprise: Five Centuries of Canadian Business*. Toronto: McClelland & Stewart, 1987.

Brooks, S. *Public Policy in Canada*. Toronto: McClelland & Stewart, 1989.

Brooks, S. "The State as Financier: A Comparison of the Caisse de dépôt et placement du Québec and the Alberta Heritage Savings Trust Fund." *Canadian Public Policy* 13, 3 (September 1987): 318–29.

Brooks, S., and A. Stritch. *Business and Government in Canada*. Scarborough: Prentice-Hall, 1991.

Brooks, S., and A.B. Tanguay. "Québec's Caisse de dépôt et placement: Tool of Nationalism?" *Canadian Public Administration* 28, 1 (Spring 1985): 99–119.

Canada. Royal Commission on Corporate Concentration. *Report*. Ottawa: Supply and Services, 1978.

Canada. Royal Commission on the Economic Union and Development Prospects for Canada. *Final Report*. Ottawa: Supply and Services, 1985.

Canada. Task Force on Program Review. *Economic Growth: Services and Subsidies to Business*. Ottawa: Supply and Services, 1985.

Canada. Task Force on Program Review. *Management of Government: Procurement*. Ottawa: Supply and Services, 1985.

Charette, M., et al. "The Evolution of the Canadian Industrial Structure: An International Perspective." In D. McFetridge (research co-ordinator), *Canadian Industry in Transition*. Toronto: University of Toronto Press, 1985.

Clarkson, S. *Canada and the Reagan Challenge*. 2nd ed. Toronto: James Lorimer, 1985.

Coffee, W., and M. Polese, eds. *Still Living Together: Recent Trends and Future Directions in Canadian Regional Development*. Montreal: Institute for Research on Public Policy, 1987.

Gorecki, P.K., and W.T. Stanbury. *The Objectives of Canadian Competition Policy: 1888–1983*. Montreal: Institute for Research on Public Policy, 1984.

Lithwick, H. "Federal Government Regional Economic Development Policies: An Evaluation Survey." In K. Norrie (research co-ordinator). *Disparities and Interregional Adjustment*. Toronto: University of Toronto Press, 1986.

Lower, A.R.M. *Colony to Nation*. 4th ed. Don Mills: Longmans, 1964.

Molot, M.A. and G. Williams. "The Political Economy of Continentalism." In M. Whittington and G. Williams, eds. *Canadian Politics in the 1980s*. 2nd ed. Toronto: Methuen, 1984.

Pomfret, R. *The Economic Development of Canada*. Toronto: Methuen, 1981.

Savoie, D. *Federal–Provincial Collaboration*. Montreal: McGill-Queen's University Press, 1981.

Savoie, D. *Regional Economic Development: Canada's Search for Solutions*. Toronto: University of Toronto Press, 1986.

Savoie, D., and J. Chenier. "The State and Development: The Politics of Regional Development Policy." In W. Coffee and M. Polese, eds. *Still Living Together: Recent Trends and Future Directions in Canadian Regional Development*. Montreal: Institute for Research on Public Policy, 1987.

The Arts

French-Language Literature in Canada

Réjean Beaudoin and André Lamontagne
Translated by
*Lynda A. Davey and Ralph Sarkonak**

INTRODUCTION

I n this chapter we present a survey of Canadian literature written in French. Taking into account the various genres, our principal objective is to demonstrate how this literature has evolved. The subject is divided into five parts: the first four trace the evolution of Québécois literature, and the last one deals with French-Canadian literature written outside Québec.

The historical development and the regional diversity of these literatures have dictated the organization of the chapter. In the first part we study the ideological basis of the literary institution in Québec in the mid-nineteenth century. The second part demonstrates the slow but constant development of writing in Québec up to the 1950s, when contemporary Québécois literature began to acquire its own particular and original flavour. The search for a collective identity, which characterizes the period of the Quiet Revolution, forms the focus of the third part. The fourth part deals with the wide range and the vitality of formal practices and themes in current literary production. Finally, the last part deals with the efforts of Acadian, Franco-Ontarian, and western Francophone writers to ensure the survival of their language and culture.

---

* English translations are provided for the titles referred to in this chapter. Italic type indicates that an English translation of the work has been published; roman type indicates that the work has not been published in English.

THE ORIGINS OF FRENCH-CANADIAN LITERATURE (SIXTEENTH TO NINETEENTH CENTURY)

The origin of French-Canadian literature goes back to the earliest period of the "discovery" and colonization of the North American continent by French-speaking Europeans. But, while the texts written before the nineteenth century—the *Voyages*[1] of St. Malo's famous explorer, Jacques Cartier, and the travel tales and missionary propaganda of the seventeenth and eighteenth centuries, such as the writings of Samuel de Champlain and Marie de l'Incarnation, the Jesuit *Relations,* Gabriel Sagard's travel accounts (which according to Jack Warwick[2] represent the "archetypical Canadian journey"), private correspondence (such as the letters of Elisabeth Bégon), and Father Charlevoix's 1744 *Histoire et description générale de la Nouvelle-France* (History and General Description of New France)—all form an integral part of the literary heritage of Québec, they nevertheless still remain French archival documents. It is only in the middle of the nineteenth century that the essential elements of a literary institution begin to appear: publishing houses, marketing, and ideological control of the production and of the reception of literary texts.[3]

From the Durham Report in 1839 to the passage of the British North America Act (1867), and in fact right up to the beginnings of the Quiet Revolution, the project of creating a national literature remained a constant goal and preoccupation of the French-Canadian intelligentsia. In the 1840s the movement was headed by liberals and other laypeople, but this changed during the 1860s when the clergy began to take an interest. The first literary review in French Canada, *Les Soirées canadiennes* (1860), reflected the influence of Henri-Raymond Casgrain, a priest with a strong following among the cultural elite and one of the first proponents of French-Canadian messianism. According to this point of view, which was developed by the Québec church as a response to the political predominance of English-speaking Canadians and the fabled atheism of the French in Europe, the conquered people of 1760 were encouraged to believe in their miraculous collective survival and their providential religious and social vocation. This was the main thesis of the literary movement that, around the middle of the nineteenth century, saw the birth of the first works to be written and published in French Canada. The clergy, who largely succeeded in imposing this mythic view of national destiny, made up the most influential and the best-organized social group: they had almost absolute control over education, the press, and literature.

A few years earlier, during the first phase of the cultural awakening of Lower Canada—its response to the Durham Report—the historian François-Xavier Garneau, the poet Octave Crémazie, and the members of the Institut Canadien—an organization of liberal forces—had been the dominant influences on French-Canadian literature. But the hardening of ideological positions in 1860 posed problems for the development of Québécois literature. Firstly, religious doctrine imposed its concept of literature in opposition to contemporary ideas about writing and texts, especially those current at the time in France. Secondly, any point of view that was critical of, or divergent from, their concept of French-Canadian literature was severely censored. Thirdly, a small number of authorized themes and cultural stereotypes tended to enclose writers' imaginations in the confines of a backward-looking representation of French Canadians as they were supposed to be or have been. The land, the patriotism, and the religious heroism of the forebears of New France were the principal themes of many works right up to World War II.

For Abbé Casgrain, "the history of Canada is indeed, for all intents and purposes, the history of religious life and civilization on the banks of the St. Lawrence."[4] Relying on the authority of François Rohrbacher's, *L'histoire universelle de l'Eglise catholique* (Universal History of the Catholic Church),[5] the Abbé wrote, "the discovery of the North American continent resulted ultimately from the Crusades. Since in taking up the Cross in order to conquer a tomb, God rewarded Christian Europe with a large part of the world."[6] Thus, New France became a chapter in the Christian epic and its citizens were accorded a place in the continuing biblical narrative of the destiny of the chosen people. Consequently, a mythic theme became part of the founding texts of Québec literature. Gabriel Dussault summarized this theme in the following terms:

> As French Canadian and Catholic people in a French Catholic nation, we are God's chosen people, chosen by Him to work for the expansion of His realm and to sow the seeds of truth in the hearts of the infidel populations around us . . . and we have inherited the promises once made to the early Church and to Israel.[7]

In 1866 the Abbé Casgrain described the literature that he envisaged:

> We will have an indigenous literature with its own seal, original works that will vividly display our nation's mark, in other words a national literature. It is even possible to guess in advance what type of literature this will be. . . . In its essence, it will be a literature of faith and piety. . . . This will be its sole reason for being and it will need no other; in the same way, our people themselves have no principles of existence without religion, without faith. The day that the people cease to believe will be the day they cease to exist. Literature, as the incarnation of the people's thought, the motor of their intelligence, will trace their destiny.[8]

The exiled poet Octave Crémazie was the first to throw a damper on the Abbé's enthusiastic attempts to create such a national literature. In a letter to the Abbé dated 1866, Crémazie writes:

> In those works that you appreciate, you salute the dawning of a national literature. Let us hope that your wish soon becomes true! But I fear that here in Canada, in this almost always indifferent and sometimes even hostile milieu which surrounds those who have the courage to devote themselves to using

their intellects, the glorious era that you invoke with all your might is still very distant. . . . You know what amateur concerts are worth: they are sometimes nice, but never beautiful. Literature created by amateurs is not worth any more than amateur music.[9]

Crémazie's point of view, developed at great length in his letters, is bold indeed. He felt that public indifference and the lack of material resources for intellectual activity made the project of a national literature premature. He distanced himself from the ideological considerations that so interested the Abbé in order to raise questions such as book prices, writers' revenues, local and European markets for Canadian literature, and the language of expression. Such issues had been excluded from a debate centred on the patriotic promotion of French-Canadian literature. Crémazie pointed out that it would be fruitless to promote works of quality without having first assured that a reasonable profit could be made from the sale of such works. But Crémazie's position constituted an exception. Messianism continued its conquest of literature and rallied to its side the most important authors of the age. The poet Pamphile Le May explained the mission given to French-Canadian writers as "one of progress, and progress is the movement of all humanity towards God."[10]

Both secular and religious writers adopted the messianic approach,[11] and its dominance was largely unchallenged.[12] Because of the discredit that had fallen on the lay bourgeoisie after the failure of the 1837 Rebellion, the French-Canadian people found themselves under the spiritual yoke of an all-powerful clergy and let themselves be convinced by their religious leaders that they had a divine mission in modern history. The birth of Québec's literary institution was strongly influenced by the intellectual climate that made the elaboration of this thesis of predestination possible.[13]

French-Canadian novelists such as Patrice Lacombe (*La Terre Paternelle*, 1846—The Fatherland), Joseph-Charles Taché (*Forestiers et Voyageurs*, 1863—Lumberjacks and Explorers), Antoine Gérin-Lajoie (*Jean Rivard, le défricheur*, 1862—Jean Rivard), Philippe Aubert de Gaspé (*Les Anciens Canadiens*, 1863—The Canadians of Old), and Jules-Paul Tardivel (*Pour la patrie*, 1895—For My Country) claimed that their novels were not imaginary narratives but nothing less than the truth. Certainly the modern reader will find many things in them besides a promise of divine election, including a sad, symbolic compensation for the immediate consequences of the military defeat of 1760. The collective shock stemming from this event gave rise to the messianic image of a nationalist discourse, focusing on the "cult of the soil"; this image would dominate French-Canadian literature, with few exceptions, until World War II.

One exception was Emile Nelligan who wrote at the end of the nineteenth century. In three feverish years between the ages of sixteen and nineteen, this adolescent, who was pathetically in love with his own despair, wrote the only poems of the entire Québec repertory before Saint-Denys Garneau that are still read today. Then he "sombra dans l'abîme du rêve"[14] (sank into the abyss of dreams). He died some forty years later in an insane asylum where he used to recite his verses to anyone who would listen and would recopy them in his best schoolboy script.

INNOVATIONS AND CONSISTENCY (FROM THE END OF THE NINETEENTH CENTURY TO 1948)

By the end of the nineteenth century, French-Canadian society had achieved a type of intellectual and social unanimity that left less and less room for divergent opinions. A few independents, the disciples of bygone liberals, were dismissed as mavericks and were progressively isolated.[15] One of them, Louis Fréchette, attacked the educational system of classical colleges (*A propos d'éducation*, 1893). Another, Arthur Buies, criticized the state of spoken and written French (*Anglicismes et canadianismes*, 1888). These were the only dissenting voices.

Buies wrote that "the French Canadian is strangely horrified by any clear and precise expression of thought. . . . As a result, art does not exist in any field whatsoever; there is only craft."[16] Buies attributed to the influence of the English language the inability of many writers to master French. Journalism, law, and political institutions suffered from a massive invasion of English idioms. Literal translations were responsible for a kind of "franglais," a bastardized mixture of French and English. As a polemicist Buies inaugurated a long literary tradition of preoccupation with the language. He went right to the heart of the question, criticizing the grand project of creating a national literature. "Among educated nations, we provide the unique spectacle of a race without an educated class . . . . And there are those who maintain that a national literature can exist under such conditions!"[17] His bitterness recalls Octave Crémazie's criticism of Abbé Casgrain's zeal some twenty-five years earlier:

> Unfortunately, we only have a society of grocers. A grocer is any man whose knowledge is limited to what he needs to earn a living, since for him, science is nothing more than a tool . . . . Such men make good fathers since they possess all the virtues suitable for an epitaph; you will have city councillors, church-wardens, members of parliament, and even ministers. But you will never create a literary, artistic and, I would even say, a patriotic society in the largest and most beautiful sense of the word.[18]

At the beginning of the century literary debates raged between proponents of regionalism and exoticism, the first remaining faithful to the land, the second avidly searching for a way out of the aesthetic and thematic narrowness of local milieux. The poets Paul Morin, René Chopin, and Marcel Dugas looked to Paris as a way of escaping suffocation. They wooed a more refined muse, but she proved to be anemic. Original works emerged instead from the pens of individuals isolated from the mainstream; writers such as Jean Aubert Loranger and the self-educated Aubert Lozeau clearly foreshadowed an important poetic maturity.

The publication in 1916 of *Maria Chapdelaine* by the French writer Louis Hémon signalled the appearance of a novel that respected the expectations of messianism. However, this novel, admirable in many respects including its literary qualities, was the victim of a serious misunderstanding that is only now beginning to be brought to light. This bestseller was first considered, not only in Québec but in the entire world, the symbol of the Québécois soul, as the expression of the virtues of "a race that does not know how to die." However, a recent rereading of this pivotal text cast doubt on this interpretation. In her discussion of "the Maria Chapdelaine myth,"[19] Nicole Deschamps shows that Hémon's novel is much more a human tragedy than a celebration of the race.

Immediately following the publication of Hémon's novel, the "cult of the soil" experienced one of its most violent rejections with Albert Laberge's *La Scouine* (*Bitter Bread*), published in 1918. This novel was banned by local church authorities and its author almost lost his job as a journalist. *La Scouine* was the first Québec naturalist novel. Laberge's art can be characterized by a vigorous prose style and a deftly composed narrative using an economy of stylistic effects. However, his work remained largely unknown by the public until it was rediscovered by critics around 1960.

In the 1930s, the appearance of a number of remarkable novels—Claude-Henri Grignon's *Un homme et son péché* (1933, *The Woman and the Miser*), Ringuet's *Trente Arpents* (1938, *Thirty Acres*), Félix-Antoine Savard's *Menaud ma tre draveur* (1937, *Master of the River*), Léo-Paul Desrosiers's *Les Engagés du Grand Portage* (1938, *The Making of Nicolas Montour*)—marked in varying degrees the end of the cult of the soil and showed a technical improvement in narrative writing. Here the "national text"[20] reveals itself in collective dispossession and individual alienation. Even in 1937, the poems of Hector de Saint-Denys Garneau, *Regards et jeux dans l'espace* (in *The Complete Poems*), unmask a stifled spirituality created by Québec's rigid Catholic tradition. They are among the starkest and most modern creations of Québec literature. Garneau died under mysterious circumstances at thirty-two; the journal and letters that he left behind, which were later published by his friends, closely examined a sick society. Soon such poets as Alain Grandbois, Alfred Desrochers, Robert Choquette, Clément Marchand, Alphonse Piché, and Rina Lasnier produced works of unflawed quality, not only in form, but in the boldness of their vision. The tired rhetorical question as to whether a French-Canadian literature existed was pushed aside by their stylistic innovations.

Though one could claim that Montréal had enjoyed an intense theatre life since the mid-nineteenth century, it would be erroneous to speak of a true Québec theatre.[21] Many theatres limited themselves to Broadway shows or to touring French repertory productions. French-Canadian theatre, limited to colleges and parish activities, was poor in every sense of the word. The historical dramas of Louis-Honoré Fréchette (*Papineau, Le Retour de l'exilé*—Return of the Exile), created in the 1880s with realistic effects that excited the public, constituted a brief exception.

Towards the beginning of the twentieth century, the musical revue (inspired by the café-concert and spurred on by artists from France) introduced a structure that was destined to compete with highly popular Parisian and New York models. At the same time, religious melodrama and visual spectacle began to define a scenic art that appealed directly to the tastes of local audiences. Popular successes resulted, the prototype being Petitjean and Rollin's *Aurore l'enfant martyre* (Aurora, the Child Martyr), which monopolized Québec stages between 1920 and 1950. Père Emile Légault's Compagnons de Saint-Laurent, founded in 1937, added some order to these carnivalesque celebrations. This company provided technical training for actors, directors, and technicians who, in their turn, were prepared to promote the works of playwrights. The period between the Depression and World War II also saw a turning point in theatrical activity, but the ultimate development of this art would not occur until the mid-1950s with the advent of the television age.

The Second World War would leave its indelible mark on other literary genres. Firstly, the German occupation of France paralyzed French printing presses, and Québec publishing houses took advantage of this situation to fill the void left by the silenced voices across the ocean.[22] In addition, the war contributed to opening the horizons of a traditionally inward-looking culture. Finally, industrialization and urbanization were stimulated by wartime demands; both continued to increase after hostilities ended. The conjunction of all these factors profoundly changed the face of literature, and the waning clerical influence allowed the new art to pass into maturity. In the postwar novel, the urban milieu replaced the country scene. But more than just a simple change of setting was involved. In Germaine Guèvremont's *Le Survenant* (*The Outlander*), Roger Lemelin's *Au pied de la pente douce* (*The Town Below*), and Gabrielle Roy's *Bonheur d'occasion* (*The Tin Flute*), all three dating from 1945, family life was depicted as coming apart at the seams. Misery took on a proletarian face, and love was no more than an illusion that faded as quickly as the young people themselves, who were hurrying towards war, money, and death. Regionalism was singing its swan song.

Change had wormed its way into a French-Canadian existence that still seemed closely attached to its legendary roots.[23] This can be seen in expanding labour unionization, intellectual debates, radio, and theatre. In 1948, a painter's manifesto, signed by a dozen disciples, aimed at casting off fear and confronting "right-thinking" authorities. *Refus global* (*Total Refusal*) was a short text of only a few hastily printed pages discretely distributed by a bookstore, but it so upset Premier Maurice Duplessis that he forced the treatise's author, Paul-Emile Borduas, into exile. But this first glimmer of light in the midst of the great darkness was not about to fade. A surrealist movement formed around Borduas and extended beyond the visual arts to include such poets as Claude Gauvreau, Gilles Hénault, Paul-Marie Lapointe, and Roland Giguère. Borduas provided an example of resistance and of vocal protest in a universe of silence and obedience and was a prophetic voice in the years before the Quiet Revolution.

The year 1948 saw the birth of Québécois drama with the publication of actual plays. Gratien Gélinas's *Tit-Coq*, a truly popular success, was performed over 200 times at the Monument National. All Québec shared the anger and the humiliation of the play's hero, an illegitimate son, who returned from the war to find that his fiancée had given in to family pressure and married a man she did not love. Gélinas's theatre owed a great deal to the burlesque tradition, which he combined with a social realism that would become the hallmark of Québec theatre.[24]

THE QUEST FOR IDENTITY AND THE AFFIRMATION OF DIFFERENCES (1950–1970)

The novel continued an evolution that was already well under way and led to works of unprecedented originality and scope by André Langevin (*Poussière sur la ville*, 1953—*Dust Over the City*), Yves Thériault (*Agaguk*, 1958), Gérard Bessette (*Le Libraire*, 1960—*Not for Every Eye*), Gabrielle Roy (*Alexandre Chenevert*, 1954—*The Cashier*), Anne Hébert (*Les Chambres de bois*, 1958— *The Silent Rooms*), and Jacques Ferron (*Cotnoir*, 1962—*Dr. Cotnoir*).[25] The energy of the sixties emerged in the works of a new generation of artists: Jacques Renaud (*Le Cassé*, 1964—*Broke City*), André Major (*Le Cabochon*, 1964—*The Pighead*), Jacques Godbout (*Salut Galarneau*, 1967—*Hail Galarneau!*), and Roch Carrier (*La Guerre, yes sir*, 1969—*La Guerre, Yes Sir!*). Gilles Dorion summarized this development in the following terms:

> the structure is reinforced, the plot becomes more solid, the description of the social milieux more skilful, the psychology of the characters more profound and true. In short, Québec novelists are finally masters of their craft. The Québec novel achieves its autonomy even at a time when the people are still searching for it.[26]

The fruitful harvest for the Québec novel led to some unexpected break-throughs on the international market. After winning the Prix Femina in 1945 with *The Tin Flute*, Gabrielle Roy became famous overnight; Marie-Claire Blais, discovered by the American critic Edmund Wilson, repeated this feat by winning the Prix Médicis in 1966 for *Une saison dans la vie d'Emmanuel* (*A Season in the Life of Emmanuel*); Réjean Ducharme narrowly missed winning the Prix Goncourt in the same year for *L'Avalée des avalés*, 1966 (*The Swallower Swallowed*). The giant French publishing houses all seemed to want a Québec writer in their stable; Jacques Godbout and Anne Hébert were signed by Seuil, and Ducharme signed a contract with Gallimard after being rebuffed by several Montréal firms due to his difficult style. But all the texts that were published and fêted in Paris were mainly sold and read in Québec. International success eluded Hubert Aquin, a separatist "writer for want of being a banker,"[27] a prophet and martyr for a political ideal that mobilized everyone in Québec who could be considered a thinker. His *Prochain épisode* (1965, *Prochain Episode*) was unanimously fêted by Canadian critics but largely ignored internationally.

Poetry played a crucial role in the popular fray of the Quiet Revolution.[28] A "national" poetic discourse, which substituted liberating speech for tragic isolation, centred on Gaston Miron (whose works, though written in the 1950s·and 1960s, were not published until 1970) and on l'Hexagone, a publishing house founded in 1953.²⁹ Such diverse poets as Jean-Guy Pilon, Fernand Ouellette, Jacques Brault, Gatien Lapointe, Gérald Godin, Paul Chamberland, and Michèle Lalonde would follow him.

But theatre was the genre that experienced the most remarkable development. After the pioneering work of Gratien Gélinas, Marcel Dubé inspired a veritable flowering of Québec theatre. Dubé began writing at an early age. *Zone* (1953), with its theme of social revolt, brought his talent to the fore. *Un simple soldat* and *Florence* (1957) explored new rhythms, a language of harsh tones and bitter poetry perfectly suited to a popular reality stripped of all melodrama. Dubé's subsequent evolution, beginning with his 1960 play *Bilan* (Taking Stock), led him to break with the violence of his early works to espouse the tortuous debates of conscience of the petite bourgeoisie. Today Michel Tremblay has become without doubt the most popular playwright in Québec. Since the first production of his seminal work *Les Belles-Soeurs* in 1968, his language and characters have remained faithful to the collective fears and anxieties of contemporary Quebeckers, and his *oeuvre* embraces theatre, television, cinema, and the novel.

Finally, it is necessary to mention the literary genre of the essay whose importance became evident during this period. Non-fiction prose has many representatives: Jean Lemoyne, Fernand Dumont, Jean-Paul Desbiens, Marcel Rioux, Gilles Marcotte, Pierre Vadeboncoeur, Jean-Ethier Blais, Jean Bouthillette, Pierre Vallières, Fernand Ouellette, Jacques Godbout, Hubert Aquin, and André Brochu.³⁰ Their works deal with all the subjects that characterize the evolution of modern Québec—from religion to politics, from language to literature.

The explosion of cultural forms and social structures took shape amid the enormous collective upheaval of the Quiet Revolution, which would irrevocably change the face of the province hurriedly trying to transform itself into a sovereign state. One cannot understand the literature of these feverish years without first admitting that intellectuals, for many years kept under the thumb of censorship, had finally found their voice in a movement of solidarity with the newly powerful middle class, the beneficiaries of educational reform and modernization of the state apparatus. Within the realm of the performing arts, popular song became part of the collective experience, transcending its earlier role as folksy family entertainment. Parallel to theatre, Québec music searched for and found original forms of expression, ranging from the troubadour Félix Leclerc to the rocker Robert Charlebois, by way of the age-old northern strains of Gilles Vigneault.

Three journals—*Cité Libre*, founded in 1950, *Liberté*, founded in 1959, and *Parti pris*, founded in 1963—were at the root of attempts to make up for lost time, a desire which characterized this period. They also served as landmarks of postwar intellectual evolution.³¹ The influence of these publications, though limited at first, grew to include various groups. In them, the voice of liberalism, secularism, sovereignty, and a hint of socialism became progressively stronger, eventually replacing the old messianism with a newborn nationalism that would pass from the cultural into the political arena between 1950 and 1970. Undoubtedly, the major achievement of these two decades was the difficult acquisition of relative autonomy in aesthetic works.

This development of Québec literature was at the price of inevitable contradictions and a difficult renunciation of certain ambitions. It became evident, for example, that Québec works would stop patterning themselves on those of the great French tradition and that they would increasingly express an originality based on their cultural and imaginative difference,[32] along with their claim to a specific socio-political content. But, at the same time, this quest for identity could not avoid a discovery of existential solitude, historical isolation, and modern-day anguish. The phantom of a former way of life, always difficult to isolate from the original legacy of European heritage, continued to haunt literary production. However, this phenomenon did not occur at a thematic level; rather, it presented itself through interventions by the author in the literary text, in publishing and commercial policies, and even in the status of the text as determined by literary canon. New forces also exerted their influence in the writing domain and other groups instituted various means of intervention in order to make their voice heard.

FROM AN UNCERTAIN COUNTRY TO AN IMAGINARY PLACE (SINCE 1970)

The contemporary Québécois novel can be divided into two main types: the popular novel and a more sophisticated type of work that involves stylistic and narrative innovations. However, this division is by no means clear-cut, and there are numerous works that blend the two in a way described by Laurent Mailhot:

> there exists a fiction in contemporary Québec literature that is situated somewhere between oral and written discourse, between tradition and modernity, between epic and criticism. . . . [these novels] combine blood and ink, life and its representation, what is transmitted and what is constructed. They are part of the story-telling tradition [Carrier, Ferron, Thériault], not far removed from theatre [monologues, choruses, divisions]. Whereas novels in the strictly literary tradition [*écriture*] affirm European intertextuality, novels of speaking [*parole*] are [North] American. The ones in the first group are wilfully intellectual, abstract, schematic, brilliant and of a studied formalism. The other ones are pragmatic, giving an appearance of *naturalness* even within myth.[33]

In 1980 Gilles Marcotte asked whether it was possible in Québec to write a "nineteenth-century novel" and have it published.[34] He argued that, because nineteenth-century traditions were summarily condemned around 1960, writers had to go back in time to reinvent these traditions. Consequently he argued that "the oldest is the most contemporary" in terms of the production of novels.[35] Elsewhere, André Belleau has judiciously noted:

Whereas modern literary discursive practice tends to question forms, reflect on language, construct and deconstruct codes—in short, abolish the difference between creation and criticism, all this assuming that the writer finally views himself as a full-fledged intellectual—Québec ideology encourages the survival of or the return to outmoded forms: neo-regionalism, naive historicity, national glorification.[36]

This conflict between nineteenth-century traditions and modern literary trends constitutes the fundamental trait of the modern Québec novel and is well illustrated in the urban novel. The city, a place of socio-cultural mixing, thus becomes the scene where individual stories are played out against a backdrop of tales of primordial conflicts. The mixture of realism and the fantastic characterizes works such as those of André Carpentier and invites comparisons with some Latin-American works of the magic realism school.[37] The playful and parodic aspects of Québec novels thus take the well-travelled road that reads the multiple discourses of modernity from many points of view.[38] There is an increasing awareness of the nature of literary communication. The writings of Pierre Turgeon, Jean-Marie Poupart, and Yvon Rivard, among others, are part of this vast enterprise in which literary parody, intertextuality, and the use of different codes transform our reading patterns. Michel Tremblay's novel cycle—*Les chroniques de Plateau Mont-Royal* (1978–1989)—is accessible to a wider reading public. Tremblay, who revolutionized Québec theatre in the 1970s, started to write novels in the 1980s in which he describes the marginal existence of the inhabitants of a poor district of Montréal. He paints a large fresco of pathetic and morally depraved characters who languish in a limbo of poverty, sexual and religious obsessions, and domestic and urban violence. Possessive mothers, religious perverts, friendly transvestites, and saintly prostitutes make up the world of *La grosse femme d'à-côté est enceinte* (1978, *The Fat Woman Next Door Is Pregnant*), *Thérèse et Pierrette à l'école des Saints-Anges* (1980, *Thérèse and Pierrette and the Little Hanging Angel*), *Des nouvelles d'Édouard* (1984, News of Edward), and *Le premier quartier de la lune* (1989, The First Quarter of the Moon).

Turning to the *roman de l'écriture*, a practical and theoretical field in which specific notions of text and of writing are imposed prior to any literary endeavour, be it discursive or fictional, the old distinction between genres loses its validity. Literary magazines (where creativity meets criticism) constitute the agents of the most noteworthy transformations and feature the most heated debates.[39] Among the names that emerge from the seventies, those of the poets and essayists Philippe Haeck, Claude Beausoleil, André Roy, France Théoret, François Charron, and the omnipresent Nicole Brossard should be mentioned.[40] But the most important development within the *roman de l'écriture* has been the emergence of feminism. The women's movement experienced continued growth and greatly extended the dimensions of intellectual debate. It established independent publishing houses, magazines, and theatrical companies. Works such as Louky Bersianik's *L'Euguelionne* (*The Euguelionne: A Triptych Novel*), a fable, novel, and myth rolled into one, and Denise Boucher's play *Les Fées ont soif* (*The*

Fairies Are Thirsty)[41] were transformed into political events. More recently, Marie Laberge's works, which take a more classical form, belong to this same struggle.

Feminist writings share several distinguishing characteristics with the textual ensemble that makes up the Québec novel of the 1980s.

> The writings of Nicole Brossard, Madeleine Gagnon, Denise Boucher, Louki Bersianik or Yolande Villemaire capture the inherent inauthenticity of language and superimpose textual networks in a "discontinuum." Their works become, each one in its own voice, the working centre for many different discourses [or types of discourses] in which laughter breaks out in the form of an incessant questioning of the collective textual body.[42]

Yolande Villemaire's *La Vie en prose*[43] is a book that sums up the different mechanisms activated by the *roman de l'écriture*.[44] Its most remarkable effect is the abolition of the distinction between the text and what is outside it. Writers play "at displaying the barrier between reality and fiction, thus producing a 'trembling reality' that is quite possibly the essence of modernity."[45]

The *roman de l'écriture* assures credibility, but commercial success still seems to belong to the *roman de parole*. These works tell true stories using a proven and recognizable artistic formula and are situated in places that are carefully established, if not always carefully described. Among the many attempts to produce a best seller, certainly the most famous is Yves Beauchemin's *Le Matou* (*The Alley Cat*).[46]

> *Le Matou* was published in Montreal on March 26, 1981. Since then, the work has enjoyed phenomenal success: more than 200 000 copies sold in Québec—where a book that sells 10 000 copies is already considered to be a best seller—and 600 000 copies in France. This success has earned it translations in several languages, a film and an album. Its author has won prizes from the *Journal de Montréal* and from the Writers' Union, the City of Montreal Prize and the Book of the Sumner Prize (Cannes 1982). . . . The critical reception of *Le Matou* by experts between 1981 and 1982 was extremely positive: few reservations were expressed regarding Beauchemin's novel.[47]

Le Matou is a long book (almost 600 pages), an additional characteristic—this one purely quantitative—that seems to indicate a turning point for Québec novels of the eighties. Family sagas in the form of epic novels keep increasing in number (Arlette Cousture, Francine Noël, Michel Tremblay) or in scope (the work of Victor-Lévy Beaulieu certainly constitutes the most ambitious project of this kind). At the same time, the short story and the novella have been experiencing a popularity that they had rarely known (Anne Hébert's *Torrent,* published in 1950, being a notable exception). Established writers such as Madeleine Ferron, André Carpentier, Gaétan Brulotte, Louis Gauthier, as well as numerous young writers have adopted these genres, and there are literary magazines and publishing houses that specialize exclusively in such works.

Since 1967 novelist Jacques Poulin has been an important though restrained voice in Québécois fiction. Rather than relying on "improbable resolutions" of history, the meaning of his writing is "lodged in the middle, in the proliferation of stories."[48] A certain anguish in his writing seems to be giving way to a new serenity, devoid of illusions, in his more recent works such as *Volkswagen Blues*[49] and especially *Le Vieux Chagrin*.[50]

There is, as well, a certain kind of poetry that—as in Poulin's writings—has turned away from flirting with trendy celebrations of modernity. It has rediscovered how topical are its concerns with subjectivity. Michel Beaulieu, Marcel Beaulieu, Marcel Bélanger, and Alexis Lefrançois illustrate this tendency, as do poets such as Pierre Nepveu and Robert Mélançon.

The Québec theatre of Jean-Claude Germain, Jean Barbeau, and Michel Garneau offers a wide variety of forms, practices, and orientations. Young authors, directors, actors, and set designers present an entire range of dramatic experimentation. After a period of tension between commitment to an authentic reproduction of an author's text and collective creation of a text, it is now possible to speak of a type of multi-media spectacle in which the text, the music, the colours, the interpretations, and the artistic management aim for, and sometimes achieve, synthesis. The work of Robert Lepage and René-Daniel Dubois fits this mould. As with poets and novelists, theatrical productions integrate an increasing proportion of theoretical reflection. The spectator, like the reader, can no longer be defined as a naive receiver of information whose knowledge and active contribution should be excluded from the creative process.

FRANCO-CANADIAN LITERATURE FROM OUTSIDE QUEBEC[51]

❑ ACADIA

Quebeckers and Acadians share the belief that it is essential to dissociate their literature from the total French-Canadian production.[52] Since the seventies, Acadians have clamoured for recognition of their own political identity, and they are revealing or rediscovering their cultural specificity. History seems to justify this reappropriation process. After numerous failures along the St. Lawrence Valley, France established its first overseas colony at Port Royal, Nova Scotia, in 1605, and the myth of the promised land of Acadia was born. This myth, in which the presence of the sea was a distinguishing feature, found its prophet and propagandist in Marc Lescarbot and his *Histoire de la Nouvelle France* (*Nova Francia*).[53] The English conquest of Acadia in 1710 put an end to the historical and missionary literature represented by the Jesuit Pierre Biard (*Relation de la Nouvelle France*—Relation of New France). With the 1755 deportation—the *Grand Dérangement*, as Acadians called it—began an era of isolation and dispersion, as well as a long period of silence in the nation's literature. For almost 100 years, Acadian literature was defined only by an oral tradition and by letters (which contemporary critics are attempting to rebuild). These ensured cultural cohesion, constituting the memory of a people endangered by extinction.[54]

In 1847, an outsider, the American poet Henry Wadsworth Longfellow, broke the silence on the Acadian drama. The important role of his poem *Evangeline* (and particularly its 1867 French translation by Pamphile Le May, which was published in newspaper serial form) in the political awakening of a people who had been brutally transformed into a minority is well known today. *Evangeline* tells the tale of a betrothed couple separated by the deportation and the heroine's lengthy search for her fiancé across the entire North American continent. Napoléon Bourassa emulated Longfellow's poem in a novel entitled *Jacques et Marie, souvenir d'un peuple dispersé* (Memory of a Dispersed Race), which enjoyed considerable success following its publication in 1866.

Faithful to the Québec example, the ensuing renewal in Acadia was marked by the submission of nationalism and literature to the doctrine of messianism. Public speeches and patriotic poems published in newspapers constituted an important part of the literary production of the late nineteenth century. Marcel-François Richard, an orator and nation-builder who participated in the first Acadian National Convention in 1881, summarized the budding ideology in the following manner: "All we need is a horse-drawn cart to make today's Acadia just like that of yesteryear."[55] This period was also marked by the appearance of folk tales and legends that, aiming to maintain popular tradition, also explicitly served rural Catholic ideology. The simple title of Louis-Joseph Arthur Melanson's novel (*Pour la terre*, 1918—For the Earth) constitutes such a point. But it was Acadian historiography that would begin to fill the almost blank pages of written memory with the messianic origins of Acadia, preaching fidelity to the French language and the Catholic Church.

The second quarter of the twentieth century was marked by certain political gains as well as the creation of conditions (albeit restricted) for diffusing ideological and cultural discourse (an increase in the number of schools, newspapers, and radio stations, but no genuine literary institution). The cult of tradition grew and became more noticeable, thanks to a diversification of literary genres. Indeed, the same voice could be heard in dawning theatre, poetry, and novel forms. Some flashes of imagination were evident, such as in the newspaper serial, written under the pseudonym Paul, recounting the adventures of *Placide*.[56] A more detailed study of this serial, in which a shrewd Acadian sleuth outwits the most dangerous New York and London criminals, illustrates that it symbolizes both rupture (in this case, of isolationism) and continuity (the glorification of the ethnic virtues of an Acadian elevated to the rank of superhero).

Antonine Maillet's *Pointe-aux-Coques* and the poet Ronald Després's *Silence à nourrir de sang* (Nourishing Silence with Blood), both published in 1958, but very different works, constituted the starting point for Acadia's cultural and literary awakening. Maillet, without a doubt the most acclaimed of Acadian authors, incarnates the wish to rediscover popular ethnic traditions and day-to-day history. Her abundant output is highlighted by the creation of the character La Sagouine (*La Sagouine*),[57] whose bastardized speech became an object of great popular esteem, and the novel *Pélagie-la-charrette* (*Pélagie*)[58] for which she was honoured with the Prix Goncourt and which describes the *joie de vivre* of a people and the strength of the nation's uniqueness. Its carnivalesque tone has often been compared to Rabelais. Maillet, wishing to dissociate herself from any notion of being backward-looking, maintains that she speaks "a larger reality, that of people of all ages and in all places."[59] However, this intention does not correspond to the reception given her work by the Acadian reading public. James de Finney's excellent study has shown that Maillet's readers have limited themselves to her work's linguistic, social, and political components. They had largely ignored the aesthetic virtues or universal traits of her writings in favour of traits that fulfill remarkably well the expectations of a people looking for a representation of themselves.[60] But do her portrayals remain within the realm of folklore? It is important to note that several years before Maillet won the Prix Goncourt—an event that raised many a Québécois eyebrow—her work was declining in popularity among Acadians, and critics were questioning its ideological effects. As Marguerite Maillet has noted,[61] these writings are partially akin to the prose of Marc Lescarbot and his vision of an idyllic Acadia, as if 200 years of isolation and humiliation could suddenly vanish. While it is true that the cultural and economic inferiority of the Acadians was a major concern in the sixties, one should keep in mind that Antonine Maillet's epic was in fact removed from real social problems.

In the wake of Ronald Després, a whole generation of poets felt it necessary to break with a misleading past. Unlike Québec, where a messianic ideology determined the establishment of a literary institution in the mid-nineteenth century, after 1950 Acadia's network of production and cultural transmission was founded on a rejection of this same ideology. But, as in Québec, revolt and the affirmation of nationhood developed by means of poetic discourse. Language will end alienation: this was the message of Raymond Leblanc's *Cri de terre* (Cry of the Earth), which in 1972 launched Editions d'Acadie. This was the first genuine publishing house of a nation uncertain of itself, a nation that Leblanc, refusing to deceive himself, could only imagine in conjunction with Québec.

Using tones that borrowed from the poetic language of modernity, writers such as Guy Arsenault (*Acadie Rock*), Herménégilde Chiasson (*Mourir à Scoudouc*), and Leonard Forest (*Saisons antérieures*), drew critical attention, not only because of the justness of their revolt, but also because of their language. This language, according to Claude Beausoleil, "even in its breaches and its affirmations carries the entire discourse of a fleeing reality."[62] This reality is part of a truly contemporary imagination. From the early eighties, Acadian poetry, experiencing at an accelerated pace the changes that occurred over a period of more than twenty-five years in Québec, took both a more formal and a more intimist turn. However, the texts of Gerald Leblanc (*Comme un otage du quotidien*—Like a Hostage of Daily Living) or Dyane Léger (*Graines de fées*—Fairy Seeds) continue to protest against the alienation that is so often part of day-to-day existence. This spirit of questioning, though still evident in theatrical productions, is fading in the novel or turning to the question of North Americanness, as in the works of Jacques Savoie. Is this because Acadian writing is maturing or does it mean that preoccupations with Acadian uniqueness are fading, resulting in, as Michel Roy puts it, a lost Acadia (*Acadie perdue*)?

❑ FRENCH-SPEAKING ONTARIO

If Paul Guay's claim is true that "the literature of a collectivity becoming aware of its own identity always begins with poetry,"[63] the origins of Franco-Ontarian literature must coincide with the launching in Sudbury of Editions Prise de parole (1973), which still publishes most of the Franco-Ontarian poets. It is true, in any case, that in the preceding centuries, no pressure was felt among Franco Ontarians to produce literature, probably because, unlike Acadia, the French presence in the province was mainly due to Québec emigration necessitated by economics. Consequently, there was a more passive acceptance of assimilation. The infamous 1912 law that forbade education in French to Francophones served to spur a growth of nationalism thirty years later and produced some literary echoes such as the novel *Flambeau sacré* (1944, Sacred Torch) by Mariline (pseudonym of Alice Séguin). This work, which condemned mixed marriages, constituted an *appél de la race*,[64] a type of rallying call to the people. Some pioneer narratives, such as Maurice de Gourmois's *François Duvalet* (1954), should also be kept in mind. However, the most noteworthy texts of the period were the first of a colossal work by Father Germain Lemieux that echoed the existence of a vast oral folklore tradition. His work of more than thirteen volumes entitled *Les vieux m'ont conté* (The Elders Have Told Me), published between 1973 and 1979, assembled the stories of miners and lumberjacks from northeastern Ontario. Ti-Jean, the most frequently encountered hero of the series, is often put in situations of conflict with fictional kings, and his calls for popular revolt can be seen as subversive, though Pierre Karsh has clearly shown that these folktales were primarily meant to have a cathartic effect.[65]

Poetry was at the centre of a veritable northern voice that emerged during the seventies. Certainly, it might be risky to look for similarities between such diverse works as those of Gaston Tremblay, Robert Dickson (the lyricist, incidentally, for the famous and now defunct band Cano), Guy Lizotte, Jocelyne Villeneuve, Richard Casavant and Patrice Desbiens,[68] but they do seem to share an elliptical style that, in some cases, tends to fuse with the subject matter itself and, in others, to break down the alienation of daily life.

In northern Ontario, theatre has also been a much-appreciated form of expression during the last fifteen years: it proposes to an isolated or dispersed population the solution of a collective awareness. Among this corpus, the works of André Paiement command attention. Paiement, often compared to Michel Tremblay because of his use of popular language, presented linguistic and socio-political issues in his *Moi, j'viens du Nord, 'stie* (Me, Christ, I'm from the North) and *Lavallélle* that never cease to provoke and to question.[67]

The novel is now challenging poetry as the dominant genre. Notable are Daniel Poliquin whose *L'Obonsawin* (1987) treats the question of native people, Hélene and her *Chroniques du nouvel Ontario* (1986, *A Saga of Northern Ontario*) and Marguerite Andersen, whose novel *Mémoire de femme* (1983, Woman's Memory) won the *Journal de Montréal* prize.

The growing vitality of Franco-Ontarian literature is due to a favourable economic situation (as opposed to that in Acadia) and to the contribution of numerous teacher-writers originally from Québec or Europe and now living in Ontario. These factors, among others, form the subject of Fernand Dorais' remarkable essay *Entre Montréal et Sudbury* (*Between Montreal and Sudbury*), which culminates in the utopian hope for a Franco-Ontarian state.

❏ WESTERN CANADA

Francophone literature in western Canada was dominated by the novel, perhaps because this genre originated with the pioneers drawn to the West by the vast spaces. In this regard, it is necessary to mention Maurice Constantin-Weyer who, though he kept his French passport, lived for several years the harsh reality of early twentieth-century Manitoba. His Homeric novel *Un homme se penche sur son passé* (*A Man Scans His Past*), which won the Prix Goncourt in 1928, recounts the northern wanderings of a French pioneer searching for the woman who abandoned him.[68] Georges Bugnet, also from France, describes in *La Forêt* (1935, *The Forest*) the difficulties of a European couple having to cope with the rigours of an Albertan winter. Jean Féron (pseudonym of Joseph-Marc Lebel), of American birth but Franco-Saskatchewan by adoption, documents in his novel *La Métisse* (1923) the conditions of another founding people. Curiously enough, the historical question of the Metis has had few repercussions in western Canadian literature, but its principal exponent, Louis Riel, integrated it into his *Poésies religieuses et politiques* (in *The Collective Writings*) and especially in a famous text dedicated "To Sir John A. Macdonald."[69]

Gabrielle Roy, who is usually seen as a Québécois writer, bridged the gap in western Canada literature between the early and latter parts of the twentieth century with novels such as *La Petite Poule d'eau* (1950, *Where Nests the Water Hen*), *Rue Deschambault* (1955, *Street of Riches*), and *La route d'Altamont* (1966, *The Road Past Altamont*). Roy's influence is evident in the works of Marguerite-A. Primeau, certainly the most famous western Francophone writer, whose novel *Dans le Muskeg* (1960, In the Muskeg) tells of an Albertan teacher who loses his illusions of a bilingual Canada. In the realm of poetry, Roger Léveillé, whose *Livre des marges* (1981, The Book of Margins) was very favourably received by the critics, should be mentioned.

But the thread of Francophone intellectual life in the West remains tenuous. This is why many authors such as Paul Savoie have migrated to Québec and others, like playwright Guy Gauthier, have opted for a complete break by choosing to exile themselves in the United States. Such a choice challenges all Francophone writers outside Québec and exposes the precarious situation of those who choose to affirm their minority status since, under these conditions, to write is to speak of one's own extinction, even if the telling is intended as a protest.

CONCLUSION

It is clear from this overview that French-language literature in Canada does not form an organic whole but rather a multicoloured patchwork of themes and formal techniques. Québécois literature is characterized by its four-century-old historical roots and especially by the dynamic and flourishing character of its recent production. These traits are due in large part to the importance and relative stability of its demographic pool and institutional networks. From the few laborious works of the nineteenth century to the hundreds of titles presently published annually, the evolution is nonpareil. Since World War II, Québec society has fully entered the modern era, and its literary production has often been at the cutting edge of the cultural avant-garde. Poetry was the first genre to be affected, but theatre and the novel were soon to feel the complex consequences of the social and psychological evolution of modern-day Québec. Today its writers have earned a place for themselves among the national literatures. The challenges that Québécois authors now set for themselves are among the most difficult as they must grapple with postmodern textual practices. Acadian and Franco-Ontarian literature is on the threshold of self-affirmation, but Francophone literature in the West must still wait for substantial political gains if its voice is to be heard and to endure.

Notes

[1] *Voyages en Nouvelle-France*, introduction and notes by R. Lahaise and M. Couturier (Montréal: Hurtubise HMH, 1977). The excellent study by F.-M. Gagnon and D. Petel, *Hommes effarables et bestes sauvages* (Montréal: Boréal, 1986) on the iconography of older editions of Cartier's writings can also provide valuable information. In an article entitled "Littérature de la Nouvelle-France" that appeared in *Etudes françaises* ("Petit Manuel de littérature québécoise") 13, 3–4, (octobre 1977): 243– 44, J. Warwick has pointed out that editions of works attributed to Cartier have been based on subsequent versions of manuscripts whose originals have been lost.

[2] Ibid., 245. Though the travel narrative is undoubtedly the sub-genre that unites most of the writings of this period, the outline of a new literary form is beginning to take shape from these narrations. Its specific characteristics have yet to be established.

[3] This subject has been treated in greater depth in R. Beaudoin's *Naissance d'une littérature. Essai sur le messianisme et les débuts de la littérature canadienne-française* (Montréal: Boréal, 1989).

[4] *Histoire de la Mère Marie de l'Incarnation, première supérieure des Ursulines de la Nouvelle-France, précédée d'une esquisse sur l'histoire religieuse des premiers temps de cette colonie* (Québec: G.-E. Desbarats, 1864), 31.

[5] Rohrbacher was a disciple of Félicité de Lamennais. The first edition of his twenty-nine-volume *Histoire universelle de l'Eglise catholique* appeared in 1849; it was cited by many authors.

[6] *Histoire de la Mère Marie de l'Incarnation*, 12.

[7] "Dimensions messianiques du catholicisme québécois au XIXe siècle," *Thèmes canadiens* (Ottawa: Association des études canadiennes, 1985), 66.

[8] H.-R. Casgrain, *Oeuvres complètes*, tome 1: 375.

[9] Octave Crémazie in a letter to Abbé Henri-Raymond Casgrain dated April 10, 1866, reprinted in *Anthologie de la littérature québécoise*, vol. 11, *La Patrie littéraire,* ed. G. Marcotte et R. Dionne (Montréal: La Presse, 1978), 254, 255.

[10] In H.-J., J.B. Chouinard, ed. *Fête nationale des Canadiens français*, 381.

[11] S. Gagnon, *Le Québec et ses historiens de 1840 à 1920—La Nouvelle France de Garneau Groulx* (Québec: P.U.L., 1978), 59.

[12] M. Brunet was the first to use the word "messianism" to criticize the dominant ideology of traditional French Canada: "At the time of Canadian romanticism, an entire school of historians, essayists, poets, and writers, whose influence can still be felt today, eruditely explained that French Canadians possessed certain inherent traits, that they were unlike other peoples, that they had a particular destiny to fulfil on the North American continent. . . . The former spokesmen of French-Canadian society let themselves be led astray by a romantic and messianic nationalism." ("Trois dominantes de la pensée canadienne-francaise: l'agriculturisme, l'anti-étatisme et le messianisme," in *La présence anglaise et les Canadiens* (Montréal: Beauchemin, 1964), 117–18, 161.)

[13] Through writings or by direct intervention, French authors influenced this ideological formation. The historian E. Rameau de Saint Père can be cited as an example. His two-volume set, *La France aux colonies*, published in 1859 to mark the centenary of the conquest, created quite a stir in Canada. E. Parent, F.-X. Garneau, J.-C. Taché, Curé Labelle, the Abbés Ferland, and C. Chauveau, Viger, Papineau enthusiastically welcomed the backing of this historian of colonial France who authorized them to formally base their patriotism on the French-Catholic heritage.

[14] "Le Vaisseau d'Or," *Poésies complètes d'Emile Nelligan* (Montréal: Fides, 1952); 41.

[15] L.-J. Papineau's political descendants who were very active following the publication of the Durham Report (1840).

[16] *Anglicismes et canadianismes*, 74–75.

[17] Ibid., 36.

[18] O. Crémazie, in a letter to Abbé H.-R. Casgrain dated 10 August 1866 (see note no. 9), quoted in *Anthologie de la littérature québécoise*, vol. 11, *La Patrie littéraire,* ed. G. Marcotte et R. Dionne (Montréal: La Presse, 1978), 258–59. The correspondence between the exiled poet Crémazie and Abbé Casgrain is very instructive on the subject in question as G. Marcotte has pointed out in his "Institution et courants d'air," *Liberté*, 134 (mars–avril 1981): 5–14.

[19] "Taking its influence into account, the only work of the last two centuries to become a myth is *Maria Chapdelaine*, this distant cousin who looks exactly like our sister, our daughter, our grandmother." L. Mailhot, "Classiques canadiens," in *Etudes françaises* 13, 3–4 (octobre 1977), 267. Nicole Deschamps elucidated this paradox in her work *Le Mythe de Maria Chapdelaine* (Montréal: Presses de l'Université de Montréal, 1980).

[20] J. Godbout coined this expression to denounce those aspects of the nationalist ideology that could restrict imagination and thought.

[21] On the subject of the dramatic arts of the period, one should consult J.-M. Larrue, "La naissance du théâtre au Québec; le jeu de la concurrence," in *Littératures* ("Cahiers du Département de langue et littérature françaises," Université McGill, no. 4, 1989): 49–68; C. Hébert, *Le burlesque québécois et américain* (Québec: Presses de l'Université Laval, 1989).

[22] E. Nardout-Lafarge, "Autonomie littéraire et rupture symbolique: le Québec et la France, 1940–1950," in *Littératures* ("Cahiers du Département de langue et littérature françaises," Université McGill, no. 1, 1988): 125–47.

[23] "If one refers to the habitual aesthetic norms—the division between genres, the respect of artistic rules, balance and clarity—our works are baroque, Romantic, sometimes affected, most often academic and very unclassical. Our first novels were not really novels, but supernatural tales or agronomic treatises; our first poems were songs, canticles, maxims; our first plays were discourses." (L. Mailhot, "Classiques canadiens," *Etudes françaises*, 13, 3–4 (octobre 1977): 268.)

[24] *Tit-coq* shows the dramatic development of the character Fridolin, the protagonist of a series of monologues written and performed by Gélinas in the thirties. Gélinas's formula is linked to the genre of the revue.

[25] The quantity and quality of creative production make any analysis quite impossible within the limited framework of this introduction. We can only indicate those specialized works in which more information can be obtained, such as A. Brochu's *L'instance*

critique (Montréal: Leméac, 1973) and G. Marcotte's *Le Roman à l'imparfait* (Montréal: La Presse, 1976).

[26] G. Dorion, "La littérature québécoise contemporaine 1960–1977: Le roman," in *Etudes françaises* 13, 3–4 (octobre 1977): 302. The author continues: "Since 1970 especially, novelists have translated a veritable collective unwinding which allows the liberating of forces that have been repressed for too long. The dam has burst" (p. 304).

[27] Aquin used this expression in an interview accorded to Jean Bouthillette; this interview is reprinted in *Point de fuite* (Montréal: Cercle du livre de France, 1970), a collection of essays and various writings

[28] C. Moisan, "La littérature québécoise contemporaine 1960–1977: la poésie," in *Etudes françaises*, 13, 3–4 (octobre 1977): 279–300; G. Marcotte, *Le temps des poètes* (Montréal: Editions HMH, 1969); P. Nepveu, *Les Mots à l'écoute* (Québec: Les Presses de l'Université Laval, 1979).

[29] J.-L. Major, "L'Hexagone: une aventure en poésie québécoise," in *Archives des Lettres canadiennes*, tome IV, *La Poésie canadienne-française* (Montréal: Fides, 1969): 175–203; and G. Marcotte, "L'Hexagone et compagnie," in *Liberté* 20, 6 (novembre-décembre 1978): 11–21.

[30] "Robert Vigneault has studied this 'birth of Québec thought,' that he has placed as occurring about 1940 but becoming particularly evident in essays published in the early sixties." F. Ricard, "La littérature québécoise contemporaine 1960-1977: IV l'essai," in *Etudes françaises*, 13, 3–4 (octobre 1977): 373. On this topic, one can also consult. *Archives des Lettres canadiennes,* tome VI, *L'Essai et la prose d'idées au Québec* (Montréal: Fides, 1985).

[31] The sociologist Marcel Rioux uses the word "rattrapage" (catching up), contrasting it with the term "conservation" to emphasize Québec's break with the "grande noirceur" (great darkness) that characterized the Duplessis era.

[32] On this topic, one can consult R. Sarkonak, ed., *The Language of Difference: Writing In Québéc(ois)*, Yale French Studies, no. 65. (1983).

[33] L. Mailhot, "Romans de la parole (et du mythe)," in *Canadian Literature*, 88 (Spring 1981): 84 (emphasis by Mailhot).

[34] G. Marcotte, "Histoire du temps" in *Canadian Literature* 86 (Autumn 1980): 96.

[35] Ibid., 97. G. Marcotte has made some interesting observations on the relation between the modern novel and Québec's cultural tradition in "La dialectique de l'ancien et du nouveau chez Marie-Claire Blais, Jacques Ferron et Réjean Ducharme," *Voix et Images*, 6, 1 (automne 1980): 63–74.

[36] A. Belleau, "Les écrivains québécois sont-ils des intellectuels?" in *Surprendre les voix* (Montréal: Boréal, 1986): 157.

[37] Cf. "Dossier comparatiste Québec–Amérique Latine" in *Voix et Images* 34 (automne 1986): 5–66.

[38] Some studies on parody: *Etudes littéraires*, 19, 1 (printemps–été 1986); *La parodie: théorie et lecture* in which J. Paterson, P. Imbert, and P. Malcuzynski provide readings of Anne Hébert, Réjean Ducharme, Jean-Marie Poupart, and Hubert Aquin.

[39] On this subject, one can consult the issue of *Voix et Images*, 10, 2 (hiver 1985) on *La Barre du Jour* and *La Nouvelle Barre du Jour*. *La Nouvelle Barre* is undoubtedly one

of the sites of Québec modernity, but other magazines (*Les Herbes Rouges, Spirale*),
including some of a shorter life span (*Stratégies, Chroniques, Coincidences*), should not be
forgotten. Another useful source is *Revue d'histoire littéraire du Québec et du Canada
français* ("Revues littéraires du Québec"), no. 6 (été–automne 1983).

[40] Nicole Brossard is a versatile feminist roundly booed by F. Hébert, "L'ombilic
d'une nymphe," *Liberté* no. 121 (janvier–février 1979): 214–27. This article was responsible for a polemic on modernity that mobilized many Québec writers.

[41] This work was performed at Montréal's Théâtre du Nouveau Monde in 1978.

[42] E. Cliche, "Paradigme, palimpseste, pastiche, parodie dans *Maryse* de Francine
Noël," in *Voix et Images* 36 (printemps 1987): 431.

[43] (Montréal: Les Herbes Rouges, 1980).

[44] On this writer, one can consult L. Robert, "Yolande Villemaire: inspirer
l'Amérique," in *Voix et Images* 33 (printemps 1986): 388–89.

[45] L. Potvin, "L'ourobouros est un serpent qui se mord la queue X 2," in *Voix et
Images* 33 (printemps 1986): 425.

[46] (Montréal: Québec/Amérique, 1981).

[47] F.J. Summers, "La réception critique du *Matou*," in *Voix et Images* 36 (printemps
1987): 383–84.

[48] G. Marcotte, "Histoires de zouaves," in *Etudes françaises*, 21, 3 (hiver
1985–1986): 16 (italics by Marcotte).

[49] *Volkswagen Blues* (Montréal: Québec/Amérique, 1984). "Jacques Poulin is in a
category by himself—like Gabrielle Roy or Réjean Ducharme—in the field of the contemporary Québec novel. Neither very talkative nor very prolific (six books since 1967), Poulin
does not saturate the literary institution either by his personality or by his public interventions." L. Mailhot, "Le voyage total," in *Etudes françaises* 21, 3 (hiver 1985–1986): 3.

[50] (Montréal et Arles: Leméac et Actes Sud, 1989).

[51] The inevitable division of French Canada into the diaspora and Québec, which constitutes the centre of publishing and is where writers born outside the province assemble,
problematizes the geographical distinction of those works now under study. Indeed, the criteria for inclusion vary from one critic to another. Those works written in French originating
in other provinces (excepting the Ottawa–Hull region) and conveying in a sufficiently
marked fashion their place of production are the ones we are including in this section.

[52] This notion, implicitly held for many years, probably found its most convincing
elaboration in J. Bouthillette's book *Le Canadien français et son double* (1972). The word
québécois became the rule around 1965 to refer to the collective identity of a national
group affirming its existence as a distinct society. The term *canadien-français* is used to
describe only those French-speaking individuals living outside Québec and is meant to
underline the common origin of all Canadian Francophone communities.

[53] *Histoire de la Nouvelle France* (Paris: Jean Milot, 1609). Note that the sea theme
is central to *Muses de la Nouvelle-France*, a poetic continuation annexed to the historical
work.

[54] On the subject of Acadian oral and written traditions, one can consult A. Maillet,
Rabelais et les traditions populaires en Acadie (Québec: Presses de l'Université Laval,

1971); A. Chiasson, *Chéticamp: histoire et traditions acadiennes* (Moncton: Editions des Aboiteaux, 1961); and C. Jolicoeur, "Légendes en Acadie" in *Si Que 3*, Etudes françaises, Université de Moncton (automne 1978).

[55] Quoted by M. Maillet, *Histoire de la littérature acadienne. De rêve en rêve* (Moncton: Editions d'Acadie (coll. universitaire, 1983)), 67.

[56] *L'impartial*, from 21 January 1904 to 21 June 1906.

[57] (Montréal: Leméac, 1971).

[58] (Montréal: Leméac, 1979).

[59] "Témoignages sur le théâtre québécois," in *Le Théâtre canadien français* (Archives des lettres canadiennes, tome V) (Montréal: Fides, 1976): 812.

[60] "Antonine Maillet: un exemple de réception littéraire régionale," In *Revue d'histoire littéraire du Québec et du Canada français* ("Frontières"), 12, Editions de l'Université d'Ottawa (été–automne 1986): 17–3.

[61] *Histoire de la littérature acadienne*, 185.

[62] C. Beausoleil and G. Leblanc, *La Poésie acadienne 1948–1988* (Les Ecrits des Forges/Castor Astral, 1988), 7.

[63] "Notre domaine littéraire franco-ontarien" in *Propos sur la littérature outaouaise et franco-ontarienne* (R. Dionne, dir.), vol. 3, Ottawa, le Centre de recherches en civilisation canadienne-française de l'Université d'Ottawa (mai 1981): 18.

[64] Title of a novel by Alonié de Lestre (pseudonym for Lionel Groulx) published in 1922.

[65] "Une lecture rassurante: Les Vieux m'ont conté," in *Revue d'histoire Iittéraire du Québec et du Canada français*, 12: 141–50.

[66] *Les Conséquences de la vie* (Sudbury: Les Editions Prise de Parole, 1977) and *L'Homme invisible/The Invisible Man* (Sudbury: Les Editions Prise de Parole, 1982) in which the two languages used translate the reality of assimilation in the form of a parody.

[67] *Théâtre*, 3 vol. (Editions Prise de Parole, 1978).

[68] (Paris: Les Editions G.P., 1928).

[69] (Montréal: Imprimerie de *L'Etendard*, 1886).

Bibliography

Beaudoin, R. *Naissance d'une littérature: Essai sur le messianisme et les débuts de la littérature canadienne-française (1850–1890)*. Montréal: Boréal, 1989.

Beausoleil, C. et G. Leblanc. *La Poésie acadienne 1948–1988*. Trois-Rivières: Les Ecrits des Forges/Castor Astral, 1988.

Belleau, A. *Surprendre les voix*. Montréal: Boréal, 1986.

Bouthillette, J. *Le Canadien français et son double*. Montréal: L'Hexagone, 1972.

Brochu, A. *L'instance critique*. Montréal: Leméac, 1973.

Brunet, M. *La présence anglaise et les Canadiens*. Montréal: Beauchemin, 1964.

Chiasson, A. *Chéticamp: histoire et traditions acadiennes*. Moncton: Editions des Aboiteaux, 1961.

Cliche, E. "Paradigme, palimpseste, pastiche, parodie dans *Maryse* de Francine Noël." *Voix et images* 36 (printemps 1987): 430–38.

Deschamps, N. *Le Mythe de Maria Chapdelaine*. Montréal: Presses de l'Université de Montréal, 1980.

Dorion, G. "La littérature québécoise contemporaine 1960–1977; II, le roman," *Etudes françaises* 13, 3–4 (octobre 1977): 301–38.

"Dossier comparatiste Québec-Amérique Latine" *Voix et images* 34 (automne 1986): 5–66.

Dussault, G. "Dimensions messianiques du catholicisme québécois au XIXe siècle," *Thèmes canadiens*. Ottawa: Association des études canadiennes, 1985.

L'Essai et la prose d'idées au Québec (Archives des lettres canadiennes, tome 6). Montréal: Fidès, 1985.

Ethier-Blais, J. "Les pionniers de la critique," *Revue d'histoire littéraire de la France,* 69e année, no. 5 (septembre–octobre 1969): 795–807.

de Finney, J. "Antonine Maillet: un exemple de réception littéraire régionale," *Revue d'histoire littéraire du Québec et du Canada français* 12 (été–automne 1986): 17–33.

Gagnon, F.-M., and D. Petel. *Hommes effarables et bestes sauvages*. Montréal: Boréal, 1986.

Gagnon, S. *Le Québec et ses historiens de 1840 à 1920—La Nouvelle-France de Garneau à Groulx*. Québec: P.U.L., 1978.

Gay, P. "Notre domaine littéraire franco-ontarien," *Propos sur la littérature outaouaise et franco-ontarienne* 111 (mai 1981): 17–22.

Hamelin, J., et N. Voisine, éd. *Les ultramontains canadiens-français*. Montréal: Boréal, 1985.

Hébert, C. *Le burlesque québécois et américain*. Québec: Presses de l'Université Laval, 1989.

Hébert, F. "L'ombilic d'une nymphe," *Liberté* 121 (janvier–février 1979): 214–27.

Hodgson, R., and R. Sarkonak, ed. *Oeuvres et Critiques* ("Le Roman québécois contemporain devant la critique, 1960–1986") 14, 1 (1989).

Jolicoeur, C. "Légendes en Acadie," *Si Que 3* (automne 1978): 39–50.

Karsh, P. "Une lecture rassurante: Les Vieux m'ont conté," *Revue d'histoire littéraire du Québec et du Canada français* 12: 141–50.

Lapierre, R. "Du meilleur et du pire: Autour de *LUEUR* de Madeleine Gagnon," *Liberté* 126 (novembre–décembre 1979): 128–34.

Larrue, J.-M. "La naissance du théâtre au Québec: le jeu de la concurrence," *Littératures* ("Cahiers du Département de langue et littérature françaises," Université McGill) no. 4 (1989): 49–68.

Marcotte, G., and R. Dionne. *Anthologie de la littérature québécoise: La Patrie littéraire.* Vol. 2. Montreal: La Presse, 1978.

Mailhot, L. "Classiques canadiens," *Etudes françaises* 13, 3–4 (octobre 1977): 263–78.

Mailhot, L. "Romans de la parole (et du mythe)," *Canadian Literature* 88 (Spring 1981): 84–90.

Mailhot, L. "Le voyage total," *Etudes françaises* 21, 3 (hiver 1985–1986): 1–5.

Maillet, A. *Rabelais et les traditions populaires en Acadie.* Québec: Presses de l'Université Laval, 1971.

Maillet, M. *Histoire de la littérature acadienne. De rêve en rêve.* Moncton: Editions d'Acadie (coll. universitaire), 1983.

Major, J.-L. "L'Hexagone: une aventure en poésie québécoise," *Archives des Lettres canadiennes: La Poésie canadienne-française.* Tome 4. Montréal: Fides, 1969: 175–203.

Marcotte, G. "La dialectique de l'ancien et du nouveau chez Marie-Claire Blais, Jacques Ferron et Réjean Ducharme," *Voix et images* 6, 1 (automne 1980): 63–74.

Marcotte, G. "L'Hexagone et compagnie," *Liberté* 20, 6 (novembre–décembre 1978): 11–21.

Marcotte, G. "Histoire du temps," *Canadian Literature* 86 (Autumn 1980): 93–99.

Marcotte, G. "Histoires de zouaves," *Etudes françaises* 21, 3 (hiver 1985–1986): 7–17.

Marcotte, G. "Institution et courants d'air," *Liberté* 134 (mars–avril 1981): 5–14.

Marcotte, G. *Le Roman à l'imparfait.* Montréal: La Presse, 1976.

Marcotte, G. *Le Temps des poètes.* Montréal: Editions HMH, 1969.

Moisan, C. "La littérature québécoise contemporaine 1960–1977, I, la posie," *Etudes françaises* 13, 3–4 (octobre 1977): 279–300.

Nardout-Lafarge, E. "Autonomie littéraire et rupture symbolique: le Québec et la France, 1940–1950," Littératures ("Cahiers du Département de langue et littérature françaises," Université McGill) no. 1 (1988): 125–47.

Nepveu, P. *L'Ecologie du réel. Mort et naissance de la littérature québécoise contemporaine.* Montréal: Boréal ("Papiers collés"), 1988.

Nepveu, P. *Les Mots à l'écoute.* Québec: Les Presses de l'Université Laval, 1979.

"La parodie: théorie et lecture," *Etudes littéraires* 19, 1 (printemps–été 1986).

Potvin, L. "L'ourobouros est un serpent qui se mord la queue X 2," *Voix et images* 33 (printemps 1986): 406–27.

"Revues littéraires du Québec," *Revue d'histoire littéraire du Québec et du Canada français* 6 (été–automne 1983).

Ricard, F. "La littérature québécoise contemporaine 1960–1977, IV, l'essai," *Etudes françaises* 13, 3–4 (octobre 1977): 365–81.

Sarkonak, R., ed. *The Language of Difference: Writing in Québéc(ois)*. Yale French Studies 65 (1983).

Summers, F.J. "La réception critique du *Matou*," *Voix et images* 36 (printemps 1987): 383–92.

Le Théâtre canadien-francais (Archives des lettres canadiennes, tome 5). Montréal: Fidès, 1976.

Viswanathan, J. "Dire le moi," *Canadian Literature* 102 (Autumn 1984): 128–30.

Warwick, J. "Littérature de la Nouvelle-France," *Etudes françaises* ("Petit Manuel de littérature québécoise") 13, 3–4 (octobre 1977): 237-61.

"Yolande Villemaire: inspirer l'Amérique," *Voix et images* 33 (printemps 1986).

Research Tools

Dionne, R., et P. Cantin. *Bibliographie de la critique de la littérature québécoise et cana-dienne-française dans les revues canadiennes* (1974–1978). Ottawa: Presses de l'Université d'Ottawa, 1988.

Fortin, M., Y. Lamonde, and F. Ricard. *Guide de la littérature québécoise.* Montréal: Boréal, 1988.

Lemire, M., *Dictionnaire des oeuvres littéraires du Québec.* 5 vol. Montréal: Fides, 1978–1986.

Mailhot, L. *La Littérature québécoise.* Paris: Presses Universitaires de France, 1974.

Mezei, K. *Bibliography of Criticism on English and French Literary Translations in Canada.* Ottawa: Les Presses de l'Université d'Ottawa/Fédération canadienne des études humaines, 1988.

The Oxford Companion to Canadian Literature. Toronto: Oxford University Press, 1983.

Répertoire des écrivains franco-ontariens. Sudbury: Les Editions Prise de parole, 1987.

St-Pierre, A., dir. *Répertoire littéraire de l'Ouest canadien.* Saint-Boniface: Centre d'études franco-canadiennes de l'Ouest, 1984.

Translated Works

Compiled by Lynda Davey

Aquin, H. *Prochain Episode*. Trans. P. Williams. Toronto: McClelland & Stewart, 1967 (New Canadian Library, 1973).

Bersianik, L. *The Euguelionne: A Triptych Novel*. Trans. G. Denis et al. Victoria: Press Porcepic, 1981.

Bessette, G. *Not for Every Eye*. Trans. G. Shortliffe. Toronto: Exile Editions, 1986.

Blais, M.-C. *A Season in the Life of Emmanuel*. Trans. D. Cottman. New York: Farrar, Straus & Giroux, 1966.

Borduas, P. *Total Refusal*. Trans. R. Ellenwood. Toronto: Exile Editions, 1985.

Boucher, D. *The Fairies are Thirsty*. Trans. A. Brown. Vancouver: Talon Books, 1982.

Brodeur, H. *A Saga of Northern Ontario*. Winnipeg: Watson & Dwyer, 1983.

Bugnet, G. *The Forest*. Trans. D. Carpenter. Montreal: Harvest House, 1976.

Carrier, R. *La Guerre, Yes Sir!* Trans. S. Fischman. Toronto: House of Anansi Press, 1970.

Cartier, J. *The Voyages of Jacques Cartier*. Trans. H.P. Biggar. Ottawa: F.A. Acland, 1924. (Publications of the Public Archives of Canada, No. 11).

Charlevoix, Father. *History and General Description of New France*. Trans. J.G. Shea. New York: J.G. Shea, 1866–1872 (6 vol.).

Chiasson, A. *Cheticamp: History and Acadian Traditions*. Trans. J.-D. Le Blanc. St. John's: Breakwater Books, 1986.

Constantin-Weyer, M. *A Man Scans His Past*. Trans. S. Brown. New York: Macaulay, 1929.

De Gaspé, P.A. *The Canadians of Old*. Trans. C.G.D. Roberts. Toronto: Copp Clark, 1905 (McClelland & Stewart, New Canadian Library, 1974).

Desrosiers, L.-P. *The Making of Nicolas Montour*. Trans. C. van Oordt. Montreal: Harvest House, 1978.

Ducharme, R. *The Swallower Swallowed*. Trans. B. Bray. London: Hamish Hamilton, 1968.

Ferron, J. *Dr. Cotnoir*. Trans. P. Cloutier. Montreal: Harvest House, 1973.

Gagnon, S. *Québec and Its Historians: 1890–1920*. Trans. Y. Brunelle. Montréal: Harvest House, 1982.

Gagnon, S. *Québec and Its Historians: The Twentieth Century*. Trans. J. Brierley. Montréal: Harvest House, 1985.

Garneau, S.-D. *The Complete Poems*. Trans. J. Glassco. Ottawa: Oberon Press, 1975.

Gélinas, G. *Tit-Coq*. Trans. K. Johnston & G. Gélinas. Toronto: Clarke Irwin, 1967.

Gérin-Lajoie, A. *Jean Rivard*. Trans. V. Bruce. Toronto: McClelland & Stewart, 1977.

Godbout, J. *Hail Galarneau!* Trans. A. Brown. Toronto: Longmans, 1970.

Grignon, C.-H. *The Woman and the Miser*. Trans. Y. Brunelle. Montréal: Harvest House, 1979.

Guèvremont, G. *The Outlander.* Trans. E. Sutton. Toronto: McGraw-Hill, 1950.

Hébert, A. *The Silent Rooms.* Trans. K. Mezei. Toronto: Masson, 1974.

Hébert, A. *Torrent.* Trans. G. Moore. Montréal: Harvest House, 1973.

Hémon, L. *Maria Chapdelaine.* Trans. W.H. Blake. New York: Macmillan, 1921, 1986.

Laberge, A. *Bitter Bread.* Trans. C. Dion. Montreal: Harvest House, 1977.

Langevin, A. *Dust Over the City.* Trans. J. Latrebe and R. Gottlieb. Toronto: McClelland & Stewart, 1955 (New Canadian Library, 1974).

Lemelin, R. *The Town Below.* Trans. S. Putnam. New York: Reynal and Hitchcock, 1948 (New Canadian Library, 1961).

Lescarbot, M. *Nova Francia or the Description of that Part of New France which is One Continent with Virginia.* Trans. P. Erondelle. London: A. Hebb, 1609 (partial translation).

Maillet, A. *Pélagie: The Return to a Homeland.* Trans. P. Stratford. Garden City, N.Y.: Doubleday, 1982.

Maillet, A. *La Sagouine.* Trans. L. de Cespedes. Toronto: Simon and Pierre, 1979.

Nelligan, E. *The Complete Poems.* Trans. F. Cogswell. Montréal: Harvest House, 1983.

Poulin, J. *Volkswagen Blues.* Trans. S. Fischman. Toronto: McClelland & Stewart, 1988.

Renaud, J. *Broke City.* Trans. D. Homel. Montréal: Guernica, 1984.

Riel, L. *The Collected Writings.* 5 vol. Trans. G.F.G. Stanley. Edmonton: University of Alberta Press, 1985.

Ringuet. *Thirty Acres.* Trans. D. Walter & F. Walter. New York: Macmillan, 1940 (New Canadian Library, 1960).

Roy, G. *The Cashier.* Trans. H.L. Binsse. New York: Harcourt, Brace, 1955 (New Canadian Library, 1963).

Roy, G. *The Road Past Altamont.* Trans. H. Binsse. Toronto: McCelland & Stewart, 1976.

Roy, G. *Street of Riches.* Trans. H. Binsse. Toronto: McClelland & Stewart, 1967.

Roy, G. *The Tin Flute.* Trans. A. Brown. Toronto: McClelland & Stewart, 1980.

Roy, G. *Where Nests the Water Hen.* Trans. H. Binsse. Toronto: McClelland & Stewart, 1970.

Savard, F.-A. *Master of the River.* Trans. R. Howard. Montreal: Harvest House, 1976.

Tardivel, J.-P. *For My Country.* Trans. S. Fischman. Toronto: University of Toronto Press, 1975.

Thériault, Y. *Agaguk.* Trans. M. Chapin. Toronto: Ryerson, 1963.

Tremblay, M. *Les Belles-Soeurs.* Trans. B. Glassco and J. Van Burek. Vancouver: Talon Books, 1974.

Tremblay, M. *The Fat Woman Next Door is Pregnant.* Trans. S. Fischman. Toronto: Talon, 1981.

Tremblay, M. *Thérèse and Pierrette and the Little Hanging Angel.* Trans. S. Fishman Toronto: McClelland & Stewart, 1984.

13

❑   ❑   ❑   ❑   ❑   ❑   ❑

English-Canadian Fiction and Poetry

Louis K. MacKendrick

INTRODUCTION

In the 1970s some Canadian literary criticism—perhaps fuelled by the 1967 centenary of Confederation—suggested several comprehensive thematic formulae by which the country's writing might be summarized. These studies, few of which approached the balance of Desmond Pacey's *Creative Writing in Canada*,[1] were fundamentally sociological and psychological in thrust. These assessments gave assurance that Canadian writing had distinctive national characteristics—that, in effect, it had a coherent identity, a word that appears often throughout studies of Canada. Such an identity, however, may be more illusory than real. The actual language used by any writer, the literary devices, the manner of enactment, and the very nature of the fictional or poetic activity hardly concerned these brave proposals of likeness. Until the 1980s, critical studies of literary individuality, technique, structure, and rhetoric were rare.

An early example of the thematic approach is the concept of a "garrison mentality," an urge to preserve an inherited (that is, British) culture as defined in Northrop Frye's conclusion to *The Literary History of Canada*.[2] At the same time, Canada's early writers resisted the influence of a relatively unmapped and, presumably, hostile territory, failing to comprehend it in its own terms. In the afterword to her book of poems, *The Journals of Susanna Moodie* (1970),[3] Margaret Atwood would declare the national mental illness to be "paranoid schizophrenia," the reflection of Canadians' continuing immigrant outlook. Frye's phrase and elaboration of culture shock were immediately absorbed by Canadian literary criticism, which at the time did not resist such inclusive concepts.

In *Butterfly on Rock* (1970),[4] D.G. Jones considered a significantly representative range of Canadian poetry and fiction, discussing variations on the prime
ideas of exile, the vitality of the land as opposed to the repressions of civilization, the resistance of the natural and irrational, the search for identity, and the
confrontation of an indifferent universe. The variety and insight of Jones's
approach did not dilute its thematic insistence. The suggestion of his title—taken
from a poem by Irving Layton—was of a fragile metamorphic beauty set against
the bleakly inorganic elemental granite. This imagistic opposition implicitly
underlay much of Jones's study, in which the Canadian sense of irony was
shown to play a considerable part in the literature.

In *Survival* (1972), leadingly subtitled *A Thematic Guide to Canadian
Literature*,[5] Margaret Atwood found Canadian prose and poetry to be focused on
the idea and image of "survival." Atwood brought forward sufficient related psychological and symbolic motifs and character types to make a substantial case.
Her book was strictly content oriented; the assumption of some demonstrable,
even convenient, literary homogeneity persisted.

In *Patterns of Isolation* (1974),[6] John Moss considered the Canadian novel
and its manifestations of the theme of exile. His examination of particular fictions in which geography was the major factor in the characters' isolation was
straightforward. However, Moss paid substantial attention to irony: the literary
device was seen as the foundation of the theme and as its expressive comple-
ment. His treatment pointed towards later Canadian critics who would focus on
style and form.

A final, later example of the comprehensive approach to Canadian writing
was Gaile McGregor's massive *The Wacousta Syndrome* (1985).[7] In studying
the linguistic symbols by which the natural environment is brought under imaginative control in Canada, in both written and visual arts, McGregor considerably
extended Frye's "garrison" and Atwood's "victim" solutions. As she focused on
techniques and concepts of displacement, the themes she discovered included the
denial of the natural, the sense of alienation and patterns of avoidance, psycho-
logically symbolic settings, the suspicion of and impossibility of transcendence,
the association of love with death, and passive role models. McGregor's extensive variations also exemplified the tendency of Canadian thematic criticism to
discover consistency in almost exclusively negative terms.

Until recently, the bulk of the critical study of Canadian literature favoured this
manner of analysis. Nevertheless, the maturing of English-Canadian fiction and
poetry has manifested a considerable variety of subjects and technical approaches.
This body of work has never been limited to, or exclusively defined by, those
themes outlined above: any such claim would be reductive and inaccurate. It
would appear as if, in acknowledging the national literature to be a legitimate
agent of Canada's self-definition, a narrow schematic constraint would be imposed
on this authentic activity from the outset. Literature never has determinable and
precise dimensions—its concerns are not predictable—and it never realizes itself so
conveniently. What follows, then, suggests the distinctive literary qualities of the

work of some selected major figures in the development of Canadian writing. This overview also often considers these writers' relation to the broader themes that many feel distinguish the enduring shape of Canadian writing.

Frye's original conclusion had used the image of Jonah entering the whale as an analogy for the immigrant travelling down the St. Lawrence River. The inherited values were subject to severe culture shock in the face of a landscape with no familiar contours, and the natural impulse was one of withdrawal—literal, symbolic, psychological. The language and values of Canada's early imaginative literature were those of the writer's native country, of an inherited literary tradition radically unsuited to "a country without a mythology"—the title of a 1948 poem by Douglas LePan.

The potentially habitable areas of Canada required considerable pioneering effort at the frontier. Such physical commitment left little time for aesthetic creation, for completely imaginative separation from the daily round. In consequence, serious Canadian writing had an early and persistent element of the realistic about it. This took several forms: a relative accuracy of representation, an unconscious revelation of a darker psychology beneath the surface, or an implicit celebration of the work ethic, which has persisted into the present. The perspective of realism encouraged an often normative and prescriptive cast of writing in Canada: the community's values were unconsciously enforced and approved in its literature—and in its reception. Behaviour apart from the approved middle way was implicitly condemned, devalued, and distrusted. Conformism of an almost religious dedication was the underlying message. It may be suggested that this presupposes the Canadian habit of self-scrutiny in its literature, an internal policing as opposed to an objective look outwards.

Another attitude that developed almost as a necessary adjunct to realism was irony, a deflation of the romantic, idealistic, or inflated, with the correspondent implication of a more balanced, realistic outlook. This perspective has persisted most emphatically throughout the maturing of the national literary consciousness, finding its structural counterpart in the tendency of Canadian writing to favour ambivalence and duality. The country's literature has seemed to have an earnestness about it as a record of actuality—or has been so received. It is not romantic. Canada's best writing is technically sophisticated, literary in the best sense, and self-absorbed.

DEVELOPMENT OF ENGLISH-CANADIAN WRITING

The present overview highlights the nature and development of English-Canadian writing in the genres of poetry, short story, and novel. The task becomes increasingly difficult, given the growing number of modern and contemporary writers, the refusal of an older defensive attitude to literature, and the increasing maturity of this body of writing. This highly selective survey can only suggest, in the most general terms, some of those authors and particular works with distinctive claims on the critical attention of the present.

❏ THE EARLY PERIOD

Much of the early Canadian literature in reprint is undeniably superior to the sentimental, elegiac, or nationalistic verse and fiction that appeared in Canadian newspapers of the time and, by the mid-nineteenth century, in several genuinely literary magazines. Such popular writing had little real stylistic discipline or distinction, and hewed strictly to standardized character, situation, and community values. Whatever the literary value of such work, in most cases Canadian content was merely nominal and topographical, and often had a tourist's perspective: witness Canada's first novel, Frances Brooke's *The History of Emily Montague* (1769), published in England.

Some Americans loyal to Britain who emigrated to the Maritimes during the War of Independence satirized the liberal and egalitarian values of their former compatriots in verse. Their essentially elitist and sophisticated English culture, however, had crossed the border with them. It was a native-born poet like Halifax's Oliver Goldsmith (1794–1861) whose verse narrative, "The Rising Village" (London, 1825),[8] demonstrated the earnest awkwardnesses of the writer who attempted to re-create the opening of a new land in retrospect. However, Goldsmith had not the experience, technical control, or language. His verbal formulae and conventional figures were obsolete in the age of romantic poetry, while his poem manifested the colonial's uncritical loyalty to an idealized British example.

❏ THE NARRATIVE POEM

With few exceptions it was in the narrative poem rather than in prose—romance, intrigue, society, and moral lessons its usual subjects—that the process of Canada's early settlement was inventively re-created. "Acadia" (1874),[9] by Joseph Howe (1804–1873), was a retrospective celebration of the civilizing process on the frontier; his elementary insight into the psychology behind the loyalty to territory somewhat offset his relatively static and conventional heroic verse form. But in the anomalous "The St. Lawrence and the Saguenay" (1856)[10] by Charles Sangster (1822–1893), the conventions of allegory were intriguingly imposed on a voyage down the St. Lawrence. The Canadian landscape was given both a religious and a geological significance in an equal degree of grimness and celebration, and in artificial Spenserian stanzas.[11]

The exemplar of the earlier Canadian narrative-documentary poem was "Malcolm's Katie" (1884)[12] by Isabella Valancy Crawford (1850–1887). This was a standard love story leavened by the immature hero's need to prove himself against the wilderness, and by a nihilistic suitor. However, the poem had a considerable density of carefully repeated symbol, metaphor, and image patterns in its unflagging vivacity. Crawford's themes were skilfully and subtly woven into an extraordinary concentration of singularly connotative phrases and words. Human and natural correspondences were constantly implied through an inventive Indian mythology. The attractive villain, Alfred, had an existential view of time that was bleak, mordant, and eloquent:

Nations immortal? Where the well-trimmed lamps
Of long-past ages? When Time seemed to pause
On smooth, dust-blotted graves that, like the tombs
Of monarchs, held dead bones and sparkling gems,
She saw no glimmer on the hideous ring
Of the black clouds; no stream of sharp, clear light
From those great torches passed into the black
Of deep oblivion.

Crawford's sophistication, range, and control were considerably in advance of
her time: her poem remains powerful and unique. Crawford's accomplished technique did not obscure her poem's focus on place, a continuing mainstay of the
national literature, nor her separation from the essentially colonial perspective of
her literary predecessors.

❑ FICTION

Canadian fiction of the earlier nineteenth century only had a capacity to present
social or adventurous vehicles of a romantic heightening, against which later,
more tutored writers reacted with instructive parables. *The Stepsure Letters*
(1862)[13] of Thomas McCulloch (1776–1843), printed in 1821–1822 and 1823,
attaches the epistolary form of fiction to the humorous illustrative anecdote or
sketch, initiating a model still identifiable in Canadian comic fiction. Through his
crippled protagonist's self-righteously conservative and materialistic values,
McCulloch commented repetitively and with ingenuous burlesque on the vanity
of human wishes. *The Clockmaker* (1836),[14] by Thomas Chandler Haliburton
(1796–1865), follows the same form of the self-contained anecdote in his satire
of Nova Scotian gullibility and economic inertia. His persona, the memorable
Sam Slick, was an American pedlar and raconteur with a genuinely inventive
vernacular that included elementary puns, epigrams ("power has a natural tendency to corpulency"), cautionary *exempla*, and unflattering analogies. Slick's
unrestrained linguistic invention may be seen in his characterization of a
Grahamite:[15]

> He was as thin as a whippin' post. His skin looked like a blown bladder arter
> some of the air had leaked out, kinder wrinkled and rumpled like, and his eye
> as dim as a lamp that's livin' on a short allowance of ile. He put me in mind of
> a pair of kitchen tongs, all legs, shaft, and head, and no belly; a real gander-
> gutted lookin' critter, as holler as a bamboo walkin' cane, and twice as yaller.
> He actilly looked as if he had been picked off a rack at sea, and dragged
> through a gimlet-hole.

Haliburton's popular character, to reappear in a succession of later books of virtually identical format, entertained and instructed with a sometimes heavy-
handed, even hectoring, pointedness. Both McCulloch and Haliburton strongly
emphasized acceptable and contributory social behaviour, the reasonable conduct of life that was often to inform later Canadian realistic fiction.

Wacousta (1832),[16] by John Richardson (1796–1852), is a lengthy Gothic curiosity with a strong basis in the actual conflicts of the War of 1812 in central North America. As historical fiction, it is marred by Romantic excess—melodrama, repetition, idealized characterization, sensationalist details, a series of gross or grotesque incidents, and feverish overwriting. Its conflicts of characters are elementary and vivid; the articulate and Byronic gentleman savage, Wacousta, is consistently more interesting and physical than his pallid and polite antagonists. However, the unambiguous polarities in the novel were an early anticipation of a continuing structural consciousness in English-Canadian literature.

Two later writers, William Kirby (1817–1906) and Gilbert Parker (1862–1932), extended the genre of the Canadian historical novel. Kirby's *The Golden Dog* (1877)[17] was sporadically loyal to actual history in his protracted treatment of the intrigues within the polite society of mid-eighteenth-century Québec City. The character types, passionately unphysical love, betrayal, witchcraft, stirring rhetoric, psychological embroidery, and Gothic trappings gained Kirby a wide audience. *The Seats of the Mighty* (1896)[18] was truer to historical fact and personalities. Parker's first-person narrative by a long-time English captive of the French in Québec, Robert Moray, progresses in a relatively unadorned style through love, disguise, honour, a droll jailer, and a measure of derring-do to Wolfe's victory over the French at Québec in 1759. Parker modulated many of the standard elements of romantic adventure, and also created an attractive and complicated villain, a vain, allusive, and intelligent games player. It is important to note that these novelists were working towards greater psychological truth beneath the romantic formulae of their stories.

The sophisticated *A Strange Manuscript Found in a Copper Cylinder* (1888)[19] of James de Mille (1833–1880) is one of the oddities of Canadian fiction that belongs to no tradition or readily identifiable type, such as local-colour fiction. It is a knowing satire of current travel literature and utopian projections; that it creates a society that takes familiar Christian values to their often irrational and inhumane extremes is another of its distinctions. Though ostensibly a "lost world" adventure, the novel is also a "frame story"[20] with literary and other learned commentary used in a very contemporary manner. It is a rigorous allegory as well as a novel of ideas, a rarity in Canadian fiction. Similarly, one vivacious novel of Sarah Jeannette Duncan (1861–1922), *The Imperialist* (1904),[21] has enjoyed a persistent life. The affected mores and characters of a small Ontario town are treated with a delicate and sophisticated irony, as Duncan bemusedly examined varieties of misdirected love, including an idealistic protagonist's dream of an economic connection with Britain. Duncan's personable narrator is both expansive and epigrammatic, sympathetic and superior, as in her genial consideration of this town:

> Centres of small circumference yield a quick swing; the concern of the average intelligent Englishman as to the consolidation of his country's interests in the Yangtse Valley would be a languid manifestation beside that of an Elgin elector in the chances of an appropriation for a new court house. The single mind is

the most fervid: Elgin had few distractions from the question of the court house or the branch line to Clayfield.[22]

The thematic consistency of the novel, and its precise awareness of current political and social currents, continue to be instructive. Even as fiction, it is an impressively exact document of its time, offering insight into the reality that was Canada. Its presentation and analysis of small-town Ontario's characters and mores is virtually a model for twentieth-century Canadian fictions of this type.

❏ THE CONFEDERATION POETS

The reputation of the so-called Confederation Poets—Charles G.D. Roberts (1860–1943), Bliss Carman (1861–1929), Archibald Lampman (1861–1899), and Duncan Campbell Scott (1862–1947)—was more immediate, commencing with Roberts's first book published in 1880. These writers treated the natural environment as objective phenomena, which they often used as metaphors; their poetry marked a dramatic advance over the sentimental, chauvinistic, or spiritualized verse of the time. The almost invariable Canadian literary attraction to nature was forcefully signalled by these writers.

Roberts's most significant contribution is the unemphatic and intensely visual aspects of his realistic sonnets about a recognizable Nova Scotian hinterland. His early work is best seen in his most celebrated poem, "The Tantramar Revisited."[23] Over a long career, his poetry lost much of its initial control, and suffered diffusion into quasi-mystical impressionism. Bliss Carman, whose familiarity with and genuine love of the changing natural world appears so much wider, brought an infectious energy and emphatic rhythm to his immensely popular songs of the open road. The increasing facility of his work did not completely eclipse evidence of an often splendid articulacy or of an engaging Gothicism as in "The Eavesdropper." Many of his sea poems, for instance, have a careful pathos and measured images, while his best-known early poem, "Low Tide on Grand Pré," uses evocative symbolism and careful repetition that are anything but fortuitous.

Archibald Lampman, whose poetry is often filled with purely sensuous lingering, the moods and atmosphere of autumn, and sometimes socialist sentiments, was the most consistently successful of these writers. Once he lost a derivative Keatsian tone, his highly accomplished sonnets best showed his deceptive control of natural language, with a careful attention to sound values and undemonstrative metaphor, as in "A Thunderstorm":

> And now from heaven's height,
> With the long roar of elm-trees swept and swayed,
> And pelted waters, on the vanished plain
> Plunges the blast. Behind the wild white flash
> Over bleared fields and gardens disarrayed,
> Column on column comes the drenching rain.[24]

Duncan Campbell Scott developed metaphorical correspondences between nature and human psychology in his often tragic romances about Indians. His poems, which toy with free-verse form, could submit to decadent colouration and tenuous allegory, but at their best manage a serious and sympathetic examination of naturalistic impulse, or attempted forms of aesthetic parable. "The Height of Land," a protracted consideration of the artistic nature, contains vividly illustrative passages:

> . . . not to be urged toward the fatal shore
> Where a bush fire, smouldering, with sudden roar
> Leaped on a cedar and smothered it with light
> And terror. It had left the portage-height
> A tangle of slanted spruces burned to the roots,
> Covered still with patches of bright fire
> Smoking with incense of the fragrant resin
> That even then began to thin and lessen
> Into the gloom and glimmer of ruin.[25]

❑ THE SHORT STORY

The short story has been identified as the most consistently accomplished genre in Canadian literature. In *Old Man Savarin and Other Stories* (1895)[26] by E.W. Thomson (1849–1924), the form first emerged with some skill and freedom from an undistinguished romance tradition. These are comic and sociologically unflattering dialect tales of Scottish and habitant life along the Ottawa River. Writing fiction at the same time was Charles G.D. Roberts, whose reputation rests as much on his animal stories as on his less consistent efforts in poetry. In *The Kindred of the Wild* (1902),[27] the first in a number of like volumes, Roberts attempted to be true to animals' naturalistic behaviour and environment, and demonstrated a heretofore unusual control of sentimental identification in this mode.

The satirical sketches and stories of Stephen Leacock (1869–1944) are of a different order. Leacock was a master of comic incongruity, hardly better seen than in his first collection, *Literary Lapses* (1910),[28] and its ever-popular "My Financial Career," or in a selection of brilliantly inventive pseudo-Euclidean "Definitions and Axioms" and "Postulates and Propositions" from "Boarding-House Geometry":

> All boarding-houses are the same boarding-house.
> A single room is that which has no parts and no magnitude.
> All the other rooms being taken, a single room is said to be
> a double room.
> Any two meals at a boarding-house are together less
> than two square meals.
> If from the opposite ends of a boarding-house a
> line be drawn passing through all the rooms in turn, then the
> stovepipe which warms the boarders will lie within that line.[29]

Leacock exploded clichés of language and character, and vigorously mocked forms of popular fiction in *Nonsense Novels* (1911).[30] His best-known books, *Sunshine Sketches of a Little Town* (1912)[31] and *Arcadian Adventures Among the Idle Rich* (1914),[32] mix whimsy, an ingenuous narrative perspective, puns, irony, and his principal device of burlesque in forms that he would successfully repeat for decades. He considered his comedy to be kindly, though there are marked differences between the broadly drawn, pastoral, and sentimental *Sketches* (whose town of Mariposa shares many of the values of Duncan's Elgin) and the urban *Adventures*, with their sharp look at the unpleasant and hypocritical values of capitalism. Perhaps the tone and texture of his wit, which would also depend on deliberate malapropism and purely inventive silliness, can be suggested in the following passage of tolerant exaggeration from *Sunshine Sketches*:

> When Mariposa was laid out there was none of that shortsightedness which is seen in the cramped dimensions of Wall Street and Piccadilly. Missinaba Street is so wide that if you were to roll Jeff Thorpe's barber shop over on its face it wouldn't reach halfway across. Up and down the Main Street are telegraph poles of cedar of colossal thickness, standing at a variety of angles and carrying rather more wires than are commonly seen at a transatlantic cable station.[33]

In this period the short story also asserted itself in the early work of Morley Callaghan (1903–1990), beginning with *A Native Argosy* (1929).[34] His flatly declarative prose conveys credible urban life and ordinary characters, often those forced to struggle with fine moral distinctions and unfamiliar feelings. Their psychology is uncomplicated; they are immediately identifiable; their encounters are simple but never simplistic. The prairie stories of Sinclair Ross (b. 1908), with their isolated characters caught up in the dustbowl of the later thirties (first collected in *The Lamp at Noon*, 1968)[35] have bleak psychological and symbolic dimensions. His portraits of stubborn dreamers battered by experience and environment into mechanical behaviour are compelling and ironic.

Ethel Wilson's stylish short fiction from the forties and fifties (in *Mrs. Golightly and Other Stories*, 1961)[36] has an often whimsical perspective and a sometimes patronizing narrative voice that anticipates the reflexive styles of the later modernist period. Even at her most exquisitely and coolly ironic, Wilson (1888–1980) crafted a deliberate and virtuoso mixture of the elevated and the commonplace, the comic and the pathetic. Her characters express and experience such juxtapositions in her well-regarded novels, such as *Hetty Dorval* (1947) and *The Innocent Traveller* (1949).[37] Her clever sophistication contrasts with the work of Hugh Garner (1913–1979), whose often formulaic fictions with their repetitively ironic closure emphasize varieties of determinism. His focus on the often unrewarding lives of the working class and the social outcasts is distinctive and sympathetic.

❑ NOVELS

Many other writers of fiction flourished in great, and often undistinguished, numbers in the early decades of the twentieth century, when the various forms of the romantic novel achieved a singular popularity. However, Canadian fiction also reflected in its own ways the growing modernist movement in literature. The novel, in looking at urban rather than rural life, became increasingly psychological and less superficial; story was internal rather than being restricted to physical event. An awareness of rhetorical style and thematic structure began to be apparent, and any regional sensibilities of fiction seemed to begin to suggest a broader Canadian perspective.

Wild Geese (1925),[38] by Martha Ostenso (1900–1963), the story of a brutally repressive farmer, Caleb Gare, obsessed with his property, still has much of its startlingly original naturalistic power. The psychological and sexual implications of her novel marked a new level in Canadian fiction, a virtual refusal of the polite conventions of character and morality that had effectively been the hallmark of the country's culture. A more influential writer was Frederick Philip Grove (1879–1948), whose European background was reflected in his novels' sometimes weighty attention to the psychological and sexual forces inherent in the human condition. His forceful, obsessive prairie characters, almost wholly subject to their passions, are blindly bent on mastery of their pioneering conditions in such novels as *Settlers of the Marsh* (1925), *Our Daily Bread* (1928), and *Fruits of the Earth* (1933).[39] They have an inevitability of tragic personality that depends on their almost willful neglect of their human needs. Grove's fictions, though sometimes stylistically awkward and strangled and lugubriously earnest, have strong and pitiful characters in elemental conflict with themselves, their society, and the environment—itself rendered with a characteristically precise and evocative skill best seen in his essays, *Over Prairie Trails* (1922) and *The Turn of the Year* (1923).[40] Significantly, the fictional pathology of Ostenso's and Grove's characters reflect a nearly current tendency in American writing.

The novels of Morley Callaghan have often had deliberate echoes of Christian stories, like the ironic, pathos-ridden *Such Is My Beloved* (1934).[41] Callaghan's narrative consistencies are a strong evocation of place, a concern with social pressures and hierarchies, forms of the quest, and varieties of innocence. His work, with its implicit moral thrust, relies on the formal metaphor; it is never far from parable. His virtually uninflected and economical narrative style often reflects the deliberate and literal thought processes of his characters.

The novels of Hugh MacLennan (1907–1990) have the strengths of persuasive historical re-creation (the 1917 Halifax explosion in *Barometer Rising*, 1941)[42] as well as unabashed commentaries on the condition of the country, such as *Two Solitudes* (1945)[43]—the latter giving a key, but incorrectly understood, phrase to many subsequent descriptions of French–English relations in Canada—and the mentality of the thirties in *The Watch That Ends the Night* (1959).[44] His fiction is selectively symbolic, artificial in dialogue, indebted to

classical and Christian mythology (*Each Man's Son*, 1951),[45] and often heavily
but sincerely instructive in tone. However, its force of conviction is cleanly com-
municated in characters and events completely appropriate to their times, and in
often reverberant description:

> I sat in silence staring at the landscape which stared back: form and colour and
> light and shade, useless to farmers, some of the oldest rock in the world crop-
> ping out of it, dark green and light green, ancient, mindless, from everlasting to
> everlasting without any purpose anyone could possibly understand, but there.[46]

The persistent Canadian literary attraction to space, and its corollary of hori-
zonless entrapment, is epitomized in two prominent prairie novels. Sinclair
Ross's *As For Me and My House* (1941)[47] repeats the bleak environmental and
personal isolation of his stories. The novel is an obsessive, even masochistic
record of repetitive passages in the dust-ridden lives of a failed minister, whose
frustrated inner life is aesthetic, and his wife, a diarist who unconsciously sup-
presses any positive emotions in their relationship. The later *Sawbones
Memorial* (1974),[48] an unusual interplay of voices, shows a dramatic relaxation
of thematic insistence compared to previous work.

In contrast to the work of Ross, the skilful admixture of different characters
and moods—from earthily profane to allegorically distant, and from socially out-
cast to the humanely inclusive—is realized in *Who Has Seen the Wind* (1947)[49]
by W.O. Mitchell (b. 1914). The novel, set during and after the Depression, trans-
lates spiritual values into the naturally symbolic and seasonal, centring on "the
prairie wind that lifted over the edge of the prairie world to sing mortality to every
living thing." Mitchell combines comically eccentric characters, as he would in the
stories of *Jake and the Kid* (1962),[50] with the conundrums of existence and
truths of the heart in a masterly, enduring fiction. His later novels, such as *How I
Spent My Summer Holidays* (1981),[51] are darker in social and personal implication, but maintain many aspects of his earlier successful formulae.

Several completely unique novels appeared in this period. *Sarah Binks*
(1947),[52] by Paul Hiebert (1892–1987), is an ingenious and immaculate burlesque of literary biography. The apparently worshipful biographer of "The Sweet
Songstress of Saskatchewan" is loyal to every cliché about the artistic personality. The novel observes the conventions of the type, literary biography, even
wittily inventing its subject's untutored verses. In 1947, *Under the Volcano* by
Malcolm Lowry (1909–1957)[53] was also published, and was subsequently
admired as an extravagantly learned and technically remarkable novel. Its simple story is of the inelegant final stages in the life of an alcoholic in Mexico. The
novel, with its recurrent symbols, imagery, motifs, and allusions, is a highly literary performance whose technical literary devices often pre-empt its narrative.
The implied search for communion or revelation, but not the stylistic complexity,
would occupy Lowry's later work, much of it assembled posthumously.

The Mountain and the Valley (1952),[54] by Ernest Buckler (1908–1984),
amplifies a pastoral story of growth and private artistic ambition through a lav-

ishly prodigal poetic style and intensive metaphorical elaboration. Buckler's uniquely self-conscious expression, however, is ironically directed at the character, David Canaan, who is distinguished only in his own estimation, and crudely limited by his rural Nova Scotian environment. *The Double Hook* (1959),[55] by Sheila Watson (b. 1909), is a spare, intensely symbolic and mythic prairie mystery, cryptic in character, event, and style, its manner as connotative and Gothic as its matter. The novel is tense, laconic, and allegorical in its dislocating amalgam of extreme human behaviour and unfamiliar beliefs: Eliot's Wasteland superimposed on western Canada.

❑ POETRY

Canadian modernist poetry effectively began with the work of A.J.M. Smith (1902–1980), F.R. Scott (1899–1985), A.M. Klein (1909–1972), and Dorothy Livesay (b. 1909). This body of writing, heavily influenced by the work of T.S. Eliot, Ezra Pound, and the Imagists, was announced in the undergraduate work of Smith and Scott at McGill University in the later twenties. It was to become imagistic, spare, erudite, significantly metaphorical, allusive, rigorously crafted, and compressed. These poets were particularly aware of the rich ambiguities and connotations of language, an emphasis that was to identify many of the best Canadian writers thereafter.

A.J.M. Smith and F.R. Scott advanced modernist Canadian poetry for decades after the later twenties—Smith particularly as critic and anthologist. His symbolist and metaphysical tendencies, and his general adherence to precise form and aesthetic sensibility, did not take a specifically Canadian direction. His is a taut and precisely connotative lyricism not separable from modernist irony, or from the intellectual socialism of the thirties:

> They say the Phoenix is dying, some say dead.
> Dead without issue is what one message said,
> But that has been suppressed, officially denied.
>
> I think myself the man who sent it lied.
> In any case, I'm told, he has been shot,
> As a precautionary measure, whether he did or not.
> ("News of the Phoenix")[56]

Scott's favoured epigrammatic expression in verse was not apparent in his pointed and devastating social satires, which implied a failure of forms of order and of rational perspective. His accessible intelligence, and metaphorical gifts, were usually apparent:

> The water's deepest colonnades
> Contract the blood, and to this home
> That stirs the dark amphibian
> With me the naked swimmers come
> Drawn to their prehistoric womb.
> ("Lakeshore")[57]

Even in her aggressively socialist poetry of the thirties, Dorothy Livesay had a characteristic, deceptively informal, personal, and sensual awareness; much of her work explores human relationships in a considerable variety of free poetic forms with a surprising loyalty to traditional practices. A.M. Klein's attentions to his Jewish and French-Canadian background and environment resulted in devotional and comic poetry of a unique density and emotion. His essentially celebratory imagination, fired by a rich and multilingual vocabulary, was generous with wittily transforming metaphor. In "Portrait of the Poet as Landscape" a characteristic underlying pathos is apparent:

> Look, he is
> the nth Adam taking a green inventory
> in world but scarcely uttered, naming, praising,
> the flowering fiats in the meadow, the
> syllabled fur, stars aspirate, the pollen
> whose sweet collision sounds eternally.
>
> For to praise
> the world—he, solitary man—is breath
> to him.[58]

Contemporary with this group was Newfoundland's E.J. Pratt (1882–1964), whose earlier lyrical forms (beginning with *Newfoundland Verse*, 1923)[59] evolved into such different, detailed, and epic poetic narratives as "The Titanic" (1935), "Brebeuf and his Brethren" (1940), and "Towards the Last Spike" (1952).[60] Pratt considered the subjection of our species to the elemental forces of nature and to our nature, the latter ironically unchanged from its primeval origins. As well, he examined how humanity turns simple beliefs into mechanical certainty. Much of his poetry, and its invariable themes of struggle, heroism, accident, and faith assumed such traditional forms as blank verse. Always it had a formally appropriate and associative language:

> Willy-nilly, he comes or goes, with the clown's logic,
> Comic in epitaph, tragic in epithalamium,
> And unseduced by any mused rhyme.
> However blow the winds over the pollen,
> Whatever the course of the garden variables,
> He remains the constant,
> Ever flowering from the poppy seeds.
> ("Come Away, Death")[61]

Pratt's work influenced that of Earle Birney (b. 1904), whose wide-ranging familiarity with mythology and Anglo-Saxon literature, international travels, openness to experimental forms, and deep understanding of metaphor, irony, and rhythm have added immeasurably to his enduring popularity and accessibility. His satires and elegies on humanity's depredation of nature, and thereby of itself, are variously acute, uncompromising, poignant, and always literate:

No one bound Prometheus   Himself he chained
and consumed his own bright liver   O stranger
Plutonian   descendant   or beast in the stretching night—
there was light

("Vancouver Lights")[62]

Canada's earlier modernist poets were countered by a group in the 1940s who stood broadly for native, unaffected, socialist, and realistic poetry of direct emotion, which continued in the fifties as assertively direct, rhetorical, anti-academic, personal, and vigorous—in opposition to the elitism, intellectualism, and austerity charged against their immediate predecessors. This group—including the epigrammatic, formal, and philosophical Louis Dudek (b. 1918) and the urban, ironic, and colloquial Raymond Souster (b. 1921)—was principally represented by Irving Layton (b. 1912). Layton has often attacked Canadian pusillanimity in satiric poems of great vigour, vulgarity, and vividness; yet his range of moods and verse forms has been considerable, and his command of pathos and eloquence is persistently demonstrated, even as early in his career as the later 1940s. He has always written on Jewish experience, the function of poetry, the life of the body, and the repression of feeling by convention and bureaucracy, among many other subjects, with sometimes swaggering imagery and self-confident power:

How to dominate reality? Love is one way;
    imagination another. Sit here
beside me, sweet; take my hard hand in yours.
We'll mark the butterflies disappearing over the hedge
    with tiny wristwatches on their wings:
our fingers touching the earth, like two Buddhas.

("The Fertile Muck")[63]

Layton's artistic contemporary, P.K. Page (b. 1916), has a whimsical sensibility, covering psychological depths with vivid colouration, a firm sense of formal composition, and inventively playful imagery often drawn from childhood and innocence. However, from within a cool irony despair is often proposed:

In the inch of noon as they move they are stagnant.
The terrible calm of the noon is their anguish;
the lip of the counter, the shapes of the straws
like icicles breaking their tongues, are invaders.

("The Stenographers")[64]

The early poetry of Leonard Cohen (b. 1934) has a decadent sensuousness, thereafter being variously concerned with mythology, religion, the Jewish condition, the urge to purity and simplification, love, a strong sense of the mystical, and a romantic balladeering. Even in his most deceptively informal work, the aesthetic has often been his subject and manner:

I once believed a single line
in a Chinese poem could change
forever how blossoms fell
and that the moon itself climbed on
the grief of concise weeping men
to journey over cups of wine . . . .
("For E.J.P.")[65]

Cohen's poetry loosely accorded with the appearance of several poets of the fifties whose unified and deliberately structured collections were centred on a particular figure or theme, mythology being one. The contrasting poetic values of unaffected expression and academic formality, for example the works of Alden Nowlan (1935–1983) and Margaret Avison (b. 1918), were to constitute a continuing creative dialogue.

CONTEMPORARY ENGLISH-CANADIAN WRITING

Modern and contemporary Canadian fiction, for long considered middle-of-the-road in emotion and expression and middle class in subject, has become significantly aware of the irrational, nonlinear, and fantastic, at first in content and, more recently, as a self-conscious aspect of narrative form. Time as theme and as structural device is more apparent; the conventions of realistic fiction are breached. In effect, as content has become more self-absorbed and inward looking, form has become centrifugal.

The novels of Robertson Davies (b. 1913) in three trilogies have evolved from urbane, well-made comedies about confused ambition, such as *Leaven of Malice* (1954),[66] into highly sophisticated and distinctive treatments of passion, mythology, psychology (principally Jungian), academic obsessions, and art. The narrative tone and manner of poised and elegant formality persists. Davies's later fiction, beginning with *Fifth Business* (1970),[67] is more intellectually engaging, though his persistent themes, the heart–mind division and the ways towards self-realization, remain broadly evident. In *The Rebel Angels* (1981)[68] and afterwards, archly discursive interpolations on appropriately eccentric and arcane topics appear. His work contrasts with that of Mordecai Richler (b. 1931), whose *The Apprenticeship of Duddy Kravitz* (1959)[69] began to epitomize his distinctive traits: strong comedy in many verbal and physical degrees, an essentially cinematic structure, a surprising facility with pathos, and questing protagonists unknowingly in need of mature hearts. Richler's grander novels, *St. Urbain's Horseman* (1971)[70] and *Joshua Then and Now* (1981),[71] experiment with temporal dislocation, avoid simplistic ethical dispositions, and continue the comic successes with eccentrics and grotesques in a society where social and role models are inevitably compromised.

The Canadian novel continued to discover the range and possibilities of narrative voice, and a deliberate commitment to artistic expression, in the contrasting work of Margaret Laurence (1926–1987) and Robert Kroetsch (b. 1927)—a claim that could be proven in the work of many other contemporary Canadian novelists. In Laurence's most familiar work, centred on the prairie region of fictional Manawaka—*The Stone Angel* (1964),[72] *A Jest of God* (1966),[73] and *The Diviners* (1974)[74]—her self-isolated, self-affirming, three-dimensional women reject the tyranny of the conventional and find their passionate natures. They have further family resemblances: vigorous mental lives, wry self-deprecation, the urge to establish independent identities. Even Laurence's peripheral characters, however eccentric, are completely authentic. The voices of her fallible protagonists are sensuously and literately convincing; familiar with emphatic biblical parallels and allusions, they warmly and fully realize themselves in rich frameworks of symbolism and metaphor.

> In summer the cemetery was rich and thick as syrup with the funeral-parlor perfume of the planted peonies, dark crimson and wallpaper pink, the pompous blossoms hanging leadenly, too heavy for their light stems, bowed down with the weight of themselves and the weight of the rain, infested with upstart ants that sauntered through the plush petals as though to the manner born.[75]

In his novels, Robert Kroetsch—also an accomplished poet and persuasive literary theoretician—plays with narrative voice and the conventional elements of fiction. His work, including *Gone Indian* (1973),[76] *What the Crow Said* (1978),[77] and *Badlands* (1975),[78] unabashedly emphasizes the process and devices of fiction. Extravagant comedy complements his reflexive stories and their incongruous picaresque characters. Realism is subverted; conventional literary practice is inverted, highlighted, and parodied, as with the intrusive, mad, and subjective Demeter Proudfoot, narrator of *The Studhorse Man* (1969):

> The biographer is a person afflicted with sanity. He is a man who must first of all be sound of mind, and in the clarity of his own vision he must ride out the dark night, ride on while all about him falls into chaos. The man of the cold eye and the steady hand, he faces for all of humanity the ravishments and the terrors of existence.[79]

Kroetsch's novels, being discontinuous with their clear dualisms and thematic direction towards beginnings and identities, are challenges to linear thinking.

The short story manifested new subtleties after the relatively undemonstrative achievements of Hugh Garner. In the later twentieth century the short story in Canada has been represented by an unusual number of skilled practitioners for whom the expression of story, or narrative technique, is becoming fundamentally important. The truly modern short story appeared with the work of Mavis Gallant (b. 1922). Her fiction, including her novels, has an emotional and figurative subtlety, from her first collection, *The Other Paris* (1956)[80] to the more recent *Home Truths* (1981).[81] She has written often of dislocated characters, self-isolating dreamers, the lack of communication, and fractured relationships. Her stories are Canadian and European in setting, often featuring the culture shock of exiles and refugees from all conditions of life, including war. Her style is smooth and undemonstrative, with a thoroughness of characterization, subtly understated effects, an immaculate communication of detail, and an often delicately ironic narrative perspective.

A new emphasis on careful rhetorical formulation could also be seen in the first volume of stories by Hugh Hood (b. 1928), *Flying a Red Kite* (1962).[82] His intricate craft and Christian themes are deceptively informal. The topical variety of his many stories, their unobtrusive formal organization, their ingenuously symbolic figures, and their consistent articulacy have been consistently noted— perhaps most particularly in *August Nights* (1985).[83] Hood's massive novel sequence, *The New Age* (1975)[84], aims to re-create the social and moral climate of much of this century in Canada. Short fiction requires sophistication in theme and technique, and Hood's stories have achieved that level.

In the sure and convincing realism of the stories of Alice Munro (b. 1931), many revealing the Gothic heart of regional Ontario (*Dance of the Happy Shades*, 1968),[85] reality itself may be paradoxically suspect. Munro's apparently unaffected narrative technique manipulates linear time, subtly enforces reverberations, parallels, and contrasts; many of her shapely stories focus unobtrusively on the act of storytelling (see especially *Something I've Been Meaning to Tell You*, 1974).[86] Even at its most offhand, the language of her narrators implies the mysteries of character. Her matter is the completely and identifiably human, the complications behind simplicity, the disorder underlying the surface of life, and the unrevealed eccentricities of behaviour and the heart (see *The Moons of Jupiter*, 1982).[87]

The work of Margaret Atwood (b. 1939), in the novel, short story, and poetry, has won a major rank in contemporary writing. Her poetry, by which she first was known, often regards isolation and psychic spaces in its flat tones, and uses suggestively psychological metaphor in an expression and theme of fragments. Her analogies have been original and grotesque; her gift is a fanciful, often chillingly unsettling dislocation of attitude and image:

> Starspangled cowboy
> sauntering out of the almost-
> silly West, on your face
> a porcelain grin,
> tugging a papier-mache cactus
> on wheels behind you with a string,
>
> you are innocent as a bathtub
> full of bullets.
>> ("Backdrop addresses cowboy")[88]

Atwood's novels, from *The Edible Woman* (1969)[89] to the recent *Cat's Eye* (1988),[90] have at their best modulated their programmatic themes with a brisk ironic comedy, as in *Lady Oracle* (1974)[91]—also to be seen in the collection of stories, *Dancing Girls* (1977).[92] Some less satisfying fictions, such as *Surfacing* (1972),[93] more closely support the formulations of *Survival* in their sometimes ponderous seriousness.

The poetry of Al Purdy (b. 1918) matured in the mid-sixties. It has an often rangy, colloquial informality that can become reflective and unusually lyrical. His comedy and casualness are deceptive; his poems have intellectual peaks and imagistic completeness, many moments of profound regret, and are more purposive than impressionistic. His manner is the process of poetic thought; his particular subjects are time and place, even when his persistent sense of deflating irony is evident:

> lost relatives of these
> whose hooves were thunder
> the ghosts of horses battering thru the wind
> whose names were the wind's common usage
> whose life was the sun's
> arriving here at chilly noon
> in the gasoline smell of the
> dust and waiting 15 minutes
> at the grocer's—
> ("The Cariboo Horses")[94]

The poetry of Michael Ondaatje (b. 1943) mixes and isolates violence, domestic incident, and exoticism in an often surrealistic amalgam. Strange, eccentric, and unpredictable oddities in behaviour, content, and syntax mark his work, especially the stunningly imaginative achievements of *The Collected Works of Billy the Kid* (1970).[95] His work persistently suggests an offbeat artistic presence, and not only in challenging, grotesque, and seemingly disconnected analogies:

> At night the gold and black slashed bees come
> pluck my head away. Vague thousands drift
> leave brain naked stark as liver
> each one carries atoms of flesh, they
> walk my body in their fingers.
> The mind stinks out.
> ("Gold and Black")[96]

CONCLUSION

At the beginning of this overview, a number of representative themes were identified in modern Canadian criticism of the body of English-Canadian fiction and poetry. These have long been thought to pinpoint some distinctive and repeated concerns expressed in the national literature. However, such themes—for example, isolation, identity, a threatening natural environment, the denial of the heroic, and emotional restraint—can equally broadly be associated with the literature of any pioneering and frontier society. Furthermore, these notions can be seen as somewhat extra-literary: they summarize aspects of literary culture often in terms of sociology. They are not peculiar to Canadian writing, nor can they be said to constitute almost archetypal certainties. Such a perspective is little more than reductive. Yet in this mode of literary analysis some contemporary Canadian literary criticism is favouring a broader range of themes and approaches. These include the notions of exile, the individual in and against society, space, postmodern attitudes and practice, and feminist literary theory and studies.

Canadian literary criticism has, at one period in its development, needed to have such apparent thematic certainties, an assurance that has been identified as somewhat defensive about, perhaps, the merit and significance of the writing itself. To a large extent this criticism has relied on paraphrase and plot; its interpretive function has been, if not discounted, at best de-emphasized. However, critical attention is now strongly directed to the literary qualities of Canadian writing, in what can be described as the recognition of the maturity and even aggressive sophistication of this material.

In short, the situation of both the literature and its criticism has changed dramatically. This writing can no longer be seen through a limited number of critical formulations or thematic models. Contemporary Canadian literature does not seem particularly dependent on the history of its development, nor does it appear to subject itself to any kind of conformity in style or subject. Even within its own national precincts, Canadian literature has become autonomous. When the work of individual writers is now compared to that of others, the point of reference may not necessarily be Canadian, but that of an international literary community. The national literature is now being appreciated, studied, and analysed by an international audience.

The present overview has considered a broad, historical core of the Canadian literary enterprise. However, this survey is only selectively inclusive, and it is inevitably foreshortened by the continuing emergence of a large number of new Canadian writers. Furthermore, the complexity of literary history has been considerably simplified in this chapter: for example, many contemporary writers are not confined to one genre, and many who are identified with the modernist mid-century period continue to produce significant work. Anthologies are appearing that represent not only a variety of Canadian regions, but also experimental forms that have evolved from traditional genres. In addition, such particular heritages as the Jewish, Italian, native Indian, and Caribbean are being represented in recent collections of cross-cultural writing. The old categories and divisions of Canadian literature have expanded with extraordinary rapidity, range, and assurance.

The proliferation of estimable writers in recent decades has been remarkable, a phenomenon that has been encouraged by federal and provincial government funding for the arts. Many of the writers considered above have been awarded relatively extensive critical attention. What may have been a parochial attention to Canadian literature in the past is disappearing. More writers are answering to exacting contemporary critical standards, and the older thematic assumptions about this body of writing are now being seen as one aspect of an ongoing historical development.

Notes

[1] D. Pacey, *Creative Writing in Canada: A Short History of English-Canadian Literature* (Toronto: Ryerson Press, 1952. Rev. ed., 1961).

[2] N. Frye, "Conclusion" in C.F. Klinck, gen. ed., *Literary History of Canada: Canadian Literature in English* (Toronto: University of Toronto Press, 1965), 830.

[3] M. Atwood, *The Journals of Susanna Moodie* (Toronto: Oxford University Press, 1970), 62.

[4] D.G. Jones, *Butterfly on Rock: A Study of Themes and Images in Canadian Literature* (Toronto: University of Toronto Press, 1970).

[5] M. Atwood, *Survival: A Thematic Guide to Canadian Literature* (Toronto: House of Anansi Press, 1972).

[6] J. Moss, *Patterns of Isolation in English-Canadian Fiction* (Toronto: McClelland & Stewart, 1974).

[7] G. McGregor, *The Wacousta Syndrome: Explorations in the Canadian Landscape* (Toronto: University of Toronto Press, 1985).

[8] O. Goldsmith, "The Rising Village," in *Nineteenth-Century Narrative Poems,* ed. D. Sinclair (Toronto: McClelland & Stewart, New Canadian Library, 1972), 1–15.

[9] J. Howe, "Acadia," in *Nineteenth-Century Narrative Poems*, 17–41.

[10] C. Sangster, "The St. Lawrence and the Saguenay," in *Nineteenth-Century Narrative Poems*, 43–80.

[11] The nine-line stanza form, created by English poet Edmund Spenser, was first employed in his *Faerie Queene* (1590). It has the distinctive rhyme scheme ababbcbcc; all lines are in iambic pentameter except the last, which is iambic hexameter.

[12] I.V. Crawford, "Malcolm's Katie: A Love Story," in *Nineteenth-Century Narrative Poems*, 157–90. The quotation is found on p. 177.

[13] T. McCulloch, *The Stepsure Letters* (Toronto: McClelland & Stewart, New Canadian Library, 1960). The *Letters* were not published in book form until nineteen years after McCulloch's death, in Halifax.

[14] T.C. Haliburton, *The Clockmaker* (Toronto: McClelland & Stewart, New Canadian Library, 1958). The epigram is from p. 83.

[15] A Grahamite was a member of a possibly fictitious American sect whose members, according to Sam Slick, avoided meat and excitement, subsisting on water and bland victuals. See p. 80.

[16] J. Richardson, *Wacousta or the Prophecy* (Toronto: McClelland & Stewart, New Canadian Library, 1967).

[17] W. Kirby, *The Golden Dog: A Romance of Old Québec* (Toronto: McClelland & Stewart, New Canadian Library, 1969).

[18] G. Parker, *The Seats of the Mighty* (Toronto: McClelland & Stewart, New Canadian Library, 1971).

[19] J. de Mille, *A Strange Manuscript Found in a Copper Cylinder* (Toronto: McClelland & Stewart, New Canadian Library, 1969).

[20] The literary device of enclosing a coherent narrative within an external framework, which itself functions as the occasion and setting for the main story related. Elements from the frame—characters, opinions, refreshments—may sporadically interrupt the narrative proper.

[21] S.J. Duncan, *The Imperialist* (Toronto: McClelland & Stewart, New Canadian Library, 1990).

[22] Duncan, *The Imperialist*, 59–60.

[23] C.G.D. Roberts, *The Collected Poems of Sir Charles G.D. Roberts*, ed. D. Pacey (Wolfville, NS: Wombat Press, 1985): 78–79.

[24] A. Lampman, *The Poems of Archibald Lampman* (Toronto: University of Toronto Press, 1974), 215. D. Lochhead, gen. ed., *Literature of Canada: Poetry and Prose in Reprint*.

[25] D.C. Scott, *Selected Poetry*, ed. G. Clever (Ottawa: Tecumseh Press, 1974), 54.

[26] E.W. Thomson, *Old Man Savarin and Other Stories: Tales of Canada and Canadians* (Toronto: University of Toronto Press, 1974). Lochhead, *Literature of Canada: Poetry and Prose in Reprint*.

[27] C.G.D. Roberts, *The Kindred of the Wild: A Book of Animal Life* (Boston: Page, 1902). Selections from this collection appear in C.G.D. Roberts, *The Last Barrier and Other Stories* (Toronto: McClelland & Stewart, New Canadian Library, 1958).

[28] S. Leacock, *Literary Lapses* (Toronto: McClelland & Stewart, New Canadian Library, 1989).

[29] Ibid., 11, 12.

[30] S. Leacock, *Nonsense Novels* (Toronto: McClelland & Stewart, New Canadian Library, 1973).

[31] S. Leacock, *Sunshine Sketches of a Little Town* (Toronto: McClelland & Stewart, New Canadian Library, 1990).

[32] S. Leacock, *Arcadian Adventures with the Idle Rich* (Toronto: McClelland & Stewart, New Canadian Library, 1990).

[33] Leacock, *Sunshine Sketches*, 14.

[34] M. Callaghan, *A Native Argosy* (Toronto: Macmillan, 1929).

[35] S. Ross, *The Lamp at Noon and Other Stories* (Toronto: McClelland & Stewart, New Canadian Library, 1989).

[36] E. Wilson, *Mrs. Golightly and Other Stories* (Toronto: McClelland & Stewart, New Canadian Library, 1990).

[37] E. Wilson, *Hetty Dorval* (Toronto: McClelland & Stewart, New Canadian Library, 1990); *The Innocent Traveller* (Toronto: McClelland & Stewart, New Canadian Library, 1990).

[38] M. Ostenso, *Wild Geese* (Toronto: McClelland & Stewart, New Canadian Library, 1985).

[39] F.P. Grove, *Settlers of the Marsh* (Toronto: McClelland & Stewart, New Canadian Library, 1989); *Our Daily Bread* (Toronto: McClelland & Stewart, New Canadian Library, 1975); *Fruits of the Earth* (Toronto: McClelland & Stewart, New Canadian Library, 1989).

[40] F.P. Grove, *Over Prairie Trails* (Toronto: McClelland & Stewart, New Canadian Library, 1957); *The Turn of the Year* (Toronto: McClelland & Stewart, 1923).

[41] M. Callaghan, *Such Is My Beloved* (Toronto: McClelland & Stewart, New Canadian Library, 1989).

[42] H. MacLennan, *Barometer Rising* (Toronto: McClelland & Stewart, New Canadian Library, 1989).

[43] H. MacLennan, *Two Solitudes* (Toronto: Macmillan, Macmillan Paperbacks, 1989).

[44] H. MacLennan, *The Watch That Ends the Night* (Toronto: Macmillan, Macmillan Paperbacks, 1988).

[45] H. MacLennan, *Each Man's Son* (Toronto: Macmillan, Macmillan Paperbacks, 1988).

[46] MacLennan, *The Watch That Ends the Night*, 265.

[47] S. Ross, *As For Me and My House* (Toronto: McClelland & Stewart, New Canadian Library, 1990).

[48] S. Ross, *Sawbones Memorial* (Toronto: McClelland & Stewart, New Canadian Library, 1978).

[49] W.O. Mitchell, *Who Has Seen the Wind* (Toronto: Bantam Seal Books, 1982). The quotation appears on p. 30.

[50] W.O. Mitchell, *Jake and the Kid* (Toronto: Bantam Seal Books, 1982).

[51] W.O. Mitchell, *How I Spent My Summer Holidays* (Toronto: Bantam Seal Books, 1981).

[52] P. Hiebert, *Sarah Binks* (Toronto: McClelland & Stewart, New Canadian Library, 1979).

[53] M. Lowry, *Under the Volcano* (Toronto: Penguin Books, 1962).

[54] E. Buckler, *The Mountain and the Valley* (Toronto: McClelland & Stewart, New Canadian Library, 1989).

[55] S. Watson, *The Double Hook* (Toronto: McClelland & Stewart, New Canadian Library, 1989).

[56] A.J.M. Smith, *The Classic Shade: Selected Poems* (Toronto: McClelland & Stewart, 1978), 77.

[57] F.R. Scott, *The Collected Poems of F.R. Scott* (Toronto: McClelland & Stewart, 1981), 50.

[58] A.M. Klein, *The Collected Poems of A.M. Klein*, comp. M. Waddington (Toronto: McGraw-Hill Ryerson, 1974), 334–35.

[59] E.J. Pratt, *Newfoundland Verse* (Toronto: Ryerson Press, 1923).

[60] E.J. Pratt, *The Collected Poems of E. J. Pratt*, ed. N. Frye (Toronto: Macmillan, 1958).

[61] Pratt, *Collected Poems*, 95.

[62] E. Birney, *Ghost in the Wheels: Selected Poems* (Toronto: McClelland & Stewart, 1977), 29.

[63] I. Layton, *The Collected Poems of Irving Layton* (Toronto: McClelland & Stewart, 1971), 28.

[64] P.K. Page, *Poems Selected and New* (Toronto: House of Anansi Press, 1974), 17.

[65] L. Cohen, *Selected Poems 1956–1968* (Toronto: McClelland & Stewart, 1968), 124.

[66] R. Davies, *Leaven of Malice* (Markham, Ont.: Penguin Books, 1980).

[67] R. Davies, *Fifth Business* (Markham, Ont.: Penguin Books, 1977).

[68] R. Davies, *The Rebel Angels* (Markham, Ont.: Penguin Books, 1982).

[69] M. Richler, *The Apprenticeship of Duddy Kravitz* (Toronto: McClelland & Stewart, New Canadian Library, 1989).

[70] M. Richler, *St. Urbain's Horseman* (Toronto: Bantam Books, 1972).

[71] M. Richler, *Joshua Then and Now* (Toronto: Bantam Seal Books, 1982).

[72] M. Laurence, *The Stone Angel* (Toronto: McClelland & Stewart, New Canadian Library, 1989).

[73] M.Laurence, *A Jest of God* (Toronto: McClelland & Stewart, New Canadian Library, 1989).

[74] M. Laurence, *The Diviners* (Toronto: McClelland & Stewart, New Canadian Library, 1989).

[75] Laurence, *The Stone Angel*, 4.

[76] R. Kroetsch, *Gone Indian* (Nanaimo, BC: Theytus Books, 1981).

[77] R. Kroetsch, *What the Crow Said* (Toronto: General Publishing, New Press Canadian Classics, 1983).

[78] R. Kroetsch, *Badlands* (Toronto: General Publishing, New Press Canadian Classics, 1982).

[79] R. Kroetsch, *The Studhorse Man* (Toronto: Random House, 1988), 165.

[80] M. Gallant, *The Other Paris* (Toronto: Macmillan, 1986).

[81] M. Gallant, *Home Truths: Selected Canadian Stories* (Toronto: Macmillan, Macmillan Paperbacks, 1986).

[82] H. Hood, *Flying A Red Kite* (Erin, ON: Porcupine's Quill, 1987).

[83] H. Hood, *August Nights* (Toronto: Stoddart, 1985).

[84] In order of appearance, to date the sequence includes *The Swing in the Garden, A New Athens, Reservoir Ravine, Black and White Keys, The Scenic Art, The Motor Boys in Ottawa*, and *Tony's Book*.

[85] A. Munro, *Dance of the Happy Shades* (Toronto: McGraw-Hill Ryerson, 1973).

[86] A. Munro, *Something I've Been Meaning to Tell You . . . . Thirteen Stories* (Markham, ON.: Penguin Books, 1990).

[87] A. Munro, *The Moons of Jupiter* (Markham, ON.: Penguin Books, 1983).

[88] M. Atwood, *Selected Poems* (Toronto: Oxford University Press, 1976), 70.

[89] M. Atwood, *The Edible Woman* (Toronto: Bantam Seal Books, 1978).

[90] M. Atwood, *Cat's Eye* (Toronto: Bantam Seal Books, 1989).

[91] M. Atwood, *Lady Oracle* (Toronto: Bantam Seal Books, 1988).

[92] M. Atwood, *Dancing Girls and Other Stories* (Toronto: Bantam Seal Books, 1988).

[93] M. Atwood, *Surfacing* (Toronto: General Publishing, New Press Canadian Classics, 1983).

[94] A. Purdy, *The Collected Poems of Al Purdy*, Russell Brown, ed. (Toronto: McClelland & Stewart, 1986), 43.

[95] M. Ondaatje, *The Collected Works of Billy the Kid* (Toronto: House of Anansi Press, 1970).

[96] M. Ondaatje, *There's a Trick with a Knife I'm Learning to Do: Poems 1963–1978* (Toronto: McClelland & Stewart, 1979), 83.

Bibliography

Atwood, M. *Survival: A Thematic Guide to Canadian Literature*. Toronto: House of Anansi Press, 1972.

Brown, E.K. *On Canadian Poetry*. Toronto: Ryerson Press, 1943.

Dudek, L., and M. Gnarowski, eds. *The Making of Modern Poetry in Canada: Essential Articles on Contemporary Canadian Poetry in English*. Toronto: Ryerson Press, 1967.

Frye, N. *The Bush Garden: Essays on the Canadian Imagination*. Toronto: House of Anansi Press, 1971.

Gadpaille, M. *The Canadian Short Story*. Toronto: Oxford University Press, 1988.

Heath, J.M., ed. *Profiles in Canadian Literature*. Toronto: Dundurn Press, 1980.

Jones, D.G. *Butterfly on Rock: A Study of Themes and Images in Canadian Literature*. Toronto: University of Toronto Press, 1970.

Keith, W.J. *Canadian Literature in English*. Longman Literature in English Series, D. Carroll and M. Wheeler, gen. eds. London: Longman, 1985.

Klinck, C.F., gen. ed. *Literary History of Canada: Canadian Literature in English*. Toronto: University of Toronto Press, 1965. Rev. ed., 3 vols., 1976.

Lecker, R., and J. David, eds. *The Annotated Bibliography of Canada's Major Authors*. Downsview: ECW Press, 1979– .

Lecker, R., J. David, and E. Quigley, eds. *Canadian Writers and Their Works, Fiction Series*. Downsview: ECW Press, 1983– .

Lecker, R., J. David, and E. Quigley, eds. *Canadian Writers and Their Works, Poetry Series*. Downsview: ECW Press, 1983– .

Marshall, T. *Harsh and Lovely Land: The Major Canadian Poets and the Making of a Canadian Tradition*. Vancouver: University of British Columbia Press, 1979.

McGregor, G. *The Wacousta Syndrome: Explorations in the Canadian Langscape*. Toronto: University of Toronto Press, 1985.

Moss, J. *Patterns of Isolation in English-Canadian Fiction*. Toronto: McClelland & Stewart, 1974.

Moss, J. *A Reader's Guide to the Canadian Novel*. Toronto: McClelland & Stewart, 1981.

New, W.H. *A History of Canadian Literature*. Toronto: Collier Macmillan, 1989.

Pacey, D. *Creative Writing in Canada: A Short History of English-Canadian Literature*. Toronto: Ryerson Press, 1952. Rev. ed., 1961.

Toye, W., gen. ed. *The Oxford Companion to Canadian Literature*. Toronto: Oxford University Press, 1983.

Theatre in English-Speaking Canada

Joan Hackett

INTRODUCTION

Theatre and drama in Canada, as in the United States, are rooted in the theatrical and dramatic traditions of Europe and the British Isles. Both countries were settled by immigrants from abroad who brought their cultures with them, and both, in the early years, depended on foreign plays and players for their entertainment. Eventually both countries evolved from theatrical dependence on others to form their own dramatic and theatrical styles, but even today those styles are not completely devoid of foreign influence. Movements, experiments, and theories from abroad, as well as plays and musicals, still infiltrate the North American theatre, but they no longer dominate it.

EARLY THEATRE: PLAYS AND AUDIENCES

From the late eighteenth century to the early twentieth, Canadian theatre consisted of amateur groups, some professional Canadian companies, and foreign (British and US) professional touring companies. The latter dominated the Canadian scene during the late nineteenth and early twentieth centuries. Most of the dramatic fare offered to the public by these groups, both domestic and foreign, consisted of melodrama, well-made plays, and musical entertainments popular in Europe, England, and the US at the time. Sprinkled here and there in the playbills of the day were productions of the classics—Shakespeare, Sheridan, Molière, and the like. But the overwhelming choice of producers and the audience they served was imported melodrama. And this audience preferred melodrama with a message—a moral one. Canadian theatregoers were usually conservative and even a bit prudish. They did not like controversial or distasteful subject matter exhibited on the stage. The avant-garde writers of the nineteenth century, especially Ibsen and Shaw, were anathema to Canadians as they were to many theatregoers in other countries.[1] Despite their unpopularity at the turn of the century, the modern dramas of Ibsen and Shaw were performed here by touring stars such as Alla Nazimova, Ellen Terry, Forbes-Robertson, and others.

But performances of plays written by Canadians were few and far between. Canadians were writing plays and having them published, but few actual productions and performances of them materialized. Evidently producers were afraid to gamble on unproven material and stayed with the "sure-fire" hits that had been done elsewhere. Some homegrown products, however, did reach the stage and gained a measure of success. An example of an early Canadian play that succeeded on the stage was *H.M.S. Parliament* by W.H. Fuller. It was a political satire that poked fun at the major politicians of the day. Although based on Gilbert and Sullivan's *H.M.S. Pinafore*, its characters, scenes, and subject matter were thoroughly Canadian. The first performance took place in Emerson, Manitoba, a small community (population 1000) south of Winnipeg in 1877.

❑ THEATRES

The theatres in which touring companies and local groups mounted their productions were very often not theatres at all, but rooms in buildings that served a number of other purposes. In some communities, especially the smaller ones, performance conditions were difficult. One example of the extreme conditions endured by touring companies and their audiences is contained in a description of the performance of *H.M.S. Parliament* in Emerson:

> The "theatre" was an old warehouse full of farming implements and boxes. The place had but two exits one of which was from the platform to the prairie, where tents had been rigged up for the company. There was not a house nearer than a mile . . . everybody came on horseback. . . . Soap and candle boxes formed the back seats, champagne and brandy boxes being in front.[2]

Amateurs did not fare much better than the travelling professionals with respect to performance conditions. They performed in a variety of makeshift theatres arranged in hotel ballrooms, lofts, town halls, stores, and saloons.

As the nineteenth century progressed, performance conditions improved for amateur and professional alike. By 1850 actual theatres and opera houses had been built in many communities—by the early twentieth century, theatre buildings could be found from coast to coast. They varied in capacity from 500 to 2000. Some were quite opulent, following a pattern established in eighteenth-century Europe; while others, less pretentious, followed the early Canadian pattern of second-storey theatres. The Opera House (capacity 1100), which opened in 1879 in Kingston, Ontario, is a good example of the more elaborate type.[3] A contemporary boasts of the theatre's grandeur in the following manner:

The auditorium . . . , when lighted up, presents a scene of great beauty. At each side of the stage there are four boxes, which are of more than ordinary size, and from which each seat in the house can be seen. These are lighted with cluster chandeliers in front of each box, fitted with damask curtains and upholstered in crimson velvet. They will be very comfortable indeed.

The proscenium arch . . . is a very elegant arch. It is most elaborately fres-coed. Directly in front of the stage is the orchestra . . . .

The parquette contains 225 iron folding opera house chairs . . . finely uphol-stered in maroon leather. . . . The iron work of the chairs is painted and gilt . . . .

In front of the gallery [reached by] a spacious staircase . . . is a handsome railing, painted and gilt.[4]

And he goes on to describe the domed ceiling and the beautifully frescoed, painted interior of the auditorium. Incidentally, *H.M.S. Parliament* played in this house in 1880, a far cry from the accommodations found in Emerson. In con-trast to the elegance and comfort of the Kingston house was a theatre (capacity 500) built in Winnipeg in 1876, located on the second floor of the town hall. There was a gallery stretching across one end of its rather plain auditorium and, like many theatres of this type, it had no emergency exits—in other words, it was a firetrap.

❑ THEATRE COMPANIES

As has been noted, unusual performance areas were the rule during the eight-eenth and early nineteenth centuries, but at least they were on dry land. What is believed to be the first theatrical performance ever to take place in Canada (1606), *The Theatre of Neptune in New France*, was performed on the water in a fleet of canoes with Neptune and his Tritons on board as the major participants in the action. It was a marine pageant performed by members of the garrison at Port Royal (now Annapolis Royal, Nova Scotia) to celebrate the governor's return from a successful expedition. This show was conceived and acted by ama-teurs. Perhaps it was a portent of things to come, because one of the strongest traditions to evolve in the country was that of amateur theatre. In both French and English Canada, soldiers in the garrisons and civilians in the towns formed amateur theatre groups.

From the late 1700s to the expansion of the railroads in the 1860s, amateur theatre flourished, but afterwards it dwindled because foreign troupes and star performers were now able to include the smaller, more remote towns in their itineraries due to the improved system of transportation. These tours enabled the public to witness performances by some of the greatest actors and actresses of the day, including Henry Irving, a great English actor and the first to be knighted; the legendary French star, Sarah Bernhardt; and Minnie Maddern Fiske, a famous American actress. In all, more than fifty star companies "hit the road" in Canada during this period. There were also Canadian stars, based in New York, who toured their homeland: Margaret Anglin, Marie Dressler, Julia Arthur, and Annie Russel, among others, performed here on several occasions.

But not all of the talented Canadian theatre folk headed for New York or London in search of fame and fortune. Some stayed at home to develop their own companies. Some of the Canadian professional pioneers were the Summers Stock Company, Hamilton, Ontario; Morrison's Stock Company, Toronto; the McDowell Company, which toured the West and parts of the US; the Tavernier-Van Cortland Company, which toured throughout Canada and parts of the US But it was the Marks Brothers who were the most prolific in their theatrical ventures and who survived longer than any other Canadian troupe. They toured the hinterlands of Canada and the US for forty-three years, from 1879 through 1922. There were seven brothers. Bob, the eldest, was the first to get into show business, and he was eventually joined by his brothers. They toured small towns in northern Ontario, then went west to Winnipeg and on to the mining towns of the US. By the 1890s their shows had become so popular that three separate companies were formed, each with its own circuit and managed by one of the brothers. They specialized in the production of melodrama because it appealed to the tastes and morals of small-town audiences. Bob Marks, a shrewd showman, knew his audience and gave it what it wanted. He explained that

> The great appetite of the masses of show-goers is for melodrama. Despite what the "experts" say, melodrama is one of the great perennials in the theatrical business. . . . For the lifetime of the Marks enterprises our people have absolutely refused to compromise on *honest and orderly* entertainment. Companies must depend on *family patronage*, and the vast majority of Canadian and American families are founded on *wholesome standards*.[5]

The Marks Brothers were in show business. They gave their audiences entertainment, not high culture, and it stood them in good stead until the 1920s. But by that time even they could not compete with the new forms of popular entertainment: movies and radio. Nor could the touring companies from abroad because of shrinking audiences and box office receipts.

THE LITTLE THEATRE MOVEMENT

Professional theatre took a nose-dive in Canada in the 1920s and 1930s. While there were attempts by a few professional Canadian stock companies to revitalize the theatre at this time, it was the amateur Little Theatre Movement that formed the core of Canadian theatre after World War I. The movement was influenced by the "art" theatres of Europe and England, non-commercial companies that presented new forms of drama and practised "new staging."[6] The fledgling little theatres of Canada embraced the ideas of the art theatres and made them their own. All of them wanted to practise the new staging. Some were determined to produce Canadian plays, and in one way or another, they all endeavoured to create Canadian theatre. This became the prime goal of the Little Theatre Movement, and it was the first concentrated effort of this kind in the country.

The most prestigious and influential of these organizations was the Hart House Theatre in Toronto, founded in 1919 and still in operation. The theatre (capacity 500) was a well-equipped, honest-to-goodness theatre in which the amateurs, aided by a professional director and technicians, could do serious work. Their goal was to encourage and stimulate Canadian theatre talent and they certainly achieved it. Among the actors and actresses who got experience at Hart House early in their careers were William Hutt, Donald Sutherland, Dora Mavor Moore, and Kate Reid.

The plays presented by Hart House included those of Canadian playwrights, along with the classics and contemporary material from abroad. The most note-worthy of the Canadian writers who got a showing there was Merrill Denison, whose plays dealt with the rugged life of northern Ontario, its harshness, and its dehumanizing effect on the individual. Later he turned to historical themes deal-ing with important Canadian events and characters from the past. Plays dealing with these same themes are popular with Canadian playwrights today. Denison, of course, was not the only writer produced by Hart House, which encouraged and produced many other newcomers. By now there was at least budding inter-est in plays written by Canadians about things Canadian, but there was still a long way to go before the playwright became a significant force in the develop-ment of the nation's theatre.

The amateurs were given further impetus and encouragement when, in 1932, the Dominion Drama Festival was inaugurated in Ottawa. Lord Bessborough, the governor general, who had convened a meeting of theatre people and other interested parties, stated the purpose of a nationwide drama festival: "Now that the Little Theatre has gained so strong a foothold in this country, there is, with-out any doubt a great opportunity for its development along national lines, with the ultimate objective of creating a national drama."[7] The Dominion Drama Festival was the brainchild of the governor general himself. He was an enthusi-astic theatregoer, as well as an amateur actor, producer, and designer. Imagine his dismay when, prior to his departure for Canada in 1931, a friend told him that theatre in Canada was dead. For a person so infatuated with theatre this indeed was devastating news. But after his arrival Bessborough discovered that, although professional theatre was moribund, amateur theatre was flourishing. So he decided that he should "do something for amateur dramatics" and this he did, with the help of others—especially Vincent Massey, who was vitally interested in the theatre.

The Dominion Drama Festival was a competition in which amateur dramatic societies participated on a local, regional, and national level. Each of these com-petitions were adjudicated by experts in the field. The best of the regional pro-ductions were invited to participate in the national finals held each year in a major city. Trophies were awarded in a variety of categories: best play, best scenery, best actor, and so on. The first national festival took place in Ottawa at the Little Theatre from 24 to 29 April 1933. One hundred and sixty-eight ama-teurs participated. They came from Winnipeg, Saskatoon, Québec City, New

Brunswick, Medicine Hat, Halifax, Vancouver, Montréal, and Toronto. Thus, the Dominion Drama Festival was launched and continued for forty years (the last was held in Winnipeg in 1970).

In a sense the DDF was the country's national theatre, because it inspired amateur productions all over the land and kept an interest in theatre alive throughout the thirties, forties, and fifties, when little or no other kind of live theatre was available. Also, many of those who participated in the DDF were to become professionals. A study of DDF programs between 1933 and 1965 revealed that no fewer than 400 individuals whose names appeared had gone into the professional ranks.[8] But the festival did not discover nor nurture new Canadian writing talent. Despite efforts by the DDF to encourage the production of Canadian plays, only a handful of Canadian playwrights were represented in the festivals.

DEVELOPMENT OF THE PROFESSIONAL THEATRE AND THE CANADIAN PLAYWRIGHT

After World War II there was an effort in Toronto by three newly-formed professional companies to put Canadian plays on the boards. The first was the New Play Society (1946–1971) founded by Dora Mavor Moore, an actress, director, and teacher who, by the end of World War I, "had indisputably become Canada's First Lady of the Theatre."[9] Her memory is honoured today by the annual Dora Mavor Moore Awards (started in 1979), given to theatre artists who have excelled in the Toronto theatre each season. The theatre she founded, as its name implied, was eager to mount the works of Canadian authors. The society produced plays by Lister Sinclair, Mavor Moore (Dora's son), Andrew Allan, Morley Callaghan, Mazo de la Roche, Henry Boyle, and John Coulter. The Crest Theatre (1954–1966) was the next to give Canadian playwrights an opportunity to see their works performed; and the third, the Jupiter Theatre (1951–1954), also produced Canadian plays in its short life span.

All three of these theatres were established prior to the formation of the Canada Council in 1957, which was to provide a momentous shot in the arm for all arts in the country. There was yet another professional theatre that opened its doors in this pre-subsidy era, which turned out to be one of the most ambitious and successful ventures in the annals of Canadian theatre: the Stratford Festival. In the summer of 1953 the city of Stratford, Ontario (population 19 500), launched its Shakespearean Festival—that it happened at all is something of a miracle. The idea to produce Shakespeare's plays in the Canadian Stratford was that of Tom Patterson, a journalist and native of the town. It was through his herculean efforts and those of a committee of Stratfordites that the Festival became a reality. Three important aims, among others, of the Festival were:

- to provide improved opportunities for Canadian artistic talent.
- to advance the development of the theatre arts in Canada.
- to conduct an annual Shakespearean Festival at Stratford, Ontario.[10]

The difficulties encountered in achieving these goals, especially the last, were monumental. Money, of course, was the main problem. It was estimated that it would take $150 000 to get the project off the ground. A fund-raising campaign was stymied by negative publicity generated by pessimistic snipers who predicted that the venture would flop mainly because "it had never been done before."[11] In fact, the financial situation became so critical that the whole undertaking was nearly abandoned. Then, in the nick of time, a large sum was given by an anonymous donor and the show went on in spite of the "crepe-hangers." Actually, there were two shows, *Richard III* and *All's Well That Ends Well*— they ran for six weeks and grossed $206 000.

The lack of money in the early years was not the only problem. The Festival Theatre was to be housed in an enormous tent. Unfortunately, by the time rehearsals began the tent was still under construction in Chicago, so they had to rehearse in a wooden shed. Tyrone Guthrie, the artistic director, described the bizarre rehearsal conditions:

> The acoustics of the building were such that the lightest whisper became an enormous booming noise. Normal speech was almost too loud to be endured by the naked ear, and totally unintelligible. Giants and giantesses seemed to be shouting through the vaults of a cathedral jointly designed by Cecil B. deMille and Orson Welles.
>
> The weeks wore on. . . . But still there was no sign of the Tent.
>
> Days pass. The words of the plays are now known . . . but no one has yet heard any lines but his own. Lips are seen to move, gigantic but unintelligible noises resound. . . . The noises made a Wagnerian accompaniment to the *miming* of two Shakespearean plays. It is an interesting new Art form; *avant garde*, but searing to the nerves.
>
> Came the dawn. Chicago telegraphed that the Tent would Reach The Yards on Tuesday.[12]

Even after the long-awaited tent had arrived there were still many obstacles to overcome. When faced with any unpleasant or nearly-impossible or situation, one of Guthrie's phrases was "Rise above it." There were many "its" to be risen above before Stratford's opening night, but rise above it they did and on 13 July 1953, in spite of the impossible odds against it, the miracle occurred. *Richard III* not only got on the boards but "at the end of the performance, the crowd rose to its feet with what was to remain the most memorable ovation in the Festival's history. Strangers embraced, tears of pride flowed, and the actors began to think the curtain calls would never end."[13]

The following night *All's Well That Ends Well* opened—its title may have been a prophetic one because, as of 1992, the Festival is still operating. Now there are three theatres: the Festival Theatre, a permanent structure, replaced the tent after 1956; the Avon, built in 1900, was purchased and renovated in 1963; and the Third Stage was installed in the Festival Exhibition Hall in 1971. The latter was renamed the Tom Patterson Theatre in 1991.

The founders of the Festival had conceived the project as a Canadian one, employing Canadian theatre people. Sixty Canadian actors, few with professional experience, were hired for that first season and formed the core of the company. Stratford provided a place at home in which Canadian talent could work. Prior to this, anyone with theatrical ambitions headed for the border or for England. It has been concluded that "no strong body of professional acting talent was based in Canada until after the founding of the Festival in 1953."[14]

Since its debut the Festival has earned an international reputation. Its audience from 1953 through 1988 (over 12 million) came from all over Canada, the US and fifty other countries. The Festival company has toured to various parts of Canada, Scotland, England, the United States, Denmark, Holland, Poland, and the Soviet Union. The unique open, or thrust, stage of the Festival Theatre has been imitated in Australia, England, and the United States. A Festival production of *Oedipus Rex* (1954–1955), done with masked and padded actors, has been imitated in other parts of Canada, the United States, and England in productions of ancient Greek tragedy. The impact of this theatre has been far-reaching: it is a world-class theatre.

Although Stratford's opening in 1953 and its subsequent success were landmarks in Canadian theatre history, the real impetus for the development of theatre throughout the country came from the government. The first step in this process was *The Report of the Royal Commission on National Development in the Arts, Letters and Sciences* (published in 1951), generally known as the Massey Report after the commission's chair. It was an in-depth examination of the cultural situation in the country. The recommendations made in this report had a great deal to do with the formation of the Canada Council in 1957. The council gave government support in the form of subsidies to the arts, which of course included theatre. Robertson Davies, a highly respected novelist, playwright, and former actor, wrote the section of the report that dealt with theatre. He reviewed the current status of theatrical activity and emphasized that there was a widespread interest in it, and that this interest was fostered by amateur groups, CBC radio drama, and a few intrepid repertory companies, as well as by intermittent tours by a handful of foreign troupes. But he went on to point out that this was not enough to feed the growing appetite throughout the country for dramatic presentations.

In a prologue to his report, Davies used the form of a letter to an imaginary playwright to paint a very grim picture of the Canadian playhouse:

> You want to be a Canadian playwright, and ask me for advice as to how to set about it. Well, Fishorn, the first thing you had better acquaint yourself with is the physical conditions of a Canadian theatre.
> Now what is a Canadian playhouse? Nine times out of ten, Fishorn, it is a school hall, smelling of chalk and kids, and decorated in the Early Concrete style. The stage is a small raised room at one end. And I mean a room. If you step into the wings suddenly you will fracture your nose against the wall. There is no place for storing scenery, no place for actors to dress, and the lighting is designed to warm the stage but not illuminate it.

> Write your plays then for such a stage. Do not demand any processions . . . sunsets . . . storms at sea. Place as many scenes as you can in cellars and kindred spots, and don't have more than three characters on stage at one time, or the weakest of them is sure to be nudged into the audience. Farewell, and good luck to you.[15]

Many of the theatres built in the nineteenth and early twentieth centuries had been torn down or converted into movie houses, so Davies's description of what was available for live performances was not far off the mark. However, this situation changed with the help of grants from the Canada Council. Between 1958 and 1970 at least one major theatre centre was built in each province; thus, a chain of professional regional theatres stretched from coast to coast. These theatres, plus the Shaw Festival at Niagara-on-the-Lake, the Stratford Festival, and a number of smaller ventures, now depend in part on government subsidy for survival.

The development of the regional theatres brought about a drastic change in the profile of Canadian theatre. Suddenly there was a great surge of live theatre performed and produced by professionals. In contrast to the precarious conditions of the past, theatre people now had many permanent homes in which to practise their craft. It was a tremendous opportunity for performing artists to develop their talents, but what of the Canadian playwright? A 1971 study of seven regional theatres revealed that between 1965 and 1971 they had produced 108 plays, 19 of which had been Canadian.[16]

But all was not lost for playwrights even though they were given back seats by the majority of Canadian theatres. In the 1970s there were other groups, lumped under the heading "alternate theatre," whose main objective was to produce and present Canadian works. These groups, which had been influenced by avant-garde experiments in Europe and the US, were smaller and more adventurous than the larger, more conservative regional organizations. Alternates sprouted up in many parts of the country, dedicated to the expression of the Canadian experience, either by the encouragement of new playwrights or by collectively creating pieces based on some facet of Canadian life. In Toronto, alone, there were three alternates of the first type: the Tarragon (1970), Factory Lab (1970), and Toronto Free (1972), which was literally "free," charging no admission.

The Tarragon, in particular, was created to foster a Canadian theatrical voice because it was felt that, at that time, "plays articulating the Canadian sensibility were the exception rather than the rule."[17] Bill Glassco, founder of the Tarragon, expressed his theatre's goal "to develop Canadian playwrights and produce their scripts, to shape a community of Canadian artists and actors to interpret these plays and to build an audience to accept [their] works."[18] "Develop" is the operative word here in that it expresses the concept of helping *potential* playwrights to learn their craft and hone their skills in a theatrical environment. At the Tarragon this was realized by working on plays-in-progress, supporting a playwright-in-residence, and assisting new writers artistically and financially.

Between 1971 and 1986 fifty new English-language plays were premiered, as well as a dozen or so French-Canadian plays in translation. Some of the playwrights whose early work was produced at one or another of these three Toronto theatres were David French, Michel Tremblay, David Freeman, Carol Bolt, Anne Chislett, and George Walker—all of them well-established playwrights today. In the West, the Globe Theatre (1966) in Regina produced Canadian plays, particularly those of its early resident playwright, Rex Deverall, whose plays dealt with events in that region.

The other alternate theatres were those that chose to do "collectives." They wanted to arouse the social and political consciousness of their audiences by doing works on historical events or on contemporary political, social, or regional issues. A "collective" is a theatre piece that grows out of the improvisation of actors alone, or in collaboration with a director or writer, or both. It is somewhat like a documentary, but researched and composed by a group rather than by an individual author. Toronto Workshop Productions (1959–1988) was founded and led by George Luscombe, the pioneer in producing collectives in English Canada. Although TWP paved the way for collective composition in Toronto, Theatre Passe Muraille (1969)—theatre without walls—became the leading exponent of this form and was responsible for spreading its gospel to alternate theatres in other parts of the country. Passe Muraille, under the stewardship of Paul Thompson, who has collaborated on over forty collectives, concentrated on sociological topics and historical events as the basis for his theatre's work. One of Passe Muraille's most successful efforts was *The Farm Show* (1972)—a mélange of songs, monologues, and short scenes that grew out of a summer's research in the rural community of Clinton, Ontario. The whole company went on location to study and absorb the speech and behaviour of the people in that area, as well as to gather not only facts, but tales and legends about local events, characters, and traditions. In other words, they immersed themselves in the fabric of the community. Working along the same lines as Passe Muraille was the Newfoundland Mummers Troupe and the 25th Street Theatre in Saskatoon. Theatres on the West Coast and in the Prairie provinces also did collectives. But today only a handful of theatres do collectives, so it would seem that this type of activity has pretty much run its course. How much the collectives influenced the development of Canadian theatre as a whole is questionable, but there is no doubt about the alternates, which worked at developing playwrights. They made a significant contribution not only to Canadian theatre but to Canadian drama as well.[19]

There were also non-alternate theatres that nurtured new playwrights. The Centaur (1969), an English-speaking theatre in Montreal, produced some fifty Canadian plays in the early years. Festival Lennoxville (1972–1982) in Québec produced nothing but Canadian plays during its ten-year run. And yet another festival in Blyth, Ontario, started in 1975 and still going, has done only *one* non-Canadian play, Agatha Christie's *The Mousetrap*. It was one of two plays presented in Blyth's first season; the other was *Mostly in Clover*, Anne Chislett's adaptation of short stories written by Harry J. Boyle, a broadcaster, writer, and native of Huron County. Much to everyone's amazement, the new Canadian play outsold the tried-and-true Christie by a large margin. This circumstance sealed Blyth's destiny—to promote and produce Canadian plays only. Since 1975 the Blyth Festival has produced fifty-nine Canadian plays, and of these, forty were premieres.

CONTEMPORARY CANADIAN THEATRE

Canadian theatre in 1991 is a sprawling tapestry of various organizations, some housed in large regional or civic theatres, others in small renovated or makeshift quarters. All, however, are vigorously engaged in producing their particular brand of theatre.

❏ THE ALTERNATES

Tarragon, Passe Muraille, and Factory Theatre, the mavericks of the 1960s and 1970s, are now looked upon as the solid citizens of Toronto's theatrical scene. They are still producing Canadian plays—new and old—as well as contemporary and classic works from abroad. In the West the former alternates that have survived are Tamahnous (which means "magic" in Chilcotin Indian) in Vancouver, now the resident company in the city's East Cultural Centre; the 25th Street Theatre in Saskatoon; and the Prairie Theatre Exchange, which has just moved into a $3.5 million theatre located on the third floor of Winnipeg's Portage Place Mall. All produce a majority of Canadian plays, especially those having to do with their own regions.

Now there are new alternates in Toronto, which are investigating the very nature of theatre: Buddies in Bad Times aims to develop the poet-playwright; A.K.A. Performance Interfaces and Video Cabaret combine theatre, video, film, electronic music, and dance. Theatre Autumn Leaf and Necessary Angel use masks, environmental settings, and epic theatre techniques, while Nightwood, a "theatre of images," uses painting, music, and novels as a basis for theatrical presentation. An alternate theatre in Vancouver, Jumpstart, creates and produces works that amalgamate the features of all the performing arts: dance, opera, and theatre.

In other parts of the country the spirit of the sixties is kept alive by The Mulgrave Road Co-op of Nova Scotia, which tours the province with collectives based on regional topics, and Touchstone Theatre in Vancouver, which sticks to the presentation of Canadian plays. In Thunder Bay there are two theatres: Kam Theatre Lab does Canadian plays only, including many original scripts; Magnus does a mixture of modern, classical, and Canadian plays. Both take plays on tour to isolated northern communities. In Ottawa, the Great Canadian Theatre Company (1975) does Canadian plays, many of them with a political slant.

❑ SPECIALIZED THEATRES

In contrast to those theatres involved with experimentation in new forms of theatre and drama, there are those in various parts of the country whose main concern is with specific audiences. The multicultural, or ethnic, theatre groups do shows in a wide range of native languages that include Chinese, Finnish, Spanish, and German; there are also Jewish, Irish, and Black groups that perform in English. "Theatre for Young People" (more commonly known as "Children's Theatre"), mainly consists of touring companies that travel to the schools in particular areas. This can be quite a gruelling experience as a company can be on the road anywhere from three to nine months, moving from one place to the next by bus and truck. One company from Sudbury travels by plane and snowmobile to northern Ontario. At each stop these companies must set up scenery, lights, props, etc., then strike all the equipment, pack it, load it, and move on. For example, "Calgary's Stage Coach Players will often carry one play for five to seven year olds, one for eight to twelves, another for high schools—and a fourth that is performed for the community at large on evenings and weekends."[20]

The plays chosen for tours are no longer of the fairy tale/fantasy variety, although Dickens's *A Christmas Carol* is still a hot item during the holidays. The Green Thumb Theatre (1974) in Vancouver focuses on developing and producing new Canadian plays for young people, and these plays deal with what is relevant to the immediate needs and concerns of their young audiences. Green Thumb has taken its plays across this country and abroad with tours in England, West Germany, Sweden, the US, New Zealand, Singapore, and Hong Kong. Another British Columbian company, the Kaleidoscope Theatre (1974) in Victoria, unlike the issue-oriented Green Thumb, concentrates on the use of music, dialogue, and dance to illustrate a particular theme. On the East Coast, the Mermaid Theatre (1972) of Wolfville, Nova Scotia, has developed another approach to theatre for young people. It deals with the local history and legends of the Micmac Indians, which are interpeted by combining music, dance, puppetry, colourful costumes, and masks into a fascinating pattern of story telling. The company also tours other parts of Canada and has gone abroad to Mexico and Wales. Toronto's Young People's Theatre (1966) is the largest children's theatre in Canada and it produces a mixture of the classics, fairy tales, and newer plays dealing with current issues. These four theatres and their programs serve as examples of the kind of work being done by approximately sixty other companies spread throughout the land, bringing theatre to young people.

❑ REGIONAL THEATRE

Perhaps the regional or civic theatres could be called the backbone of today's Canadian theatre. These theatres offer their audiences a series of five or six plays a year. In addition to these mainstage seasons, a number of "regionals" tour shows to outlying areas in their provinces and sometimes beyond into other parts of the country. Some include theatre training schools, experimental theatre,

theatre for young people tours, and summer seasons in their activities. Several also support a playwright-in-residence. They make a very substantial contribution to the cultural life of their communities.[21]

❏ AMATEUR THEATRE

In spite of the demise of the Dominion Drama Festival in 1970, amateur theatres remain very much a part of today's theatrical picture. They seem to be busier than ever, producing plays and musicals for audiences in their own communities. In some provinces they have an opportunity to participate in drama festivals similar in format to those formerly held by the DDF. New Brunswick, British Columbia, Alberta, Nova Scotia, Ontario, Manitoba, and Newfoundland sponsor province-wide competitions for little theatre groups, and those seven provinces, plus Saskatchewan, also host an annual high-school drama festival. The Powerhouse Theatre (1963) in Vernon, BC, is an example of how a community theatre operates and competes in a provincial drama festival. The company usually does a season of three plays and also competes in the British Columbia Drama Festival. In 1988 they did *Play Memory* by Canadian playwright Joanna Glass for that year's festival and then worked their way through ten regional competitions and the finals in Victoria. The director of the play, Sarah Perry, describe competing in those ten regionals as "absolutely hair-raising." However, the experience did not stop her or her group from taking the show across the country to the Great Canadian Drama Festival in Halifax, Nova Scotia, where it won Best Play. Nor did it deter them from a chance to participate in yet another competition: in the summer of 1989 they headed for the International Amateur Theatre Festival in Monaco.[22] Perry and her company of nineteen put a tremendous amount of time and effort into preparing, performing, and touring *Play Memory*. Multiply this group, with its dedication and energy, many times over and you will get an idea of the strength of Canadian amateur theatre.

❏ COMMERCIAL THEATRE (TORONTO)

While all kinds of theatre is available to audiences throughout the country, the theatrical hub is Toronto " . . . indisputably the centre of English-language theatre in Canada."[23] There are 120 professional producing companies in the city and a dozen dance companies. "Toronto sees over 300 live theatre and dance productions in a year. Every theatre goer, from the conservative to the *avant-garde*, has a choice of productions to visit. In short, Toronto's theatre community is excitingly alive and growing."[24] Most of the 120 companies are non-profit organizations, depending in part on government funding to cover their expenses. But there is also a fairly healthy non-subsidized commercial theatre in the city. There are about a dozen dinner theatres offering a show and a meal for a set price; musicals or light comedies are the main offerings at these theatre-restaurants. On a larger scale, the Royal Alexandra (capacity 1497), the O'Keefe Centre (3000), the Elgin (1600), the Winter Garden (1100), and the

Pantages (2100) are the theatres where visiting attractions from other parts of Canada and abroad are shown, usually for limited runs. The Royal Alexandra is the most successful commercial theatre in the city. It was built in 1907 and renovated in 1963 by millionaire businessman Ed Mirvish. He and his son, David, own and operate the theatre and they have done very well with it. The theatre has a subscription list of 51 000 (1985) and has housed some remarkable productions in recent years: Stratford's *The Mikado* (1983) and *Cyrano de Bergerac* (1984); a Canadian production of Tom Stoppard's *The Real Thing* directed by Guy Sprung (1985); and productions by East Germany's Berliner Ensemble (1986) and the English Shakespeare Company (1987).

David Mirvish describes the role of the Royal Alex in Toronto as follows:

> This theatre was built as a major first-class touring house whose purpose was to show the most successful works of Broadway and the West End. And it did that for many years. So to do an original play that doesn't have a reputation, without a star in it, and expect 12 000 people to come every week, you have to then ask: What is the magic you will supply?[25]

He expresses the fear many producers, both professional and amateur, have of an unknown, untried work, but in spite of this he and his father want to produce more original works at the Royal Alex. In the 1988/89 season, they took a step in that direction by mounting their own production of *Les Misérables* (not exactly an untried commodity, as it had been a success in London and New York), which proved to be very popular with the Alex audience—in fact, it was a tremendous hit.

The O'Keefe Centre opened in 1960, and has been a touring house for Broadway musicals as well as the home of the National Ballet and the Canadian Opera Company (both subsidized). In recent years the ballet and opera companies have not been satisfied with the O'Keefe. The situation is not likely to improve since plans for a new Ballet Opera House, which had been projected to open in 1994, were disrupted when the new NDP provincial government reversed the financial commitment made by the previous government.

In 1981 the Ontario government bought and renovated two old vaudeville houses, the Elgin and the Winter Garden. The Elgin opened in 1985 with an all-Canadian production of the English hit musical *Cats*. This was a milestone in Canadian commercial theatre. The box office receipts before the show opened were $4 million—enough to pay the producers' production costs. Better still, the show was a smash hit after it opened and played to standing-room-only crowds.

In the fall of 1989 a third refurbished vaudeville theatre (vintage 1920), the Pantages, opened its doors with a local production of *Phantom of the Opera*. Like *Cats* it was a commercially successful venture.

Another theatre complex, the St. Lawrence Centre for the Arts, opened in Toronto in 1970 and is an important performance space in the city. There are two theatres in the Centre, the Bluma Appel Theatre and a smaller space, the Jane Mallett Theatre. The Bluma Appel Theatre has been used by various non-profit companies: Toronto Arts Productions, Centre Stage, and now the Canadian Stage Company (Toronto Free Theatre amalgamated with Centre Stage). But in addition to dramatic presentations, the Centre also accommodates music, dance, film, forums, and debates—it is in essence a multi-purpose cultural centre, described as a "vibrant showcase for the work of the most accomplished artists from this country and abroad."[26]

Toronto theatres and production companies offer something for everyone: large and small musicals, comedies, dramas, experimental multi-media shows, ethnic plays, and plays for young people, as well as opera and ballet—a virtual feast for any theatregoer.

CONCLUSION

Canadian theatre has come a long way since *The Theatre of Neptune in New France*. However, instead of evolving slowly in a linear pattern from the days of the early settlers, it has developed and come into its own only recently. Its growth started with the efforts of those groups that after the First World War set out to create Canadian theatre and to produce Canadian plays. Then, in the 1950s, a growing desire by many Canadians for a stronger cultural expression of themselves and their country was manifested in the Massey Report (1951), which in turn led to the creation of the Canada Council (1957). The Council and the financial support it provided led to what might be called a cultural explosion in the 1960s and 1970s. Of course, Canadian theatre was a part of that explosion, and it is still expanding and growing.

What, then, are the characteristics of this Canadian theatre? Most of it is non-profit and subsidized in part by government funds. There is comparatively little commercial theatre, much of it confined to the Toronto area. Canada does not have a national theatre, per se, but it does have a nationwide theatre that is diverse in its activities. There are conservative theatres and experimental theatres; the plays range from contemporary hits to all-Canadian plays to new experimental presentations. Almost all of these groups tour all or some of their offerings to outlying communities in their areas. Many tour to other parts of Canada and abroad. A number of them support their own theatre schools and a few have a playwright-in-residence.

What about the future of Canadian theatre? Right now it is strong and vibrant. It is by no means stagnant or self-satisfied, and it is striving to accomplish many new goals. As long as it continues to grow, change, and explore, Canadian theatre will remain a strong and exciting contributor to the cultural life of the country.

Notes

[1] M. Edwards, *A Stage in Our Past: English Language Theatre in Eastern Canada* (Toronto: University of Toronto Press, 1968), 67.

[2] F. Graham, *Histrionic Montréal* (Montréal: John Lovel and Son Publishers, 1902) as quoted in Edwards, *A Stage*, 40.

[3] Many of the theatres built in this era were called "opera houses" because that term connoted respectability, whereas the term "theatre" was still tainted with the puritanical view that a theatre was a place of the devil.

[4] *Daily News*, 2 Jan. 1879, as quoted in E. Waldhauer, *Grand Theatre 1879–1979* (Kingston: Grand Theatre,1979), 2–3. The proscenium arch frames the opening in one wall of the auditorium through which the audience can view the stage and the actors performing on it. The orchestra (pit) is an area directly in front of the stage floor and lower than it, used by musicians who play for opera, musicals, or incidental music for straight plays. The parquette is the main floor of the theatre extending from in front of the stage to the parquette circle, which is part of the main floor underneath the upper galleries.

[5] R.W. Marks as quoted in Edwards, *A Stage*, 43.

[6] The art theatre not only reacted against the commercial drama of the era but also against the prevalent practice of mounting plays in overly detailed naturalistic settings. Simplified and symbolic settings were designed and developed. For instance, two or three columns, some steps, and a platform could represent an entire palace or temple. This came to be known as "new staging" or "new stagecraft."

[7] Bessborough speech 10 Oct. 1932, Rideau Hall, Ottawa, as quoted in B. Lee, *Love and Whisky: The Story of the Dominion Drama Festival and the Early Years of Theatre in Canada 1602–1972* (Toronto: Simon and Pierre, 1973), 96.

[8] Lee, *Love and Whisky*, 281.

[9] J. Pettigrew and J. Portman, *Stratford: The First Thirty Years* (Toronto: Macmillan, 1985), 19.

[10] *Stratford Festival Story 1953–1966* (Stratford, ON: Mirror Press Limited, 1966), 1.

[11] T. Guthrie, R. Davies, and G. MacDonald, *Renown at Stratford* (Toronto: Clarke, Irwin, 1953), 12.

[12] Ibid., 20–21.

[13] Pettigrew and Portman, *Stratford*, 6–7.

[14] E. Benson and L.W. Conolly, *English-Canadian Theatre* (Toronto: Oxford University Press, 1987), 38.

[15] Roberton Davies as quoted in Pettigrew and Portman, *Stratford*, 16.

[16] Benson and Conolly, *English Canadian Theatre*, 84.

[17] P. Michael, "The Tarragon Theatre Story," *Performing Arts in Canada.* 23, 1 (July 1986): 29.

[18] Bill Glassco as quoted in ibid., 29.

[19] R. Usmiani, "The Alternate Theatre Movement," in *Contemporary Canadian Theatre: New World Visions,* ed. A. Wagner (Toronto: Simon and Pierre, 1985), 49–59. Most of the information on the alternates is drawn from Usmiani's article.

[20] D. Foon, "Theatre for Young Audiences in English Canada," in *Contemporary Canadian Theatre,* 254. All information on theatre for children is drawn from Foon's article, 253–61.

[21] Most of the information on these theatres is from M. Czarnecki, "The Regional Theatre System," in *Contemporary Canadian Theatre,* 47.

[22] L. Donnelly, "A Play on Memory," *Performing Arts in Canada* 25, 2 (April/Spring 1989): 19–20.

[23] A.M. Ashley and B. Neil, "Ontario," in Wagner, ed., *Contemporary Canadian Theatre,* 142.

[24] S.B. Hood, "Paranoia, Dry Lips and a Dora," *Performing Arts in Canada* 25, 4 (Dec./Winter 1989): 8.

[25] David Mirvish as quoted in N. Hunt, "Charting the Progess of the Whirling Mirvishes," *Performing Arts in Canada* 25, 2 (April/Spring 1989): 13.

[26] *St. Lawrence Centre Magazine* 1, 2 (Jan. 1986): 1.

Bibliography

Ashley, A., and B. Neil. "Ontario." In A. Wagner, ed. *Contemporary Canadian Theatre: New World Visions*. Toronto: Simon and Pierre, 1985.

Benson, E., and L.W. Conolly. *English-Canadian Theatre*. Toronto: Oxford University Press, 1987.

Berger, J. "A Coat of Many Colours: The Multicultural Theatre Movement in Canada." In A. Wagner, ed., *Contemporary Canadian Theatre*.

Blyth Festival Souvenir Book. 1985.

Blyth Festival Souvenir Brochure. 1987.

Budnick, C. "Theatre on the Frontier: Winnipeg in the 1880s." *Theatre History in Canada* 4, 1 (Spring 1983): 25–40.

Citron, P. "The Blyth Festival: The Little Acorn That Grew." *Canadian Theatre Review* 45 (Winter 1985): 63–68.

Czarnecki, M. "The Regional Theatre System." In A. Wagner, ed. *Contemporary Canadian Theatre*.

Des Landes, C., and W., Learning. "The Canada Council and the Theatre: The Past 25 Years and Tomorrow." *Theatre History in Canada* 3, 2 (Fall 1982): 165–92.

Doherty, B. *Not Bloody Likely: The Shaw Festival 1962–1973*. Toronto: Dent, 1974.

Donnelly, L. "A Play on Memory." *Performing Arts in Canada* 25, 2 (April/Spring 1989):18–20.

Doolittle, J., and Z. Barnich with H. Beauchamp. *A Mirror of Our Dreams: Children and Theatre in Canada*. Vancouver: Talonbooks, 1979.

Edinborough, A., ed. *The Festivals of Canada*. Toronto: Lester and Orpen Dennys, 1980.

Edwards, M. *A Stage in Our Past: English Language Theatre in Eastern Canada*. Toronto: University of Toronto Press, 1968.

Filewood, A. *Collective Encounters: Documentary Theatre in English Canada*. Toronto: University of Toronto Press, 1987.

Foon, D. "Theatre for Young Audiences in English Canada." In A. Wagner, ed. *Contemporary Canadian Theatre*.

Friedlander, M. "The Enduring Vitality of Community and Grass Roots Theatre." In A. Wagner, ed. *Contemporary Canadian Theatre*.

Fulks, W. "Albert Tavernier and the Guelph Royal Opera House." *Theatre History in Canada* 4, 1 (Spring 1983): 41–56.

Gardner, D. "Canada's Eskimo Lear." *Theatre History in Canada* 7, 1 (Spring 1986): 99–118.

Garebian, K. *William Hutt: A Theatre Portrait*. Oakville, ON: Mosaic Press, 1988.

Guinness, A. *Blessings in Disguise*. Glasgow: Fontana/Collins, 1986.

Guthrie, T., R. Davies, and G. MacDonald. *Renown at Stratford*. Toronto: Clarke, Irwin, 1953.

Hood, S.B. "Paranoia, Dry Lips and a Dora." *Performing Arts in Canada* 25, 4 (Dec./Winter, 1989): 8–9.

Hunt, N. "Charting the Progress of the Whirling Mirvishes." *Performing Arts in Canada* 25, 2 (April/Spring 1989): 10–14.

Lee, B. *Love and Whisky: The Story of the Dominion Drama Festival and the Early Years of Theatre in Canada 1602–1972*. Toronto: Simon and Pierre, 1973.

Michael, P. "The Tarragon Theatre Story." *Performing Arts in Canada* 23, 1 (July 1986): 29–30.

Newman, A. "Opera for All." *Performing Arts in Canada* 25, 4 (Dec./Winter 1989): 11–12.

O'Neill, P.B. "Saskatchewan's Last Opera House: Hanley 1912–1982." *Theatre History in Canada* 3, 2 (Fall 1982): 137–47.

Perkyns, R., ed. *Major Plays of the Canadian Theatre 1934–1984*. Toronto: Irwin, 1984.

Perkyns, R. "Two Decades of Neptune Theatre." *Theatre History in Canada* 6, 2 (Fall 1985): 148–86.

Pettigrew, J., and J. Portman. *Stratford: The First Thirty Years*. 2 vols. Toronto: Macmillan, 1985.

Pigott, C. "Blyth Spirit." *London Magazine* (May/June 1987): 34–37, 64–70.

Rubin, D., ed. *Canada On Stage: Canadian Theatre Review Yearbook*. 8 vols. Downsview, ON: CTR Publications, 1974–1982.

Rubin, D., and A. Cramer-Byng, eds. *Canada Playwrights: A Biographical Guide*. Toronto: CTN Publications, 1980.

St. Lawrence Centre Magazine 1, 2 (Jan. 1986).

Smith, M.E. "Shakespeare in Atlantic Canada." *Theatre History in Canada* 3, 2 (Fall 1982): 126–135.

Stone-Blackburn, S. *Robertson Davies, Playwright: A Search for the Self on the Canadian Stage*. Vancouver: University of British Columbia Press, 1985.

Stratford Festival Story 1953–1966. Stratford, ON: Mirror Press Limited, 1966.

Stuart, E.R. *The History of Prairie Theatre: The Development of Theatre in Alberta, Manitoba and Saskatchewan*. Toronto: Simon and Pierre, 1984.

"A Trip to the Blyth Festival." *Can Play: The Newsletter for Canadian Playwrights* 3, 3 (Feb. 1987): 1–7.

Usin, L.V. "A Local Habitation and a Name: Ottawa's Great Canadian Theatre Company." *Theatre History in Canada* 7, 1 (Spring 1986): 71–90.

Usmiani, R. "The Alternate Theatre Movement." In A. Wagner, ed. *Contemporary Canadian Theatre*.

Wagner, A., ed. *Contemporary Canadian Theatre: New World Visions*. Toronto: Simon and Pierre, 1985.

Waldhauer, E. *Grand Theatre 1879–1979*. Kingston: Grand Theatre, 1979.

Wasserman, J., ed. *Modern Canadian Plays*. Vancouver: Talon Books, 1985.

Whittaker, H. "Shakespeare in Canada Before 1953." In B.W. Jackson, ed., *Stratford Papers on Shakespeare 1964*. Toronto: Gage, 1965.

Canadian Music

Edward Kovarik
Paul McIntyre

INTRODUCTION

A country's culture is reflected in its music. In the case of Canada, an examination of its music must include that of its native peoples as well as that of its various immigrant groups. We also need to examine music in its various forms: folk, popular, and classical. As with so many dimensions of Canadian culture, it is impossible to understand Canada's music without understanding its relationships to Europe and the United States.

MUSIC OF THE OLDEST CANADIANS

Canada's native peoples—the Inuit of the Far North and the many dozens of Indian tribes that once roamed the country south of the tree line—could not avoid being affected by their contact with European traders and settlers. Native music, like other aspects of native life, came under tremendous cultural pressure. In a few instances European instruments (violin, accordion, harmonica) and musical forms (jigs and reels) were taken over; more important the many native cultures that accepted Christianity naturally accepted Christian music as well. In the twentieth century this process of acculturation has been further accelerated by the spread of radio and TV broadcasting.

In recent years, however, various attempts have been made to preserve and restore the native cultures. In addition, reports from several generations of anthropologists are available; thus, we can form a reasonably good idea of what native music was like prior to the coming of the European. The dominant form, common to most North American tribes, was ceremonial dancing and chanting accompanied by the rhythmic beating of a drum. Rattles of various sorts were sometimes used in addition to the drum, but the only melody instrument known was the human voice, solo or in group unison. Beyond this standard practice, however, the melodies, texts, and rhythmic patterns employed in these ceremonies differed from place to place and from tribe to tribe; the uniqueness of these repertories was a source of local pride and distinction. The ceremonies also differed widely in their setting and social function: among the settled agricultural tribes of the East, planting and harvest rituals were held in the tribal longhouse; among the nomadic prairie tribes of the West, weather and hunting dances were performed in the open air.

In addition to ceremonial music, the native musical cultures included a great deal of "personal music"—songs sung within the family or in small social groups. These included play and game songs sung to and by children, lullabies, women's work songs, and the like. The Inuit had various categories of songs for different social occasions: hunting, whaling, the reception of visitors, etc. Songs were often treated as personal or family property, to be sung only by those to whom they "belonged," although they might be exchanged with guests. The songs were generally strophic in form,[1] and their texts were usually laced with nonsense syllables. In melodic style they varied a great deal: many were of limited range and frequent note repetition (almost like chanting), but some included wide-ranging, even exuberant, vocalizations.

The best-known example of Canadian Indian music is not Indian at all. This is the "Huron Carol," a popular Christmas carol that begins "'Twas in the moon of winter time, when all the birds had fled. . . . " The original words are a telling of the Christmas story in the language of the Huron Indians, set down somewhere near present-day Georgian Bay in the early seventeenth century by one of the first French Jesuit missionaries, Jean de Brébeuf, who was later martyred and canonized as a saint. It was these Catholic missionaries and their Protestant counterparts who first captured the sounds of the native languages in written form. The music, however, is not an Indian melody, as many people assume, but rather an old French folk tune, which sounds modal[2] and exotic to our ears simply because of its antiquity.

THE FOLK MUSIC OF THE FIRST EUROPEAN SETTLERS

As with native music, so also with folk music—the pressures of the modern-day mass media have substantially disrupted the traditional oral transmission from one generation to the next. Luckily, many songs have been preserved through recordings made by folk-song researchers in the first half of the twentieth century. Some of this material has been transcribed and published; much of it still resides on wax cylinders and reels of tape at Laval University in Québec City and at the National Museum in Ottawa.

The richest heritage of Canadian folk song is to be found, naturally enough, in the earliest settlements: in Newfoundland (settled in the sixteenth century) and Québec (settled in the seventeenth century.) Ontario and the Maritime provinces, founded not long afterwards, also preserve important repertories of folk song, whereas the western half of the country, settled much more recently, contributes relatively little.

Though Newfoundland remained an independent British colony outside of Canada until 1949, it was actually one of the first areas of North America to be settled, probably not long after its "discovery" by Giovanni Caboto (John Cabot) in 1497. Much of this settlement was the outgrowth of temporary fishing camps; thus, it took the form of small, isolated coastal communities—called "outports"— a situation that contributed to the growth and preservation of homemade music. The settlers and their descendents, chiefly of English and Irish extraction, culti- vated two types of unaccompanied vocal music: the ditty, or light song, often with satirical or bawdy lyrics, and the more serious ballad, or narrative song, which often recorded an actual local event such as a shipwreck. The importance of the coastal fishery to the economic life of Newfoundland was captured in numerous sea shanties, some of which have achieved widespread popularity outside of Canada. Instrumental dance music was also cultivated, along with an unusual style of wordless vocalizing—an imitation of instrumental music employed when no instruments were available—which was called "gob music" or "chin music."[3]

The early French settlers of Québec brought with them a number of traditional tunes, some in an ancient modal style that predates the development of the modern major and minor scales (the "Huron Carol" mentioned above was one of these). Other songs in the simpler style of the eighteenth century were brought over later or composed in Québec. Often old tunes continued in use but were given new words to reflect recent events.

An important subspecies of French-Canadian folk song consists of the songs sung by the voyageurs or coureurs de bois (runners of the woods), the canoe handlers who in the seventeenth and eighteenth centuries provided the major means of transportation into the interior of the continent. Although occupied chiefly with the fur trade, these canoeists occasionally carried passengers, and it is from these passengers that the world first heard about Canadian folk song. The earliest travellers' reports date back to the eighteenth century. In 1804, the Irish poet Thomas Moore memorized some of the songs and composed his own Canadian boat song in the same vein. In 1823 a collection called "Canadian Airs" was published in London, but with the original French texts replaced by free English paraphrases. In this collection and in similar ones published later in London, New York, and Paris, the rough tunes were smoothed out, "prettied up," and embedded in a conventional piano accompaniment.

A more purist approach was taken by Ernest Gagnon, the first great Canadian scholar of folk song, who published his *Chansons populaires du Canada* (1865) without editorial changes or additions. Gagnon set the tone for a number of other serious collectors, who worked at first in Québec and later (after the turn of the twentieth century) in other parts of eastern Canada. In Ontario and the Atlantic provinces they found many original lumbering songs (reflecting the economic importance of this activity), as well as many local variants of well-known ballads, both English and French.

Another tradition that transcends the language barrier is folk fiddling, which remains popular even today in rural areas of Ontario, Québec, and the Atlantic provinces. As music for dancing, it fulfilled an important social function, in which the fiddle was often supplemented by concertina, accordion, or harmonica (plus, in recent times, guitar or banjo). A peculiarly French tradition is "clogging," in which the fiddler, sitting down, taps out an accompaniment of rhythmic patterns with his feet.

In Canada's West, those songs not brought in from the East often reflected local conditions; thus the popularity of railroad work songs and cowboy songs. Many of these, of course, are shared with the American West and may have originated south of the border, but one old favourite, "Red River Valley," has been traced to the Red River settlement near what is now Winnipeg, Manitoba.

Over the last hundred years or so, a great deal of music has been brought to Canada by the waves of new immigrants who have settled in various parts of the country, both east and west. These groups include German Moravians, Ukrainians and other eastern Europeans, Afro-Americans, Orientals, and Caribbean peoples. Much of this music, however, has remained within the immigrant communities, making little impression on the country at large.

EARLIEST STAGES IN THE DEVELOPMENT OF ART MUSIC

The cultivation of art music in Canada began in earnest after the middle of the eighteenth century, principally in the urban centres of that time: Montréal, Québec City, and Halifax. There the first music shops opened for business, dealing in imported sheet music and musical instruments. There, too, could be heard the occasional performance of light musical comedies such as those popular in contemporary France. The best known of these musical theatre pieces is *Colas et Colinette* by the French-born Joseph Quesnel (1746–1809). Quesnel had been caught running guns to the Americans during the Revolutionary War and was interned in Halifax (1779). Upon his release, he settled near Montréal and began raising a large family. By profession an import-export trader, he was a passionate amateur in literature and music, although in eighteenth-century Québec he found little beyond what he managed to supply for himself. To a friend he wrote:

I made my way to Canada and here
Was welcomed with all manner of good cheer:

I'd no complaint. But music? Oh, the pity!
At table, naught but some old drinking ditty;
In church, two or three worn-out old motets
Sung to a gasping organ out of breath.
Oh, hideous all. So for my heart's release,
See me composing music! First a piece
For some religious business—grave or gay.
Was it or was it not for Christmas day?[4]

Quesnel wrote both text and music for *Colas*, which was performed in Montréal in 1790 and in Québec City in 1805 and again in 1807. Like most light operas of the time, it consists of long stretches of spoken dialogue interspersed with an occasional song—mostly solos and an occasional duet or trio. There are only a handful of characters: the young lovers mentioned in the title, the girl's guardian, and the old Bailli ("bailiff," or village magistrate), who would like to win Colinette for himself. In recent years *Colas et Colinette* has come to be recognized as an important part of Canada's cultural heritage; the work has been restored and performed, and a recording of the music has been made. Quesnel's text survives, complete, but of the music only the voice and second violin parts have been found. The task of restoration—supplying the other parts of the score and writing an overture—was undertaken by the Toronto composer Godfrey Ridout (1918–1984) in 1963.

Another colourful figure in early Canadian musical life was German-born Theodore Molt, who settled in Québec as a music teacher in 1823 when he was in his late twenties. After two years he sold his possessions and returned to Europe, but a year later he was back in Canada again. He claimed to have studied with a number of masters—Beethoven, Carl Czerny, and Ignaz Moscheles. He certainly met Beethoven (although he probably did not study with him), for he brought back to Canada a souvenir in Beethoven's own handwriting, a canon (a brief fragment of music that could be sung as a round), one among the many that the old Viennese master was accustomed to give out to visitors. Molt spent the rest of his life teaching music in Québec City, Montréal, and Burlington, Vermont, where he died. He composed a little and wrote several instruction books in harmony and piano playing.

Throughout the first half of the nineteenth century, art music in Canada expanded along with the growing population, and it soon began to include home-grown efforts at composing, publishing, and instrument building. Many of the earliest compositions and publications were religious music: plainchant and Latin-texted motets in Catholic Québec, and hymn settings in Protestant English Canada. Piano making began in the 1820s, mostly in small shops run by a single master; the craft did not become a major industry until the end of the century. One of the most notable of Canadian instrument makers was the organ building family of Casavant, first established at St. Hyacinthe, Québec by Joseph Casavant in 1840 and then reestablished on the same site in 1879 by Joseph's two sons; it is still going strong today.

FROM THE TIME OF CONFEDERATION

The second half of the nineteenth century witnessed the emergence of several important new centres of musical activity, most notably Ottawa and Toronto. Publishers in these and other major cities began turning out a wealth of light salon music, chiefly songs and short piano pieces by a host of European, American, and Canadian composers now mostly forgotten. Singing societies were founded in the larger cities, and festive concerts of choral and orchestral music were sometimes put together for special occasions. The performers were mostly amateurs or local music teachers; the director was usually a church organist or British Army bandmaster, either of whom might well have received his training outside of the country.

A notable exception to the general pattern was the checkered career of Calixa Lavallée (1842–1891), the most famous musician of nineteenth-century Canada. The son of a violin maker and music dealer, he learned to play several instruments, and while still in his teens he became a military bandsman with the Union forces during the American Civil War. After the war he worked in Boston and New York City; he returned to Montréal in 1872 and a year later his friends raised money to send him abroad to study. He spent two years at the Paris Conservatory, had works published and performed there, and then returned to Canada full of ideas and hope. The rest of his life was spent in a losing struggle for recognition and financial success. After six unrewarding years in Montréal and Québec City, Lavallée emigrated to the US, where in the 1880s he became an important figure in the Music Teachers' National Association (at the time no similar organization existed in Canada). When he died in Boston in 1891, Lavallée left behind a small selection of songs and piano pieces, several concert overtures for band, and the published piano-vocal scores of two stage works, the melodramatic musical satire *TIQ* (The Indian Question Settled at Last), and a musical comedy called *The Widow*. In recent years this latter work has been orchestrated and performed a number of times; it is not only an important document of Canada's musical past, but also great fun to see and hear.

The Canadian public may not recognize Calixa Lavallée's name, but they still hear his music regularly, for he is the composer of the national anthem, "O Canada." The anthem grew out of a National Festival of French Canadians held in Québec City in June 1880. The music committee for this event, which included most of the prominent French-Canadian musicians of the time, thought first of holding an open competition to choose a new patriotic song, but soon decided instead to entrust the task to their most gifted colleague. Lavallée went to work with a will and quickly produced a series of melodies, all of which were immediately rejected by the committee; finally he found one that both he and they knew was right. A distinguished jurist, Adolphe-Basile Routhier, was then invited to write the words. The new anthem was first performed by massed bands on 24 June (the Feast of St. John the Baptist, patron saint of French Canada), and it was repeated on several occasions over the next few days. Its popularity in English Canada dates from about twenty-five years later (1905), when several English translations of Judge Routhier's words were published almost simultaneously.

As Lavallée's problematic career indicates, the cultivation of art music in nineteenth-century Canada was left largely in the hands of amateurs. Young men and women drawn towards music as a career had to go abroad, not only to pursue their studies but also to seek performance opportunities unavailable at home. Composers were constrained by the needs of their society and by the resources available; for example, since there were no permanent orchestras before about 1890, very little orchestral music was written prior to this date. There was, however, plenty of other music: religious choral music (especially in Québec), band music (prompted by the British regimental bands that had long been a part of the Canadian scene), and, needless to say, great quantities of light piano music and sentimental songs, all intended for amateur performance.

AT THE TURN OF THE TWENTIETH CENTURY

The decades surrounding the turn of the twentieth century brought some important changes in Canadian musical life, including the founding of the first orchestras and the establishment of regular concert series in the major cities. To these places, as well, came a succession of touring recitalists, chiefly singers and pianists, who set a new standard of excellence for local musicians and audiences. The first private music schools and colleges were also founded, although for many decades to come foreign-born and foreign-trained musicians continued to enjoy a real or imagined superiority over the local product. Indeed, the most gifted native-born composers and performers usually found it necessary to spend a few years in London, Paris, Leipzig, or Berlin to complete their musical training.

Canadian musicians prominent in the period 1870–1930 included two internationally successful opera singers, the finest cornet player in North America, and three composers who achieved considerable local success. Dame Emma Albani (ca. 1847–1930), the oldest of this group, was one of the most celebrated sopranos of her time. Born Marie Louise Lajeunesse at Chambly, near Montréal, she claimed to have taken her stage name from an old Italian family; cynics, however, have suggested that she took it from the town of Albany, New York, where she achieved her first success outside of Canada. Albani studied at the Paris Conservatory, made her debut in Italy, and spent most of her long career as a featured singer at the Covent Garden Opera in London. In her prime (and after) she made numerous concert tours, which usually included a triumphal return to her native city.

The other opera singer was Edward Johnson (1878–1959), a leading tenor who became general manager of the Metropolitan Opera Company in New York City. Johnson began as a singer of oratorio and musical comedy, but abandoned this career to study opera in Paris and Italy. After seven years on the Italian stage (where he billed himself as "Edoardo Di Giovanni," the last name a literal translation of "Johnson"), he returned to the US, where he sang with Chicago's Lyric Opera and with the Met; he became general manager in 1935 and held that position for the next fifteen years. After his retirement he returned to Toronto, where he remained active as chairman of the Toronto Conservatory.

The cornetist was Herbert L. Clarke (1867–1945), who came to Toronto from Massachusetts as a young boy and grew up playing both violin and cornet. For nearly thirty years (ca. 1890–1920) Clarke was the solo cornetist in bands directed by Patrick Gilmore, Victor Herbert, and John Philip Sousa, and he also composed and recorded numerous cornet solos.

The leading Canadian composers of this period were the Montréal natives Guillaume Couture (1851–1915) and Alexis Contant (1858–1918), and Wesley Octavius Forsyth (1859–1937) of Toronto. Couture completed his musical studies in Paris, Forsyth in Leipzig and Vienna. Contant studied with Albani and Lavallée in Montréal, but was prevented from going to Paris by his father, who was concerned about the effect such exposure might have on his son's religious faith. Contant thus became the first prominent Canadian composer to be trained entirely at home. Forsyth remained an internationalist throughout his life: he made his career in Toronto as a teacher and administrator but also served as musical correspondent for journals in Britain and the United States, while his light classical compositions—chiefly songs and short piano pieces—won him success throughout the English-speaking world. Couture and Contant lived out their lives in the Montréal area, where they taught music and performed as organists and choirmasters. Both composed mass settings and other sacred choral works, and both wrote a modest amount of secular music as well, including some music for orchestra. Of the two, Contant seems to have developed the stronger, more personal style.

BETWEEN THE WORLD WARS

At the close of World War I the only orchestra to be found anywhere in the country was in Québec City, and that ensemble usually managed to present a grand total of two concerts per season. Earlier orchestras in Montréal and Toronto had ceased activities under the pressures of wartime, and so neither of Canada's major cities had a regularly functioning orchestra of its own until the late twenties. Elsewhere in the country orchestral activity was sporadic at best.

This is not to say that Canada was a land without music. Good teachers could be found in nearly every city, and choral societies on the British model flourished. Often the best musician in town was the church organist—typically a pipe-smoking Englishman, thoroughly trained in the musical needs of the Anglican or Presbyterian service. The establishment in 1909 of the Canadian Guild of Organists, later the Royal Canadian College of Organists, or RCCO, provided one of the earliest musical networks in a vast country: examiners going out from the larger cities were able not only to assure a reasonably high standard of playing and general musicianship, but also—and perhaps more important—to stay in touch with what was happening in the smaller centres. Similar benefits accrued from the examinations conducted annually throughout the country by the Toronto Conservatory of Music, which in 1947 became the Royal Conservatory, or RCMT.

Other communication networks indirectly aided the cause of music in the period between the wars. Beginning in 1927, the Canadian Pacific Railway (CPR) held a series of music festivals in Victoria, Banff, Calgary, Regina, Winnipeg, Toronto, and Québec City. While these were primarily promotions for the CPR hotel chain, they managed in the five years of their existence to focus a spotlight on the work of serious Canadian composers and performers at a time when the need for such attention was great.

Of more lasting impact on the growth of music in Canada was the work of the Canadian Broadcasting Corporation (CBC), established in 1936, and its predecessors. The power of radio to communicate over vast distances was recognized early in Canada—initially by the CPR and its counterpart, the Canadian National Railway, each of which had its own radio network in the late twenties and early thirties. Through these and other sources, Canadians everywhere were able to hear fine music, often for the first time in an age of still primitive recording techniques; broadcasts by major American orchestras and by the Metropolitan Opera of New York gave Canadian listeners a foretaste of musical excellence at a level not yet to be found in their own country. The CBC began creating its own musical organizations in some of the larger cities, with the result that, by the end of the forties, CBC orchestras of various sizes could be found in Halifax, Québec City, Montréal, Toronto, Winnipeg, and Vancouver. Together these constituted not only a direct benefit to professional musical development, but also an interesting precedent for indirect government subsidy of the arts.

Throughout the inter-war years, the figure of Ernest Campbell MacMillan (1893–1973) stands tall. Born near Toronto, the son of a musically gifted Presbyterian minister, he excelled early as a church organist, proceeded to further studies in London, Edinburgh, and Paris, and was later made Doctor of Music by Oxford University. Trapped on German soil at the outbreak of World War I (he had been attending the Wagner Festival at Bayreuth, in Bavaria), he spent the next four years in a prisoner-of-war camp near Berlin—in the process learning German and conducting the camp orchestra. On his return to Canada, he became active as an examiner for the RCCO and the RCMT, crisscrossing the country by train and leaving the mark of his enthusiasm and the memory of his high expectations everywhere he went. He became principal of the Toronto Conservatory, dean of music at the University of Toronto and, in 1931, conductor of the revived Toronto Symphony Orchestra. Following his knighthood by King George V in 1935, "Sir Ernest" became synonymous in Canada with musical leadership and erudition.

A companion figure of the period, of nearly equally high profile, was the English-born organist and composer Healey Willan (1880–1968), who lived and worked in Toronto from 1913. Best known for his Anglican service music, including many lovely choral motets, and for his virtuoso organ pieces, Willan in later life also composed an important body of orchestral music and two large operas; to the end of his career, however, he retained the lush, late romantic musical style of his youth in Edwardian England.

The leading Québec composer of this period was Claude Champagne (1891–1965). Born in Montréal of a French-Canadian father and an Irish-Canadian mother, he studied and later taught music (piano, violin, harmony) in his native city. He spent most of the 1920s (when he was in his thirties) studying at the Paris Conservatoire, had orchestral works performed in Paris, returned to Canada late in 1928, then managed almost single-handedly to keep musical life going in Montréal through the first half of the Depression decade (1930–1935). Later, as professor at McGill University and assistant director of the Montréal Conservatory, he taught most of the younger generation of French-Canadian composers. His own compositions are few in number but highly regarded. His *Symphonie gaspésienne*, inspired by the folk music of the Gaspé Peninsula, is typical of his search for a Québec voice within the mainstream of imported French culture.

The musical life of Montréal picked up somewhat in the late thirties, thanks in large part to the efforts of Wilfrid Pelletier (1896–1982), a Montréal-born pianist and conductor who had studied in Paris during World War I. Although Pelletier's career unfolded largely in New York City, where he conducted for many years at the Metropolitan Opera, he also gave his support at important moments to the development of a permanent orchestra for his native city, most notably in 1935, when he became artistic director of the newly formed Montreal Symphony. He was succeeded in 1940 by the Belgian-born Désiré Defauw (1885–1960), who concurrently led the Chicago Symphony during part of his Montréal tenure.

By the mid-1940s, then, Canada's two major cities had orchestras of their own—ensembles of which they could be justly proud, whatever might be their international standing. The great British conductor, Sir Thomas Beecham, one of many international figures who conducted both orchestras at that time, was heard to remark that if you put the strings of the TSO together with the winds and brass of the MSO, you might have one good orchestra.

RECENT TIMES

The years following the close of World War II were kinder to music in Canada than the decades between the wars had been. This may be traced, in part, to the arrival in Canada of large numbers of central European immigrants, including many highly trained musicians. Their presence led to a broadening of musical taste, and a movement away from the narrow provincialism of the country's colonial past: the British ways of English Canada and, in Québec, the compulsive emphasis on French culture to the virtual exclusion of all else.

In the Toronto area, three of the most conspicuous newcomers were Arnold Walter (1902–1973), Nicholas Goldschmidt (b. 1908) and Herman Geiger-Torel

(1907–1976). Walter revamped the curriculum of the newly renamed Royal Conservatory and founded an opera school there in 1946. Goldschmidt served as first director of the opera school and then went on to a distinguished career as organizer and administrator of music festivals throughout the country, including the Centennial celebrations of 1967. Geiger-Torel brought his considerable expertise as opera producer and stage director to the opera school, and began preparing talent for a CBC Opera Company (established in 1948) and for its successor, the Toronto-based Canadian Opera Company, whose touring wing would soon bring opera to all parts of the country.

Not surprisingly, in these years a number of Canadian singers emerged who went on to international careers of distinction. Among these should be mentioned the sopranos Lois Marshall (b. 1924) and Theresa Stratas (b. 1938), the contralto Maureen Forrester (b. 1930), the tenors Leopold Simoneau (b. 1918) and Jon Vickers (b. 1926), and the bass-baritones Louis Quilico (b. 1925) and Victor Braun (b. 1935). A number of other Canadian performers achieved international recognition in the second half of the twentieth century. The pianist and conductor Mario Bernardi (b. 1930), having served as music director at the Sadlers Wells Opera in London during the mid-1960s, returned to Canada in 1968 as founding music director of the newly formed National Arts Centre Orchestra, an ensemble that he led to international distinction during the next fifteen years through tours and recordings. The pianist Glenn Gould (1932–1982), universally renowned for his playing of Bach and for his mastery of some of the most difficult piano music of the early twentieth century, became something of an international cult figure, having retired from the public platform at the age of thirty-two, thereafter confining his playing activities to the recording studio. From this time forward his sparkling prose also enlivened Canadian music criticism.

The National Arts Centre Orchestra was far from the only success story in the orchestral field during the postwar period. Unlike their predecessors of an earlier time, the symphony orchestras of Toronto and Montréal had both survived World War II intact and were thus well-positioned for the period of growth that followed. MacMillan left the Toronto Symphony in 1956 at the end of his twenty-fifth season; he was succeeded by the Czech-born Walter Susskind (1913–1980), who gave place nine years later to Seiji Ozawa (b. 1935). A similar pattern unfolded in Montreal, where the Russian-born Igor Markevitch (1912–1983) served as artistic director of the orchestra from 1958–1961; he was succeeded by Zubin Mehta (b. 1936) who served until 1967. Artistic improvements in both orchestras were matched by audience growth and greater financial security. During the same period, similar developments could be observed, if on a smaller scale, in other cities such as Québec, Winnipeg, and Vancouver. Important chamber ensembles active in this period included the Orford String Quartet (1965–1991) and the Canadian Brass (formed in 1970).

While the CBC continued to have a role in these developments, it had long since become evident that a more direct kind of government involvement would be needed if music and the arts in general were to flourish in Canada. A Royal Commission on National Development in the Arts, Letters and Sciences, established in 1949 under the chairmanship of Vincent Massey, held public hearings in all parts of the country over the course of two years. Addressing the problems arising from Canada's vast distances and from its vulnerability to cultural penetration from the South, the Massey Commission recommended in 1951 that the federal government become a direct patron of the arts, acting not through a ministry of culture but rather through a separate, arm's-length agency.

The government dragged its feet for five years (direct or even indirect government subsidy of the arts being then as now a fiercely debated subject), but at length was prompted into action by the unlikely coincidence of the deaths, within six months of each other, of two of the wealthiest men in Canada. Death duties on these two estates amounted to $100 million, a substantial sum even today and an embarrassment of riches for a Canadian government in the mid-1950s. "What shall we do with a hundred million?" asked Sir Ernest MacMillan, rhetorically.

The government's response was to establish, in 1957, a Crown corporation called the Canada Council, funded initially by the income from half of the windfall (the other half being put directly into university construction), later by annual parliamentary subsidy. Over the decades of its existence, the Council has played an incalculably important role in the development of all the arts in Canada. In the case of music, this has meant that even cities of modest size now have their own professional orchestra, that musical organizations in the largest cities now perform to international standards, and that, through commissioning programs, large numbers of musical compositions have been written and performed that might otherwise never have seen the light of day.

The postwar years were also kind in other ways to the growth and maturation of musical composition in Canada. The Canadian League of Composers, founded in Toronto in 1951 by John Weinzweig (b. 1913) and a few of his students, has grown over the years to number more than 200 members from all parts of the country. Often perceived in its early years as a tool of the avant-garde, the League nowadays admits to membership composers of all stylistic persuasions, from archconservative to ultramodern. It functions as a lobby group to promote policies that support composers' needs. The League has been most influential in the program policies of the CBC and of organizations supported by Canada Council grants, and can claim full credit for the establishment and maintenance of the Canadian Music Centre, a library and distribution service for the works of Canadian composers.

With 200 or more active composers to choose from, it is not easy to single out a few names for special mention. Among the Toronto group of the postwar generation, Harry Freedman (b. 1922), Harry Somers (b. 1925), and John Beckwith (b. 1927) have sought, each in his own way, a personal expression of their shared Canadian identity. In Montréal, Jean Papineau-Couture (b. 1916), a grandson of Guillaume Couture, and Clermont Pepin (b. 1926) together form a link between the more traditional, self-conscious provincialism of Champagne and his contemporaries, and the equally self-conscious internationalist, avant-garde tendencies of a younger group, whose spiritual leader for many years was Serge Garant (1929–1986).

Musical composition in Canada has been greatly enriched over the past half century by the arrival of a number of highly-gifted European-trained composers; the best known of these is probably Oskar Morawetz (b. 1917), who came to Toronto in 1940 and whose music, while very much of our time, is also deeply rooted in his Czech heritage. Traffic to and from the United States has not been wanting: Michael Colgrass (b. 1932) moved to Toronto in 1974 at the height of a successful American career, while Canadian-born Sydney Hodkinson (b. 1934) has found an equal success south of the border. The leading theatre composer in Canada is Louis Applebaum (b. 1918), whose score for the Hollywood movie *The Story of G.I. Joe* won an Oscar nomination in 1946, and who has pursued an important second career as an arts administrator at various levels of government. Among Canada's many active women composers, two of the most prominent of the older generation are Violet Archer (b. 1913), who studied with both Bartok and Hindemith in the forties, and Jean Coulthard (b. 1908), who has gained widespread recognition for her works in small forms. An important younger woman is Alexina Louie (b. 1949), who has successfully incorporated aspects of her Chinese heritage into a series of highly colourful orchestral works. In a class by himself is R. Murray Schafer (b. 1933), who has developed a considerable international following, not only for the breadth and originality of his compositions, but also for his writings in musicology and modern music education and for his research into noise pollution of the sonic environment, which he calls the "soundscape."

THE JAZZ AND POP SCENE

In the course of the twentieth century, popular music evolved in Canada as it did in the US and elsewhere. The light classical salon music popular in the first decades of the century gave way in the 1920s to the raucous beat of the jazz age and then to the smoother big band era of the thirties and forties. One of the icons of popular culture during this period was the dance band known as Guy Lombardo and his Royal Canadians. Guy, short for Gaetano (1902–1977), formed the band with his brothers when they were teenagers in London, Ontario; later they played in Cleveland and Chicago before settling in New York City in 1929. The band's distinctive mellow sound and quiet beat (dubbed "the sweetest music this side of Heaven") quickly won it a large radio audience. From the 1930s to the 1960s the Lombardo group made hundreds of recordings, including many original songs and medley arrangements by Guy's brother Carmen. During these years the band also became a permanent fixture of the yearly New Year's Eve celebrations broadcast across the US and Canada from the grand ballroom of the Waldorf Astoria Hotel in New York.

Other influential figures in popular music around the middle of the century were the composer-arrangers Percy Faith (1908–1976) and Robert Farnon (b. 1917). Faith studied in Toronto as a classical pianist and then went to work for CBC Radio in the 1930s. He moved to Chicago in 1940 and became one of the most successful music directors of network radio in the US. Later he repeated his success as an arranger and conductor for Columbia Records; he also produced a number of film scores. Farnon worked under Faith in Toronto during the 1930s, later became music director for the Canadian "Army Show" during World War II, and went on to a distinguished career in records and films. Active as a composer as well as an arranger,[5] Farnon eventually settled on the island of Guernsey, where he became the focus of a British-based "Robert Farnon Appreciation Society."

Singers and singer-songwriters dominated the pop scene in the years following World War II. Robert Goulet (b. 1933) was active in radio and TV in Toronto in the 1950s; he burst into American consciousness in 1960 as Lancelot in Lerner and Loewe's *Camelot*, playing opposite Richard Burton and Julie Andrews. Meanwhile, an Ottawa teenager named Paul Anka (b. 1941) had already taken Canada, the US, and Europe by storm with his first major-label single "Diana" (1957). Anka, who wrote most of his own material, was one of the leading teen idols of the period 1957-1962; later he carved out a stable career as a songwriter and middle-of-the-road balladeer. His song "My Way" was written for and popularized by Frank Sinatra. More recently, Canada's most successful popular singer has been Anne Murray (b. 1945), who began her career in her native Nova Scotia and achieved international recognition as a recording artist in the 1970s.

The urban-folk movement of the 1960s raised powerful echoes in Canada. Three of the most prominent singer-songwriters of this period were the Canadians Leonard Cohen (b. 1934), Gordon Lightfoot (b. 1939), and Joni Mitchell (b. 1943). Cohen, more highly regarded as a poet and novelist than as a musician, actually anticipated the folk movement in his poetry of the late 1950s; Lightfoot began by writing songs for Ian and Sylvia and for Peter, Paul, and Mary; later he achieved recognition as a performer and eventually—like Bob Dylan in the States—made the transition from folk to pop music. Mitchell, too, began her career as a songwriter and only gradually became a powerful and convincing performer; in recent years she has explored a variety of pop and experimental jazz styles.

Traditional jazz is represented in Canada by a handful of world-class artists, including pianist Oscar Peterson (b. 1925), vibraphonist Peter Appleyard (b. 1928), and clarinetist Phil Nimmons (b. 1923); the interface between jazz and traditional art music has been explored at length by composer-clarinetist Norm Symonds (b. 1920). One of the finest of modern-day big bands is Toronto's Boss Brass, founded in 1968. Among Canada's many rock musicians, three of the most durable are Randy Bachman (b. 1946) of the Guess Who and Bachman-Turner Overdrive, Neil Young (b. 1945), and Bruce Cockburn (b. 1945). A recent sensation in the country and western genre is young k.d. lang from Alberta. In a special category are the singer-songwriters, or chansonniers, of French-speaking Québec, who work apart from English Canada in a distinct and somewhat isolated cultural milieu. They flourished during the urban-folk movement of the 1960s, particularly in big-city cafés such as Montréal's Chez Bozo, and some of them were in the forefront of the movement towards Québec nationalism. Since the 1970s, however, political themes have usually taken second place to purely artistic considerations, particularly among the younger generation of singers. Among the best-known of the chansonniers are two older, somewhat conservative figures, Gilles Vigneault and Monique Leyrac (both born in 1928), and the younger and musically more adventurous Robert Charlebois (b. 1945). Charlebois in particular has begun to expand and transform the traditional French songs by admitting cross-cultural stylistic elements and a broadened range of subject matter.

CONCLUSION

Canada has a fairly rich and well-explored heritage of native and folk music, and Canadians have made important contributions to modern popular music, urban-folk, and jazz. In the area of concert music, Canada is somewhat of a Johnny-come-lately, still better known for its performers than for its composers. The latter, however, are beginning to thrive within Canada (thanks in no small part to government support of various kinds), and some of them are being performed and recorded outside the country. Of the particular strengths of Canada's musical community, one is its warm reception of immigrant composers and performers, both from the US and abroad. Another is its unabashed use of "nationalist" materials, including folk songs, in various kinds of choral and instrumental settings ranging from the simple and practical to the elaborate and highly artistic. Canada's vigorous musical past conjures up images of an even more impressive musical future.

Notes

[1] That is, they consisted of a series of stanzas all sung to the same music. New stanzas often supplemented or replaced old ones as the songs passed from one "owner" to another. For examples, see the bibliographies in the article "Indians" in H. Kallman, G. Potvin, and K. Winters, eds., *Encyclopedia of Music in Canada* (Toronto: University of Toronto Press, 1981), 449–52.

[2] "Modal" tunes are not based on the modern major or minor scale. The "Huron Carol" is in the Aeolian mode, which runs from A to A on the piano keyboard, using only the white keys. It is equivalent to the "natural minor" scale.

[3] The practice is described at length in K. Peacock, *Songs of the Newfoundland Outports* (Ottawa: National Museum of Canada, 1965).

[4] English translation by J. Glassco, printed in *Encyclopedia of Music in Canada*, 789.

[5] G. Lees, "The Influence of Robert Farnon," *Canadian Composer* 180 (April 1983), 28–33.

Bibliography

Beckwith, J. and F. Hall, eds. *Musical Canada: Words and Music Honouring Helmut Kallmann*. Toronto: University of Toronto Press, 1988.

Canadian Music Centre: publications (Toronto).

Canadian Music: A Selective Guidelist for Teachers (1978).

Catalogue of Canadian Choral Music (1978).

Catalogue of Canadian Keyboard Music (1971).

Catalogue of Canadian Music for Orchestra (1976), and *Supplement* (1979).

Directory of Associate Composers (1989).

Catalogues and other reference works dealing with the music of Canadian composers whose scores have been deposited at the CMC. Unpublished works are available on loan from the Centre.

Canadian Musical Heritage Society publications (Ottawa: 1983–1989)—eleven volumes of piano and organ music, chamber music, choral works, and popular songs in English and French.

Gagnon, E. *Chansons populaires du Canada*. Québec City, 1865, 1880.

Kallmann, H., G. Potvin, and K. Winters, eds. *Encyclopedia of Music in Canada*. Toronto: University of Toronto Press, 1981.

Lees, G. "The Influence of Robert Farnon." *Canadian Composer* 180 (April 1983): 28–33.

Peacock, K. *Songs of the Newfoundland Outports*. Ottawa: National Museum of Canada, 1965.

Proctor, G.A. *Canadian Music of the Twentieth Century*. Toronto: University of Toronto Press, 1980.

Walter, A., ed. *Aspects of Music in Canada*. Toronto: University of Toronto Press, 1969.

16

❏ ❏ ❏ ❏ ❏ ❏ ❏

Landscape Painting in Canada

Sandra Paikowsky

INTRODUCTION

The history of Canadian art is as multi-faceted and complex as the country itself. It represents the aesthetic achievement of a country and a people whose essential common denominator is diversity. Similarly, the history of Canadian art can be understood through a variety of approaches: chronology, biography, patronage, education, geography, subject matter, and formal concerns, to cite the most obvious.[1] However, the development of Canadian art, like the growth of Canada itself, must be understood in light of all of the issues, for each in its own way has contributed to the visual appearance of Canadian art and to the aims and ambitions of the women and men who have produced our cultural heritage.

For the purposes of this study, we focus on the image of the landscape, particularly as it is portrayed in painting. Landscape painting has been the most popular and dominant art form in Canada for almost 200 years. And even in the last decade, when video and installation have gained particular prominence, references to nature have still remained an essential component within the visual imagery.

In the context of this overview, we do not discuss the art of native peoples because of the distinctiveness of their cultural traditions; thus, our use of "Canada" and "Canadian" has built-in limitations. As well, it must be remembered that the term "nationalism" has a distinct and different meaning in Québec than in other parts of Canada. The emphasis here on Toronto and Montréal painting is not reflective of a centrist bias, but rather an acknowledgement that they were the most active Canadian art centres until the later twentieth century because of population, art schools, patronage, and exhibiting opportunities. Furthermore, only a small proportion of Canadian landscape artists can be cited in this overview.[2]

CHARACTERISTICS OF LANDSCAPE PAINTING

Landscape painting, like other visual art forms in Canada, was greatly influenced by outside aesthetic traditions, especially those of France and Britain, and to an ever increasing degree, the United States. By drawing upon the visual approaches and attitudes to nature in long-established international art, Canadian artists were seeking their own identity at the same time as they were seeking to know and understand the environment in which they worked and lived.

The landscape as both reality and myth has become our national symbol (we do have a maple leaf on our flag) and even in the mid-nineteenth century when more than half of the population lived in urban areas, images of the Canadian wilderness were our most prolific visual icons. Only in Québec were representations of the village or town consistently integrated into paintings of the rural landscape. Despite the vastness of Canada, the toughness of the terrain, and the unwelcoming topography, the landscape was approached by artists with a mixture of awe and ease. Nature signified the "Other," a place to visit but one rarely inhabited. However, the image of the landscape in Canadian painting has never expressed the sense of fear and isolation that has been so dominant a theme in Canadian literature. Canadian painters recognized and emphasized the notion that nature was available to everyone. The artists had relatively easy access to the rural environment and the audience intuitively recognized the "truth to reality" presented in landscape painting, even if they had never visited the places that were painted.

Interestingly, representations emphasizing the human figure in the landscape were never as popular a theme here as they were in the United States or Europe. The figure in Canadian landscape painting tends to be an observer rather than an active participant, particularly until the end of the nineteenth century, although she or he is always at ease in nature. The figure is often presented in small scale in comparison to the elements of the landscape—a device intended to imply the majesty of nature but not to exclude a human presence. While the figure may often assume an anecdotal role and not affect the formal composition of the work, it does act as a mediator between the viewing audience and the painted subject.

THE EIGHTEENTH CENTURY

The first landscape painters in Canada were British military officers stationed in Québec and the Maritimes. As topographical drawing was a part of their basic training, producing water-colour views of their new surroundings became a popular pastime. Artists from France had come to Québec somewhat earlier, and their portrayal of the landscape was limited to the background settings of religious altarpieces and narrative votive paintings. British soldiers such as Thomas Davies (ca. 1737–1812), George Heriot (1759–1839), and James Pattison Cockburn (1779–1847) sought out such picturesque sites as rushing rivers, rapids, and waterfalls and reproduced the scenes in tightly controlled and precisely drawn water colours, the most portable of artists' materials. Usually horizontal in format, a calm, clouded sky often occupied the upper half of the image. The landscape was frequently described in deep, receding planes with the main subject strategically placed in the centre of the middle ground. Trees and foliage framed the view on each side and in the open foreground. This popular compositional formula evoked a sense of limitless space without sacrificing a detailed rendering of each natural element. The paintings were often reproduced and published in England as engravings. These, the first "postcards" of Canada, were remarkable for their careful description of the natural elements and their detailed mapping of the Canadian topography. But more important, these neatly arranged views of spectacular scenery established the validity and style of a landscape tradition in Canada.[3] This objective approach to nature would form the basis of landscape painting for generations to come.

Thomas Davies (c. 1737–1812), *View of the Great Falls on the Ottawa River, Lower Canada*, 1791. Watercolour over graphite on wove paper. 34.6 x 51.4 cm. National Gallery of Canada, Ottawa.

THE NINETEENTH CENTURY

By the early nineteenth century, portrait painting began to challenge the landscape as the most popular subject matter. Only very occasionally did these portrait images contain some reference to the landscape setting where the sitters resided. Unlike the grand-manner portraits of England and the United States, the emphasis here was primarily on the sitter's face and costume—the subjects' place in society rather than the place they lived. In Québec, however, the rollicking habitants of Dutch-born Cornelius Krieghoff (1815–1872) are as important as the place they occupy. His populated landscapes suggest that he was perhaps more interested in local costumes and customs than in the appearance of rural Québec, which may explain why the same figures are repeated in numerous pictures despite the change in the landscape setting. However, Krieghoff introduced the notion of narrative into Canadian landscape painting, even though he rarely suggested the true hardship of habitant life in Québec. Krieghoff was also one of the few painters to ever depict the Canadian winter landscape. In general, his images reflected a new maturity through their animated composition, which strongly contrasts with the static scenic views of earlier artists. Rather than relying upon horizontal bands of receding planes, Krieghoff often presented the landscape in diagonal planes moving to the side edges of the paintings. The figures were usually placed in the foreground, moving in an opposite direction to that of the setting. Through colour and light, nature was portrayed as having some emotional qualities. By the early nineteenth century, the image of Canadian landscape in paintings was beginning to develop a personality, a sense of specificity, but one that did not deny the desire for an objective rendering of the various phenomena of nature.

Paul Kane's (1810–1871) interest in the native peoples of western Canada was the *raison d'être* of his numerous landscapes. A Toronto artist whose travels led him to the West in the mid-1840s, he was more concerned with the plight of the Indians and their vanishing way of life than in simply recording their environment. His figures are less anecdotal than Krieghoff's, although sometimes just as romanticized. Like Krieghoff, Kane's landscape views were treated with emotive light and shadow with an intense tonal range that suggested the romantic traditions of European landscape painting. Similarly, Joseph Légaré from Québec City (1795–1855) often exaggerated the light and colour of his landscape views to intensify their emotional content. Portraying such dramatic local subjects as fires and rock slides, as well as "pure" landscapes, his work contained both romantic tendencies and a direct response to the horrific events in his own community.

By the mid-nineteenth century, Canadian landscapes could best be described as "view" paintings, that is, panoramic investigations of the facts of the Canadian countryside. Vistas of impressive natural phenomena, the rolling, pastoral landscape lying just outside the city or the isolated, lonely lakes and rivers far from urban centres, were all components of the early Canadian artist's desire

Cornelius Krieghoff (1815–1872) *Habitants Crossing the Ice at Quebec*, 1857. Oil on canvas. 12 1/4 x 18 1/4 in. (31.1 x 46.4 cm). Gift of Dr. and Mrs. Matthew J. Boylen. The Beaverbrook Art Galley, Fredericton, NB, Canada.

Joseph Légaré, *Après l'incendie du Faubourg Saint-Roch survenu le 28 mai 1845: Les ruins,* 1845. Oil on canvas. 81.4 x 111.2 cm. Musée du Québec. Accession no. 58.534. Photo, Patrick Altman.

for a self-mapping of Canada. These essentially factual and realistic analyses of the places where painters travelled reached their most intensive period at mid-century, just as Canada itself was seeking to secure its own identity through the instrument of Confederation.

The idea of a national spirit in art became the linchpin of Canadian painting for much of the nineteenth century. And it was the image of the landscape that could best be evoked to reflect the nationalist aspirations of the public and the aesthetic ambitions of the painters. The physical size of Canada and the grandeur and variety of its terrain, as well as the potential of its natural resources, gave the Canadian landscape a symbolic role for artist and audience alike. The landscape was the ideal metaphor for the new country, and it played the role traditionally ascribed to history painting, providing us with images of dignity, inspiration, and moral strength. Unlike portrait painting, landscape imagery made no references to economic and social conditions or to cultural materialism. It was the visual embodiment of Canada's democratic aspirations.

By mid-century, rather than being a single assemblage of distinct parts—as in late-eighteenth and early-nineteenth century landscape painting—images of nature became more evocative of a totality of vision. As a result, nature could function as the appropriate vehicle for both visual truth and emotional meaning. The earlier objective recordings had by now given way to a more expressive, heroic landscape.

The growing sophistication of Canadian landscape painting was influenced by many forces. British and American paintings were more frequently exhibited in the developing museums and galleries; art education became more readily available to both women and men; and European paintings, although collected privately, were often placed on public view. As well, European artists now emigrated to Canada (rather than merely visiting) and helped transplant established styles and aesthetics. Most important, the artists themselves banded together in professional associations to present exhibitions of their work. Painters and collectors involved in the Art Association of Montreal and the Ontario Society of Artists were instrumental in the eventual founding of the Montreal Museum of Fine Arts and the Art Gallery of Ontario. All of these factors allowed Canadian artists to broaden their vision of the possibilities of landscape painting and to recognize more clearly the potential for an individual approach to the subject.

Photography also assisted the artists in reevaluating landscape painting, and it encouraged the pursuit of the "truth" of the scene. Photography played an essential role as an *aide-mémoire* (as did the water colour) when the landscape painters travelled outside their urban studios. It helped them to produce large oil paintings far from the sites of their on-the-spot sketches, often some time after the fact. The photograph was an essential tool for helping the artist express a basic tenet of nineteenth-century aesthetics: that art was firmly rooted in fact. Yet photography did not alter the style of painting because the aesthetic basis of the photograph itself was formulated by painting.

The Ontario and Québec landscapes of Daniel Fowler (1810–1894), Otto Jacobie (1812–1901), and Allan Edson (1846–1888), among others in the 1870s, reflected a close attention to detail in a careful investigation of nature that is both familiar and knowable. Their images have an increased sense of tactility, which gives the landscape a greater intimacy and suggests that nature indeed has an inner life. Landscape painting at mid-century reflects a new sense of the immediacy of nature, which is made emphatic by the use of bright, dappled light and colour. These works showed a marked resemblance to aspects of the American Hudson River School painting in the fascination with the discovery of the vibrant world of the rural environment. Rather than portraying vast areas of nature as the early topographers did, the artists tended to concentrate on intimate views of a selected aspect of the landscape, such as a hidden glade or a small stand of trees. Unlike earlier paintings, the main focus of interest and the largest forms were placed towards the foreground, near to the viewer and easily accessible. Close-up views now occupied almost all of the pictorial space. The sky, if portrayed at all, emphasized the contrast between the far and the near.

In the 1880s, landscape painting in Toronto and Montréal had even greater ambitions. Artists were encouraged by the recovery from the depression of the 1870s, the success of their local art societies, and the recent founding of both the Royal Canadian Academy in 1880 and the National Gallery of Canada, which opened in 1882. Artists expressed both the new expansiveness of their own community and of the country through the production of epic landscape paintings. John Arthur Fraser (1838–1898) and Lucius O'Brien (1832–1899), among others, imbued their images with a sense of heroic grandeur. They painted in eastern, central, and western Canada, and their subjects were as representative of nationalist aspirations as the country itself. The artists, like the early topographers, selected potentially spectacular subjects such as waterfalls, rock cliffs, and mountains. But they manipulated their images to stress the expressive symbolic content of such monumental sites. Now the foreground was often filled with rocks and foliage to subtly act as a barrier to the main subject, allowing the viewer to become a witness to, rather than a participant in, nature. The middle area often described a quiet lake or bay while the primary focus, the largest object in the picture, dominated the central background. This compositional device, with its careful change in scale from one part of the view to the other, reinforced the grandeur of the scene. The absolute stillness of the image similarly created the desired monumentality of the subject. While nature is never described as overwhelming, and there is always some trace of human presence, the emphasis on the drama of the subject underlines both the spiritual and the sublime meanings of the landscape.[4]

Landscape painting in Canada at this point again displays ties with American aesthetic attitudes to nature, influenced somewhat by luminist painting in the

Allan Aaron Edson, Canadian, Stanbridge, 1846–Glen Sutton, 1888. *Giant Falls*, 1872. Watercolour. 55.7 x 45 cm. Purchase, Dr. F.J. Shepherd Bequest. Photo, Marilyn Aitken. MMFA, 1963.1434.

eastern United States.[5] The works of Fraser and O'Brien describe an increased response to the sensation and poetics of light—to make the real appear even more real, to make natural objects even more intense, and to emphatically heighten the lyricism of the theme. The sweeping panorama format, the plunging pictorial space, and the eloquent tranquillity of the subject exemplify the more subjective approach to nature then occurring in both Canadian and American painting. The sense of idealism and of optimism in these large-scale pictures were important aspects of the national spirit in the art of both countries. However, Canadian painting of the period did not espouse the quasi-religious and transcendental concepts of luminism. Perhaps because of the traditional pragmatism of Canadian art it did not share the utopian vision of American painting. Because of our ties to Britain and France, Canada, unlike the United States, did not see itself as the "new Eden." Nevertheless, the landscape was a metaphor for the growth and expansion of the new unified country.

National pride in Canada was also exemplified in the 1880s by the completion of the trans-Canada railway. The patronage of artists by the Canadian Pacific Railway allowed them to discover a new landscape theme: the mountains, and the company found a new vehicle to publicize its achievement. Because of the difficulties of *plein-air* painting in the Rockies, artists produced their large, heroic landscapes in their studios in Montréal and Toronto, aided by small water colour sketches done in the West and photographs supplied by the C.P.R. and the firm of William Notman. Sometimes paintings were produced solely from photographs when the artist had either not visited the site or had been able to record only a

Lucius Richard O'Brien. Canadian, 1832–1899, *Mount Hermit Range, Selkirk, B.C., near Glacier Hotel*, c. 1887. Watercolour, graphite, scraping out on wove paper. 35.8 x 51.5 cm (sheet). Art Galley of Ontario, Toronto.

partial view of the area. Despite the loss of immediacy and freshness in the transfer from water colour and photograph to oil painting, the works still expressed the dignity and solemnity of this new frontier desired by both artist and patron. However, by the end of the nineteenth century, the epic landscape had become overly familiar, and the national aspirations of Canadian landscape painting were satisfied—at least for the time being.

While the panoramic vistas of the Canadian wilderness were indeed the most popular theme at the turn of the century, both Homer Watson (1855–1936) and Ozias Leduc (1864–1955) preferred the quiet rural settings of the respective villages where they lived. Both scrutinized the familiar with an intense respect for the innate power of nature. Watson's southern Ontario farmlands and Leduc's Mont Saint-Hilaire outside of Montréal encouraged each to look at the landscape through art, not nature. And despite their different cultural backgrounds, both viewed the familiar with a romantic, almost nostalgic attitude. While Leduc often concentrated on a close-up view of one aspect of the mountain and Watson's images were more open, both regarded ordinary natural phenomena as symbolic of an indecipherable universe. Unlike other Canadian landscapists, Watson and Leduc described nature as it existed in a single moment, enveloped in a single light, colour, and movement. Their consistency of vision gave an aura of timelessness to the transitory.

Homer Ransford Watson (1855–1936), *After the Rain*, 1883. Oil on canvas. 32 x 49 1/4 in. (81.3 x 125.1 cm.). Gift of Lord Beaverbrook. The Beaverbrook Art Gallery, Fredericton, NB, Canada.

THE TWENTIETH CENTURY

At the beginning of the twentieth century, many painters, especially in Montréal and Toronto, began to turn their attention back to Europe for their first taste of modern ideas. Numerous artists had attended the Parisian academies since the mid-nineteenth century, but few had any contact with the new tenets of modernism.[6] Both the conservative French Barbizon and the Dutch Hague schools of atmospheric landscape painting of the mid-nineteenth century did effect some change in early twentieth century Canadian art. Artists here responded to the emphasis on naturalism and the non-heroic subject. Specimens of such European styles were avidly collected in Montreal and Toronto, but Canadian examples fared less well. Painters such as Horatio Walker (1858–1938), William Brymner (1855–1925), and Elizabeth McGillivray Knowles (1866–1926) were strongly affected by the Barbizon concern for *plein-air* effects of early-morning and late-afternoon light to impart a particularly nostalgic mood to the rural Canadian landscape. The founding of the Canadian Art Club (1907–1915) in Toronto encouraged subjective painting that would also enliven entrenched academic traditions. This exhibiting society was intended to show the work of modern artists. Many had abandoned Canada because of its upholding of conservative art, while those who had stayed had received little support for their

William Brymner, *October, Rivièvre Beaudet*, 1914. Oil on canvas. 96.8 x 125.7 cm. Musée du Québec. Accession no. 41.220. Photo, Patrick Altman.

interest in new aesthetic approaches. Clarence Gagnon (1881–1942), W.H. Clapp (1879–1954), and Berthe Des Clayes (1887–1968), for example, showed some acquaintance with impressionism which, while considered an avant-garde style in Canada, was finished in France by 1880.[7] Although impressionist attitudes were not truly understood and accepted in Canada, Canadian landscape painting became both more generalized and intimate, with limited tonal palette and poetic atmosphere, because of impressionism's influence. The impressionist notion of overall unity of light and tone had some effect on Canadian art and provided the landscape with a more modern appearance. Another important development in this country as a result of impressionism was the inclusion of buildings and people in landscape images as active participants, not as spectators or anecdotal details. The landscape for many artists was not an exclusive subject matter but one that could reflect the familiar fabric of Canadian life.

The work of Maurice Cullen (1866–1934) displays the greatest familiarity with impressionism, especially its sense of intimacy. Cullen's tempered, inhabited winter landscapes with their broken brush stroke, luminous atmosphere, and spontaneous, direct treatment of form express many of the formal concerns of French painting and its belief in the facts of experience and the sensations this belief can evoke. But Cullen, like other Canadian, British, and American impressionists, could not accept the Parisian notion of total passivity before nature.

Maurice Cullen, Canadian, 1866–1934, *Lévis from Québec*, 1906. Oil on canvas. 76.7 x 102.2 cm. Art Gallery of Ontario, Toronto. Gift from the Albert H. Robson Memorial Subscription Fund, 1946.

Canadian impressionists generally refused to deny the integrity of the subject, which would entail a rejection of the established values of their conservative culture. While Canadian artists began to take a more relaxed attitude to the landscape, and describe it as a source of ordinary pleasure rather than as symbolic metaphor, there was a hesitancy here to abandon the entrenched notions of naturalism for a purely perceptual art. The idea that art could be the primary content of painting was perhaps too threatening in a community where painting was still trying to find a secure position. The belief in the legitimacy of "art for art's sake" would not gain wide acceptance in Canada until the 1940s.[8]

However, the inhabited landscapes of James Wilson Morrice (1865–1924) exhibit an exceptional understanding of international trends of the time. An expatriate who returned to Montréal annually until 1914, Morrice imposed a design on nature, rather than taking the more traditional approach of looking for design in nature. His soft, low-toned colour, extreme simplification, and clarity of form, as well as his equal emphasis on all the elements of the image, gave his landscape paintings immense subtlety and sensuousness. The delicacy of Morrice's treatment of nature gained him great admiration in Europe (rare for a Canadian) and made him the most progressive Canadian artist of his generation.

James Wilson Morrice, Canadian, Montréal, 1865–Tunis, 1924. *Ice Bridge Over the St. Charles River*, 1908. Oil on canvas. 60 x 80.6 cm. Gift of the artist's estate. Photo, Brian Merrett. MMFA, (1925.333).

THE GROUP OF SEVEN

At the end of World War I, landscape painting in Canada gained intense momentum, due largely to the efforts and successes of the Group of Seven and Tom Thomson (1877–1917), who died before the group received its official name in 1920. The artists, J.E.H. MacDonald (1873–1932), Lawren Harris (1885–1970), A.Y. Jackson (1882–1974), Fred Varley (1881–1969), Arthur Lismer (1885–1969), Frank Carmichael (1890–1945), and Frank Johnston (1888–1949) set out to establish a national school of painting. This idea had occurred to others in the 1880s but not with the same determined ideology. The Group of Seven was actually Toronto-based and their reputation was made essentially on representations of the Ontario wilderness. Thus, it was their attitude to landscape painting rather than the places they painted that made them a national movement in the 1920s. In the next decade, many of the group worked in the Arctic and the West as well as Québec and Nova Scotia, although their ideals remained unchanged. However, by then the group had lost some of their homogeneity.[9] Despite individual differences and training, the group and Thomson believed that the landscape could suggest the sense of place that was Canada (as exemplified by Ontario).

Tom Thomson 1877–1917, *Afternoon, Algonquin Park*, c .1914. Oil on canvas. 63.2 x 81.1 cm. McMichael Canadian Art Collection. In Memory of Norman and Evelyn McMichael. 1966.16.76.

A.Y. Jackson 1882–1974, *Lake Superior Country*, 1924. Oil on canvas. 117.0 x 148.0 cm. McMichael Canadian Art Collection. Gift of Mr. S. Walter Stewart, 1968.8.26.

The preceding international tendencies of Canadian landscape painting had been criticized for failing to evoke this feeling.

Canada's participation in World War I gave the country a new sense of identity and rapidly brought the nation into the twentieth century. The group accepted as a matter of fact the appearance of nature in their works, and claimed that this gave their art a national purity. Actually, their approach to painting was greatly influenced by European modern styles, especially post-impressionism as it was defined in France, England, and Scandinavia. Unlike previous Canadian landscape painters, the group strongly emphasized the insignificance of humankind in the face of nature, and rarely, if ever, referred to a human presence directly or indirectly. Wilderness scenes became the ideal of physical and psychological survival. The painters hoped to evoke emotions in the viewer that would lead to a glorification of the Canadian wilderness at a time when the opening of the national parks system encouraged Canadians to vacation regularly in their own countryside.

While the Group of Seven advocated the role of art in the service of nationalism, espousing its educational value and taking a stance against the importance of art's own intrinsic value, their portrayal of the landscape was radically different from earlier treatments in Canada. Their wind-swept trees, rocky shores, and weathered underbrush have become national icons, but such subjects were considered extremely daring at the time. The group used large, flattened, outlined forms, intense, decorative colour, and energetic brushwork to create a spontaneous atmosphere. Its graphic quality and strong design gave the work great immediacy and visual appeal. The lack of sentimentality and artifice in their painting, still prevalent in academic painting in Canada in the first quarter of the twentieth century, made the group's work appear startlingly fresh and candid. The painters' advocacy of a new kind of image and a new kind of painting reflected their strong engagement with nature. The forthrightness and directness of the group's landscapes also reflected a change in the image of the artist from the "Victorian dandy" to "the man in the canoe." Canadian art and the Canadian artist developed a new self-consciousness that greatly increased its autonomy within the country's cultural life.

The group's approach to landscape painting, particularly in Ontario and Québec, was subsequently fostered by the Canadian Group of Painters (founded in 1933 and continuing until the early 1960s), although its primary purpose was that of an exhibiting society. Both CGP members and other artists were less nationalistic in approach than the Group of Seven, and they made art itself more of a primary goal.[10] Canadian painting thus became somewhat less concerned with defining itself in terms of the country and more interested in becoming part of an international art community. However, the CGP abandoned neither the subject matter nor the painting style of the group. The notion that their work was Canadian was exemplified by the places that were painted and by the fact that the work was produced by Canadians for a Canadian audience. Interestingly, the work of the Group of Seven has never gained a reputation outside of Canada, despite its fame at home.

Two artists in particular worked away from the mainstream momentum of the group: Emily Carr (1871–1945) in Vancouver and David Milne (1882–1953) in up-state New York and rural Ontario. While Carr's work is closer to the approach of the group and she shared their belief in the power of nature, her attitudes were less dogmatic in support of nationalism. As well, her painting reflects the influence of European expressionism, which was a suitable style for her deep belief in the elemental spiritual forces of nature. Carr's dramatic compositions, dark, heavy colour and dense forms, used to express the energy of the landscape, suggest her close identification with the British Columbia forest. She became a participant in natural existence rather than an observer as had been the case with the Group of Seven.

David Milne's primary concern was that of picture making in and for itself. He transferred his feelings for nature into an aesthetic feeling for form, colour, and line. While he had a great reverence for nature as the agent of renewal, he had little interest in portraying its supernatural spiritual force as did Carr. Nor did he have any interest in the nationalist content of art. Milne's intimate landscapes were a fusion of reality and aesthetic abstraction. His reductivist approach to

Emily Carr, *Forest, British Columbia*. Oil on canvas. VAG 42.3.9. Vancouver Art Gallery, 750 Hornby Stret, Vancouver, BC V6Z 2H7.

David B. Milne, 1882–1953, Canadian, *Painting Place*, 1930. Oil on canvas. 51.3 x 66.4 cm. Vincent Massey Bequest, 1968. National Gallery of Canada, Ottawa. Reproduced under license of The David Milne Estate, 1992, copyright.

describing only essential shapes, creating spatial ambiguity, and using non-natural colour suggest that his landscapes were highly personal and non-symbolic. The inner content of these compressed landscapes was his own perceptions, and their intimacy was in marked contrast to the Group of Seven's pursuit of nature's rhetorical grandeur.

INFLUENCE OF MODERNISM

By the mid-1930s, Milne's attitude to nature as the stimulus of art where the landscape was the means and not the end had become much more prevalent in the work of many artists all across Canada. The influence of European and American modernism slowly replaced nationalist aims. The founding of the Contemporary Arts Society (1939–1949) in Montreal by John Lyman (1866–1967) particularly emphasized the individual aesthetic investigation of nature in which the only symbolic content was the artist's empathy for the subject.[11] The CAS could be regarded as a reply to the nationalism of the Group of Seven and a return to internationalist aims in both pictorial form and content.

The landscape portrayed was no longer the uninhabited wilderness but the cultivated countryside. More important, artists began to view the landscape as just
another subject matter, like figure painting, still-life, or urban images, which
were greatly increasing in popularity in the 1930s and 1940s. As national aspirations in painting lost their hegemony, so did landscape painting.

The landscape images of Montréaler Goodridge Roberts (1904–1974), for
example, reflect this modernist interpretation of nature. Like Milne, his concern
lay with his own response to what is seen; to extract from nature, not to imitate
it. The sensations of nature, the particular play of light and dark, clear colour,
and simplified form were the means of giving the landscape its sense of place.
The process of painting became the method to impose a visual structure on the
landscape and, at the same time, to describe the role that art could play in sharp-
ening our awareness of the appearance of reality.

For many artists in Canada during the 1930s and 1940s, the landscape gained
greater importance as the setting for images of the figure and of the portrait.
André Biéler (1896–1989), Edwin Holgate (1892–1977), and Prudence Heward
(1896–1947), among many others, frequently transposed the figure from the
anonymous interior to a natural setting. Rather than looking like a stage prop, as

William Goodridge Roberts (1904–1974), *Green Day in the Laurentians*, 1945.
Watercolour on paper. 55 x 71 cm. Galerie d'Art Concordia/Concordia Art
Gallery, Montréal. Gift of Dr. and Mrs. Max Stern. 963.12. (c) William Goodridge
Roberts 1991/VIS*ART Copyright Inc.

nature often appeared in early portraits, the mood and attitude suggested by the human figure was reflected in the landscape. This implied that both the human and natural world could co-exist in a mutually interactive environment.

ABSTRACT ART

Beginning in the late 1940s, the next thirty years of Canadian art were dominated by abstract painting. The movement away from a naturalist interpretation of the landscape towards non-representational images had, however, emerged slowly in the late 1930s. Abstract work by Lawren Harris of the Group of Seven, Bertram Brooker (1888–1955), and Jock MacDonald (1897–1960), for example, was strongly influenced by natural imagery. However, a more important concern was the search for the mystical and spiritual content of the landscape. The symbolic meaning of the cosmos, not Canada, determined both the imagery and the aesthetic vocabulary of their painting.[12]

Starting in the early 1950s, such international styles as surrealism, constructivism, and then abstract expressionism influenced both the ideas and appearance of Canadian painting. As had occurred frequently in the history of Canadian art, painters banded together to encourage and promote new aesthetic viewpoints. Painters Eleven in Toronto, the Automatistes and Plasticiens in Montréal, and the Regina Five slowly created an audience for non-objective painting in Canada, and in their own regions influenced the acceptance (albeit late) of abstract painting as a legitimate tendency in Canadian art. The move away from representational art to various types of non-objective painting describes the painters' concentration on the formal values and emotional content of art without obvious reference to recognizable, realistic imagery. Thus the landscape *per se* was abandoned. Rather than describing the landscapes of external reality, abstract painting could be said to embody the landscape of the mind, of inner reality.

It is possible to view the paintings of many non-objective artists in terms of the concerns of landscape pictures. For example, the sense of scale, the play of light and shadow, as well as the expansive movement found in non-representational painting related, in abstracted form, to many of the concerns found in landscape painting. Indeed, artists such as Paul-Émile Borduas (1905–1960), Jack Shadbolt (b. 1909), and Gershon Iskowitz (1921–1988) were directly affected by the open, limitless space of the rural countryside. But since most non-figurative artists were not interested in producing abstract landscape as such, it is perhaps unfair and untruthful to the intentions of the painters to attempt to overemphasize covert references to the landscape in their work. However, if nature was the spark for defining and presenting the sensations of the emotions and the inner mind, this occurred because nature was traditionally regarded as exemplary of universal truths. Certainly, countless abstract artists made direct references to the landscape in the titles of their paintings. While in some cases the landscape may have provided the initial stimulus for the idea of the image, just as frequently the title was chosen because the final image of the painting evoked the emotional sensations aroused by the contemplation and experience of nature.

However, this is not to say that landscape painting was abandoned wholesale from the late 1940s to the late 1970s. Artists previously engaged with landscape painting continued to develop their work. However, the landscape by now had changed from being a theme to becoming a motif for the investigation of particular aesthetic problems. Younger artists such as John Fox (b. 1927), Dorothy Knowles (b. 1927), and Ivan Eyre (b. 1935) used the formal vocabulary of art to explore through divergent means the possibilities of paint itself to redefine different approaches to painting nature. In western Canada particularly, and perhaps prompted by its changing topography, landscape painting found a new energy as described in the lyrical, abstracted work of Takao Tanabe (b. 1926), Gordon Smith (b. 1919), and Otto Rogers (b. 1935), among many others. In central and eastern Canada, a realist approach to the representational landscape could be found in the work of Jack Chambers (1931–1978), Alex Colville (b. 1920), Mary Pratt (b. 1935), and Christopher Pratt (b. 1935). Their immediate heightened references to the natural world describe a dramatic reply to the ideology of non-objectivism.[13]

Dorothy Knowles, *Summer Days*, 1969. Acrylic on canvas. 142.2 x 184.8 cm. Accession no. 72.1. Collection of the Edmonton Art Gallery. Purchased with funds donated by the Women's Society. Photo, Eleanor Lazare.

Alex Colville, *Boy, Dog and St. John River*, 1958. Synthetic resin and oil on masonite, 60.9 x 81.3 cm. London Regional Art and Historical Museums. Photo, Larry Ostrom. Art Gallery of Ontario.

CONTEMPORARY DEVELOPMENTS

By the 1980s, Canadian artists were actively participating in the international return to figurative painting—a term that includes the landscape as well as the human figure. The landscape image now became again a viable focus for Canadian painting. Essentially, the new nature pictures are imaginary landscapes, where the facts of nature are combined with the freedom of abstraction. Unlike earlier, more traditional landscape imagery, recent paintings of nature rarely refer to a specific time or place. Perhaps because of the dominance of urban culture and our unfortunate divorce from nature, these artists seek to re-experience the landscape to better understand our own place in the modern world. Rather than being a description of Canada, the work is more concerned with our membership in the global community. At the same time, many of these artists have rediscovered the traditions and the earlier impulses of Canadian landscape painting. While not interested in repeating what has gone before, there is a keen awareness of their own art history.

Contemporary trends in landscape painting generally tend to investigate the relationship between nature and culture more than portraying the traditional view of nature as the Other. Influenced by such diverse sources as film, photography, and television, as well as the timeless values of landscape painting itself, recent images of nature do not necessarily describe a first-hand experience of the rural environment. That is not to say that artists deny the importance of such an experience and many do make studies from nature in *plein-air* as did the earliest landscape painters in Canada. Rather, this current attitude suggests that landscape painting, like other forms of the visual arts, is open to the innumerable and sometimes contradictory impulses that have defined the face of late twentieth-century life.

While contemporary landscape imagery may display the sense of nostalgia that is inherent in all landscape painting, it is not necessarily nostalgic for an image reminiscent of ideal places and ideal times. Recent images of nature have a concreteness and materiality that seem to stress the psychological presence of nature within a culture that continues to disclaim its authority. Perhaps because of the dramatic increase in the number of artists now working in Canada and the intensely individual approach each takes to the subject, landscape painting now

Paterson Ewen, *The Great Wave: Homage to Hokusai*, 1974. Acrylic paint on gouged plywood. 90 x 96 inches. Art Gallery of Windsor. Photo, Saltmarche, Toronto.

has a greater variety and openness of definition than had ever occurred previously in Canadian art. Nature is seen as multi-dimensional and functions as the source for a myriad of images and a complexity of emotions and ideas.

Among the numerous painters working within a contemporary landscape convention, Paterson Ewen (b. 1925) exemplifies many of the new attitudes to nature. Approaching the landscape through his interest in meteorological phenomena, his work implies an atavistic response to nature. His vocabulary of emphatic colour, rough surfaces, intentionally awkward drawing, and flat, eccentric compositions creates a charged world of energy, noise, and light. By turning nature inside out, the objective natural forces that shape our landscape have become the vehicle for aesthetic emotional expression.

CONCLUSION

The tradition of landscape painting in Canada has taken many routes over the last 200 years, a path filled with both success and failure. For generations, it described geographical and cultural similarities as well as differences within this country. At the same time that it expressed the aims and ambitions of Canada, it also reflected the artists' individual search to better understand and interpret the world they inhabited. The future of Canadian landscape painting cannot be predicted, any more than one can predict the future of the nation. However, the potential of art, regardless of its subject matter, lies in its value as a source of stimulation and reflection. In whatever direction our artists may take landscape painting, it will continue to serve as a metaphor for our attitude towards this country and, most important, as a metaphor for how we see ourselves.

Notes

[1] For an introduction to methodologies in art history, see W.E. Kleinbauer, *Modern Perspectives in Western Art History* (New York: Holt, Rinehart and Winston) and J.M. Thompson, *Twentieth Century Theories of Art* (Toronto: Oxford University Press, 1990).

[2] The most complete information on Canadian landscape painters of all periods is generally to be found in exhibition catalogues published by Canadian art galleries and museums. Such texts may refer to a single artist or a group; a historical period or movement; or take a thematic approach. Information on each artist mentioned in this chapter can be found in monographic studies such as books, exhibition catalogues, and periodical articles.

[3] For a study of early landscape painters, see M. Allodi, *Canadian Watercolours and Drawings in the Royal Ontario Museum* (Toronto: Royal Ontario Museum, 1974) and her *Printmaking in Canada: The Earliest Views and Portraits* (Toronto: Royal Ontario Museum, 1980).

[4] Many of these concerns are discussed in D. Reid, "Our Own Country Canada," *Being an Account of the National Aspirations of the Principal Landscape Artists in Montreal and Toronto 1860–1890* (Ottawa: National Gallery of Canada, 1979).

[5] For a discussion of American painting styles, see B. Novak, *American Painting of the Nineteenth Century* (New York: Praeger, 1969).

[6] For the European context, see G.H. Hamilton, *Painting and Sculpture in Europe 1880–1940* (Baltimore: Penguin Books, 1972).

[7] Among the many discussions of impressionism, see J. Rewald, *The History of Impressionism* (New York: Museum of Modern Art, 1973).

[8] The influence of modernism in Canadian painting is discussed in T. Fenton and K. Wilkin, *Modern Painting in Canada* (Edmonton: Hurtig Publishers, 1978).

[9] For a history of the Group of Seven, see D. Reid, *Le Groupe des Sept/The Group of Seven* (Ottawa: National Gallery of Canada, 1970).

[10] For this period, see C. Hill, *Canadian Painting in the Thirties* (Ottawa: National Gallery of Canada, 1975).

[11] For a history of the CAS see C. Varley, *Contemporary Arts Society/La Société d'art contemporain. Montréal 1939–1948.* (Edmonton: The Edmonton Art Gallery, 1980).

[12] See A. Davis, *The Logic of Ecstasy: Canadian Mystical Painting 1920–1940* (London, ON.: London Regional Art Gallery, 1991).

[13] For a survey of Canadian art since 1950, see D. Burnett and M. Schiff, *Contemporary Canadian Art* (Edmonton: Hurtig Publishers, 1983).

Bibliography

Ainslie, P. *Images of the Land: Canadian Block Prints.* Calgary: Glenbow Museum, 1984.

Allodi, M. *Canadian Watercolours and Drawings in the Royal Ontario Museum.* Toronto: Royal Ontario Musuem, 1974.

Allodi, M. *Printmaking in Canada: The Earliest Views and Portraits.* Toronto: Royal Ontario Museum, 1980.

Bell, M. *Painters in a New Land: From Newfoundland to the Klondike.* Toronto: McClelland & Stewart, 1973.

Bringhurst, R., et al. *Visions: Contemporary Art in Canada.* Vancouver: Douglas and McIntyre, 1983.

Burnett, D., and M. Schiff. *Contemporary Canadian Art.* Edmonton: Hurtig Publishers, 1983.

Davis, A. *The Logic of Ecstasy: Canadian Mystical Painting 1920-1940.* London, ON.: London Regional Art Gallery, 1991.

Duval, P. *High Realism in Canada.* Toronto: Clarke, Irwin, 1974.

Fenton, T., and K. Wilkin. *Modern Painting in Canada.* Edmonton: Hurtig Publishers, 1978.

Glenbow Museum. *With Lens and Brush: Images of the Western Canadian Landscape 1845–1890.* Calgary: Glenbow Museum, 1989.

Hale, B. *Toronto Painting 1953–1965.* Ottawa: National Gallery of Canada, 1972.

Harper, J. R. *Painting in Canada: A History.* Toronto: University of Toronto Press, 1977.

Hill, C. *Canadian Painting in the Thirties.* Ottawa: National Gallery of Canada, 1975.

Lord, B. *The History of Painting in Canada: Toward a People's Art.* Toronto: NC Press, 1974.

McTavish, D. *Canadian Artists in Venice 1830–1930.* Kingston: Agnes Etherington Art Centre of Queen's University, 1984.

Musée du Québec. *L'Art du paysage au Québec (1800–1940)/Landscape Painting in Québec (1800–1940).* Québec: Musée du Québec, 1975.

Reid, D. *A Concise History of Canadian Painting.* Toronto: Oxford University Press, 1988.

Reid, D. *Le Groupe des Sept/The Group of Seven.* Ottawa: National Gallery of Canada, 1970.

Reid, D. "Our Own Country Canada." *Being an Account of the National Aspirations of the Principal Landscape Artists in Montréal and Toronto 1860–1890.* Ottawa: National Gallery of Canada, 1979.

Sparling, M. *Great Expectations: The European Vision in Nova Scotia 1749–1848.* Halifax: Mount St. Vincent University Art Gallery, 1980.

Tippett, M., and D. Cole. *From Desolation to Splendour: Changing Perceptions of the British Columbia Landscape.* Toronto: Clarke, Irwin, 1979.

Varley, C. *The Contemporary Arts Society/La Société d'art contemporain. Montréal 1939–1948.* Edmonton: Edmonton Art Gallery, 1980.

Wilkin, K. *The Collective Unconscious: American and Canadian Art 1940–1950.* Edmonton: Edmonton Art Gallery, 1980.

Canadian periodicals with articles relevant to Canadian landscape painting:

Artmagazine
Artscanada
C Magazine
Canadian Art
Journal of Canadian Art History/Annales d'histoire de l'art canadien
Journal of Canadian Studies
Racar
Vanguard
Vie des arts

Epilogue

Kenneth McNaught

The theme of crisis recurs throughout this wide-ranging volume. This is not surprising. From the 1760s to the present day, Canada has been an experiment every bit as much (although very different) as has that often-proclaimed first new nation, the United States. While never afflicted with a civil war such as that which sundered and refashioned the United States, successive Canadian generations have seldom been spared warnings of a crisis, real or apprehended.

In 1838 Lord Durham depicted "two nations warring within the bosom of a single state," and prescribed assimilation of the French Canadians as a solution. In 1965 an interim report of the Royal Commission on Bilingualism and Biculturalism blew the whistle loud and clear: "Canada, without being fully conscious of the fact, is passing through the greatest crisis in its history," and prescribed greater recognition of the French fact, including equality of French and English as the languages of the "two founding races." In 1991 a prominent social scientist from Laval University told Québec's National Assembly that Québec would achieve the constitutional jurisdictions he deemed necessary only when it held a knife to the throat of English Canada. The National Assembly went on to provide for a referendum on Québec sovereignty in 1992 in the event that no acceptable restructuring of the constitution was offered by the rest of the country. At the time of writing that knife remains poised.

What are we to make of this apparently unending sequence of crises? The essays in this book, without being written to any comprehensive prescription, present Canada as an adventure, and there can be no real adventure without crisis. At the same time, the book's cumulative portrayal of the adventure is quintessentially Canadian, certainly in tone. A quiet confidence pervades all of the essays. While questions are raised about many aspects of policy, condition, and achievement, there is no flag waving. Even when the essayists touch upon critical issues, the mythology of the Peaceable Kingdom intervenes to soften perceptions of conflict. Somehow an acceptance of continuity and of legitimacy underpins the whole. Perhaps survival and *survivance* are more potent concepts—and less contradictory—than might seem likely in this crisis-prone country.

The several authors make frequent reference to the impact of the American republic on nearly every aspect of Canadian life. Yet their analyses of economic affairs, culture and communications, politics, and even geography lead the reader to an almost surprised recognition that the differences are even more significant than the obvious similarities. Of course, each reader will read between the lines. My own reading leads me to endorse much and also to rethink some earlier conclusions.

Despite the geographically determined intra-American comparisons, Canada's history is relatively free-standing. Many scholars, however, argue that Canadians define themselves (if at all) simply as not American. This negative, even timid, perception, it is said, shows up especially in reluctance to acclaim the achievements of individual Canadians until New York, London, or Paris has rendered judgment. Again, it is argued that Canadian respect for authority reflects a lingering colonial mentality. Some of the essays in this volume reflect such views; overall, however, they either reject the view or raise serious doubts about their worth. References to the adverse effects of Canada's imperial–colonial past, and implicit assumptions about its present position as senior province in the American economic empire, pose questions for which (by my reading) answers may be found scattered throughout the volume.

It is surely remarkable that Canada—whether French, British, or independent—has always been a monarchy. The Canadian Crown and its gradual evolution symbolize the concept of the common good in a manner difficult for an elected head of a republic. It represents, too, a high regard for continuity. Foreign observers seldom miss the conservative features of Canadian society and politics. Some, especially Americans, have seen Canada as overly deferential to authority, lacking in individual initiative, too ready to rely upon governments for everything from personal security and economic development to cultural enterprise. Such condescending assessments, I think, rest upon the assumption that change, even violent change, is usually beneficial. Moreover, such views almost always equate individualism with values established by the marketplace: competitive as opposed to collectivist. The essayists in this volume, by and large, refrain from sharply etched conclusions. They do, however, provoke such basic questions. Fortunately, an epilogist may ignore the illusory constraints of objectivity.

I have suggested that Canadians attach importance to continuity. One might well go further. Canadian symbols—and there are more of them than is commonly believed—consecrate the notion that the legitimacy of institutions and political methods, acceptability of literary work and of what used to be called "manners and morals," spring from unbroken roots. Québec's official motto *"Je me souviens,"* the RCMP, and constitutional monarchy all suggest this unmistakably. None of this should be surprising. Canada was not the child of revolution. The country evolved gradually from a European background and, unlike the United States, never defined itself as not-Europe. In this respect, Canada's long colonial–imperial existence was as much a liberating as a restricting one. Constitutional, cultural, and economic links meant that well into the twentieth century British and French ideas about society, arts and letters, and politics were regarded as part and parcel of Canadian life, rather than as imports. Indeed, Mark Twain and Henry James were more "foreign" than, say, Charles Dickens, Anthony Trollope, or even Victor Hugo. Moreover, Canada's best-selling authors, from T.C. Haliburton to Ralph Connor, were perfectly at ease with the allegedly restrictive colonial setting. Widely-read Canadian authors such as William Kirby, Gilbert Parker, Agnes Laut, Stephen Leacock, Sara J. Duncan, and L.M. Montgomery show little sense of repression. The notion that Canadian literature reveals a garrison mentality and depicts its subjects as victims does not withstand close inspection. Nearer to the mark is the impression of a distinct confidence. As Carl Berger has shown in *The Sense of Power*, that confidence was often expressed as pride in the growing importance of Canada as senior auxiliary kingdom in the powerful British Empire.[1] Imperialism, like heartland–hinterland relationships within Canada, was always a two-way street. It kept doors open to a larger world; both its benefits and costs were reciprocal. The Imperial legacy is a Canada with a marked European ambience, a country still reluctant to lock itself into a fortress North America where foreign ideas and customs can so readily be labelled un-American.

The essential conservatism of Canadians—both Anglophone and Francophone—is revealed in a number of the book's essays. From socio-economic policy and the parliamentary system to foreign policy, the theme of continuity stands out in startling clarity. Even in the country's present constitutional floundering it is apparent that Canadians are considering how best to ensure preservation of historic values and purposes. For federalists the goal is to maintain by cautious adjustment the Canadian experiment; for *nationalistes* it is to fulfil ancient aspirations of *notre maître le passé*. One is not surprised to hear Jacques Parizeau, chief Péquiste proponent of Québec sovereignty, explain that in his independent state there would be little need of substantial legal change because "we like English laws." What *would* be surprising would be for English Canada to accept the proposals being bandied about, at the time of writing, for an American-style constituent assembly to rewrite the constitution. Although populism has made brief appearances on the Canadian stage, each emanation has been short-lived. Invariably Canadians seem to return to a kind of Burkean view of representative democracy: elected politicians are charged with the accountable responsibility for formulating and implementing constitutional adjustments as well as for ongoing policy.

One way of approaching contemporary Canadian tremors is to recall a remark made by Sir John A. Macdonald during the 1864 Québec Conference, which produced the resolutions embodied in the British North America Act: "Thus we shall have a strong central government under which we can work out constitutional liberty as opposed to democracy, and be able to protect the minority." As with many of Macdonald's succinct assessments, this one carries some heavy implications. Two such are very relevant today: his view of democracy and the importance of minority rights.

Macdonald was no stranger to the rough-and-tumble of democratic politics, but he was also a close observer of the American Civil War. In 1864 that war was about to enforce the will of the majority and to sharply restrict the power of the states. Macdonald understood well that American concepts of populist, majoritarian democracy were antithetical to British-Canadian ideas of constitutional government, as well as to Canadian views on the essential importance of the provinces. Anticipating what later observers would identify as a deep difference between Canadian and American attitudes, he employed the word "individuality" to describe the distinctiveness and rights of the provinces. The rights of individuals he assumed to be protected by the continuance in Canada of centuries-old constitutional liberty, and extendible by precedent. Thus, Macdonald laid the greatest stress not upon individualism but upon *collectivités*—provinces and the minorities within them, whose rights should be specifically prescribed.

In a very real way Macdonald anticipated the future. The Canadian Charter of Rights and Freedoms does spell out individual rights, nearly all of which existed by precedent already. It pays more attention to group rights, especially to those of minority groups. The present debate about the relative precedence of the Québec and Canadian charters has not to do with individualism and protection against governmental infringements but, rather, with the rights of minority language groups.

The notion of individualism deserves further comment. It is often remarked that, while the proclaimed purpose of American government is to ensure the individual's right to pursue life, liberty, and happiness, that of Canadian government is to provide peace, order, and good government. The apparent contrast is ambiguous; the ambiguity is best cleared up by noting that in the constitutional language of the 1860s, the phrase "peace, welfare, and good government" was synonymous with the phrase actually chosen. While it is clear that a fundamental aspect of Canadian socio-political attitudes is the belief that there can be no real liberty without order (Montréal, 1970 and 1990, provides only the most recent evidence), it is also evident that Canadians view positive government in a much more friendly light than do Americans. Several of the essays herein make the point that Canadians have no inborn suspicion of government. That this is so is revealed not only in the readiness with which they have accepted quick use of state force to suppress resort to violence in pursuit of socio-political change—the other side of the coin is of at least equal importance.

For many reasons Canadians are more collectivist, more European, than are their American cousins. One reason for this is found in the long interaction between Canada's geographic and population patterns. Vast distances separated relatively sparse settlements. From the day of substantial British governmental assistance to United Empire Loyalist emigrés (not to mention the paternalism of New France's Jean Talon), to the extraordinary leap across the thousand miles of rocky shield north of Huron–Superior, and thence across the prairies and mountains to the Pacific, Canadians have looked to their governments to plan and underwrite the costs of community well-being and economic development. And, as industrial capitalism burgeoned in towns, forests, and mines, it became clear that the British connection carried with it much more than economic–military implications.

A steady stream of British immigrants brought with them strong notions about the positive state. The sparkling course of political thought running from Bentham through Shaftesbury, Disraeli, T.H. Greene, L.T. Hobhouse, the Fabians, and the Labour party joined with that of militant industrial unionism to counterbalance the influence of the aristocrats of imperial federation. Because democratic socialism came to Canada in the cultural baggage of British immigrants, it could not be labelled alien, although attempts were made to do just that. The same ideas went to the United States and, along with the heavy influence of German socialists there, could be, and were, pilloried as un-American. The result was clear by the 1930s: the Socialist party of the United States died just as Canadian socialist-labour-farmer parties amalgamated in the Co-operative Commonwealth Federation (to become, in 1961, the New Democratic Party).

In the twentieth century, Canada's European tilt was enhanced by regular interaction among democratic socialist parties of western Europe and the Commonwealth. Since 1945, especially, this political ambience has been further nourished by the several million new Canadians who recognize an approach to government and society with which they are comfortably familiar. Various facets of that approach are touched upon in this book's essays: maturation of the welfare state, the mixed economy's array of public enterprises in services, cultural activities, natural resource development, and even manufacturing. Together, these Canadian socio-political characteristics express a conviction that people may act collectively rather than recoiling from government as a threat to what the late Brough Macpherson called "possessive individualism."[2]

In the present crisis it is worth remembering that many basic Canadian attitudes to society and government—especially in the fields of culture and the relationships among order, liberty, democracy, and social justice—are shared by Francophone and Anglophone alike. If British thinking about free-market capitalism underlies Anglophone collectivism (both NDP and Liberal), it is equally true that French-Catholic liberal thought, especially of the 1920s and 1930s, informed the evolution of Québec attitudes towards government and society. Beyond question, this European intellectual connection underlay Québec's secularizing Quiet

Revolution and René Lévesque's democratic socialism. Québec Liberal and Péquiste leaders now call into question the social justice implications of *maîtres chez nous*. Like the Mulroney Conservatives in Ottawa, they lean towards an "un-Canadian" (one has to invent the term) reliance upon free-market forces. Thus, there are contrapuntal elements in the contemporary constitutional confrontation, forces that have little, if nothing, to do with the constitution. These elements, in political terms, are right and left; they are clearly evident in Québec as they are across the rest of Canada.

Inside Québec, the rhetoric of independence has been appropriated by the beneficiaries of the Lesage-Lévesque years. Today, Québec's schools of business process more graduates than do those of all the other provinces combined. Their graduates, greatly assisted by legislation requiring francization of economic life, now manage most of Québec's commercial, financial, and industrial activity and, not least important, all governmental administration. But in the very process of completing one aspect of the Quiet Revolution they appear willing, even anxious, to jettison Lévesque's egalitarian social justice concerns. The business-oriented supporters of Jacques Parizeau, like those of Robert Bourassa—the Belangers, Campeaus, and Allaires—wish to roll back rather than extend the social activism of government. Privatization and fiscal cutbacks, hostility to labour unions and to the aims of aboriginals, and restructuring of the economy in harmony with American corporate principles amount to a profound transformation of the sovereigntist movement. By mid-1991, opinion polls showed a weakening of support for the sovereignty option. The original Lévesque alliance was perhaps coming to suspect that the drive for a unilingual, egalitarian, and independent Québec had been commandeered by a new business class that sees francization primarily as guarantor of its management rights in a society ever more closely integrated in a North American economic bloc. In the 1988 federal election, Québec voters determined the outcome by supporting the proposed Canada–US Free Trade Agreement. In 1991, opposition to extension of that agreement to include Mexico appears to be rooted in the same body of opinion that had swept Lévesque to power in 1976.

Beyond Québec, as Canadians reeled before an array of constitutional commissions, hearings, and proposals for populist constituent conventions, there has appeared a similar, unmistakable apprehension. Nearly unanimous dismay at an absence of leadership suggested that Anglophones also suspected hidden agendas behind vague talk of preserving unity by whittling down Ottawa's powers—by turning Canada into a mere community of communities. As in Québec, but even more intensely in the rest of the country, the social and economic ramifications of a continental economic bloc seemed to be foreshadowed by massive cutbacks in federal transfer payments in support of provincial services; in unemployment insurance; in the CBC and other areas of culture and communications; together with tentative forays against the principle of universality in the social-security structure. Such policy thrusts, combined with deep cuts in passenger rail service and extensive privatization of Crown corporations, suggested to many Anglophone Canadians that Prime Minister Mulroney's government had opted for a kind of Reagan–Bush–Thatcher neo-conservatism. A policy of allowing the market alone to establish socio-economic decisions could, in the eyes of many, mean that the restructuring of Canada would take place (perhaps *was* taking place) largely at the behest of US-based trans-national corporations. That such business organizations prefer to deal with governments whose powers are limited seems consonant with a constitutional reformation that would leave Ottawa greatly weakened and the provinces somewhat strengthened.

It is not far-fetched to suggest that in 1991 much of the public confusion about why the Meech Lake Accord was rejected and why an alternative approach is elusive stems from a failure of leaders to endorse both the collectivism and sense of national purpose that lie at the heart of Canadian society—a good deal of which is shared by Francophones and Anglophones. A recent immigrant writing to a Toronto newspaper got closer to defining the Canadian identity than do some of today's high-wire political balancers. Canadians, he wrote, should not be upset when they define themselves negatively: "I came to Canada *because* of what it was not." Not surprisingly, the most original proposal for ameliorating the constitutional squabbles was drawn from a European precedent. The government of Ontario, underlying the need to stress what Canadians have in common, proposes a social charter to be added to the Charter of Rights and Freedoms. Modelled on that of the European Community, such a charter would specify a wide range of social-security and employment rights. Premier Rae's proposal would, as it were, define Canada positively as not America.

Few people inside or outside Québec ever read the fine print of Meech; all, however, knew well that the accord would guarantee Québec as a "distinct society" whose special status would be enhanced by several of the accord's provisions. Anglophone nervousness sprang from two sources. First, Meech Lake was presented by Robert Bourassa inside Québec as adding substantial powers to that province; indeed, it would convey to Québec an unrestricted "right of self-determination." Outside Québec, however, the accord was portrayed as simply recognizing and buttressing Québec's existing special position within the federal state. Lack of clear agreement about the accord's actual purpose brought into play an underlying Canadian antipathy to declarations as such.

Anglophone rejection of Meech grew not from the manner of the accord's inception—private inter-governmental negotiation is, after all, consonant with all of Canadian history—but from deep-rooted suspicion of declarations that define little while implying much. In short, Canada is a non-declaratory society. The country's independence has never been declared; it was achieved incrementally by the simple and often contradictory process of exercising authority in one area after another. This functional approach to socio-political requirements led from achieving fiscal independence in 1859—when A.T. Galt simply imposed a tariff on imports (including those from Britain) and thus took over an imperial jurisdiction—to a separate Canadian declaration of war in 1939. That 1939 precedent was but one in a long series of functional steps. Canada's membership in the

League of Nations in 1919, separate from that of Britain, and acquisition of an independent treaty-making right by simply not asking for a British countersignature to a 1923 fisheries treaty with the United States, were other such steps. Even the 1931 Statute of Westminster, often identified as declaring the independence of all the British dominion, in fact merely recognized what had already occurred. Again, the last, undeniable step—of patriating the constitution in 1982—was taken not by declaration but by two acts of the British Parliament: the Constitution Act, which was a series of amendments (including the Charter of Rights) to the British North America Act, and the Canada Act, by which the Westminster Parliament announced that no future British legislation "shall extend to Canada as part of its law."

That Canada's constitution is, in fact, an amended nineteenth-century imperial law illustrates not only an ingrained appreciation of continuity: the central processes of government themselves remain unwritten, part of the custom of the constitution. Nowhere does the Constitution Act describe the office of the prime minister, nor does it say anything about a Cabinet, let alone whether ministers should also be members of Parliament. Aversion to declarations, it seems, extends to written constitutions.

A near absence of theory, aversion to abstractions, as well as a sort of comfortable acceptance of contradictions and even illogicality in political–constitutional affairs are perhaps counterpart to features evident in Canadian writing and painting. Critical analyses of Canadian culture stress irony, humour, and put-downs of pomposity. They have also discerned a distinct preference for the concrete, for writing about *things* as a means of perceiving relationships. In painting, Canadians have shown a preference for landscape rather than portraiture. The essentially European romanticism of a Lucius O'Brien and the Scandinavian-based symbolism of the Group of Seven are infused with spiritual humanism, even political purpose; but the romance and the symbols are achieved through the specifics of rocks, trees, and rivers.

Distaste for grand and hazy declarations, like preference for pragmatic evolution by precedent, is revealed not only in suspicion of theories and written constitutions. Its counterpart is quiet political confidence, a confidence made remarkable by the proximity of an identity-seeking, hand-on-heart republican neighbour. That confidence is revealed especially in the evolution of a multi-party political format quite distinct from the rigid two-party (some have said one-party) pattern in the United States. Evolution of the Canadian party pattern stems from the country's British-European parliamentary system. Direct accountability of governments to legislative majorities sustains not only a view of democracy different from the American—it underpins a greater confidence in government. The growth of democratic socialism in Canada, which has done much to entrench the multi-party system, resulted not only from the immigration and cultural ingredients mentioned earlier. It was due also to the opportunities provided by the parliamentary system itself. The possibility that a minor party electing only two or three members can immediately influence, even topple, a government has meant the chance of life denied such parties by the separation of powers written into the American Constitution. To this unwritten constitutional opportunity is due a very un-American political phenomenon: a series of minority governments at both provincial and federal levels, akin to, yet distinguishable from, the European addiction to coalition government.

Canada's multi-partyism reflects another distinctive feature: a relative readiness to tolerate dissent—a readiness which, in turn, depends upon confidence in the country's basic institutions. The flip side, of course, is public support of the quick use of state force to suppress violence as a political weapon. Even apprehension of violent insurrection has justified governmental alacrity in calling out the police or army. For Canadians, order has always been a *sine qua non* of Macdonald's "constitutional liberty." While repressive power has sometimes been abused by government, overreaction has nearly always been succeeded by extraordinary lenience towards participants in social violence. For the present Québec–Canada crisis, the significance of this particular ingredient of the Canadian experience is all but overlooked.

While economists employ their shaky statistics and crystal balls to tally the costs of Québec secession, no one wishes to contemplate the more horrible costs of predictable social violence. Canadians cherish the myth of their Peaceable Kingdom. Like northerners and southerners during the American secession crisis of 1860–1861, neither Quebeckers nor other Canadians believe that a unilateral declaration of independence by Québec (exercising its unrestricted right to self-determination) would entail violence. This is the most precarious of assumptions. Canadian history is packed with evidence that governments will employ force to sustain constitutional liberty, to oppose unconstitutional action—and there is no constitutional right of secession from the Canadian federal union. While anything comparable to the American Civil War is inconceivable, a break-down of social order is not. Ottawa, faced with the responsibility of protecting its own property and also the rights and property of opponents of secession—both Anglophone and Francophone—during a period of protracted negotiation would face a situation beside which that of October 1970 would pale.

Beyond Canada's own historical experience, a glance around the world of today affords little consolation. The break-up of failed federal states is everywhere accompanied by an atrocious variety of violence. Moreover, the principal cause of such violence is racial nationalism. Contemplating the purposes of Québec's unilingualism, the seas of blue and white flags on St. Jean Baptiste Day, the *nationaliste* rhetoric of rejection, it is difficult to set aside either history or contemporary comparisons. The question, then, is whether Canada's long tradition of functional, piecemeal adjustments can survive an all-out assault, or whether that tradition will evaporate in the midst of uncharacteristic populist conventions and rewriting of the constitution, or even break-up of the country.

As several of the essayists in this book imply, Canada's present difficulties concern more than Québec's constitutional powers. They concern also the long-delayed resolution of aboriginal claims to land and self-government, trans-provincial recovery and control of the environment, and demands of the West for more effective influence in Ottawa. None of these problems can be properly defined, let alone satisfactorily resolved, by an emasculated federal government. Moreover, emergence of such complex questions highlights the central theme of Canadian studies: Canadian identity. Let me conclude with a brief look at three facets of that identity not touched upon above: provincialism, multiculturalism, and nationality.

It is no accident that few commentators, other than the savants of the Business Council on National Issues, dwell long upon Canadian individualism. Sir John A. Macdonald's version of individuality characterized provinces rather than people. His notion that the country would be formed by cultural, social, and economic purposes originating in the provinces was prescient. To take but one example: Canada's collectivist flagship, national health insurance, was pioneered so successfully by the Douglas government of Saskatchewan that the federal government was virtually compelled to spread it across the land. The crucial role of provincial governments—and they are much more powerful, relatively, than American state governments—is sometimes lost sight of by those who exaggerate regionalism. Thus one hears of Western alienation or the anxieties of the Maritimes. A closer look reveals sharp differences in cultural life and economic interest within each region. And those differences are focused much more by provincial governments and the evolution of their political communities than by imaginary regional boundaries. Again, just as community of regional political–economic interest is more an intellectual artifact than an observable reality, so too is the dubious idea of regional culture. Thomas Raddall and L.M. Montgomery are more accurately depicted as Nova Scotia and Prince Edward Island writers than Maritime writers. Ethel Wilson, Laura Salverson, and Sinclair Ross are profoundly British Columbia, Manitoba, and Saskatchewan writers rather than Western writers. Reduced *ad absurdum*, should we describe Morley Callaghan and Roch Carrier as writers from the St. Lawrence Lowlands region? The defining role of the provinces has been, and will remain, crucial—even as most provinces seek to retain a strong federal government to underpin their individuality—as will the common purposes that emerge from shared experience.

In many respects, multiculturalism, as official policy, is antithetical both to provincial individualities and to the shared federal experience. It seems, almost consciously, to encourage a split in the Canadian polity; to enhance perception of what Ramsay Cook has called the country's "limited identities." Seen by its authors as counterbalancing Hugh MacLennan's "two solitudes" and reinforcing John Porter's "vertical mosaic," multiculturalism is under attack by a growing number of Canadians. Emphasizing racial and cultural differences, claim the critics, multiculturalism in fact marginalizes ethnic groups, locating them by hyphenated definition outside either of the charter-group mainstreams. The critics allege that, as a flawed conception, multiculturalism is of advantage only to ethnic spokespersons who exploit the subsidies available for folk festivals and multicultural media.

Canadian nationality is rooted not only in acceptance and entrenchment of provincial and other individualities. It is the product and heir to an unbroken European lineage. That lineage has been enriched, especially since 1945, by many streams from every other continent. Perhaps the major lure for post-World War II immigrants, beyond improvement of their economic opportunities, has been that of "peace, order, and good government," the modest purposes of a conservative, democratic society. Yet, if Canada is modest, it is also confident. The historian, Frank Underhill, once defined a nation as a "body of people who have done great things together in the past and who hope to do great things together in the future."[3] In war and in peace his definition applies to Canada. Despite the current emphasis on difference, Canadians do have many things in common, many shared values and traditions, which both identify them and link them to an outside world, past and present. Malcolm Ross put his well:

> A.M. Klein was the first to "naturalize" for all of us the rich idiom of the Talmud, Torah and the Chassidic mysteries. Into the mainstream of our literature came other Jewish writers, and first- and second-generation writers of Polish, Hungarian, Icelandic, Mennonite and Japanese origin. . . . This phenomenon meant not only enrichment of the writer's palette; it also meant an incredible extension of the sense we have of our position in time. . . . We are not really a young people, even if we are rather a young nation; we are as old as the British, the Poles, the Hungarians, the Children of Israel. As John Moss tells us, "Unlike the immigrants to the United States . . . newcomers to Canada are neither absolved [n]or relieved of their participation in the world they left behind."[4]

An equally indicative cultural web has been spun within the other arts as observed by the Montréal art historian, Francois-Marc Gagnon:

> From the beginning, artists in Canada have refused to operate in a vacuum, to cut themselves off from their European roots, whether French, English, Scottish or Ukrainian. . . . The French influence, completely lacking in the United States, is too overwhelming in Canadian art not to maintain an essential distinction between the art forms of the two countries [and] this is true not only for Québec and French Canadian artists but for all Canadian artists. Moreover, federal institutions like the Canada Council, the Art Bank and the National Gallery have succeeded in creating among contemporary Canadian artists a sense of community that goes beyond the language barrier. . . . [5]

As Ross put it, Canada is not really young. It has had plenty of time for an emotional element to develop within its political nationality. The present perils faced by Canadians originate in a *nationalisme* very different from (if still an aspect of) the complex Canadian nationality. It is perhaps appropriate to close with the muted optimism of a sensitive Montréal journalist, Lysiane Gagnon, who wrote in the spring of 1991: "Québec may have her coat on, but her boots are still in the closet. And not only her boots: her wallet. And not only her wallet: family belongings, old pictures, love letters, cases and bags filled with history and emotions you can't easily leave behind."[6]

Notes

[1] C. Berger, *The Sense of Power: Studies in the Ideas of Canadian Imperialism, 1867–1914* (Toronto: University of Toronto Press, 1970).

[2] C.B. Macpherson, *The Political Theory of Possessive Individualism: Hobbes to Locke* (London: Oxford University Press, 1962).

[3] F. Underhill, *The Image of Confederation* (Toronto: Canadian Broadcasting Corporation, 1964), 2.

[4] M. Ross, *The Impossible Sum of Our Tradition: Reflections on Canadian Literature* (Toronto: McClelland & Stewart, 1986), 190–91.

[5] F.-M. Gagnon, "Art, Contemporary Trends," *The Canadian Encyclopedia*, 2nd ed. (Edmonton: Hurtig Publishers, 1988), 123.

[6] L. Gagnon, "Quebec Has Its Coat on, but Is Lingering in the Doorway," *Globe and Mail* (9 February 1991), D3.

A Guide for Student Research

William S. Jackson

CANADIAN STUDIES

GOVERNMENT PUBLICATIONS
Government of Canada Publications. Ottawa: Canadian Government Publishing Centre, Supply and Services Canada, 1953– .
Jarvi, Edith. *Access to Canadian Government Publications*.

INDEXES AND ABSTRACTS
Canadian Business Index. Toronto: Micromedia Ltd., 1980– .
Canadian Magazine Index. Toronto: Micromedia Ltd., 1986– .
Canadian News Index. Toronto: Micromedia Ltd., 1977– . Monthly with annual cumulations. Sources nine major Canadian newspapers.
Canadian Periodical Index (an author and subject index). Ottawa: Canadian Library Association. 1948– .
  (1920–1937).
  (1938–1948).

CD/ROM AND/OR ELECTRONIC INFORMATION SERVICES
Canadian Business and Current Affairs. (CBCA) (online and CD/ROM) Toronto: Micromedia Ltd., 1980– .
Can/Ole. Ottawa: Vendor.
Infoglobe. Toronto: Vendor.
Infomart. Toronto: Vendor.
Micromedia. Toronto: Producer.
Sport Discus (online and CD/ROM). Ottawa: Sport Information Resource Centre, 1949– (theses and monographs); 1975– (journal articles).

GENERAL REFERENCE WORKS
Campbell, Henry C., ed. *How To Find Out About Canada*. Oxford: Pergamon Press, 1967.
Canada Yearbook. Ottawa: Supply and Services, 1905– .
Canadian Almanac and Directory. Toronto: Copp Clark Pitman, 1847– .
Canadian Books in Print. Author and title index. Toronto: University of Toronto Press, 1967– .
Canadian Books in Print. Subject index. 1973– .
The Canadian Encyclopedia. 2nd ed. Edmonton: Hurtig Publishers, 1988.
Canadian News Facts: the Indexed Digest to Canadian Current Events. Toronto: Marpep Publishing Company, 1967– .
Canadiana. Canada's National Bibliography.

Canadiana 1867–1900: Monographs. Ottawa: National Library of Canada, 1980. Microfiche. National retrospective bibliography.

Colombo, John Robert. *Colombo's Canadian References.* Toronto: Oxford University Press, 1976.

Corpus Almanac of Canada: The Annual Handbook of Current Business and Governmental Affairs. Toronto: Corpus, 1966– .

Encyclopedia Canadiana: The Encyclopedia of Canada. Toronto: Grolier of Canada, 1977.

Land, Brian. *Directory of Associations in Canada.* Toronto: University of Toronto Press, annual.

Ryder, Dorothy E. *Canadian Reference Sources: A Selective Guide.* 2nd ed. Ottawa: Canadian Library Association, 1981.

POLITICS AND GOVERNMENT

REFERENCE WORKS

Bibliography: Canadian Political Parties, 1791–1867, 1867– . Montreal, 1967.

Canadian Annual Review of Politics and Public Affairs. Toronto: University of Toronto Press, 1960– .

Canadian Government Programmes and Services. 2nd ed. Don Mills: CCH Canadian Limited, 1971– .

Canadian Review of Studies in Nationalism: Bibliography. vol. 1 (1974)–vol. 14 (1987). Charlottetown: 1974–1987. Bibliography incorporated into the serial *Canadian Review of Studies in Nationalism* starting in 1988.

Canadian Urban History: A Selected Bibliography. Gilbert A. Stelter, comp. Sudbury: Laurentian University, 1972.

Federalism and Intergovernmental Relations in Canada and Other Countries: A Supplementary Bibliography. Kingston: Queen's University, Institute of Intergovernmental Relations, 1979.

Grasham, W.E. *Canadian Public Administration: Bibliography.* Toronto: Institute of Public Administration of Canada, 1973, with supplements in 1974, 1977, 1980, and 1985.

Gregor, Jan. *A Bibliographic Guide to Canadian Government and Politics.* Windsor, 1974.

Heggie, Grace F. *Canadian Political Parties, 1867–1968: A Historical Bibliography.* Toronto: Macmillan, 1977.

Lakos, Amos. *Comparative Provincial Politics of Canada: A Bibliography of Select Periodical Articles, 1970–1977.* Waterloo: University of Waterloo, 1978.

Lambert, Ronald Dick. *Nationalism and National Ideologies in Canada and Quebec: A Bibliography.* Revised edition. n.p. 1975.

Maddaugh, Peter D. *A Bibliography of Canadian Legal History.* Toronto: York University, 1972.

Moulary, Josiane. *Referendum Québécois: Bibliographie.* Montréal: Editions Bergeron, 1983.

Northern Politics Review: An Annual, 1983– . Calgary: University of Calgary, 1984– .

Smandych, Russell C. *Canadian Criminal Justice History: An Annotated Bibliography.* Toronto: University of Toronto Press, 1987.

BOOKS

Asch, Michael. *Home and Native Land: Aboriginal Rights and the Canadian Constitution*. Toronto: Methuen, 1984.

Banting, Keith and Richard Simeon, eds. *And No One Cheered: Federalism, Democracy and the Constitution Act*. Toronto: Methuen, 1983.

Bell, David and Lorne Tepperman. *The Roots of Disunity*. Toronto: McClelland & Stewart, 1979.

Bercuson, David, ed. *Canada and the Burden of Unity*. Toronto: Macmillan, 1977.

Bercuson, David and Philip Buckner, eds. *Eastern and Western Perspectives*. Toronto: University of Toronto Press, 1967.

Black, Edwin. *Divided Loyalties: Canadian Concepts of Federalism*. Montréal: McGill-Queen's University Press, 1975.

Brodie, M. Janine. *Crisis, Challenge and Change: Party and Class in Canada Revisited*. Ottawa: Carleton University Press, 1988.

Cook, Ramsay. *Canada, Quebec and the Uses of Nationalism*. Toronto: McClelland & Stewart, 1986.

Cook, Ramsay, ed. *French Canadian Nationalism*. Toronto: Macmillan, 1969.

Cook, Ramsay. *The Maple Leaf Forever*. Toronto: Macmillan, 1971.

Dacks, Gurston. *A Choice of Futures: Politics in the Canadian North*. Toronto: Methuen, 1981.

Dewitt, David and John Kirton. *Canada as a Principal Power*. Toronto: John Wiley, 1983.

Doran, Charles. *Forgotten Partnership: U.S.–Canada Relations Today*. Baltimore: Johns Hopkins University Press, 1983.

Forbes, Ernest. *The Maritime Rights Movement, 1919–1927: A Study in Canadian Regionalism*. Montréal: McGill-Queen's University Press, 1979.

Gibbins, Roger. *Regionalism: Territorial Politics in Canada and the United States*. Toronto: Butterworths, 1982.

Manser, Ronald. *Public Policies and Political Development in Canada*. Toronto: University of Toronto Press, 1985.

Matthews, Ralph. *The Creation of Regional Dependency*. Toronto: University of Toronto Press, 1983.

McRoberts, Kenneth and Dale Posgate. *Quebec: Social Change and Political Crisis*. Toronto: McClelland & Stewart, 1980.

Panitch, Leo, ed. *The Canadian State: Political Economy and Political Power*. Toronto: Univerity of Toronto Press, 1977.

Richards, John and Larry Pratt. *Prairie Capitalism: Power and Influence in the New West*. Toronto: McClelland & Stewart, 1979.

Shortt, Adam. *Canada and Its Provinces: A History of the Canadian People and Their Institutions, By One Hundred Associates*. Toronto: Brook and Company, 1914–1917.

Silver, A.I. *The French-Canadian Idea of Confederation, 1864–1900*. Toronto: University of Toronto Press, 1982.

Smiley, Donald. *Canada in Question: Federalism in the Eighties*. 3rd ed. Toronto: McGraw-Hill Ryerson, 1980.

Stevenson, Garth. *Unfulfilled Union: Canadian Federalism and National Unity.* Toronto: Gage, 1982.

MEDIA IN CANADA

REFERENCE WORKS

Burrows, Sandra and Franceen Gaudet. *Checklist of Indexes to Canadian Newspapers.* Ottawa: National Library of Canada, 1987.

CARD. *Canadian Advertising Rates and Data. The Media Authority.* Toronto: Maclean-Hunter, 1928– .

Gilchrist, J. Brian. *Inventory of Ontario Newspapers: 1793–1986.* Toronto: Micromedia Limited, 1987.

Sotiron, Minko. *An Annotated Bibliography of Works on Daily Newspapers in Canada: 1914–1983.* Montréal: M. Sotiron, 1987.

BOOKS

Canadian Broadcasting Corporation. *CBC—A Brief History of the Canadian Broadcasting Corporation.* Ottawa, 1976.

Nolan, Michael. *Foundations: Alan Plaunt and the Early Days of CBC Radio.* Toronto: CBC Enterprises, 1986.

Rutherford, Paul. *The Making of the Canadian Media.* Toronto: McGraw-Hill Ryerson, 1978.

Rutherford, Paul. *When Television Was Young: Primetime Canada, 1952–1967.* Toronto: University of Toronto Press, 1990.

Stewart, Sandy. *From Coast to Coast: A Personal History of Radio in Canada.* Toronto: CBC Enterprises, 1985.

Stewart, Sandy. *Here's Looking at Us: A Personal History of Television in Canada.* Toronto: CBC Enterprises, 1986.

Vipond, Mary. *The Mass Media in Canada.* Toronto: James Lorimer, 1989.

HISTORY AND LITERATURE

REFERENCE WORKS

Aitken, Barbara B. *Local Histories of Ontario Municipalities, 1927–1987: A Bibliography.* Toronto: Ontario Library Association, 1989.

Annual Bibliography of Ontario History. Toronto: Historical Society, 1980– .

Artibise, Alan Francis J. *Western Canada Since 1870: A Select Bibliography and Guide.* Vancouver: University of British Columbia, 1978.

Aubin, Paul. *Bibliographie de l'Histoire du Québec et du Canada, 1946–1965.* Québec: Institut québécois de la recherche sur la culture, 1987.

Aubin, Paul. *Bibliographie de l'Histoire du Québec et du Canada, 1966–1975.* Québec: Institut québécois de la recherche sur la culture, 1981.

Beaulieu, André. *Guide d'Histoire du Canada.* Québec: Presses de l'université Laval, 1969.

Bibliography of Canadian Bibliographies. 2nd ed. rev. and enlarged. Toronto: University of Toronto Press, 1972.

Bishop, Olga B. *Bibliography of Ontario History, 1867–1976: Cultural, Economic, Political, Social.* Toronto: University of Toronto Press, 1980.

Campbell, Catherine. *Canada's Two Heritages: The Effect of the Two Predominant Heritages on French Canadians and English Canadians As Revealed in Their Writings of Present Century, a Bibliography to the End of 1952.* London: University of Western Ontario, 1954.

Canadian Who's Who. Toronto: University of Toronto Press, 1910– .

Dictionary of Canadian Biography. 1966– . Toronto: University of Toronto Press, forthcoming.

Fleming, Patricia. *Upper Canadian Imprints, 1801–1841.* Toronto: University of Toronto Press, 1988.

Granatstein, J.L. and Paul Stevens. *Canada Since 1867: A Bibliographic Guide.* 2nd ed. Toronto: Hakkert, 1977.

Hann, Russell G. *Primary Sources in Canadian Working Class History, 1860–1930.* Kitchener, Ont.: Dumont Press, 1973.

Jarrell, Richard A. *Bibliography for Sources in the History of Canadian Science, Medicine and Technology.* Thornhill, Ont.: HSTC Publications, 1979.

Light, Beth. *True Daughters of the North: Canadian Women's History: An Annotated Bibliography.* Toronto: OISE, 1980.

Mennonite Heritage Centre. *Resources for Canadian Mennonite Studies: An Inventory and Guide to Archival Holdings at the Mennonite Heritage Centre.* Lawrence Klippenstein, Adolf Ens, and Margaret Franz, eds. Winnipeg: The Centre, 1988.

Messier, Jean-Jacques. *Bibliographie Relative à la Nouvelle-France.* Montréal: Editions Univers, L'Aurore, 1979.

Morgan, Henry James. *Bibliotheca Canadensis: or, A Manual of Canadian Literature.* Ottawa: G.E. Desbarats, 1867.

Ontario Historical Society. *Index to the Publications of the Ontario Historical Society.* 1899–1972. Toronto, 1974.

Oxford Companion to Canadian History and Literature. Toronto: Oxford University Press, 1983.

Reader's Guide to Canadian History. Toronto: University of Toronto Press, 1982. Volume 1. *Beginnings to Confederation.*
Volume 2. *Confederation to Present.*

Review of Historical Publications Relating to Canada. 22 vols. Toronto: University of Toronto Press, 1896–1918.

Stelter, Gilbert A. *Canadian Urban History: A Selected Bibliography.* Sudbury: Laurentian University Press, 1972.

Thibault, Claude. *Bibliographia Canadiana.* Don Mills: Longmans, 1973.

Who's Who in Canada: An Illustrated Biographical Record of Men and Women of the Time in Canada. Toronto: International Press, 1911– .

York University. Libraries. *Catalogue, Canadian Pamphlet Collection.* Toronto: York University, 1984. "Collection consists of pamphlets published primarily in Quebec and Ontario throughout the years 1900–1969." C.f. Introduction.

BOOKS

Baillargeon, Samuel. *Littérature Canadienne-française*. Rev. ed. Montréal: Fides, 1965.

Ballstadt, Carl. *The Search for English-Canadian Literature*. Toronto: University of Toronto Press, 1975.

Berger, Carl, ed. *Approaches to Canadian History*. Toronto: University of Toronto Press, 1967.

Berger, Carl. *The Writing of Canadian History*. Toronto: Oxford University Press, 1976.

Bothwell, Robert, Ian Drummond, and John English. *Canada, 1900–1945*. Toronto: University of Toronto Press, 1987.

Finlay, J.L. and D.N. Sprague. 2nd ed. *The Structure of Canadian History*. Scarborough: Prentice-Hall, 1984.

Francis, R. Douglas, Richard Jones, and Donald B. Smith. *Destinies: Canadian History Since Confederation*. Toronto: Holt, Rinehart and Winston, 1988.

Francis, R. Douglas, Richard Jones, and Donald B. Smith. *Origins: Canadian History Before Confederation*. Toronto: Holt, Rinehart and Winston, 1988.

Friesen, Gerald. *The Canadian Prairies: A History*. Toronto: University of Toronto Press, 1984.

Harris, R. Cole and John Warkentin. *Canada Before Confederation*. Toronto: University of Toronto Press, 1974.

Innis, Harold. *The Fur Trade in Canada*. Toronto: University of Toronto Press, 1930.

Morley, William F.E. *Ontario and the Canadian North*. Toronto: University of Toronto Press, 1978.

Parr, Joy. *The Gender of Breadwinners: Women, Men and Change in Two Industrial Towns, 1880–1950*. Toronto: University of Toronto Press, 1990.

Rawlyk, G.A., ed. *The Atlantic Provinces and the Problems of Confederation*. St. John's: Breakwater Books, 1979.

Strong-Boag, Veronica and Anita Clair Fellman, eds. *Rethinking Canada: The Promise of Women's History*, 2nd ed. Toronto: Copp Clark Pitman, 1991.

ECONOMICS

REFERENCE WORKS

Canadian Business and Economics: A Guide to Sources of Information. Ottawa: Canadian Library Association, 1984.

Harvey, Fernand. *Les Classes Sociales au Canada et au Québec: Bibliographie Annotes*. Québec: Institut supérieur des sciences humaines, Université Laval, 1979.

Labour Companion: A Bibliography of Canadian Labour History Based on Materials Printed from 1950–1975. Halifax: Committee on Canadian Labour History, 1980.

Primary Sources in Canadian Working Class History, 1860–1930. Kitchener, Ont.: Dumont Press, 1973.

BOOKS

George, Peter. *Survey of Economic and Social History in Canada, 1976*. Ottawa: Committee on Economic History, Canadian Economics Association, 1977.

GEOGRAPHY

REFERENCE WORKS

Burpee, O. Lawrence Johnston, ed. *An Historical Atlas of Canada*. Toronto: Thomas Nelson, 1927.

Fraser, J. Keith. *List of Theses and Dissertations on Canadian Geography*. Ottawa: Department of the Environment, 1972.

Historical Atlas of Canada. Geoffrey R. Matthews, cartographer. Toronto: University of Toronto Press, 1987– .

Kerr, Donald Gordon Grady, ed. *An Historical Atlas of Canada*. 3rd rev. ed. Don Mills, Ont.: Nelson, 1975.

NATIVE PEOPLES

REFERENCE WORKS

Abler, T.S. *A Canadian Indian Bibliography 1960–1970*. Toronto: University of Toronto Press, 1974.

Bradley, Ian Leonard. *A Bibliography of Canadian Native Arts: Indian and Eskimo Arts, Craft, Dance and Music*. Agincourt, Ont.: GLC Publishers, 1977.

Krech, Shepard. *Native Canadian Anthropology and History: A Selected Bibliography*. Winnipeg: University of Winnipeg Press, 1986.

Stevens, Tina. *Native Peoples Annotated Bibliography: A Listing of Books, Films, Videos, Newspapers, Journals for and Approved by Native People*. London, Ont.: Library Service Thames, 1988.

Verall, Catherine. *Resource/ Reading List 1987: Annotated Bibliography of Resources by and About Native People*. Toronto: Canadian Alliance in Solidarity with the Native Peoples, 1987.

Wai, Lokky. *The Native Peoples of Canada in Contemporary Society: A Demographic and Socioeconomic Bibliography*. London, Ont.: Population Studies Centre, University of Western Ontario, 1989.

Whiteside, D. *Aboriginal People: A Selected Bibliography*. National Indian Brotherhood, 1973.

ARTS AND HUMANITIES

REFERENCE WORKS

Ball, John and Richard Plant. *A Bibliography of Canadian Theatre History, 1583–1975*. Toronto: Playwrights Co-op, 1976.

Ball, John Leslie. *A Bibliography of Canadian Theatre History: Supplement, 1975–1976*. Toronto: Playwrights Co-op, 1979.

Bradley, Ian L. *A Selected Bibliography of Musical Canadiana*. Rev. ed. Agincourt, Ont.: GLC Publishers, 1976.

Canada. *Catalogue of the National Gallery of Canada*. Ottawa: National Gallery of Canada.

Canada. *Directory of Museums, Art Galleries and Related Institutions.* Ottawa: Statistics Canada.

Canada on Stage. 1982/1986– Toronto: PACT Communications Centre, 1989– .

Canadian Literature: Littérature Canadienne. A Quarterly of Criticism and Review. no.1 (summer 1959–). Vancouver: University of British Columbia, 1959– .

Creative Canada: A Biographical Dictionary of Twentieth-century Creative and Performing Artists. Toronto: University of Toronto Press, 1971–1972.

Directory of Canadian Museums and Related Institutions. Ottawa: Canadian Museums Association, 1984– .

Edinborough, Arnold. *The Festivals of Canada.* Toronto: Lester & Orpen Dennys, 1981.

Egoff, Sheila Agnes. *The New Republic of Childhood: A Critical Guide to Canadian Children's Literature in English.* Don Mills, Ont.: Oxford University Press, 1990.

Gilpin, Wayne. *Directory of Musical Canada.* Edmonton: Canadian Music Press, 1978.

Gnarowski, Michael. *A Concise Bibliography of English-Canadian Literature.* Rev. ed. Toronto: McClelland & Stewart, 1978.

Kallman, Helmut, Gilles Potvin, and Kenneth Winters, eds. *Encyclopedia of Music in Canada.* Toronto: University of Toronto Press, 1981.

Lecker, Robert and Jack David, eds. *The Annotated Bibliography of Canada's Major Authors.* Vol. 1– . Downsview, Ont.: ECW Press, 1979.

Leggat, Portia. *Union List of Architectural Records in Canadian Public Collections.* Montréal: Centre Canadien d'Architecture, 1983.

MacDonald, Colin Somerled. *A Dictionary of Canadian Artists.* Ottawa: Canadian Paperbacks, 1967– .

MacMillan, Keith and John Beckwith, eds. *Contemporary Canadian Composers.* Toronto: Oxford University Press, 1975.

Mezei, Kathy. *Bibliography of Criticism on English and French Literary Translation in Canada, 1950–1986.* Ottawa: University of Ottawa Press, 1988.

Music Directory Canada. Toronto: CM Books, 1982– . Annual.

Proctor, George A. *Sources of Canadian Music: A Bibliography of Bibliographies.* 2nd ed. Sackville, NB: Mount Allison University, 1979.

Sedgwick, Dorothy. *A Bibliography of English-language Theatre and Drama in Canada, 1800–1914.* Edmonton: Nineteenth Century Theatre Research, 1976.

Watters, Reginald Eyre. *A Checklist of Canadian Literature and Background Materials, 1628–1960.* 2nd ed. rev. and enlarged. Toronto: University of Toronto Press, 1972.

BOOKS

Benson, Eugene Patrick. *English-Canadian Theatre.* Toronto: Oxford University Press, 1987.

Contemporary Canadian Theatre: New World Visions. Toronto: Simon & Pierre Publishing Company, 1985.

Ford, Clifford. *Canada's Music: An Historical Survey.* Agincourt, Ont.: GLC Publishers, 1982.

Harper, J. Russell. *Painting in Canada: A History.* 2nd ed. Toronto: University of Toronto Press, 1977.

Theatre History in Canada. vol. 1 (spring 1980). Toronto, 1980– .

Tippett, Maria. *Making Culture: English-Canadian Institutions and the Arts Before the Massey Commission*. Toronto: University of Toronto Press, 1990.

CANADIAN PERIODICALS

An excellent source for ordering information and other important data regarding the following periodicals, magazines, or newspapers is *CARD: Canadian Advertising Rates and Data: The Media Authority*. Toronto: Maclean-Hunter.

BUSINESS

Atlantic Report. Atlantic Provinces Economic Council. Halifax, Nova Scotia.

Bank of Canada Review. Bank of Canada. Ottawa, Ontario.

Business Quarterly. London, Ontario.

CA Magazine. C.I.C.A. Toronto, Ontario.

Canadian Banker. Toronto, Ontario.

Canadian Business. Toronto, Ontario.

Canadian Journal of Economics. Downsview, Ontario.

Financial Post. Toronto, Ontario.

Financial Times of Canada. Toronto, Ontario.

Investor's Digest. Toronto, Ontario.

Labour Magazine. St. John's, Newfoundland.

Northern Miner. Toronto, Ontario.

INTERNATIONAL PERSPECTIVE

Behind the Headlines. Toronto, Ontario.

Canada and the World. Oakville, Ontario.

International Perspectives. Department of External Affairs. Ottawa, Ontario.

GOVERNMENT

Canadian Journal of Political Science. Ottawa, Ontario.

Canadian Parliamentary Review. Ottawa, Ontario.

Canadian Public Administration. Toronto, Ontario.

Canadian Public Policy. Guelph, Ontario.

Policy Options. Halifax, Nova Scotia.

Studies in Political Economy. Ottawa, Ontario.

CANADIAN PERSPECTIVE

Alberta (Western) Report. Edmonton, Alberta.

Canadian Forum. Halifax, Nova Scotia.

Canadian Speeches. Woodville, Ontario.

Equinox. Camden East, Ontario.

Harrowsmith. Camden East, Ontario.

Journal of Canadian Studies. Peterborough, Ontario.

Queen's Quarterly. Kingston, Ontario.
Saturday Night. Toronto, Ontario.

HUMANITIES

Acadiensis. Fredericton, New Brunswick.
Alberta History. Calgary, Alberta.
BC Studies. Vancouver, British Columbia.
Canadian Historical Association. *Historical Papers.* Toronto, Ontario.
Canadian Historical Review. Toronto.
Canadian Journal of Philosophy. Calgary, Alberta.
Dalhousie Review. Halifax, Nova Scotia.
Humanist in Canada. Ottawa, Ontario.
International History Review. Burnaby, British Columbia.
Royal Society of Canada. *Proceedings and Transactions.* Ottawa, Ontario.

ARTS

Archivaria. Ottawa, Ontario.
Canadian Architect. Don Mills, Ontario.
Canadian Art. Toronto, Ontario.
Canadian Composer. Toronto, Ontario.
Canadian Musician. Toronto, Ontario.
Canadian Theatre Review. Downsview, Ontario.
Journal of Canadian Art History. Montréal, Québec.
Modern Drama. Downsview, Ontario.
Museum Quarterly. Toronto, Ontario.
Opera Canada. Toronto, Ontario.
Performing Arts in Canada. Toronto, Ontario.
Theatre History in Canada. Toronto, Ontario.

LITERATURE

Antigonish Review. Antigonish, Nova Scotia.
Canadian Fiction Magazine. Toronto, Ontario.
Canadian Poetry. London, Ontario.
Journal of Canadian Fiction. Montréal, Québec.
Studies in Canadian Literature. Fredericton, New Brunswick.

INFORMATION/MEDIA

Books in Canada. Toronto, Ontario.
Canadian Journal of Communication. Montréal, Québec.
Canadian Journal of Information Science. Downsview, Ontario.
Canadian Library Journal. Ottawa, Ontario.
Feliciter. Ottawa, Ontario.
National Library News. Ottawa, Ontario.
Quill and Quire. Toronto, Ontario.

EDUCATION
Canadian Journal of Education. Ottawa, Ontario.
Canadian Modern Language Review. Welland, Ontario.
CM (Canadian Materials). Ottawa, Ontario.
Education Canada. Toronto, Ontario.

SOCIAL SCIENCES
Canadian Dimension. Winnipeg, Manitoba.
Canadian Ethnic Studies. Halifax, Nova Scotia.
Canadian Human Rights Advocate. Maniwaki, Québec.
Canadian Journal of Behavioural Sciences. Chelsea, Québec.
Canadian Journal of Criminology. Ottawa, Ontario.
Canadian Journal of Law and Society. Calgary, Alberta.
Canadian Journal of Native Studies. Brandon, Manitoba.
Canadian Journal of Political and Social Theory. Montréal, Québec.
Canadian Journal of Sociology. Edmonton, Alberta.
Canadian Journal of Women and the Law. Ottawa, Ontario.
Canadian Journal on Aging. Toronto, Ontario.
Canadian Review of Sociology and Anthropology. Montréal, Québec.
Canadian Social Trends. Statistics Canada. Ottawa, Ontario.
Canadian Woman Studies. North York, Ontario.
Windspeaker. Edmonton, Ontario.

CONSUMER
Canadian Consumer. Toronto, Ontario.
Canadian Living. Toronto, Ontario.
Chatelaine. Toronto, Ontario.
Toronto Life. Toronto, Ontario.

HEALTH SCIENCES
Canada's Mental Health. Ottawa, Ontario.
Canadian Journal of Psychology. Old Chelsea, Québec.
Canadian Journal of Public Health. Ottawa, Ontario.
Dimensions in Health Service. Ottawa, Ontario.
Journal (Addiction Research Foundation). Toronto, Ontario.

ENVIRONMENT
Alternatives. Waterloo, Ontario.
Canadian Geographer. Sherbrooke, Québec.
Canadian Geographic. Vanier, Ontario.
Great Lakes Reporter. Toronto, Ontario.
Nature Canada. Ottawa, Ontario.

Name Index

Subject Index